# « TUG OF WAR »

## THE TENSION CONCEPT AND THE ART OF INTERNATIONAL NEGOTIATION

*TONY ENGLISH*

# « TUG OF WAR »

## THE TENSION CONCEPT AND THE ART OF INTERNATIONAL NEGOTIATION

*TONY ENGLISH*

Common Ground

First published in Australia in 2010
by Common Ground Publishing
at The Social Sciences
a series imprint of The University Press

The National Library of Australia Cataloguing-in-Publication data:

Tug of War: The Tension Concept and the Art of International Negotiation
A. W. English

Includes index.
Bibliography.

978 1 86335 673 2 (pbk.)
978 1 86335 674 9 (pdf)

1. International negotiation in diplomacy, hostage release and business.
2. Communication in management.

658.4052

Cover illustration: Johannes Torrentius, *Emblematic Still-Life*, 1614. © Rijksmuseum, Amsterdam.

For my Darling. She knows who she is.

# TABLE OF CONTENTS

# LIST OF FIGURES

## ACKNOWLEDGEMENTS

Diplomats, hostage release specialists, business managers and other veteran negotiators contributed to the project. Dr Ashton Calvert, the Australian Secretary for Foreign Affairs and Trade at the time, and Mr Peter Henderson, a former Secretary, suggested I interview their short list of Australian diplomatic negotiators, several of whom turned out to be excellent informants. In the frenzied world of international business, people were generous with their time. Arish Turle put me in touch with hostage negotiators who spent many hours trying to educate me when they could have been doing easier things.

I met my informants in interesting places. In England alone, there were two clubs in London's Pall Mall, a flat in Pimlico, a 15th century farmhouse in Kent and a local pub about the same age; and a hotel called 'Angel-On-The-Hill' at Bury St Edmunds, Suffolk. The smells and noises of Sydney's fresh produce market filled Warehouse H, where I started an interview at 8 a.m. with a man who had been at work for three hours and would be there for at least another ten. At the Australian Embassy in Washington, the Deputy Ambassador banned calls and visitors to her office for two and a half hours, which must be a record for a city obsessed with contacts and networks. There was a modest but beautiful house by the sea at Ulladulla, on the south coast of New South Wales. I visited the Carter Center in Atlanta. Wherever I went, my informants were hospitable and good-humoured. Several interview tapes are enriched by laughter, popping corks, tinkling glasses and interruptions by family members and waiters. All this made me think twice about reducing my 'findings' to a set of clever statistics that would squash the life out of the study and turn a silk purse into a sow's ear.

The Australian Research Council funded some of the fieldwork. Flinders University gave me a few months to work on the book. I am indebted to the many informants and other people who read the manuscript and advised me how to improve it without retreating from my approach to the topic. In particular, Peter Lenz applied his hawk eye and soaring mind's eye to the exercise. Don Round gave expert advice on Chapter 9. Kathryn Otte and her colleagues at Common Ground managed the publishing process with finesse and patience.

For use of copyright graphics, my thanks to the Albright-Knox Art Gallery at Buffalo, the Rijksmuseum at Amsterdam, the M. C. Escher Company, the *Far Eastern Economic Review*, the *Negotiation Journal* and *Business Horizons*.

My wife Linda, son Cain and daughter Megan have been bemused champions.

## THE AUTHOR

Tony English teaches international management in the Business School at Flinders University, Adelaide, Australia. He came late to academia after a 30-year non-career as a colonial civil servant, factory worker, development project manager, executive headhunter, education consultant, and international management coach. He has taught negotiation skills to learners from sundry countries and cultures. He and his family have lived for many years in Papua New Guinea, New Zealand, Kiribati, Indonesia, the Philippines and Sri Lanka. Tony holds a BA in anthropology, a postgraduate diploma in adult education, a Master of Education (First Class Honours), and a PhD awarded for a thesis exploring the way international managers learn to understand and work within unfamiliar contexts. He is trained in mediation. He has published in the *International Journal of Organizational Analysis*, the *Asian Business Review*, the *Taiwanese Journal of Australian Studies*, *The Australian*, *The Australian Financial Review*, *Quadrant* and *Penthouse*. Tony has his best ideas when kayaking and fishing but cannot remember them very well and never takes a pen and paper to record them.

# Introduction

## Crossing Beaches

This introduction has two main purposes, intertwined. The first is to sketch my research philosophy and the influence of my personal history, assumptions and biases; the second is to outline the core of my thinking about international negotiation. I am impatient with social scientists who covet the label 'objective' so much that they try to camouflage subjective influences when they should declare them. Avoiding the first person singular is a standard ploy. Virginal objectivity is impossible as we watch, record and interpret human behaviour, but we can become better at collecting information and sifting it for patterns, aberrations and meanings.

In this book, I explore the significance of patterns in veteran practitioners' reports of their experience in three realms of international negotiation: diplomacy, hostage release, and business—perhaps 'other business' would be better, as hostage negotiation and associated services is a burgeoning industry. I argue that tensions, in the sense of complex relationships defined by polar oppositions, are prominent in every negotiation I have studied, and that 'tension management' is what the negotiator does to identify and try to manipulate tensions for the benefit of one or more parties. On those premises I build a negotiation model for analysts who might or might not be practitioners, always conscious that my model is but one way of representing negotiation, and that there is always the possibility—albeit remote—of finding a tension-free negotiation.

Perhaps my interest in the tension construct derives from my dualistic thinking as a Catholic child sweating in fear of eternity in hot sulphur within the earth's bowel as the alternative to a seat at the right hand of God, lolling above me on a cumulus lounge. The staging point of Purgatory was my best chance as I tried to avoid mortal as opposed to venial sin. Those ideas lasted until I decided people invented religion to house hopes of immortality and so cope with fear of oblivion. If no death, then no religion. Tensions, tensions everywhere.

The negotiation study derived from my finding, during earlier research into how international managers make sense of unfamiliar contexts, that many informants tended to talk about the content and context of managerial problems in terms of tensions; that is, dilemma, conflict, contradiction, paradox, and other terms founded on perceived oppositions (English 1995, 2001).[1] 'Issues' in the sense of points of contention or problems were replete with tensions, which are intellectual constructs and not to be confused with 'tension' as a popular term for anxiety (although the circumstances expressed by my construct may cause psychological stress). Explicit and implicit attempts to modify tensions or take them into account were labeled 'tension management'. Chapter 1 roughs out the tension and tension management; later chapters refine them.

After I noticed tensions in the transcripts I could see them in much management and other literature but could also see they were not well-understood, let alone unified by theory. I decided a systematic study of variations on the tension might assist managers to define problem scenarios before making decisions, or during transactions, or post mortem. In this book, the meaning of 'scenario' is close to "a sketch of a plot or play; giving particulars of the scenes, situations etc." (Oxford English Dictionary 1980). The term relates to sketches of the past, present and future, and is therefore broader than in the management literature, where scenarios are usually guides to planning based on forecasts of variable business influences and conditions (e.g. Schoemaker 1995).[2] Here, a scenario is a sketch expressed as a set of tensions. I will explain it in detail in Chapters 4 and 5.

After developing a tension-based model of context for management problems, I designed and delivered executive courses based on the model. They seemed to work (English 2001). Parts One and Two of this book

---

1. An 'informant' is a person who gave me information, usually in an interview. The information may be particular to the person's experience of a case, or may be general (e.g. about Chinese negotiators). Some social scientists say a given person is an 'informant' when providing the latter type of information, but a 'respondent' when providing the former type (Levy & Hollan 1998: 335–336). Most researchers use 'informant' as I do, and 'respondent' to mean a person who takes part in a survey.

2. In his press briefing of 12 February 2002, perhaps US Defense Secretary Donald Rumsfeld should have cited Schoemaker. Rumsfeld said "As we know, there are known knowns. There are things we know we know. We also know there are known unknowns. That is to say, we know there are some things we do not know. But there are also unknown unknowns, the ones we don't know we don't know." Schoemaker says: "When contemplating the future, it is useful to consider three classes of knowledge: 1. Things we know we know. 2. Things we know we don't know. 3. Things we don't know we don't know" (1995: 38).

explore the origins and elements of the model, refined for analysis of negotiation as a form of management. To seek an agreement the negotiator must plan, organise, lead, control and coordinate human activity in a cross-cultural environment. This makes a manager of the negotiator.

The tension construct, the idea of tension management, and my model of context emerged from the more inductive approach of my earlier study. To make sense of my data for that study, I extracted patterns and developed tension theory as I went along. I believe I had an open mind at the outset about what I would find, and certainly no conscious purpose in looking for what I would later call 'tensions' (which does not mean there was no subliminal interest that steered me on a selective quest). This is in the spirit, if not always the practice, of inductive research by social scientists (Neumann 2003). Of course, another researcher with a different open mind might find other, more important themes and patterns than the tension-based ones that engage me.

In the later negotiation study, the tension construct was there at the outset, as I suspected my theory would help me to understand negotiation, founded as it is on actual or potential conflict over content and process. That is, to develop theory in the first study I relied on what I saw as induction, more or less; in the second I used the theory as a deductive guide to another area of human life that seemed inherently suitable. I refined the theory as I tried to make sense of the 'facts' of negotiation reported by informants. Like a fisherman who targets tuna but knows there are other fish in the sea, I explored the negotiation literature for explicit and implicit examples of tension-based thinking to see if there was any support for the theory.

As I designed my study, I crossed the boundaries of many disciplines in my reading about and around negotiation, and became even more aware of the tension and its management in diverse scholarship, religious practice, and other human activity. As this general observation supports the specific idea of negotiation as tension management, I survey the ubiquitous tension in Chapter 2 as a prelude to focusing on tensions in the negotiation literature. After completing a draft of the book I discovered the work of philosopher Morris Cohen on the polarity concept as a metaphysical principle and "a heuristic principle directing our enquiry in the search for adequate explanations" (1949a: 12–13). He does not refer to 'tensions' but in effect he sees some links—Heraclitus, Plato, Socrates, Aristotle, Hegel—that I had already seen between the tension construct and philosophy across time and culture. This discovery was heartening. As explained in Chapter 2, my construct embraces but is not limited to Cohen's thinking on the nature and significance of polar relationships.

I found several negotiation studies that included explicit use of the tension concept (e.g. Babbitt 1999; Cutcher-Gershenfeld & Watkins 1999, Janosik 1997, Mnookin, Peppet & Tulumello 1996, Watkins & Winters 1997). To my horror, some used *my* term 'tension management' under the influence of Lax and Sebenius (1986), whose work I discovered long after I created the phrase for my PhD thesis (English 1995). The horror waned

3

when I realised my global concept, with its complex and ever-changing variations, subsumed theirs. This discovery assured me that negotiation as tension management could be seen and exploited as a generic construct. In general, negotiation writers who touch on the idea are enlightened but constrained. It was an obvious step for me to explore the potential for a more systematic, unified understanding of negotiation as management of inherent tensions. Perhaps negotiation analysis and tertiary courses could be founded on an explicit grasp of tensions and their relationship to issues and context. One of my main challenges would be to apply the tension construct to analysis of real negotiations without squashing round characters into flat ones, or altogether purging live *people* from my study. At present, too much negotiation writing is a cemetery.

Although my analytical model applies to negotiation in general, the scope of my project had to be international to satisfy my identity as someone who has spent most of his life working across national and cultural borders, mainly in island communities of the Pacific and Asia. Perhaps I am the counterpart of the 19th century misfits who struggled, as non-Romantic beachcombers, to navigate "the boundary between the old world and the new that ran down the very centre of their lives" (Dening 1980: 129). I will touch on the beach metaphor from time to time, albeit lightly, because it can illuminate international negotiations in particular and negotiations in general. When I use it again, I hope to be less cryptic (perhaps less auto-erotic) than most contributors to *On the Beach*, the proceedings of the Conference of the Cultural Studies Association of Australia in 2000 (CSAA 2000). One abstract, written by a university lecturer in English, makes my point: "The romanticising of linear notions of 'time' into 'timelessness' suggests the existence of presumed pre-commodified entities.... However ... one consequence of the Western traveller's presence is to change that which they most desire to remain unchanged." All of which warns me to try to make sense and to avoid the ethnocentric 'notion', common in universities throughout the world, that only Western variations on the beachcomber are naïve and destructive. My study of negotiators' behaviour does not romanticise 'non-West' as I do not wish to insult anyone by denying the human side of being human.

The relationship between context, tension, and tension management—all to be defined later, when the definitions are needed—is crucial to my understanding of how my informants negotiate across international and cultural boundaries. I will also define 'boundary play' when necessary; also seven 'marks' (skills, inclinations, senses) evident in the practice and commentary of all informants, albeit in different measure for each person but stronger than observed in lesser negotiators: anticipation, diagnosis, drama, empathy, flexibility, opportunism and potency. These concepts are refined and unified in Part Four, where I relate tension management to psychological models of intelligence.

Within two realms of negotiation—diplomacy and hostage release—I concentrate (in Part Three, Chapters 6 and 7) on specific sub-types because they entice me more than others, and because appropriate informants were available to provide reportage from which I could extract patterns and speculate on their meaning and significance. As pointed out by Dening, this is where the researcher's imagination comes into play: "Imagination is the ability to see those fine-lined and faint webs of significance" (1998: 209). His comment about what historians do could well apply to this study, based as it is on informant accounts of transactions involving them: "The one thing historians never do is observe the past. All we observe is the past transformed in some way into history" (207). In that sense, my informants allow me to observe *their* history which stems from *their* experience of particular transactions. Whether or not other people involved in the same transactions would offer a different history invites another study, related to this one but beyond my current interest and resources. Whether or not other people can see different patterns and meanings than I see in the reportage is another problem which prompts me, in Chapters 6 and 7, to give raw accounts of that reportage for two cases. I then use the tension model to analyse each account, but in the meantime the reader may see other patterns and meanings, and use them to judge my observations and suppositions. It is not my task to present a forest that blocks other people's view of the trees. Nor do I want to dilute the colour in the original transcripts: "I think ethnographers [read 'social scientists'] should be criticized if they take the exciting material of real people's lives and turn it into deadly dull reading" (Bernard 2002: 346).

For each of the two realms, I present one detailed case involving an informant as player, but I did seek ideas from all informants about international negotiation skills and processes. In one case (Chapter 6) the ideas are in full because I reproduce the entire interview transcript.[3] Hugh Davies, for five years the lead British negotiator for the return of Hong Kong to China, recounts the intricacies and intrigues associated with designing a handover ceremony that would suit both the British and Chinese at a most sensitive point in their relationship. Moreover, he talks about patterns of Chinese negotiating style and diplomatic practice beyond the handover case. The ideas and experience of most informants illustrate Part Four (Chapters 8–10). At the Carter Center in Atlanta, colleagues of the former President explained his approach to informal 'Track 2' diplomacy. In hostage negotiation, Terry Waite, a Briton held captive for four years in Beirut, described a transaction involving Colonel Kaddafi of Libya. Mr Waite also offered snippets based on his dealings with other people in diverse settings. In the business realm, Robin Talbot told me of deals he negotiated in Latin America and the United States as CEO of a business chain, and he described his generic learning about international negotiation over a lifetime

---

3. The transcript might interest narrative analysts, whose "methodological approach examines the informant's story [verbatim] and analyzes how it is put together, the linguistic and cultural resources it draws on, and how it persuades a listener of authenticity.... We ask, why was the story told *that* way?" (Riessman 1993: 1). Also see Druckman (2002: 312).

of doing deals.[4]

These story-tellers all seemed to have a strong sense of transactional context and the need to recognise and manage tensions within it. It is not clear if these traits are natural or acquired through trial and error. Whatever the case, they have been honed—these people are all inquisitive about international negotiation and have an intellectual thirst that complements their pragmatism. They all told stories that I have tried to retell, especially in the two detailed case studies, in the spirit of Bernard's praise of phenomenology: "There is still no substitute for a good story, well told, especially if you're trying to make people understand how the people you've studied think and feel about their lives" (2002: 23).

My informant sample shows I am more fossicker than open-cut miner. As a casual student of military matters, I am more curious about guerrilla tactics than blitzkrieg. As a hunter, I am inclined to throw stones into a few bushes to see if something moves, rather than organise a beating-party to flush out every creature that lives in the forest. As a fisherman, I cast my lure only where my reading of the beach says there might be fish. To me as photographer, the film drive that permits ten shots per second is like fishing blind with a grenade or net, or carpet-bombing by grid: "If there was anything out there, we sure as hell got it." Rather than survey a large statistical (probability) sample, I wanted to use interviews to delve into the experience of a small judgment sample of veterans and select whatever data would give me the best insight into international negotiation without giving equal space and weight to everyone. Like Henry Mintzberg, doyen of managerial researchers, my interest lies less in large samples, statistical analysis, frequency and 'truth' than in the richness of individual lives and the meaning we can draw from them, based on attempts to understand how informants see and manage their reality. In the social sciences this type of search for meaning is at the core of phenomenology, narrative analysis, grounded theory and most ethnographic research (Hammersley & Atkinson 2000). Discovered, inferred or constructed meaning might or might not be relevant to other people in similar circumstances. In the jargon of the flock of deskbound academics who see the world as numbers, and are lambing fast, my limited sample has low external validity (which does not mean my tension-based model of negotiation is wrong).

Software is now available to analyse interview transcripts and other written sources, but qualitative research is still slow sculpture with no quickfire equivalent of statistics packages. If done well it tends to take longer than quantitative research and to generate fewer papers per capita, which creates anxiety for many academics. Quantity outweighs quality in promotion or tenure rounds in the modern university, where the annual quota of publications works against scholarship (Conger 1998). One colleague says he needs only a bottle of cognac, a computer, a statistics package and access to a public database to build the pile of papers demanded of

---

4. Robin Talbot is not his real name.

him. His method is more prolific than mine but it also looks too much like sausage production. He wonders why I torture myself for years on a single work, playing with what he calls "intangibles"—he means "uncountables". Another Henry, more lethal than Henry Mintzberg, got it right when he criticised academic researchers for avoiding intangibles because they are hard to pin down: "Things are done because one knows how to do them and not because one ought to do them" (Kissinger 1977: 29).

My need to see the eye colour of interesting people outweighs my need for promotion (if not for cognac), so I opted to meet and interview a few international negotiators seen as exemplars by their peers and associates. Of course, what you think of the peers and associates, not just the exemplars, will affect your opinion of my judgment as in 'judgment sample': for instance, Hugh Davies' boss Chris Patten, the last British Governor of Hong Kong; or Terry Waite's boss, the Archbishop of Canterbury; or the Australian Secretary for Foreign Affairs and Trade. My informants are almost all Western males, even though I attempted to recruit others, but the negotiation model presented in this book accounts well for cultural, political, historical and other influences in specific negotiations. For example, there is much evidence in Fang (1999) for the tension concept in Chinese approaches to negotiation, which he says are distant from what he calls "Western" approaches. As for the influence of gender, I could not have drawn conclusions from such a small sample even if there had been more female informants. In any case, my experience and reading tell me Howard Raiffa is still right when he says there is no convincing evidence of intrinsic differences between men and women as negotiators (1982: 122–123).

Concerning negotiator competence and my judgment, this study has limitations, but the tension concept's potential to deepen our insight into negotiation does not depend on the reality of personal success or failure in the selected cases. My interest is less in proven results than in the process and content reported by the players. For the most part, the reports are accounts of successful performances on a single stage; the players tell stories that include themselves as characters. Like many a résumé, some of the stories may have a creative and self-protective touch, which would do no damage to my position that tensions and their management are at least at the heart of my veterans' *thinking* about negotiation. My informants may have failed in some respects, but who will dwell on failure to a stranger who plans to write about the play but was not there to see it? Iklé (1964: 236) thinks it is easier for an observer to describe faults than virtues in negotiators, but harsh self-criticism by the latter is another matter. There is no good reason to doubt any informant's account but reportage *is* founded on the hindsight that sometimes "makes the past our puppet" (Dening 1998: 211).

The problem of hindsight is compounded by evidence that individual participants or observers may see and frame the same events with bizarre differences (Goffman 1974). The professional negotiator Herb Cohen, in his best-seller *You Can Negotiate Anything*, says that we see transactions through the filter of personal history: "You and I do not see things as they are. We see things as *we* are" (1980: 159). These points raise another factor that cramps findings in this sort of study, much more than in physics, chemistry or ballistics. No matter how hard I might resist, my preconceptions, experience and interests must influence heavily, if not dictate, the themes and meanings that I draw from interviews.

I am starting to realise why most of my colleagues seek refuge in the number-crunching that bolsters their sense of scientific detachment as they seek incremental findings based on other people's incremental findings. But increments and safety do not concern me any more than numbers in this study. My purpose is to develop a new, tension-based model that encourages researchers to revel in uncertainty, not try to deny it, while looking for manageable order in the chaos of negotiation as an open system. I generate theory that quantitative researchers might choose to test in their own way—I do not dismiss statistics packages, as long as other people use them to dredge for meaning rather than massage it to suit the method. Wright makes a case for qualitative research as a flexible generator of theory, "while quantitative methods are most useful for testing the generalizability of particular factors" (1996: 77). She says we will miss out on a lot "if we are straight-jacketed into looking only at that which can be measured" (63). Terrence Hopmann, a 30-year veteran of quantitative research, argues for qualitative method as a richer way of getting at the nuances of the negotiation process and overcoming the basic assumptions "that the actors are motivated by instrumental rationality and engage in some sort of formal bargaining process, and that the goals and moves may be quantified and subjected to systematic analysis" (2002: 74).

Like Henry Kissinger, who ought to know, Hopmann warns us to think with care about our ends before we settle on familiar means. To study negotiation, we use social science method because we are social scientists, but there are other ways. Negotiation academics swoon when I say the most lucid and rigorous study is a novel—Francis Walder's *The Negotiators* (1960), about attempts to negotiate a peace treaty at St Germain in 1570 between the Catholic supporters of Charles IX of France and the reformed church Huguenots. Novelists can explore aspects of negotiation that elude the social scientist, such as hidden agendas, ego-trips, trysts, and secret deals made away from the main game. Darkness entices novelists but academic researchers tend to ignore or deny it because they cannot delve into it with confidence. At least one anthropologist is flexible. In the first chapter of *Naven*, a composite study of a New Guinea tribe's culture from three points of view, the maverick ethnographer Gregory Bateson says social science is but one means of exploring culture; he also exalts the novelist who uses creative composition to the same end (1936).

Bateson's attitude reminds me that some colleagues think me a masochist because I carry the double burden of qualitative method and eclecticism. I have worked and studied within and across the boundaries of anthropology, international development, management, international relations and adult education. In addition to academic literature from those fields and others, I draw on journalism, novels and the visual arts. Again, my base is the beach as a transitional zone. This is an advantage for my study because too much academic writing suffers from narrow focus—the researcher sees negotiation through a strangling method and the drinking-straw of a sub-discipline. For example, negotiation is too volatile, too complex and too human to be beaten into order (and sterility) by game theorists who draw their conclusions from the behaviour of players in tidy experiments: "Game theory ... deals only with the way in which ultrasmart, all-knowing people *should* behave in competitive situations, and has little to say to Mr X as he confronts the morass of his problem" (Raiffa 1982: 2). The main game for these theorists is not negotiation but mathematics and logic, and they find it convenient to assume negotiation is successful only because the players are rational, or unsuccessful because they are irrational. Howard Gardner's work on "multiple intelligences" has convinced him "it is dangerous to assume that negotiation is purely a rational process" (2000: 322). A masterly negotiator in Walder's novel says he tries to seem rational even when he is not. Those who must look through a tube should choose a kaleidoscope, not a straw, if they want to grasp the reality of negotiation as a complex system, rich in human surprises that do not always make sense.

In *Communication and Negotiation*, Putnam and Roloff (1992) see a narrow focus even in the open and diverse world of communication studies: "The topics in this volume illustrate the way communication researchers have coalesced around demarcated zones ... [that] provide only minimal treatment of the emerging areas of international and cross-cultural negotiation, multiparty disputes, and interorganisational bargaining" (13). Too many negotiation researchers yearn to pin down one element of an elusive topic—to seize control of it, to claim they own a bird because they have managed to grab one of its feathers. One result is a bogus sense of panoramic authority. The conductor of a symphony orchestra would be daft to wander into a jazz bar and try to seize control of a jam session because he is a maestro.

I try to avoid insularity by probing several disciplines as I develop a speculative and somewhat elastic negotiation theory that seems credible at macro and micro levels, and compatible with aspects of more specialised research in negotiation. The final chapter looks at how the theory might be useful to international negotiators in any realm. Tension management as a generic concept may encourage a stronger sense of theoretical unity and a readiness to cross boundaries. It might also help some negotiation academics to overcome their fear that someone will accuse them of "admitting the unknown [i.e. uncountable or unobservable] as a crucial part of the pertinent data and interpretations.... Anality may be at the heart [!] of this tendency" (Edelman 2001: 105).

I do not seek to disparage quantitative method to defend the limitations of my own, and I certainly do not want to be lumped with the writers who wear blinkers as they defend another bastion, interpretivism, with its sometimes whimsical research and murky concepts. Perhaps a blend of quantitative and qualitative method generates the deepest insights in some studies. Testable hypotheses, probability sampling, quantitative analysis and other elements of positivist design might destroy or strengthen my concept of negotiation as tension management, and my proposition that people who learn to define tension scenarios will become better analysts and perhaps better negotiators. Perhaps positivists can better extract persuasive association of variables, even cause and effect, from sometimes baffling circumstances; but to interpret patterns is always qualitative.

In summary, what claims do I make for my research and this book? My earlier research, reading, observation, and reflection left me in no doubt that tension-based thinking is very common. In the ethnographic tradition, and knowing my search is 'theory laden', I explore a non-probability sample of people and cases for evidence of tensions in international negotiation; I locate enough examples to propose that the tension and tension management can be abstracted from negotiation. This is not new as the concepts, usually with other labels, have been explored since thinking began. But my study of the tension itself, as well as its place in negotiation, goes further. I assume analysts who refine and order their normal human grasp of tensions and the forces that generate them are likely to become better at what they do, just like a surgeon with a sharper scalpel and a better knowledge of surgery. To set the scene for analysts to refine their understanding, I deduce tension properties that make sense but are not explicit in the interviews. From my study of the tension itself, I create a model of the negotiation context; I redefine negotiation in general, and international negotiation in particular, to include tensions and their management; I relate tension management to theories of intelligence. It would not make sense to prescribe tension management for negotiators, because that is what they do anyway; but even though my main purpose is to help non-playing observers to observe better, negotiators might become better tension managers if they use the model and theory to analyse their practice.

Certainly, my method is meant to be a long way from hard science. A positivist might want to design research to test my propositions and claims to theoretical sense, and to assess my findings for validity, reliability, and so on. The test that matters more to me is the opinion of analysts, whether or not they are professional negotiators, and whether or not they know or care about mainstream negotiation theory. Does the model make sense to them? Do they think it useful? Does it help them to hone their sense of context, knowing their understanding cannot ever come close to being complete at any given time or immutable over time? Might it serve to unify fragmented approaches to negotiation analysis? "Yes" to one or more of those questions does not prove the model depicts the essence of international negotiations, only that it may be a useful framework for dealing with them. "No" might not mean the model is wrong, only that the analyst cannot see its origins or is uncomfortable with it. Anyway, correctness "is scarcely the point, for models are not to be judged as correct or incorrect but only as more or less useful as a means of analysis" (Gulliver 1988: 253).

# Part I

**《 Tensions, Life and Negotiation 》**

## « Tensions, Life and Negotiation »

*Truth is not the contrary of falsehood; to betray is not the contrary of to serve; to hate is not the contrary of to love; trust is not the contrary of distrust, nor honesty of deceit.*

Francis Walder, The Negotiators, 1960

*Theory cannot equip the mind with formulas for solving problems, nor can it mark the narrow path on which the sole solution is supposed to lie by planting a hedge of principles on either side. But it can give the mind insight into the great mass of phenomena and of their relationships, then leave it free to rise into the higher realms of action.*

Carl von Clausewitz, On War, 1832

## *Preamble*

I readily see tensions at the heart of negotiation because I tend to see them whenever I watch people trying to understand and manage their lives. Negotiation is just another human activity; but, like marriage and warfare, it intensifies our sense of actual or potential conflict and therefore our need to extract manageable order from a vast swirl of information that may have inherent order but at least appears to be chaotic. The three chapters of Part One link my general view of human 'managerial' behaviour with negotiation in particular. Chapter 1 outlines the research that generated my angle on international negotiation and explains broadly what I mean by 'tension'. To justify the tension as a reliable anchor for the model presented later (in Part Two), Chapter 2 shows how tension-based thinking pervades human attempts to order and manage diverse situations, including academic analysis, musical composition, and the interplay of earthly and spiritual realms. In a return from the general to the particular, Chapter 3 dredges the negotiation literature and finds a lode: tension-based ideas pervade the field but they are ad hoc and usually implicit; the authors do not see the generic construct that could go some way towards unifying and refining their ideas.

# Chapter 1

## « Fundamentals of the Tension »

### THE TENSION IN INTERNATIONAL MANAGEMENT IN GENERAL BEGETS A STUDY OF NEGOTIATION IN PARTICULAR

During my doctoral research in Australia, Thailand, Malaysia and Indonesia, I asked seventy-eight managers and trade officials to tell me about managerial problems that concerned outsiders in unfamiliar countries, and to place those problems in the local business context (English 1995, 2001). The group comprised forty-eight Caucasian Australians; the others were an even distribution of Thais, Indonesians, Americans, Britons, Canadians and Malaysians. My concern was managerial problems in general, not negotiation specifically, although problems relating to language in particular were identified in that arena. My later research focused on international negotiation, largely because the model of context that issued from the original project continually gave me insight into negotiation dynamics as a practitioner and teacher. The model generated a second project which explored negotiation as management, so its origins are worth telling to show the continuity between the projects.

In the original data there were many explicit and implicit references to dilemma, contradiction, contrast, conflict, paradox, quandary, counterpoint, alternatives and other binary relationships, all generated by political, cultural, ethical, personal or other forces identified by my informants. I gave the generic label 'tensions' to the myriad dilemmas and related concepts found in the interview transcripts. The tension is an analytical construct that captures the influence of cultural, political and other contextual forces on human behaviour. Tensions are not passive dyads. For analogy, think of an object wandering into the field of gravity between two planets. As they 'compete' for influence over the object their relative pulling power affects its path and stability. The analogy will do for the time being, but it is about physical forces and inanimate objects and therefore has limited application to the behaviour of human beings, for whom tensions are about consciously or subliminally perceiving, processing and reacting to influences symbolised by the two planets.

During the original research, many tensions were evident when informants talked about the choice of local partners by foreign businesses wanting to set up joint ventures in Asia. David Abbey, an Australian engineer based in Jakarta as head of a construction alliance, said many Western businesses courted trouble by not defining the relationship they wanted to have with their Indonesian partner:

> Do they want a partner who has lots of equity but does nothing except get them into the system? It has to be handled very carefully, because it's very difficult to get rid of a partner, especially a powerful one. You're better to take time to do the right research in the first place so as to avoid a situation where you have to extricate yourself down the track. Then again, there are arguments for and against having a powerful partner. A passive, powerful partner wants a free ride. You have to decide how much equity you can reasonably give. Powerful and active is probably better than passive and weak.

According to Abbey, the foreign business must control its investment by choosing a local partner who will be neither too powerful nor too weak, and neither too passive nor too active in daily operations; and the foreigner must find the right balance between giving that partner too much equity and not enough. The plot is replete with contrasting possibilities and potential conflict that must be perceived, processed, understood and managed. The foreigner perceives and grapples with a tension between the ideas of too much equity and not enough. In a figurative sense, the two poles compete with one another for influence within the mind of the perceiver, whose task is to find an appropriate balance between them and negotiate a workable arrangement with the partner.

I also explored the training role of expatriate managers and found it rich in tensions. Under most joint venture agreements approved by government authorities throughout Asia, expatriates are expected to train local people to take over specified positions held by outsiders. Informant opinion on this issue further illustrates the dilemmas and conflicts that dominated the interviews. Several informants said many foreigners did not want to jeopardise their expatriate positions by training local people so well that the trainers phased themselves out. Mike Krishnan, a Malaysian national and Executive Director of Antah Holdings in Kuala Lumpur, said expatriate managers do not always perform well as trainers even if their training skills are excellent:

Expatriates come out of the home position, perhaps without really wanting to, and see themselves out of the mainstream, and worry about where they'll fit in when they get back. They have to try to hang onto the overseas position until they're sure they have one to go back to at home. They might respond well to change, and be good at educating and delegating, but they fear undermining themselves.

Michael Noakes, an Australian mining executive based in Jakarta, raised the same issue. He said fear of redundancy generated "a real dilemma, because you have to train people to take over from you, and it [the fear] works against the mindset that you need if you are to be a good coach". The expatriate must train local people, yet strike the right balance between two demands of the job that are in tension; that is, in these people's minds there is competition between the ideas of training too well and not well enough.

Whenever experienced expatriates talked to me about head office they criticised colleagues who were supposed to support the field but were said to be too ignorant of local conditions to understand issues like those described above. Moreover, most people at head office could not fathom the multiple roles of expatriates, especially in new ventures where the managing director might also be chief engineer, accountant, personnel manager and office skills trainer. Tom Critchley, former Australian Ambassador to several Asian countries, said advanced telecommunications compounded the problem of ignorance. Contact had become easy and immediate. Therefore the diplomat and the expatriate business manager had lost much of their customary autonomy and were subject to continual and sometimes capricious interference by head office managers who wanted to centralise control. This matches Yates's finding of a tendency for new technologies to be used to extend managerial control, while the real gains from advances in international communications "await innovative thinking about the underlying managerial issues" (1989: 274–275). The lament of an Australian banker in Jakarta was typical of expatriates. Ready contact by telephone, fax and email made it too easy for headquarters staff to demand progress despite the political, cultural and other factors (including traffic snarls and fitful electricity supplies) that hindered efforts to meet schedules appropriate for Sydney or London but fanciful for most of Asia. Officials and local partners would coddle senior people during fleeting visits. After skimming across the surface, some visitors would bemoan the expatriate's lack of drive, return to headquarters as instant experts, and use technology to inflict cross-border torment. In many cases the result was a broad 'them and us' tension in expatriate minds, impeding communication between headquarters and the field: 'Do we do what is good for us, or whatever is good for them?' The two perceived poles of the tension are rich in meaning as they 'compete' for influence over the perceiver's behaviour.

Tension was the leitmotif no matter how I arranged the transcripts and interview notes through the normal qualitative process of code, cut and paste. My colleagues concurred, and advised me to use tension as the core concept for further analysis and reporting. As I continued to explore the data for inherent tensions I realised that, where implicit or explicit tensions were identified, informants tended to talk about contextual forces at three distinct but interactive levels: personal; within their own organisation; and in the macrocosm beyond the organisation. For instance, data on the training issue concerned the expatriate's personal career, the expectations of his or her organisation, and the demands of the host government. Concerning alliances, managers focused on their own capacity to control their organisation's investment in the face of political and other external forces.

In the second study I gathered thirteen cases on negotiations about international business alliances, hostage release, the Hong Kong Handover, the Torres Strait Treaty between Papua New Guinea and Australia, the 1998 Kyoto conference on greenhouse gas emissions, and Track 2 diplomacy by ex-president Jimmy Carter. As with the previous study, the interview transcripts and notes for the negotiation cases included many explicit and implicit tensions. I will not go into them here as I will distil them systematically from selected cases in Part Three.

## THE FORMAL TENSION IN BRIEF: POLES, COMPETITION AND COMPLEMENTARITY

The tension is 'two complementary phenomena that compete for influence over the perceiver's mental and other behaviour'. The perception and associated behaviour may be conscious or subconscious. A phenomenon is any concrete or abstract thing that a person perceives and interprets explicitly or implicitly. Two phenomena 'compete' as tension poles in the sense that the influence of one pole over a person is relative to the influence of the other pole, like the influence of the two planets on the straying object. To go beyond that limited metaphor, the 'competitive' influence of the poles depends on human perception and processing—the poles are not entities that jump up and challenge one another to a duel or a wrestle, independent of a perceiver. At the risk of encouraging diversion into arguments about how many angels can dance on the head of a pin, I offer another metaphor: 'Influence' depends on perception, just as a motorist coming upon conflicting red and green lights can detect a tension between them only if his eyes are open.

Tensions are expressed in a simple, manageable way that reflects the nature of tension-based thinking. A double-headed arrow (↔) represents the relationship between the poles, which must be nouns (perhaps with a qualifier) because the essence of the tension is a perceived relationship between two phenomena. For example, a business negotiator knows a bribe to a corrupt official will revive a dormant negotiation with a promising ally. The CEO tells the negotiator to pay, but to do so would breach the negotiator's moral code. The negotiator must deal with this tension between corporate practice and personal ethics, generated by endemic corruption and the pressure on the company to make a profit. *Personal ethics* ↔

*corporate practice* summarises this ethical tension, and expresses the negotiator's moral discomfort with the CEO's order to bribe bureaucrats at an overseas post. Within the frame of *that* negotiation, the poles compete for influence in the perceiver's mind, and neither makes sense without the other—hence they are complementary.

There are many other examples. *Domestic mindset ↔ international mindset* denotes a common tension in organisations that operate across national borders. A novice expatriate adjusting to an unfamiliar cultural context would be dealing with the tension *home context ↔ unfamiliar context*. For this person in the throes of culture-shock, the extremes represent incompatible frames of reference, and each pole takes its meaning from the other—hence the relationship is competitive and complementary. Therefore the terms 'pole' and 'polar' denote both unity and separation.

The arrow-shaft represents the relationship between poles, however different some relationships may be from others. In some cases it signifies rigid separation, depending on particular circumstances and individual perceptions. The poles of *life ↔ death* are clear-cut when I think of my great-uncle, blown apart on the Somme in 1916, but not when I think of a patient on a life-support machine. Most people would agree that left and right are converse, and that plus is the converse of minus. Some poles are not clear opposites. For example, *study loan ↔ new car* depicts a scholarly petrol-head's struggle to decide whether to use a lottery prize to buy a new car, redeem a study loan, or buy a used car and reduce the loan. Some variation on the tension relationship comes into play as soon as we decide to face—or are forced to face—pairs of options, alternatives, or choices; so too, if we compare ideas, things or actions as a prelude to a decision or conclusion. However insignificant, fleeting or even trivial a tension may be, it is still a tension because the poles compete with and complement one another as they influence the behaviour of anyone who experiences and must deal with the relationship.

Tension poles have arbitrary labels with rich meaning for people who deal with the problem at hand. A hostage negotiator trying to gauge the amount a kidnapper will accept to release a foreign manager in Colombia must deal with many tensions, including *no payment ↔ full payment*. This 'content' tension reflects the issue of payment—how much and under what conditions. It is not just a numerical statement of extremes delimiting a scale of payment choices. The extremes are competing positions, and in most hostage negotiations the consequences are dire if either pole dominates behaviour and so precludes compromise. Refusal to pay anything may lead to indefinite captivity or worse; full payment may encourage other kidnappings or a demand for more money because the kidnapper sees the negotiator as an easy touch. At the outset, the kidnapper demands a specific ransom. The balance of power lies with the kidnapper in *negotiator control ↔ kidnapper control*. The negotiator as tension manager must move the balance of power from the right pole towards the left one: "You are trying to get from a position where you've got virtually zero per cent of control to a

point where you've got at least fifty per cent" (Jacob Crowe, hostage negotiator interviewed in London). This tension primarily concerns the negotiation *process*. The two tensions link content and process, themselves in tension. The negotiator must induce the kidnapper to accept a figure and other conditions representing a compromise between the two poles of the first
tension, but in doing so must not allow content to distract him from process, or vice versa.

After I noticed these kidnap-related tensions I discussed them in a conference paper (English 2002); later a specialist writer on hostage negotiation made a similar point: "Whatever the negotiator gives ... he must always make the concession on the condition that he gets something in return. In this way the negotiator exerts increasing control and diminishes
the captor's own sense of control over the situation" (Griffiths 2003: 149).
No matter who is more skilful and who prevails, the manoeuvres of both
parties illustrate the tension management that seems to be inherent in all
negotiation.

The tactics chosen to manage a transaction are not tensions, but as part
of the immediate context they may generate or intensify tensions. For example, the bribery tactic required by the CEO in the ethics case has helped
create *personal ethics* ↔ *corporate practice*, with meaning specific to this
transaction.

I reiterate that the tension as defined in this book should not be confused with 'tension' used as a popular term for anxiety, edginess, suspense,
ill-feeling, stress, and so on. This is not to say a tension cannot be associated with anxiety, or that psychology is devoid of tensions fitting the definition. To the contrary, there are myriad examples in that field, including *approach* ↔ *avoidance* and *abstraction* ↔ *concreteness*. *Mania* ↔ *depression* expresses competition and complementarity between extreme phenomena in
bipolar disorder, which is interesting also because it is a good example of a
tension located within the individual.

Whether or not tensions originate within or outside the individual, they
make no sense—probably do not exist—unless they affect at least one person's abstract or concrete behaviour. The affect varies. For example, *unity*
↔ *fragmentation* expresses a content issue in negotiations between the separatist Tamil Tigers and the Sri Lankan government (Gunatilleke 2001).
This tension may be associated with killing and maiming among soldiers,
quarrels among politicians, calm discussion between negotiators, and dis-
passionate analysis by journalists who see circumstantial evidence of the
tension in others but do not care if the country bonds or splits.

So far I have wanted to say only enough about the tension to flag its potential as a helpful construct for trying to understand how people impose
manageable order on their lives, including the way they negotiate. To reinforce the general purpose, Chapter 2 roams wide. Chapter 3 combs the negotiation literature for explicit and implicit reliance on the tension
concept. This leads to a tension-based model of negotiation in Part Two,

and a recommended way of using that model to analyse particular negotiations.

↔ ↔ ↔

# Chapter 2

## 《 The Tension Pandemic 》

I propose the tension construct as a tool for analysing negotiations in order to identify, understand and perhaps forecast—'predict' is too confident—contextual influences on negotiator behaviour. As a way into an informed focus on the tension in negotiation, this chapter explores the construct's broader significance as a way of formalising the 'raw' tensions that permeate our lives. This should encourage analysts to cast their net wide when they search for influences on particular transactions. To build a sense of the tension's ubiquity and nuances, the chapter wanders across many disciplines and types of human activity, then draws conclusions about the formal and informal nature of the tension and how we use it, consciously or otherwise, accurately or otherwise, to impose manageable order on our lives, including the way we interpret our own and other people's behaviour.

Again, the tension is 'two complementary phenomena that compete for influence over the perceiver's mental and other behaviour'.[1] Neither of the two poles in tension makes sense without the other, and each pole competes for influence on the way we interpret our world and act within it. The relationship between idealism and materialism is a good example from philosophical dualism; so too is the mind-body problem. In these cases my main interest is not in whether mind and matter are independent entities,

---

1. In later chapters I will relate the tension to negotiation as a form of management. My purpose here is more general.

but how the two ideas give meaning to one another as they compete for influence on how we interpret our own and other people's experience. Perhaps at the other intellectual extreme are the hard facts of physics, such as laws about actions and reactions, and theories about polar relationships in magnetism. Scientists use tension-based words and other symbols to describe, label and explain phenomena. Whether or not physics is closer to hard facts than philosophy is irrelevant to my purpose; my concern is the way we think and express ourselves when we try to interpret and manage our abstract and physical worlds.

In explicit or implicit forms, the tension is embedded in the fine arts, music, belief systems, religion, scientific analysis, and many other aspects of behaviour in any cultural setting, although culture may influence the way we notice, interpret and deal with tensions. Tensions abound in the formal study of culture itself, but the modern literature of anthropology and other disciplines did not give birth to tension-based studies. Some post-modernist academics and literati seem to think paradox and contradiction are their discovery—one which compels them to eradicate mindless binary 'reductionism' and substitute the possibility of infinite interpretations of fiction, poetry, history, politics, paintings, and so on. Rather, the tension construct is on record in European philosophy that is more than 2000 years old. In Plato's dialogues (c. 400 BC) Socrates demands "Yes" or "No" responses to his questions about the nature of excellence. There is no choice but to make one response or the other as the two possibilities compete for influence in the mind of the respondent. The tension pervades the writings of Aristotle, Plato's student and critical colleague. His "golden mean" is "the rational and virtuous course between extremes of excess" (Speake 1979: 125). A balanced person is one who reacts to the pull of contrasting tendencies, such as asceticism and profligacy, by steering between the two. In a droll piece entitled "Philosophy and Sport", China specialist H. A. Giles (1911) says ancient Chinese philosophers obsessed about counter-tendencies in human nature and argued a lot about whether we are born evil or good, or both, or as *tabula rasa*.

In more recent European philosophy, Hegel's dialectic holds that the pursuit of truth requires us to recognise and eliminate contradictory propositions which steer us in one wrong direction or the other, or perhaps both (1821). This reconciliation process is commonly and accurately expressed as thesis–antithesis–synthesis, although the terms may not be Hegel's (Kimball 2002: 122).

In the mid-20th century, the American philosopher Morris Cohen distinguished his theory from Hegel's when he built an intellectual system on the polarity principle, "suggested by the phenomena of magnetism where north and south poles are always distinct, opposed, yet inseparable" (1949a: 11). (That looks like a tension in which extremes, in this case conceptual opposites, compete with and complement one another.) No polar concept in a pair "can exist or have meaning without the other, just as the opposite blades of a scissors ... cannot function except in pairs, united in opposition.... The idea that the nature of things depends upon the equilibrium of opposing forces, and therefore the way to get at the nature of things is to reason from opposing considerations, came to be a permanent part of my philosophical outlook" (1949b: 170). The polarity principle is about checks and balances. Cohen says every natural event "must have a cause which determines that it should happen, but the cause must be opposed by some factor which prevents it from producing any greater effect than it actually does" (1949a:12).[2] He extrapolates to society: "A social movement has just the effect or influence which it in fact has, because of the presence of certain opposing or balancing factors necessary to produce the definite result" (12).

Influenced by mathematics and the hard sciences, Cohen came to see the polarity principle not only as metaphysical but also "a maxim of intellectual search.... Terms and relations, matter and form, immediate and mediate truth, are like north and south poles, strict correlatives, clearly distinguishable and inseparable — the existence of each is necessary to give meaning to the other" (1946: 4). His movement from metaphysics to investigative tool interests me because I propose that tension-based thinking is a credible way of defining and interpreting influences on behaviour when people negotiate.[3] That is not to say my tension construct is twin to Cohen's polarity principle. Rather, the former subsumes the latter. For a start, his poles are always conceptual opposites (north and south, activity and passivity, action and reaction, fixed and flux), whereas my tension poles may be conceptual opposites ($life \leftrightarrow death$, $male \leftrightarrow female$) but are not necessarily so ($study\ loan \leftrightarrow car$). Cohen's poles are all in equilibrium or approaching it, as with some tensions in my system; but other tensions may have strong and weak poles that do not balance and perhaps cannot do so, depending on context. If $life \leftrightarrow death$ concerns a man who is almost defunct, with no hope of recovery, the former pole cannot win or neutralise the battle for influence on the patient. When he dies the tension ceases to exist for him; one pole has eclipsed the other.

Cohen's theory seems to be about the nature of the world — almost a theory-of-everything; Hegel is more concerned with a way of seeking truth by expunging ignorance and error. Cohen distinguishes the polarity principle from Hegelian dialectic:

> The effort to eliminate false alternatives or one-sided views is characteristic of the Hegelian philosophy.... [but] the principle of polarity leads to a more emphatic denial of identity between opposite categories.... The opposition between contrary categories is neither absorbed nor in any way transcended by their unity.... The opposing considerations involved in all existences (like

---

2. Cohen seems to assume magnetic poles are balanced because they pull against one another. But opposite poles attract. Therefore the magnetism analogy should not be taken too literally. What matters is the idea of balance and complementarity between opposing forces, not strict correlation with magnetism.

3. See Larsen (1959) for a detailed study of Cohen's informal extension of the principle from metaphysics to method.

the north and south pole of a magnet) are different aspects which never become identical though they necessarily coexist. (1949a: 13–14).

That is, Cohen's poles are true and absolute, like their balanced relationship, and cannot contradict one another if they are defined logically. Hegel's poles comprise an inadequate proposition and an opposing one—also
inadequate—that it generates; both are tenuous and incompatible, and
must lose their identity as truth is found by seeking synthesis and thereby
cancelling the tension between them. The new-found synthesis then becomes a thesis that generates its opposite, and so on. Both Cohen and Hegel identify and define tensions, but only Hegel is an ardent tension manager, intent on destroying tensions to create others that bring truth closer.

Cohen and Hegel both knew of Heraclitus, the weeping Greek philosopher of the 5th century B.C. (Cohen 1953: 165; Speake 1979: 135). He des-
paired at people's ignorance of *logos*,

> the universal principle through which all things are interrelated and all natur-
> al events occur.... A significant manifestation of the *logos* ... is the underlying
> connection between opposites. For example, health and disease define each
> other.... His understanding of the relation of opposites to each other enabled
> him to overcome the chaotic and divergent nature of the world, and he asser-
> ted that the world exists as a coherent system in which a change in one direc-
> tion is ultimately balanced by a corresponding change in another.
> (Encyclopaedia Britannica 2006)

He uses tension-based thinking to give meaning to his world as he distils
order from perceived chaos; or perhaps it is more accurate to say he copes
with such chaos by imposing intellectual order on it.

Heraclitus, Hegel and Cohen might be wrong in their ideas about the
way the universe works and how to arrive at truth. My interest is less in
their correctness than in the variations on the tension construct that influence the way they manage their intellectual and other behaviour.

The ideas of Heraclitus link early developments in Western dialectic
with Taoist philosophy, in which *yin* and *yang* symbolise female and male
principles of existence that compete for influence on the universe; yet
there is "a flow of complementary yet opposite energies through which all
trends eventually reverse themselves" (Morgan 1986: 257). Unlike Hegel's
contradictions, this relationship is a better match with Cohen's polarity
principle as it sees unity in opposition and does not demand resolution. In
Figure 2.1, the perfect embrace of the larger fields, and the small circles
within them, suggest that male and female contain the essence of one another and that neither makes sense without the other. The total symbol
embodies the universe.

**Figure 2.1:** Yin-Yang

Opposition and complementarity associated with gender are expressed in the ultimate corporate merger when another Greek, the mythological Hermaphrodite, son of Hermes and Aphrodite, melds with the nymph Salmacis as she seduces him. 'He' has male and female attributes thereafter. The sense of symbolic completeness associated with competing, complementary phenomena is everywhere in Greek mythology. One excellent example is in Robert Graves's notes on the myth of Sisyphus. He says a pair of capital C's, the second in reverse, could "be read as the conjoined halves of the lunar month and all that these implied—waxing and waning, increase and decline, blessing and cursing" (Graves 1996: 208).

The explicit and implicit tensions in these philosophies and myths of existence embody revitalisation in some cases and absolute progress in others. The latter connect with modern theories of economic and social progress inspired by evolutionary science. Marx and Mao said society evolves through the pressure of tensions founded on competition for wealth and power between those who have a lot and want more, and those who have little and also want more. In Darwin's theory of evolution, species evolve through competition between animals with traits that make individuals more fit or less fit to survive. Bigger teeth, thicker fur and other mutations have competitive advantage only in the sense that they give individuals a better chance to breed in a particular environment. If you are fitter you are likely to win the breeding war against animals with shorter teeth or scanter fur. Survival of the fittest is about the increase of those most fit to breed and pass on their traits as they win the mating game against less-fit challengers. *Fitness* ↔ *unfitness* sums up the relationship. This formal tension might seem unduly lean but in fact it contains rich meaning for anyone who understands Darwin's theory and issues associated with it (*evolution* ↔ *creation*, *philosophy* ↔ *science*, and so on).

A philosophy of evolutionary progress pervades development economics, which pins polar tags on nations and leaves no doubt about the 'better' pole: countries are developed or underdeveloped, rich or poor, North or South, tigers or basket-cases. A tension is at the heart of Lloyd George's *The East-West Pendulum* (1992): dominance in technology and international trade since the 17th century has moved from East to West, but is now moving from West to East. China's burgeoning power is founded on a struggle that may be expressed as *command economy* ↔ *market economy*, which embodies much more than economics. It is also about an ideological clash demanding delicate management of a patchwork nation as it starts to pull away from rigid Party control towards a more open society. Without the transition, China might gain and hold the influence it craves in global trade and politics, but many variables could cause the engine to stall—for example, environmental carnage, strife between rich and poor, or the collapse of already shaky banks. International insecurity and other problems beyond China's control could lead to failing supplies of energy and raw materials. A rush along the continuum towards a market economy could encourage people to defy the Party and so generate rifts in an empire that has always been a cultural, social, and ethnic collage with suspect glue. If this happens the Party might still hold enough power to force a retreat towards the command economy. In short, *command economy* ↔ *market economy* brims with the rich meaning of the polar labels and their relationship.

The trend in that tension will influence the role of China as an international player within and beyond Asia. The field of international relations in general is replete with examples of the tension as defined in this book, as well as the 'strained relationships' idea of tension. The former type, my main concern, tends to be associated with the latter and probably causes it in most cases. Good examples are central to Huntington's contentious prediction of a clash between major cultural groupings (e.g. *Islam* ↔ *West*) to fill the tension gap created by the demise of ideological struggle at the end of the Cold War (1993). Kissinger founded his early book, *The Necessity for Choice*, on the identification, analysis and management of international issues that can be summarised as sets of polar tensions (1960). Eban (1998) examines the ethical dilemmas of diplomats who must face "the confrontation between power and conscience" (39) as they attempt to reconcile the doctrine of state sovereignty with the principle of universal human rights. I will return to international relations and the tension construct when I focus on negotiation literature in Chapter 3.

As I searched for tension labels to use in the previous paragraphs I realised that without tension-based thinking in linguistics the dictionary of synonyms and antonyms on my desk would not exist (which is not to say all tension labels are antonyms). David Crystal's *English as a Global Language* has a tension at its heart: "The need for intelligibility and the need for identity often pull people—and countries—in opposing directions" (1997: 116). *Intelligibility* ↔ *identity* is illustrated well in a *Far Eastern Economic Review* article on government moves to expand English radio services in Shanghai but restrict broadcasting in English to Chinese presenters who are not married to foreigners: "But this is China, a country where the arm of openness and reform is frequently wrestled by the arm of tradition and insularity" (Vincent 2001: 58). The article embodies many associated tensions and is illustrated by a photograph in which a Chinese policeman, taut and vigilant, guards the sturdy gate of the US Embassy in Beijing. He ignores a tiny, carefree Caucasian girl who rides by on her a tricycle. The case is not unusual, as verbal and graphic tensions are easy to find in the press.

**Figure 2.2:** A Tension in China
*Source: Vincent (2001: 58)*
Reprinted from the Far Eastern Economic Review.

The tension construct is prominent in the hard sciences, far removed from the popular press. For example, in physics the essential concern is force and counterforce when energy acts on matter. At a broader level, the umbrella tension between convergent and divergent thinking in scientific research, said to be played out as a battle between creative radicals and compliant, incrementalist mainstreamers, is the topic of a famous paper by Kuhn (1977). Cybernetics, the study of control and communications in mechanical and living things, crosses the boundaries of the 'hard' and 'social' sciences. In the domain of culture, cybernetics has influenced the tension-based thinking of the French anthropologist Claude Lévi-Strauss (1969) and his followers. He believes that "the most fundamental operation of the mind is to operate in terms of binary oppositions (that is, to continually divide things into two categories, to dichotomize—for example: raw vs. cooked; sacred vs. profane; and, the most fundamental opposition of all, nature vs. culture)" (Langness 1987: 145). Substitute 'nurture' for 'culture' in the last phrase and you have the tension that embodies perennial debate about cause and effect in child development, criminology, education, gender politics, and so on.

Not all anthropologists see the world in the same way as Lévi-Strauss but tension-based analysis is common in their field. In another evergreen model, in this case with more implicit tensions, Edward Hall locates cultural groups on a continuum denoting their degree of preference for contrasting communication styles: one extreme is high-context (implicit, non-verbal, reserved) and the other is low-context (explicit, verbal, candid) (1976). Japanese are at the former extreme, Swiss at the latter. Although Hall does not say so, the styles would be in tension if members of the two groups were negotiating. In theory, the Swiss would push right away for a detailed written contract without holes, whereas the Japanese would prefer to talk less and work reservedly around the issues towards an oral agreement or a more general written contract, which the players might refine in later sessions. Negotiation would be difficult because the Swiss would pull the communication style in one direction and the Japanese would pull it the other way. Of course, experienced players would manage the tension by modifying their styles.

A good example of a tension that frames complexity is in *Crab Antics*, Peter Wilson's study of colonial-inspired stratification on the Caribbean island of Providencia:

> [The book] concerns the identification and interrelationship of the two primary principles of the social structure—*reputation* and *respectability* (2)…. [The] dialectic turns on social and cultural opposition, on the relation between the *respectability* of European white stratification and the *reputation* of indigenous black differentiation…. [The two terms] stand for … complexes of value, behavior, and relationships…. The relationship between these complexes is expressed in a continuous dialectic of action and reaction, of imposition and evasion, of boasting and gossiping, of climbing up and pulling down. (1973: 222–223)

The simple statement *respectability* ↔ *reputation* shows how two simple labels can enclose richness of meaning for those who understand them and their relationship.

Needham (1973) comprises eighteen papers by anthropologists who explore symbolic classifications based on left versus right as a principle of sociocultural organisation and management. Things classified as left, such as confused and wandering spirits of the newly dead, tend to be negative; those classified as right, such as spirits that have ceased to wander on earth and have passed into some sort of happy hunting ground, tend to be positive. In that example, the managerial task of living people would be to use flawless ritual to steer a confused and therefore dangerous spirit away from the pull of earthly wandering, through a grey zone and into the sodality of benign spirits on high. Metcalf (1982) describes such a tension and its management. He says the Berawan of Borneo believe the soul of a live human can wander from the body "and travel about in other worlds. At death, the physical association becomes only looser. Now the soul cannot re-enter or reanimate the body; that is what makes it a corpse…. Unable to go forward or backward, the soul's condition grows only worse, parallel with the body's" (94–95, 99). The soul becomes desperate and malevolent. In such shape it is barred from the realm of the dead, and must be appeased through ritual until it mends its ways. Eventually, dry bones say the ritual has worked and the soul has been invited into the other realm.

Hertz's seminal study of 1909 [1973] depicts "primitives" using concepts of left (negative, profane) and right (positive, sacred) to define and manage the temporal and spiritual elements of their existence, with no clear gap between them. For them the "whole universe is divided into two spheres: things, beings and powers attract or repel each other, implicate or exclude each other, according to whether they gravitate towards the one or the other of the two poles" (1973: 8). Their world is about managing tensions between phenomena separated by a continuum, by a grey area that denies a clear difference between the conceptual extremes of sacred and profane, of positive and negative, of left and right. Hertz's conceptual framework of "primitive" symbolic classification is his own design, and may be flawed in its detail and the extent to which it reflects conscious and unconscious behaviour; but it does provide insight into the way 'believers' in all societies use tension-based thinking to order and manage the nexus between temporal and spiritual, and to suppress fear of annihilation at death (*temporal ↔ spiritual, annihilation ↔ immortality*).

There is much anthropological evidence that time and culture do not bind the tension construct. On the other hand, some might object on the grounds that anthropology is a Western discipline founded on Western constructs; but the argument is feeble. The explicit tension construct may be a Western invention, and the meaning of labels such as 'male' and 'female' may be misapplied, but cultural triggers and manifestations of the tension are global and reported not only by anthropologists.[4] For example, a postgraduate student from Beijing told me tension as defined in this book is the essence of the ancient Chinese concept, dear to Mao Tse Tung, of *muo* (spear) and *dun* (shield): you identify opposing forces in human relations and apply effort where there is the best chance of tipping events in your favour. Only a foolhardy scholar would argue for *muo-dun* or *yin-yang* as Western constructs imposed on Chinese culture.

To take another example, 'moiety' is indeed a Western anthropological label for each of two social units dividing some societies on the basis of lineal descent; strict rules govern interaction between members of the two lines. No matter who created the label, it would be naive to dispute the *fact* of such a division, with its profound implications for identity, power, marriage and inheritance. There would be no argument from members of the exogamous *Tarangau* (fish hawk) and *Maningulai* (sea eagle) moieties with whom I lived in the New Ireland District of Papua New Guinea in the early 1970s. Nor would they dispute my view of their *malanggan* ceremonies, which centre on the carving and display of ancestral and supernatural

---

4. Even when anthropologists decry the transfer of European binary notions to other societies, the challenge is to the labels, their meaning or their relationships, not necessarily to all binary constructs. For example, in Marilyn Strathern's study of gender among the Mt Hagen people of Papua New Guinea, she identifies 'male' and 'female' but explains why the labels denote less deterministic and more elastic ideas about what it is to be either a man or a woman than might prevail elsewhere. (Strathern 1990)

figures, as ritual attempts to reconcile the competing but complementary demands of homage to the spirit world, on the one hand, and on the other hand the society's need to reinforce its identity and earthly prosperity through a medley of artworks, initiations of young men and displays of largesse. New Ireland abounds with tensions consistent with the generic definition.

Contrast, conflict and complementarity imbue the scripture and oral traditions of probably all religious systems. There are the natural and the supernatural, sacred and profane, good and evil, saint and sinner, life and death, heaven and earth, paradise and damnation, reward and punishment, understanding and mystery, safety and danger, threat and appeasement, inclusion and exclusion, and giving and receiving. In Buddhism the Middle Way resolves conflict between asceticism and self-indulgence; the Hindu god Shiva is both destroyer and procreator. In none of these cases does one pole make sense without the other as they vie for influence over the way people interpret and manage their lives.

Religious schism is a form of tension that steers the temporal relationship between the parties. An Islamic example is the division between the Sunni and Shiite sects, who have wrangled over the status of Mohamed and his successors for 1400 years. Saddam Hussein favoured the Sunnis and persecuted the Shiites in Iraq, but their relative influence on the way Iraqis live their daily lives seems to have reversed since the US invasion of 2003. Since Saddam's demise, signs of cooperation between the two sects in the face of a perceived common foe—the Coalition of the Willing—have given way to civil war. Another tension in Islam is the battle between reformers and fundamentalists, as examined by Lucien Pye (1985: 266–282).

The relationship between the moieties of New Ireland is complicated by an imported tension denoting rivalry for local influence between Protestant and Roman Catholic missions, causing some villages to split (Lewis 1969: 28). As a government official in 1971 I had to manage the complex manifestations of this tension when it disrupted local government meetings and projects in the area.

Like schisms and other religious rivalries, heresies encapsulate tensions. For instance, the Manichean Christians of the 3rd to 5th centuries saw God and Satan as coeternal, and always at war over their good and evil designs on human life. To anyone who understands Manicheanism and its context, *Satan ↔ God* reeks of battle and carries other rich meaning about the heresy.

A recent study of Bali by journalist Cameron Forbes contains many examples, given by the players themselves, of *evil ↔ good* and its management. He talks to a Hindu priest who links a volcanic eruption with flawed ritual and the struggle between good and evil spirits for control over Balinese lives:

> Pegeh remembered 1963 and the great ceremony and the time that God produced the eruption. "There were stones and ash. Maybe there was an imbalance in life, and God wanted to cleanse the universe. Maybe there was a lack

of something in the ritual or maybe it was the ritual itself. If things are not totally balanced, maybe the evil spirits are the stronger." (Forbes 2007: III)

When I lived in Bali in 1978-79, I thought the Balinese were obsessed, more than any other people I had met, with the need to control and balance the benign and malicious forces that define their world. The obsession is the source of all ritual, from placing small daily offerings where someone has fallen over, to splendid cremations and temple ceremonies. Chequered black, white and grey sarongs symbolise the search for balance. In temples, gardens, hotel foyers and alleys, statues of mythological characters are dressed in them. The sarongs are worn during some ritual, and some players wear them in earnest dance-drama based mainly on the Hindu Mahabharata. A frequent performance is the battle between the black witch Rangda—malicious, fanged ruler of haunted graveyards—and the Barong, a jaw-snapping leonine fantasy who practices white magic and champions the people as they try to ward off evil.[5] The battle is always in flux. In Bali, the dramatic arts are part of the perpetual flow of ritual designed to manage *evil ↔ good*.

In his classic work on the nature of religion, Mircia Eliade (1959) probes "the polarity sacred-profane [that] is often expressed as an opposition between real and unreal or pseudoreal" (1959: 12-13). Similar tensions are found in Herman Melville's novel of 1851, *Moby Dick*. For example, in the introduction to the 1957 reprint, literary commentator Newton Arvin psychoanalyses the narrator, Ishmael: "One pole of his mind is a passionate interest in prosaic fact, in tough and meaty information.... [whereas] the other pole is a profound, anxious, unquiet, but resolute preoccupation with the ultimate and insistent questions of existence itself" (Melville 1957: viii). Although Arvin does not say so, the White Whale could be Siva incarnate: "[Moby Dick is] a creature that must be regarded with mingled terror and veneration, with alternative gratitude and resentment, as a paradoxical source of much good ... and of much evil and suffering" (x). My desk calendar for 22 June 2008 quotes Melville: "There is no quality in the world that is not what it is merely by contrast. Nothing exists in itself."

The tension between good and evil is at the core of much great fiction. In English, an obvious work is R. L. Stevenson's *The Strange Case of Dr Jekyll and Mr Hyde* (1886). It is founded on the idea of an *evil ↔ good* tension inherent in the individual, and explores the disaster of a man who mismanages the conflict by abandoning morality and yielding to evil without any hope of retreating from it under the influence of the other pole. As an umbrella summary, *evil ↔ good* is rich in specific meaning to anyone familiar with the novel. This formal tension suggests links with Aristotle's golden mean and the tension in Greek mythology between profligate worship of Dionysus, the god of wine, and homage to Apollo, the sun-god who doubles

---

5. Covarrubias (*Island of Bali*, 1937, p. 355) thinks the Barong and Rangda derive from the Tantric Buddhist lore of Nepal, Tibet and northern India.

as patron of poetry and music, the ultimate expressions of order and beauty.

The most quoted passage in English literature is probably the first line of the soliloquy in Act III of Shakespeare's *Hamlet*: "To be, or not to be: that is the question." Hamlet muses on the human struggle with a tension that on the one hand draws us to cling passively to life, with its familiar problems and torments, and on the other hand to retaliate by suicide, and so launch ourselves into the hidden and possibly worse realm of death:

> For who would bear the whips and scorns of time ...
> To grunt and sweat under a weary life,
> But that the dread of something after death,
> The undiscover'd country from whose bourn
> No traveller returns, puzzles the will
> And makes us rather bear those ills we have
> Than fly to others that we know not of?

In the context of the soliloquy within the play, *life* ↔ *death* and *passivity* ↔ *action* have deep, cynical meaning about human existence.

Almost as often quoted is the first paragraph—at least the first twelve words—of *A Tale of Two Cities* by Charles Dickens:

> It was the best of times, it was the worst of times, it was the age of wisdom, it was the age of foolishness, it was the epoch of belief, it was the epoch of incredulity, it was the season of Light, it was the season of Darkness, it was the spring of hope, it was the winter of despair, we had everything before us, we had nothing before us, we were all going direct to Heaven, we were all going direct the other way—in short, the period was so far like the present period, that some of its noisiest authorities insisted on its being received, for good or evil, in the superlative degree of comparison only. (1859: 1)

Dickens frames the confused mood of pre-Revolutionary France and England as a set of informal tensions between extreme opinions about the condition and future of society in France and beyond.

Communication through the fine arts is replete with tensions. With variation due to history and cultural origin, what is music without consonance and dissonance, sound and silence, tonality and atonality, harmony and disharmony? What matters is the relationship between sounds-at-odds: "To say that a consonance is a pleasant-sounding chord, and a dissonance unpleasant, is making the case much too simple" (Copland 1957: 54). With aesthetic effect in mind, composition and performance are about the maestro's management of these musical tensions. At least one whimsical chef thinks about his art in that way: "Each dish is a symphonic collision, every flavour and texture has a counterpoint.... 'I love the sense of brinkmanship on the palate....' He ... gets satisfaction from putting opposites together and making sure they get along with each other" (Chenery & Sellick 2002: 15). Style magazines link indulgence in fine food with trendiness in the rag trade, an interest of Alan Snyder, Director of the Centre for the Mind, a joint venture of the Australian National University and the University of Sydney. He sees fashion as a balance between unique expression and plagiarism, reflecting a normal human tendency: "... we clearly have a propensity to unconsciously steal ideas as well as do something unique with them. And I believe it is the tension between these two opposing forces that drives the creative output of society" (2000: 30).[6]

In the visual arts, the unity of the tension and the interplay of the poles are fundamental to design, which is largely about creating order from the chaos of influences on the artist's worldview. All great artists of any 'ism' have a creative eye for balance and harmony of form, colour, texture, tone and space that carry meaning linked with symbolic content, whose messages may burrow deeper the more our intellect tries to dig them out. My interest in artists and others who cross real and symbolic beaches has steered me to rich tensions in the Tahitian works of Paul Gauguin, perhaps the ultimate beachcomber and 'noble savage' fantasist—at least until he arrived in Tahiti and started to understand its reality.

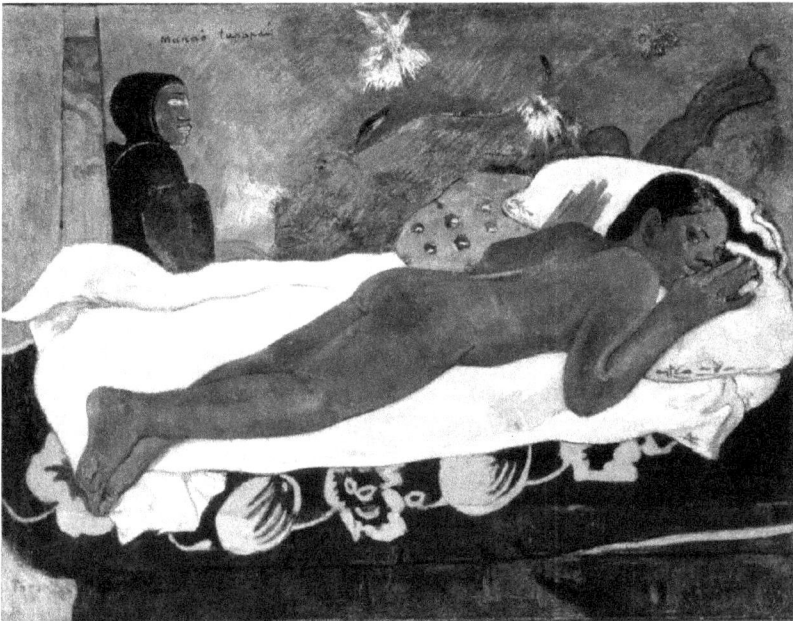

**Figure 2.3:** Paul Gauguin: *Mana'o Tupapa'u* [Spirit of the Dead Watching], 1892
Oil on burlap mounted on canvas.
Framed: 92.075 x 113.03 x 6.35 cms; support: 72.39 x 97.4725 cms.
© Albright-Knox Art Gallery, Buffalo, New York. A. Conger Goodyear Collection, 1965.

The tension-based thinking in Gauguin's journals matches his paintings. For example: "There is so much prostitution [in Tahiti] that it does not exist. We call it that, but they do not think of it as that. One only knows a thing by its contrary, and the contrary does not exist" (Gauguin 1923: 105). (This sounds like Melville, who went to the South Pacific long before

---

6. Is it theft if it is unconscious?

Gauguin and may have influenced him.) Before I read Greg Dening's comments on Gauguin's paintings I had made my own findings; but I cannot express them better than Dening:

> [The] Tahitian wilderness was ... a different order of things in which the oppositions that held in a civilised world—between human and divine, living and dead, male and female, child and adult, landscape and person—did not operate in Tahiti, in a Maohi world.[7] In his paintings, Gauguin mediated these oppositions, made them mysterious, enlarged them with his crazy imagination. He did this with colour, imported mythology, symbol and the mysterious titles of his paintings.... *Mana'o tupapa'u* [Spirit of the Dead Watching, Figure 2.3] is the most disturbing painting of all.... [The nude girl] is *taata vahine*, man-woman, a primitive mirror of the *mahu* [man-woman] in Gauguin himself. The fear in her eyes? It is more a vision that crosses in a very Tahitian way the boundaries of life and death, spirit and flesh, sacred and profane. (1998: 16–17)

The core tension *spirit world* ↔ *temporal world* (or *darkness* ↔ *light*) is symbolised by the figures of a black-clad ghost in human form and a naked, vulnerable girl. Gauguin uses symbolic colour and content to stress the girl's fear of the ghost and the swirling murk that threaten to drag her into the dark realm of the dead as she clings to the lit world of the living. To express her fear, says Gauguin in a letter to his wife, "the general harmony is sombre, sad, frightening, sounding to the eye like a death-knell: violet, dark blue, and orange-yellow" (Wadley 1978: 13). The flowers resemble sparks because "the Polynesians believe that the phosphorescences of the night are the spirits of the dead. They believe in them and dread them." The painting expresses polar influences that Gauguin infers from the girl's demeanour and from his perhaps distorted grasp of Tahitian culture. As in many of his works, there is also a sense of local people pulled between their own and alien cultures, and similar messages about him as an intruder trying to cross the metaphorical beach.

I sometimes find it hard to see deep meaning in paintings, no matter where they sit on the naturalist–abstract spectrum; but some figurative gems draw me in at once if they integrate content and design in ways that evoke rich tensions. My new-found favourite is the Rijksmuseum's *Emblematic Still-Life* (Figure 2.4), one of few surviving works by the Dutchman Johannes Torrentius (1589–1644). I did not know of this delicious tondo until I read *The Wreck of the Batavia: Anatomy of a Massacre*, by Simon Leys (2005). Leys writes of the artist's influence on Jeronimus Cornelisz, the assistant supercargo who became a despotic butcher when he took control of the crew and passengers of the Dutch East India Company ship, Batavia, after it was wrecked in 1629 in the desolate Abrolhos Islands off the southwest coast of Terra Australis. She had sailed off course en route to Java from Europe after rounding the Cape of Good Hope into the Indian Ocean. I will focus on the painting by Torrentius and not go into the

---

7. 'Maohi' is not 'Maori' misspelt. It refers to the ancestors of the Polynesian peoples and to modern Tahitians of Polynesian origin.

savagery that his alleged Satanism might have inspired in Cornelisz, who knew him and perhaps needed to escape his orbit.

**Figure 2.4:** Johannes Torrentius: *Emblematic Still-Life*, 1614
© Rijksmuseum, Amsterdam.

Torrentius was a lecher, pornographer, drunkard and blasphemer. He was also an exquisite artist who "boasted that he painted with the personal help of the Devil" (Leys 2005: 40). Apart from one pornographic print and probably one painting (Figure 2.4), his works were seized and burned in 1627 when he was imprisoned for heresy, Satanism and immorality.[8] In

8. I say "probably one painting" because the dating of this work is inconsistent. Leys (2005: 41–42) and the Rijksmuseum website (2008) say it was painted in England for King Charles I after he arranged for Torrentius to serve only two years in prison. If so, it does not make sense for the Rijksmuseum's commentary to suggest the painting survived the bonfire of 1627. Charles's seal is on the back but this may indicate only that he collected the work, not that it was painted at court after the release of Torrentius. The Rijksmuseum website also dates the work at 1614, which is more convincing for two reasons. First, "T. 1614" is on the horse's bridle. Second, in 1630 Sir Dudley Carleton, British Ambassador to The Hague, listed the painting in a letter to the Secretary of State with other works taken to England by Torrentius (Dodgson & Cust 1915: 248). It is therefore most likely that the painting was in Holland from 1614, avoided the fire of 1627, and went to England with Torrentius after his release.

austere Calvinist Holland, these charges may have been provoked by his membership of the secretive Rosicrucian society, with its philosophical footing in mysticism, alchemy and the occult. The painting was discovered in 1913 being used in a shop as a lid on a barrel of sultanas. Leys mentions the Rosicrucian connections of Torrentius but does not go into their significance for the painting, so we are left with a graceful but cropped analysis of the work. Like various other commentators, Leys sees it as a fairly obvious allegory of temperance: a horse's bridle hovers over a glass presumably used to dilute wine from the pitcher on the left with water from the jug on the right; two pipes suggest we not smoke too much. Leys does not translate the Dutch maxim on the music sheet below the pipes, but the Rijksmuseum says it means "If you ignore the tempo, you will succumb to untempered evil" and that "it is a warning that one should maintain a sense of proportion in life, just as in music. The bridle is a warning to keep desire in check. This still life is a song in praise of temperance...." (Rijksmuseum 2008).[9] I cannot understand why a lecherous drunkard would praise temperance, with or without Satan's help.

A warning to mediate between profligacy and austerity, a reminder of Aristotle's golden mean, does not draw the observer far enough into the painting's design and content. The prominent pitcher and jug do create a nuanced tension between indulgence and restraint, but the painting is about much more than temperance symbolised by diluted wine. I decided to explore beyond Leys's analysis when I realised that he did not mention the rich male-female tension, so obvious in the priapic pitcher and shapely jug. The former is metallic, cold, dark, functional, and a bit awkward; the latter is warmer, made of clay, balanced beautifully, and coloured like honey.[10] The pitcher has a superficial shine; the jug glows mellow from within. The pitcher is flawed by what looks like a musket-ball hole that would spill some of the wine where it should not go. The jug looks delicate, serene, and reliable. Perhaps I discover too much in the painting, like a wine-writer besotted by a glass of fermented grape-juice; but the larger-bowled pipe beside the male pitcher suggests overindulgence in smoking and other wickedness, compared with the slightly smaller pipe on the right, beside the virtuous female jug.

At ninety degrees to the horizontal tension *male ↔ female*, Torrentius has painted a vertical tension between a Satanic face—mocking the symbolic bridle from which it glares—and the call for self-control expressed on

---

9. There are various other translations, some reflecting the metaphor of musical discipline. The Web Gallery of Art says "That which exists out of measure [beat?] perishes in evil immeasurably" (2006). Whether or not they allude to music, all seem to warn against lack of self-control. A Dutch website says "That which exists without limitation, perishes in unlimited evil" (AMORC 2006). Martin (2005: 565) says "That which is without measure is immeasurable evil."

10. Sir Dudley Carleton (see footnote 8) refers to "a tynne pot and an errthen pot" (Dodgson & Cust 1915: 248). The "errthen pot" looks wooden to me but I will not question Sir Dudley; anyway, it is warmer than the pitcher.

the music sheet, which threatens to curl up and quash its own message. Is the music a symbol of harmony and self-discipline, at odds with the reality of disharmony and indulgence inspired by diabolical thwarting of Calvinist authority in 17th century Holland? The unobtrusive heart on the part of the bridle closest to the pitcher seems twice provocative: first, the heart is a Rosicrucian symbol; second, Calvin's personal seal was an outstretched hand holding a heart to symbolise his self-sacrifice to God (Carvill 2005).

The more I puzzle over this painting the richer it becomes in tensions that do not represent a plea for temperance; to the contrary, they suggest it is a remote and boring ideal.[11] Torrentius seems to use the tension-based cosmology of the Rosicrucians to express his cynicism about human nature.[12] As it would take a complete book to explore the Order of the Rose and Cross, I will link the painting only with the core Rosicrucian concept of polar oppositions that characterise the universe, which is dominated by a male-female tension similar to *yin* ↔ *yang*. As with the latter, the symbolic relationship between the two opposites is usually enclosed by a circle to express an ideal of unity, complementarity and completeness.

Rosicrucian graphics are much more complex than the *yin-yang* symbol but similar in principle and broad structure. For example, in *The Emerald Tablet of Hermes* the sun (male) and moon (female) are depicted within a circle, "pouring their life substance into a chalice, thus uniting [not diluting] their opposite natures. The chalice is supported by Mercury the hermaphrodite, both male and female. [This is] another union of opposites…. [Planets and other figures] are also arranged in a balanced and polarised fashion" (Courtis 1998).

Many other Rosicrucian graphics are based on similar tensions, reinforced by the geometrical symbols of the circle, the triangle and the cross that are also apparent in the painting by Torrentius. A rare circular border encloses the two main tensions in a cross; the bridle, pitcher and jug suggest an equilateral triangle. On the music sheet the abbreviation ER+, which is not musical notation, alludes to Rosicrucianism. A Dutch commentary says it signifies Torrentius's status of "*Eques Rosae Crucis*" — Latin for "Knight (literally "horseman") of the Rose Cross" (AMORC 2006). The commentary does not make the obvious link with the bridle on high, the vehicle for the devilish face that looms from the dusk to dominate the painting.

---

11. The only author I have found who notices the sexual symbolism is Martin (2005: 565), but he sees only temperance-inspired "lessons [that are] clear and explicit" about indulgence in sex and wine. He does not mention smoking.

12. If the work was painted in 1614 it may be argued that Torrentius could not have based it on a deep grasp of Rosicrucian symbolism because the first public document linked with the society is a manifesto, the *Fama Fraternitatis Rosae Crucis*, published only that year in Germany. The first Dutch translation was in 1615. On the other hand, there is plenty of evidence that Rosicrucianism was in Holland at least 20 years earlier. If the manifesto did influence Torrentius, it is possible he knew German and read the original in 1614 before it was translated into Dutch, or had a German speaker explain it to him in Dutch or another common language.

In keeping with the nuances of *sacred* ↔ *profane* I could explore the wine-water tension much further, perhaps looking for connections with the Sermon on the Mount and the mixing of wine and water in Christian ritual. Yet the goblet between the two vessels seems to contain neither red nor white wine, only water, which raises doubts about the dilution argument. Perhaps the goblet represents the Rosicrucian chalice into which the male and female life substances are poured to reconcile the tension between them. Then there is the Dutch word *roemer* for the type of goblet in the painting. Does it allude to the poet and fellow Rosicrucian, Roemer Visscher, who was born forty-two years before Torrentius and died in 1620?

There is much more room to speculate about tensions in this profound work. However, the main point is made: through its shape, structure and content, the painting evokes a rich blend of tensions that goes well beyond a platitudinous call for temperance expressed by two vessels, a goblet of diluted wine (or improved water), a bridle, two pipes, and a mini-homily set to music. Torrentius expresses the deeper tensions in a Rosicrucian framework but, more than most Rosicrucians, he seems sceptical of human effort to manage opposing forces in the universe—the Devil always intrudes as we strive to reconcile and harmonise. This struggle to identify, organise and manage tensions seems basic to human nature, no matter how the battle plays out in diverse times and places.[13]

**Figure 2.5:** M. C. Escher: *Day and Night*, 1935.
© 2009 The M. C. Escher Company, the Netherlands.

---

13. Having said all that about the paintings by Gauguin and Torrentius, I do not want the reader to think I confuse the recipe with the casserole, or even that a great chef follows a recipe, consciously or otherwise. A great chef who does use a recipe will transcend it, just as the two artists have transcended any political, philosophical or other musings that may have inspired the paintings.

A simpler and more explicit play on tensions is in prints by the Dutch artist Escher, whose work explores "relative and paradoxical points of view, [challenging] the models of reality stored within the human brain with images that contradict them: staircases that ascend downward ... and reversible patterns of figure and ground" (Hampden-Turner & Trompenaars 1994: 294–295). For example, *Day and Night* (Figure 2.5) embodies a continuum that unifies the tension: there are subtle transitions between the extremes of daylight and darkness, between dark birds and white ones flying in opposite directions, between fields that become birds, and vice versa. This work is based on oppositions. Yet the transitions and metamorphosis seem to belie the idea of clear opposites, even though Escher says "it really is very simple: white and black, day and night—the graphic artist lives on these" (quoted in Ernst 1985: 17). This print is less about the poles than what goes on between them. The continuum dominates as we are drawn to one extreme and then the other by the two directions of flight that meld around the middle of the picture.

Other birds—hawks and doves—are metaphoric extremes in a tension involving politicians who favour violence on the one hand and peaceful solutions on the other. Abdurrahman Wahid, the beleaguered former President of Indonesia, was a dove engaged in a contest of wills with hawkish army generals. As the military has been powerful in Indonesian politics since independence from Holland after the Second World War, the doves' preference for negotiation with separatists in the province of Aceh made little contextual sense without the complementary hawks. According to "a senior palace official ... there is always a tug of war between negotiation and military operations" (McBeth 2001: 28). Bernard Fall's *Street Without Joy* (1964) shows how the sapped French coloniser of Vietnam mismanaged the tension between a ground-level political strategy and reliance on conventional military force against the Viet Minh after World War Two. The colonial party was not going to last forever and was over long before the French forces trudged toward their defeat at Dien Bien Phu in 1953; but the party might have lasted a little longer and ended better if the French had not misconstrued *military strategy ↔ political strategy*.

In her philosophical study of photography, Susan Sontag (1977) alludes to tensions created when political ideology meets the visual arts. In 1970s China, she says, photographers depict only what the Party says is good and right: "The limits placed on photography in China only reflect the character of their society, a society unified by an ideology of stark, unremitting conflict" (174). Chinese photographic style embodies binary extremes without room for compromise: there is a clear right and wrong line of argument in any debate; there is no continuum. In societies where photography is more than propaganda, it captures subjects, puts them to new uses and gives them "new meanings which go beyond the distinctions between the beautiful and the ugly, the true and the false, the useful and the useless, good taste and bad. Photography is one of the chief means for producing that quality ascribed to things and situations which erases these distinctions: 'the interesting' " (174–175).

Armand Mattelart, another French academic, shares Lévi-Strauss's interest in communication and the human tendency to dichotomise. He says the glitz and glamour of the media have obscured our understanding of the way we communicate (ABC 2000). Moreover, "the problem is that the tensions which have marked the history of communicational thought are never reconciled." He then lists specific tensions that ought to be explored for the complex polar relationships that stamp human communication: physical and immaterial networks; biological and social frames of reference; nature and culture; micro and macro perspectives; village and global focus; actor and system; individual and society; free will and socioeconomic determinations. We must analyse the polar relationships, not stress "opposition and dichotomies [because this] leads to a loss of the sense of the complexity of the phenomenon". Mattelart's ideas reflect a point that is central to the process of tension management in international negotiation, to be explored further in Chapters 4 and 5. That is, the poles in a tension have no significant meaning distinct from the relationship between them. The tension is about the nature of the poles themselves, whether or not they are conceptual opposites, and whether or not they are discrete or phase into and out of one another—poles together rather than poles apart.

Poles and their relationships have made the tension a powerful analytical construct in psychiatry and psychology. For example, bipolar disorder is concerned with the oscillation between manic and depressive personality extremes within the individual. The mattoid, the person of erratic mind, is a compound of genius and fool, with each extreme taking its turn to prevail. In a classic study of personality, Thomas (1966) challenges the classification of people as *either* introvert *or* extravert. Rather, he sees people moving on a continuum according to circumstances; and, like Freud, he emphasises "the continuity between the normal and the abnormal" (Thomas 1966: 140, xlii). The psychotherapeutic system of Carl Jung, Freud's disciple turned rival, is founded on the idea that psychic life is about competing poles which must be balanced to avoid or cure psychosis, neurosis, and other disturbances. He is interesting for this principle, which justifies a wade through his reported dreams even though they are so complex, vivid and detailed that they seem like fiction created to prove a point. Like Freud, he saw sexuality as a tension-begetting force but cast his net a little wider, always concerned with human ability to manage "the problem of opposites, of good and evil, of mind and matter, of life and darkness" (Jung 1963: 221). Spiritual tensions in particular may be destructive because they lure people to extremes: "Wherever the psyche is set violently oscillating by a numinous experience, there is a danger that the thread by which one hangs may be torn. Should that happen, one man tumbles into an absolute affirmation, another into an equally absolute negation. *Nirvandva* (freedom from opposites) is the Orient's remedy for this" (151). And this: "To the Oriental, good and evil are meaningfully contained in nature, and are merely varying degrees of the same thing" (258). Jung refers to "psychological bisexuality" (349). The *anima* and *animus*, obviously inspired by aspects of *yin-yang*, are the feminine element of a man's unconscious and the masculine element of a woman's. These unconscious "regulators of behaviour" are in tension with the conscious elements of male and female intellect and emotion (349).

In most tensions within and beyond psychiatry and psychology, the continuum seems closer to reality than does a stand-off between categorical opposites. A good example, associated with another bird metaphor, is found in factionalism within political parties. Members seek a personal comfort zone or strategic location on the Left Wing–Right Wing continuum. For instance, factions in the Australian Labor Party include the Far Right, the Centre Left, and so on. One imagines zealous Right-wingers and Left-wingers flying in circles, clockwise in one case and anti-clockwise in the other. The chances of collision are high, an image that typifies the relationships along the party continuum. 'Numbers men' analyse and try to influence the distribution of support for policy and opinion in an exercise of tension management.

It is already clear that examples of tension management are as easy to find as examples of the tension itself. With aesthetic effect in mind, musical composition is about the maestro's management of the musical tensions specified above. The psychiatrist treats bipolar disorder by manipulating the tension between manic and depressive personality traits. In an intensive care unit, a doctor applies a well-considered set of managerial actions to stop the patient's condition from moving the wrong way along the continuum in *life ↔ death*.

It is no surprise that much management and organisational literature deals with tensions, but the authors do not notice the potential for turning the concept into a generic analytical and managerial tool. It is a rare textbook on strategy and decision-making that does not include a 'how to do it' section on SWOT analysis, a technique for assessing business risk by examining Strengths and Weaknesses within the organisation and Opportunities and Threats in the external environment. The macro pairings are de facto tensions that usually subsume independent lists within the four categories. Analysts tend to ignore the complementary nature of the polar categories. There are sometimes prescriptions for dealing with particular weaknesses and threats, but there is a conspicuous lack of suggestions for managerial action that would convert a Threat into an Opportunity, or a Weakness into Strength; or examples of mismanagement with the opposite effect. An astute tension manager is more concerned to identify and manipulate the relationships than to isolate and try to deal with individual items in the lists.

Handy (1994) has a general concern with framing and managing paradoxes in organisations. Hofstede's cultural value dimensions characterise nations according to their apparent location on five continua that influence management: small power distance versus large power distance; collectivism versus individualism; femininity versus masculinity; weak uncertainty avoidance versus strong uncertainty avoidance; and long-term orientation versus short-term orientation (1980, 1994). In a more recent study, Hofstede argues that attitudes and values are evaluative, by definition, because they have a positive and a negative pole (1998: 484–485). He identifies six dimensions that reflect employee perceptions of organisational units: process oriented versus results oriented; employee oriented versus job oriented; parochial versus professional; open system versus closed system; loose versus tight control; and normative versus pragmatic (483). I will revisit Hofstede in more detail in Chapter 3 when I look at examples of the tension in negotiation literature, and argue that his five cultural values dimensions, like Hall's communication dimension, are most valuable if treated as dynamic tensions that draw people in opposite directions rather than static scales used to pinpoint national traits.

Hampden-Turner and Trompenaars explore cultural influences on the resolution of seven universal dilemmas (1994). For example, "achieved status *versus* ascribed status" concerns the question of whether the status of employees should depend on personal achievement or on other characteristics such as age, seniority, gender, education, potential, or strategic role. McGregor's theory of contrasting management styles can be expressed as 'X [domineering] versus Y [participative]' (1960). Even though McGregor does not say so explicitly, the poles are on a continuum, and they compete for influence over individual managers and organisational culture. To me, a trainer who induces a manager to move away from a domineering style towards a more participative one, or vice versa, is a tension manager; so is the learner.

In a study of the difficulties faced by school principals and staff during performance appraisal, Cardno and Piggot-Irvine (1997) focus on recognising and managing "the fundamental dilemma of a tension between concern for the goals of the organisation and concern for relationships among individuals in the organisation" (72). The "dualities paradigm" of Evans and Doz (1992) deals with opposing forces that the manager can and ought to balance, but the paper does not deal with the influence of tensions that cannot or should not be balanced (see Kelly 1993), nor does it define the tension or go into its generic complexities.

The analytical model of Evans and Doz is similar to Kurt Lewin's force-field analysis, which takes a holistic view of human behaviour and is inspired, like Morris Cohen's philosophy, by the magnetic field (Lewin 1951). In Lewin's "field theory" the complex influences on behaviour are analogous to forces of attraction and repulsion between magnetic poles. Life is largely about how we react to the positive and negative factors that vie for influence on us (*+ve* ↔ *-ve*, or *north* ↔ *south*). Managerial models extend the analogy to say organisational situations needing change are locked in equilibrium by sets of forces that both foster and hinder transition to a desired condition—the umbrella tension *stasis* ↔ *change* is easy to see. Managerial models based on polarity are usually more limited than the tension construct in their tendency to deal only with force categories that are clear conceptual opposites, and to assume equilibrium between them until a manager—or a consultant—intervenes. In my system, to be described later in detail, the tension poles are not always conceptual opposites, and tensions tend to be in flux, not equilibrium.[14]

The title of the 1999 annual meeting of the Academy of International Business was *The Janus Face of Globalization*. Janus, the Roman doorkeeper of heaven, has one face that looks forward and another that looks backward: "Janus-faced has come to mean having two contrasting aspects. In the context of globalization, one face promises economic abundance, freedom of political expression, and cultural diversity while the other threatens economic insecurity, political instability and cultural decay" (Kate Wagstgold, email to Academy members, 4 March 1999). The two faces pulling against one another symbolise a struggle within people as they strive for a realistic grasp of the future and seek ways of controlling it. That is, they try to manage the tension. In similar vein, *The Lexus and the Olive Tree* examines efforts to manage the tension created by the desire of countries and smaller communities to maintain control of their destiny as global trade and communications weaken local autonomy (Friedman 1999).

International marketers and managers are obsessed with "globalization *versus* customization" (Hoang 1997); that is, finding the most profitable balance between global integration and responsiveness to local factors such as culture and economics (Gregersen, Morrison & Black 1998). My formal definition of the generic tension fits Deresky's summary of the problem: "a firm's structural choices always involve two opposing forces: the need for differentiation (focusing on and specializing in specific markets) and the need for integration (coordinating those same markets). The way the firm is organized along the differentiation–integration continuum determines how well strategies—along a localization–globalization continuum—are implemented" (2006: 286). Managers must deal with associated tensions between centralisation and decentralisation of control, between conservatism and transformation of organisational structure and strategy, and with the tendency for either structure or strategy to dominate thinking about organisational change, even though it makes more sense to integrate them and reduce the damage caused by defensive rivalry between planners who think one should hold sway.

Business managers suffer perennial torment as they seek the most profitable balance between cooperating and competing with others who want a slice of the pie: "Business is cooperative when it comes to creating a pie and competitive when it comes to carving it up.... There is a duality in every relationship—the simultaneous elements of cooperation and competition.

---

14. My lengthy experience with diverse organisations has made me sceptical of equilibrium, which may be a fantasy created by academics who draw fat fees by scaring people into hiring them as rebalancing ('re-engineering') consultants.

War and peace. Co-opetition" (Nalebuff & Brandenburger 1996: 4, 39).[15] In the search for sustainable profit based on constructive relationships, co-operation implies competition, and vice versa. Although they pull against one another they are complementary in a positive way if the players find the right combination, the right spot on the continuum.

Thus, tensions and their management are evident and prominent in diverse domains and cultural settings. Within a cultural group, individuals might disagree on the details or even the existence of one or more tensions in a given situation; also, individuals may be inconsistent from one situation to the next. Even so, research by Peng and Nisbett (1999) and Nisbett, Peng, Choi and Norenzayan (2001) does indicate broad cultural propensities in the way people see and react to contradictions. Therefore we must not assume people of different cultures perceive, interpret and deal with tensions in the same way. For example, Chinese and Americans might not see the same tensions. Even if they do, the Chinese may be less inclined to resolve contradiction because they do not think it necessary, desirable or even possible to do so. The Chinese tend not to question their assumption that the world within China (*nei* [inside]) is superior to the external world (*wai* [outside]), which creates a tension (*nei* ↔ *wai*) between internal and external influences on culture, human relationships, and pretty well everything else: "*Nei* and *wai* are opposites, just like good and bad and black and white, and the two are forever different, forever opposed" (Ching 1998: 32). If Chinese people do choose to manage tensions through compromise, they are likely to be influenced by the Buddhist and Confucian ethos of 'the middle way' and so temper their views and behaviour to ensure harmonious personal relationships with significant people.

This random journey has led us at least to a sound assumption that the tension and its management exist wherever people try to understand and cope with the minutiae and grander features of their universe. Some examples of the tension are subtle and implicit but others are obvious and explicit, in particular when scholars use dualistic thinking to make sense of their data or their philosophy, even though they rarely say 'tension' and do not even define the generic construct on which they seem to rely, let alone explore its dynamics.

Apart from the broad observation that tensions exist for us to find if we look for them, what else can we draw from the survey itself or deduce about the nature of the tension? Four prominent inferences are consistent with the overview of tension analysis and management in Chapter 1. The first and most obvious is that people use tension-based thinking to help turn perceived chaos into order as they strive to manage their lives. Second, as tensions are about perceptions of context, both facts and fantasies can generate tensions, which are facts in their own right. The third is that tensions exist and influence us whether or not we notice and articulate them *as*

---

15. In the next chapter (on negotiation literature) I cover Lax and Sebenius (1986), which is founded on the same proposition. A predecessor is Walton and McKersie (1965).

46

tensions. The fourth inference is that tensions vary according to polar types, the relationships between the poles, and relative significance—that is, some tensions matter more than others. A grasp of the four inferences is important because a refined knowledge of the tension can improve the analysis and perhaps the practice of negotiations.

First, imposing order on perceived chaos. To 'order' means to identify and organise relevant information without trying to deny the uncertainty and change inherent in context as an open system. In 'imposing order' we perceive tensions within ourselves and beyond, and express them more or less formally and systematically. We need to interpret, order and manage a perpetual deluge of information, certainly when we are awake and perhaps when we sleep. The examples in this chapter suggest an innate tendency to sense and react to tensions as a way of ordering and controlling our world, and to state them in binary form when we talk or write about them at levels of abstraction and formality that vary according to purpose and need. Whether we are New Guinean villagers, Greek philosophers or modern academics, we tend to employ tension-based thinking as we try to find manageable order in chaos. This is not to say people think only in ways represented by the tension construct, or that there is no other way of finding or imposing order; but there is plenty of evidence that this way is salient, and that it goes beyond a mere tendency to reduce complexity and chaos to 'dead dichotomy'—static lists of contrasts, in perfect symmetry, that simply mark the extremes of our vision and ignore their interaction. Hertz's pairings under the symbolic categories of left (negative) and right (positive) are exemplary. We can infer from his scheme that tension-based thinking is fundamental to our attempts to define and control a dynamic struggle between benign and malignant influences on our lives. Moreover, the left-right principle suggests the metaphor of arms in a physical embrace that symbolises complete and integrated framing of situations we need to manage; we focus on what we think matters—perhaps being wrong—and cull 'noise' as we try to extract manageable order from chaos.

The asymmetry of left-right framing appears to be deep-seated. McManus's research across many disciplines leads him to conclude that human preoccupation with symbolic, asymmetric distinctions between left and right derives from the evolved asymmetry of the brain and an associated capacity to actually make such distinctions (2002: 353). Although left-right classificatory systems are not symmetric the broad categories are intimately related, as are the specific pairings subsumed by them, and I hold that the capacity to distinguish, described by McManus, is as much about defining and managing relationships as it is about distinctions; further, that it epitomises our disposition to tension-based thinking, with its traits of competition and complementarity.

McManus sees tension between symmetry and asymmetry. We readily (but not always accurately) see symmetry of limbs, eyes, flowers and so on, and we find it generally in nature despite McManus's evidence that "the asymmetries of life are everywhere in our world" (357). We seem to search for symmetry as we define our world according to the way things ought to be—in perfect balance: "Symmetry ... is beloved of humans, who cover so many artifacts with complex symmetrical systems" (353). At the same time we tend to feel uncomfortable with the 'perfection' of symmetry, perhaps because it suggests banality, perhaps because the stasis of symmetry is at odds with the random and mutable lives of individuals and humankind. A feeling for asymmetric but unified composition and design pervades the work of artists and artisans, although there are superb examples of symmetric buildings and other works, such as Japanese masks and Ibo face-carvings. McManus gives several examples that seem to be reactions against symmetry. For instance, he describes a deliberate flaw in the complex carvings on an otherwise perfectly symmetric Japanese gate (356). An Indian dealer in Persian carpets told me the weaver always includes a flaw. In both cases the stated reason is to downplay any claim to human perfection and so appease one deity or another. Whatever the reason, these examples suggest that *symmetry* ↔ *asymmetry* influences the way we order and manage our world, including the way we define tensions. I will revisit this point when I describe tension characteristics in Chapter 4.

When we consider the variety of realms in which people impose order through tension-based thinking, we must not misread the *expression* of tensions as the creation of tensions themselves. We might say the composer creates tensions in music, that Escher creates the tensions in his prints, and that the chef creates the tension between sweet and sour flavours. It seems more likely that these people sense tensions in their world and express them in ways that reflect creative talent and knowledge in a particular field, just as Lévi-Strauss's analytical framework based on *raw* ↔ *cooked* reflects his intellectual bent as an anthropologist. The composer of music does not create *point* ↔ *counterpoint* but understands the tension and applies it in discerning combinations. Escher was not the first to notice the complexities embodied in *Day and Night* but he did come up with an original way to express them. The chef plays with our palate by expressing competition and complementarity in dishes, but does not invent the idea of contrasting flavours. Bipolar disorder is a psychiatrist's way of expressing a tension observed in a patient's behaviour. The expert does not create tensions in any of these cases; rather, he or she perceives them, and then expresses them in an ordered way that prompts us—as diners, patients and so on—to share the perceptions and perhaps gain a deeper understanding of their origins.

The second key inference: As tensions are about perceptions of context, both facts and fantasies can generate them. Indisputable facts may generate some tensions while others may issue from error, such as wrong information, misunderstanding or misperception. For example, the specific meaning of *life* ↔ *death* varies according to the circumstances of the struggle to survive, but it is a fact that the human body eventually stops functioning for one reason or another, however we explain it. The moieties of New Ireland are a fact. So is raw mental vacillation constructed as bipolar disorder. Point and counterpoint exist in music. On the other hand, *divorce* ↔ *marriage* might express a court battle founded on one partner's wrong belief that the other has been unfaithful. Perhaps I could prove that Lévi-Strauss based his theory of the raw versus the cooked on mistakes, or that Wilson misunderstood Providencia, but *raw ↔ cooked* and *respectability ↔ reputation* would still exist as formal tensions that express the way the two anthropologists interpret behaviour. Heaven and hell might not exist but if we are believers our lives will be influenced no less by *heaven ↔ hell* than if those destinations are facts. Whether or not evolution and creation are fact or fiction, the rivalry between the two explanations for our existence is real to people who believe in one or the other, or cannot make up their minds about which one to believe in, or have only a detached interest in the quality of argument. Tensions are about competitive, complementary relationships between facts, or what some or all people think are facts.

So, someone who is wrong about the 'facts' can experience a tension; that is, the raw tension issues from fancy but is real to the player and to the analyst who creates a formal construct from it. In the divorce case mentioned above, *infidelity ↔ fidelity* and *divorce ↔ marriage* denote real tensions generated by wrong perceptions of infidelity. In the woman's mind, the idea of infidelity contrasts with and dominates the idea of fidelity, just as she is drawn towards divorce away from marriage and acts to engineer the transition.

To the third major inference from the survey: As influences on human behaviour, tensions exist only if people experience them, but they can influence us whether or not we notice and articulate them *as* tensions. At first glance this point may seem to drag us into the land of questions about angels on pinheads, or whether thunder exists if no one hears it, and so on. Yet the answer is obvious enough—the formal *construct* can be invoked only by someone conscious of a raw tension in himself or in others, or in the physical world; but the raw tension can exist without being noticed, let alone formally defined. Although we might not be conscious of a tension that influences us, an observer might infer it from our behaviour or we might do so in hindsight. Again, the psychiatrist sees the patient experience bipolar disorder even if the patient does not see it and perhaps even denies it. Or take a collectivist team negotiating with one that comprises members who tend to be individualistic. All players might notice that the overall style of the transaction is pulled towards collaboration by the first team and combativeness by the other. At the same time, no member of either team may be conscious of the associated tension, expressed as *collectivism ↔ individualism*, but it does exists and does influence negotiation style. A tension analyst might watch the group and record the transaction style as *combativeness ↔ collaboration* linked with *collectivism ↔ individualism*. (Detailed notes would link the two tensions and clarify the dynamics that the double-headed arrows represents for *this* transaction.) Thus we can distinguish between the constructed tension and the raw tension, which the players might not even notice, let alone construct. The first is a formal statement and summary of the second. The next chapter will revisit the style tension in negotiation.

Note that the psychiatrist does not need to have bipolar disorder to diagnose it in others, which is a principle that applies to all tensions, including those influencing negotiation. An independent analyst or one or more negotiators may see a tension affecting others without necessarily experiencing that tension; but an astute negotiator observing the tension in other players is using it to make sense of what he sees and will take it into account for tactical or other reasons.

To the fourth inference: Tensions vary according to polar types, the interaction of the poles, and the relative significance of each tension—that is, the influence of a given tension compared with others in the situation being analysed. As the last point is self-evident I will not elaborate here but will give examples in Chapter 4 when I introduce a tension-based negotiation model and discuss ways in which negotiators may reduce or intensify the influence of some tensions.

There is much literature on polar concepts but it tends to restrict the poles to binary oppositions that are clear conceptual contrasts, contradictions or negations (e.g. Needham 1987, Cohen 1949a, Hegel 1821, Hertz 1909/1973); whereas the tension concept in this book includes them but is less constrained. Some tension poles are clear conceptual contrasts, and in that sense they are symmetric (*yin ↔ yang, night ↔ day, left ↔ right*). Others are obviously asymmetric because they are different but not in clear contrast (*respectability ↔ reputation, intelligibility ↔ identity*; in Chapter 1, the indebted student tries to decide what to do with a lottery prize—*study loan ↔ new car*). Some poles may be conceptual contrasts, but because they are on a continuum and phase into and out of one another there is no clear point where one phenomenon gives way to the other (*individualism ↔ collectivism, sourness ↔ sweetness, command economy ↔ market economy*). It follows that the presence of one phenomenon does not exclude the other. For example, *negative emotions ↔ positive emotions* may embody a tendency for me to be more influenced by positive than negative emotions, but the presence of one in my life does not exclude the other at a given time.

In another sense that concerns polar *interaction*, all poles are separated by a continuum. On it we locate their relative influence on behaviour at a given time and try to work out and perhaps manipulate the dynamics of their relationship. As implied by the formal definition of the tension, the relationship between the phenomena (the poles) is always dynamic, even when the contest is even, because they compete for influence.

When the poles compete for influence on human behaviour, their relative pull at a given time may be equal or unequal, and constant or variable; if variable, the weight of their influence moves along the continuum, either oscillating or shifting clearly towards one pole. Take *study loan ↔ new car*. The student may be indecisive if the strength of the poles is equal and constant; if it is unequal and constant, the student may become more and more inclined to make a choice but the pull might not be strong enough to have that effect. If the relative influence of the poles oscillates, the student may continually change his mind; if the transition to one pole is clear and re-lentless, the student is likely to make a decision and stick to it.

In this chapter I have travelled wide and deep to show the normal place of the tension in our lives, whether or not we recognise it in any formal sense. The raw tension influences human behaviour in myriad settings; as an analytical device the tension is powerful because the formal construct reflects a way we tend to interpret and act upon our world—perhaps well, perhaps badly—as we try to survive and prosper with varying degrees of success and failure. Yet the actors and analysts who rely on the tension do not seem to understand it very well. This does not mean a person cannot be a great negotiator without grasping and consciously using the tension con-struct as an analytical device, just as a great writer need not dwell on formal grammar. But if we can better understand the tension, it follows that we will at least refine our repertoire for trying to read our own and other people's behaviour at any time and in any place. On the other hand, I might sing like a cat in agony even if I have a vast repertoire of songs.

As this book is about negotiation, we must ask if there is enough mean-ing in all this to enlighten analysts who are interested in the behaviour of the players. This, at least: negotiators are people, so they tend to identify and try to manage tensions in contexts that are replete with actual or po-tential conflict and are therefore tension-rich.

The tension pandemic does not *prove* that something expressed as the tension construct is inherent or genetic or universal; but it is evidence to that effect. Although we may see the pandemic as evidence that we impose tension-based order on chaos because we are predisposed to do so, by nature or nurture, there must be doubt about the judgment of individual analysts who rely on a formal construct to identify and define tensions. We are not reporting hard science here, so I present tension-based analysis as *one* way to frame and try to interpret the influence of relationships between phenomena. It cannot be proven right in itself or at the expense of other frameworks, no matter how credible it seems to be. On the other hand, a survey of negotiation literature and a few case studies will bolster my claim that we can usefully interpret negotiation as a form of tension management.

↔ ↔ ↔

# Chapter 3

## « Tensions in the Negotiation Literature »

### A MEDLEY IN NEED OF ORDER

Raw tensions are facts that characterise negotiation, whether or not the players are conscious of the poles 'competing' for influence on the course and results of the transaction. My concern here is not with the whole of the negotiation literature but a selection of works that include good examples of tension-based thinking used to organise and analyse negotiation process and content. Later chapters relate the tension in some depth to literature on framing in negotiations, and to aspects of cognition.

The negotiation literature is replete with tensions and their management but the treatment is very limited, rarely explicit and always ad hoc; no one even recognises the tension as a generic construct, let alone one that warrants study in the interests of better analysis and practice. Even where tensions are recognised the discussion is enlightening but constrained; yet some treatment does evoke an expanded, systematic application. The best example is by Lax and Sebenius (1986), who know their analytical focus on cooperation and competition between parties to negotiation is not new; but, they claim, analysts who see both cooperation and competition tend to examine them separately:

> A deeper analysis shows that the competitive and cooperative elements are inextricably intertwined.... There is a central, inescapable tension between cooperative moves to create value jointly and competitive moves to gain individual advantage. This tension affects virtually all tactical and strategic choice. Analysts must come to grips with it; negotiators must manage it (Lax & Sebenius 1986: 29-30).

Their term "tension management" refers to the way we create and maximise joint value with allies while making sure we negotiate our rightful share of the creation as we seek the right balance between competition and cooperation (co-opetition).

Nalebuff and Brandenburger (1996), influenced by game theory, seem to draw on the main theme of Lax and Sebenius but do not refer to tensions or tension management. They advise us to control our competitive impulses so that we create value of some sort while making sure the tactics we use to get our share do not impede value-creation. This is a version of the 'win-win' prescription, which assumes negotiators can and want to overcome their need to be in control, and in most cases their need to be *seen* to dominate. These writers' use of the tension concept is interesting but they seem to be overly rational and idealistic in their analysis and prescription. They ask too much of negotiators. Ideals have merit as a set of behavioural guidelines but should not be confounded with the reality of human behaviour, which is often less than consistent and rational. We struggle with *ideals* ↔ *actions* in negotiations just as we do in other realms. My wife believes me when I claim to espouse Christianity's Ten Commandments without being a Christian, but she also says I spend a lot of time breaking several of them.

Although Lax and Sebenius miss *ideals* ↔ *actions*, they come close to a grasp of the centrality of the tension construct in negotiation. Unfortunately they limit their analysis to a single tension that does not convey the kaleidoscope of negotiation in business or other realms. The analyst and practitioner might identify, explore and try to manage an array of other relevant tensions—highly specific to a given negotiation—that may be subordinate to a dominant tension. In the approach of Lax and Sebenius, this would be the tension between cooperative creation of value and competitive claiming of value. But, like all authors I have read, they do not consider exploring and applying the generic tension in the analysis and practice of negotiation. It is a pervasive construct that is significant far beyond the particular tension, albeit important, identified by them. In addition, Allred (2000) says Lax and Sebenius are vague about how to actually manage the tension.

Similar limitations are found in other negotiation literature that includes explicit tensions. Several contributors to Mnookin and Susskind (1999) explore "the tensions of agency" (2) associated with the role of the negotiation agent in relation to the principal. Perhaps the most powerful of these explicit tensions involves the search for a mutually acceptable balance between the interests of the principal and those of the negotiating agent. In that volume, Cutcher-Gershenfeld and Watkins include explicit verbal and graphic tensions associated with the complex role of the agent; these tensions must be "managed" (1999: 47). They "take issue with the practice of treating the roles of principals and agents as dichotomous and mutually exclusive" (27). The authors do notice the continuum between the roles, and allude to a process of tension management; but they do not go beyond the relationship between agent and principal to consider the generic value of the tension concept in analysing and managing negotiations.

Early in one of the best-known papers in the field, Weiss uses double-headed arrows to summarise aspects of negotiation as a set of ranges that vary across cultures (1994). For example, "Protocol may range from informal to formal; the desired outcome may range from a contract to an implicit understanding" (53). He focuses on the range of possibilities rather than the relationship between the extremes, and does not refer to 'tensions'; but his brief discussion of these ranges does suggest managed or spontaneous movement along a continuum, and therefore implies the extremes are in tension because they are clearly complementary and compete for influence on the players' behaviour. The same relationship applies to the culture-based "scripts" about the meaning and method of negotiation (*own script* ↔ *other script*) that players bring to any transaction. A sense of the need to manage this tacit tension underlies eight strategies suggested by Weiss as feasible ways to deal with variation in a negotiator's familiarity with another's culture. For example, a negotiator who is moderately familiar with a counterpart's culture *might* adapt to the other person's negotiation script: "Negotiators often modify their customary behaviour by not expressing it to its usual degree, omitting some actions altogether, and following some of the counterpart's ways" (55). This strategy might impair negotiation if even two players try to use it in a simple transaction (56) and cause a wreck if people of several cultures try it in a more complex one; but my purpose here is not to describe or analyse Weiss's paper much beyond saying how *own script* ↔ *other script* underpins his model, and that the tension construct adds life and meaning to it.

The cultural drivers of this tension are strong in my research cases, but politics, personality, profession, fear of being a puppet, and other forces also spur the players to engineer the script in order to hold reasonable control over the negotiation process. Because the influence of *own script* ↔ *other script* is so strong I look for it in every transaction and advise other analysts and practitioners to do so.

Salacuse (1998) relates cultural influences on negotiating style to a list of ten dimensions. They are clear tensions because they are about the relative influence of the poles on the players during a given negotiation. He does not define culture even though it is central to his study, and the paper—despite its title—is less about how people negotiate than how they *say* they see negotiation; but a more significant problem is an assumption that poles are mutually exclusive. For example, a negotiator who focuses on gaining a "contract" (one pole) may also focus on developing personal "relationships" (other pole) so that one outcome reinforces the other—the poles are complementary, not exclusive. My intention is not to attack Salacuse but to present his paper as one that would have been enriched by a detailed grasp of the tension construct.

There are plenty of tensions in the works of scholars involved with or influenced by Harvard's Program on Negotiation and its flagship, the *Negotiation Journal*. Many of these works include explicit and implicit examples, and are often concerned with the need for negotiators to manage the tendency to defend rigid positions when it usually makes more sense to move their focus to underlying interests (*positional focus ↔ interest focus*). Provis (1996) says many authors misjudge the nature of positions and interests, and do not see that their relationship and role are often too complex for a routine change of focus. I will return to this point when I discuss the elements of my formal model of negotiation in Chapter 5. My immediate purpose is to give examples of tension-based ways of thinking, not to dispute the content of the works from which they are drawn.

In *Getting to Yes*, probably the most influential book on negotiation, Fisher, Ury and Patton (1991) do not call the conflict between positions and interests a 'tension' but that is surely the essence of the relationship. 'Tension management' would describe the process of negotiators acting to focus away from rigid positions towards underlying interests. Pairs of adjectives that label potential agreements of different strengths are tensions—for example, the broad categories "Stronger" and "Weaker" subsume "substantive" in contrast with "procedural", and "comprehensive" versus "partial" (72). A table showing differences in the interests of the parties to negotiation is a set of tensions: "form" versus "substance", "economic considerations" versus "political considerations", "hardware" versus is in Fisher, Kopelman and Schneider (1994)—several tables on "currently perceived choices" are sets of pluses and minuses that encapsulate case studies in international relations. A table of contrasting positions and interests summarises the Sikh-Hindu conflict in the Punjab as a set of tensions (in nature if not by name) that encapsulates the core issues of sovereignty and water supply (40). Watkins and Winters (1997) include tension-based graphics and discussion on international dilemmas and attempts to manage them—for example, American envoy Richard Holbrooke's mediation in the Balkans.

Tension-based thinking is also found throughout Fisher, Schneider, Borgwardt and Ganson (1997). For example, Chart 4-9 is a two-column checklist of frequent differences of interest between parties in cross-border negotiations, so that one party's concern with "form" is paired with the other party's concern with "substance"; "ad hoc results" are paired with "the relationship"; "precedent" with "this case", and so on (64). The authors say "a way to contrast these different positions and interests is to write out in parallel columns statements of position that identify the dispute" (63). Chart 4-10 is a "tool" for "looking behind opposing positions for interests that may be reconcilable" (65). It is organised according to the positions and underlying interests of "Their Side" and "Our Side". In a case study of the Antiballistic Missile Treaty, the point is made that a brief based on a positional bargaining approach "presents a dilemma for the negotiators by setting up a stark dichotomy between tough and flexible, or 'hard' and 'soft' approaches to negotiations" (100). Overall, in coverage of issues, style, strategy and tactics, the book contains much discussion and many charts that embody the tension construct.

In international negotiations, perceived incompatibilities in cultural identities, combined with political, economic and other considerations, may generate a tension in which a "fortress" mentality struggles with the "bridging" attitude essential to good communication (Salacuse 1993). The negotiator cannot hope to manage this tension without a thorough grasp of the key contextual forces that combine with culture to generate or bolster the fortress mentality in a given negotiation. The way culture in particular interacts with other forces to create implicit tensions is apparent in Faure and Rubin's collection of cases on international disputes about water supply (1993). They contain many examples of the fortress mentality and the rigid positions that are extreme forms of Fisher's "mindsets"—"persistent structures of the mind [that] affect ... international interaction" (1988: 2–3).

In another sense, the idea of a fortress is associated with the intensity of hostage negotiation, which abounds in tensions. For example, Womack and Walsh (1997) present a graphic model of the relationship between negotiator and hostage-taker. The model is replete with convincing tensions (e.g. deception versus truth) but the authors do not appear to recognise the generic construct as an analytical umbrella.

The same applies to Lewicki, Saunders and Barry (2006), a renowned academic textbook on negotiation. It abounds in discussion of implicit and explicit tensions, including Hofstede's cultural dimensions and their significance for international negotiators. Their summary of Janosik (1987) refers explicitly to tensions and dialectics that characterise contradictory values within a society. For example, there is a tension between two proverbs (Lewicki et al. say "parables"): " 'Too many cooks spoil the broth' and 'Two heads are better than one.' These parables offer conflicting guidance for those considering whether to work on a task alone or in a group. This reflects a dialectic, or tension, within the Judeo-Christian tradition regarding the values of independence and teamwork" (Lewicki et al. 2006: 418). To bring out the richness of meaning in this tension in a specific negotiation, I would express this struggle for influence over individuals and groups as *independence ↔ teamwork*, relate it to *individualism ↔ collectivism*, and group it with other relevant tensions to bring out the character of the transaction. Neither Janosik nor Lewicki et al. consider going anywhere near that far. The tensions are not defined systematically as tensions and the possibility of a generic tension is not recognised.

Hofstede's cultural dimensions are relevant to negotiation because they reflect the influence of value differences on cross-cultural relationships (Hofstede 2001, 1994). Values are one element of culture; they are "broad tendencies to prefer certain states of affairs over others. Values are feelings with an arrow to it: they have a plus and a minus side" (1994: 8). We may criticise Hofstede for equating cultural groups with nations, and for aspects of his research method, but there is evidence that his framework can guide us to cultural differences that may have significant influence on real negotiators (Brett 2001; Hofstede & Usunier 1999). 'May' is crucial. Experienced negotiators know culture always influences individuals and groups, but it is often over-estimated at the expense of other influences (Lewicki et al. 2006: 413), perhaps because academic focus has distorted its relative weight.

The tension-based model of international negotiation presented later in this book absorbs some of the five dimensions identified by Hofstede. Because they are prominent in the negotiation literature, it is worth looking at what Hofstede says they imply for international negotiators. Lewicki et al. (2006) summarise Hofstede's (1989) detailed speculation on what each dimension implies for negotiation. I would add that when negotiators with cultural tendencies located at different points on the dimension come together, this creates a tension that represents complementary and competing influences on the negotiation process. The tensions are:

1. *Power Distance (from small to large)*: "The extent to which the less powerful members of institutions (like the family) expect and accept that power is distributed unequally" (Hofstede 1989: 195). Where power distance is large, decisions tend to be taken at the top (e.g. Malaysia); where it is small, decision-making tends be distributed throughout the organisation (e.g. New Zealand). International negotiators from cultures with large power distance "may need to seek approval from their supervisors more frequently, and for more issues, leading to a slower negotiation process" (Lewicki et al. 2006: 416).

2. *Individualism versus Collectivism*: In collectivist cultures (e.g. Indonesia) people are oriented towards "strong, cohesive ingroups [that offer protection] in exchange for unquestioning loyalty" (Hofstede 1994: 260). In individualist cultures (e.g. Australia) "ties between individuals are loose: everyone is expected to look after himself or herself and his or her immediate family only" (261). (Most Australians would reject "only.") As negotiators from collectivist societies tend to focus on relationships, "changing a negotiator changes the relationship, which may take a long time to rebuild. Contrast this with individualist societies, in which negotiators are considered interchangeable, and competency (rather than relationship) is an important consideration when choosing a negotiator" (Lewicki et al. 2006: 415). This dimension absorbs Hall's (1976) continuum of low-context to high-context communication style, which has been shown to be a function of individualism and collectivism (Gudykunst & Ting-Toomey 1988; Gudykunst & Kim 1997).

3. *Masculinity versus Femininity*.[1] In a feminine society (e.g. Finland) "social gender roles overlap: both men and women are supposed to be modest, tender and concerned with the quality of life" (Hofstede 1994: 261). In a masculine society (e.g. Japan) the "roles are clearly distinct: men are supposed to be assertive, tough and focused on material success; women are supposed to be more modest, tender, and concerned with the quality of life" (262). In summary of Hofstede (1989), Lewicki et al. say "this dimension influences negotiation by increasing the competitiveness when negotiators from career success [masculine] cultures meet; negotiators from quality of life [feminine] cultures are more likely to have empathy for the other party and to seek compromise" (2006: 416).

4. *Uncertainty Avoidance (from strong to weak)*: This is "the extent to which the members of a culture feel threatened by uncertain or unknown situations" (Hofstede 1994: 263). Negotiators from countries with strong uncertainty avoidance (e.g. Greece) "are less comfortable with ambiguous situations and are more likely to seek stable rules and procedures when they negotiate" (Lewicki et al. 2006: 416). Those from cultures with weak avoidance (e.g. USA) "are likely to adapt to quickly changing situations and will be less uncomfortable when the rules of the negotiation are ambiguous or shifting" (416). Smith (2002: 127) says: "Hofstede ... asserts that critics have frequently misinterpreted the dimension as referring to risk avoidance. He notes that one can reduce uncertainty either by taking risks or avoiding them." Therefore we should not assume negotiators from a country with weak uncertainty avoidance are always more likely to take risks with style, and other aspects of negotiation process and content, than players from the other end of the dimension.

Several years after his original study, Hofstede added a fifth dimension that Lewicki et al. (2006) do not mention: *Long-term Orientation (LTO) versus Short-term Orientation (STO)*. It expresses "the extent to which a culture programs its members to accept delayed gratification of their material, social, and emotional needs" (Hofstede 2001: xx). Negotiators from STO nations (e.g. Canada) may be concerned with quick results and the bottom line rather than "perseverance towards slow results" (Hofstede 1994: 173) associated with relationship building and a structured problem solving approach in LTO nations, such as China (2001: 366-7). Independent research shows a strong correlation between LTO and a problem solving approach in negotiations (Graham, Mintu & Rodgers 1994).

The dimensions raise many questions about stereotyping and the difference between what people do compared with their expressed ideals. An hour spent observing the action at the Hong Kong or Shanghai Stock

---

1. Lewicki et al. (2006) substitute "Career Success" and "Quality of Life" for "Masculine" and "Feminine" without explaining why, although they seem to think values thought to be masculine promote career success and acquisitiveness at the expense of values thought to be feminine, such as warm relationships, nurturing, and so on. Earlier editions of their book use Hofstede's terms. The change makes sense because the original labels seem to be founded on stereotypes that might misrepresent and offend men in particular, and obscure the fact that some female negotiators are much more ruthless, uncompromising and self-serving than most men. Note Raiffa's conclusion that there is no convincing evidence of intrinsic differences between men and women as negotiators (1982: 122–123).

exchange leaves no doubt that many Chinese investors seek something other than the delayed gratification of LTO. Also, as the research was based on nations, should we assume Malaysian Chinese negotiators have the same tendencies as Malaysian Tamils or ethnic Malays? Do the practitioner's tendencies change with experience in international negotiation? To what extent do individuals match the norms? We must consider such questions for each negotiation if we wish to use Hofstede's framework, but this does not detract from its value as a guide to cultural differences that *may* influence particular players or groups (Brett 2001). Kahane says prudent generalisations about culture are risky but necessary in negotiation (2003: 11). Smith says it is unreasonable to argue against relating individual behaviour to broader cultural context: "My point [is] to question whether we need to resist these temptations.... What is the use of characterizing cultures as a whole if we cannot then use our characterizations to gain a more fine-grained understanding of what goes on within them?" (2002: 122).

The literature tends to be vague about how to use Hofstede's dimensions to practise and analyse negotiation. The negotiation model in the next chapter reflects my view of them as dynamic tensions with poles that draw negotiators one way or the other, not as descriptive, static scales on which nations are located according to their reported traits. Hofstede's measures of central tendency are based on the responses of real people who carry values into negotiations and bring them into play, and I therefore disagree with Janosik's apparent view that his dialectic approach can handle individuals and their variations within cultures, whereas Hofstede's approach cannot do so. For example, it is normal to see push and pull between an 'individualist' negotiator who wants to go straight to the content and a 'collectivist' who wants to focus first on relationships as an element of process. We may see this difference within a team or 'across the table'. In either case, two formal tensions come to mind: *individualism* ↔ *collectivism* (reflecting Hofstede to the extent that it concerns cultural propensity) and *content* ↔ *process* (my creation). My model includes them, as they need to be recognised by analysts and managed by practitioners.

A thread of 'compete or cooperate' connects Hofstede's dimensions with negotiation style, often dissected into more or less complex categories and graphics based on the dual concerns model (e.g. Blake & Mouton 1964; Pruitt & Rubin 1986). The model has four (sometimes five) styles that blend high and low concern for one's own and others' interests, and weigh assertiveness against cooperativeness. A typical summary is in Miall, Ramsbotham and Woodhouse (1999), who place the five styles on a two-dimensional figure with Concern for Other on the vertical axis and Concern for Self on the horizontal one:

> high concern for Self and low concern for Other ... is a 'contending' style. Another alternative is to yield: this implies more concern for the interests of Other than Self. Another is to avoid conflict and withdraw: this suggests low concern for both Self and Other. Another is to balance concern for the interests of Self and Other, leading to a search for accommodation and compromise. And there is a fifth alternative, seen by many in the conflict

resolution field as the one to be recommended where possible—high regard for the interests of both Self and Other. This implies strong assertion of one's own interest, but equal awareness of the aspirations and needs of the other, generating energy to search for a creative problem-solving outcome. (5)

Style is complex; but, despite variation between models in the number of dimensions and the way labels are defined, and whether or not the styles are distinct alternatives, style comes down to behaviour, at a point in time or in a pattern over time, that locates a negotiator on a continuum between competition and cooperation (*competition ↔ cooperation*). This tension has rich meaning and is consistent with depictions of style in which the extreme competitor strives to win the lion's share of the pie, to dominate, to bully, and is more concerned with the self than with the other. In contrast, the cooperative stylist wants the fairest agreement, may be subordinative or accommodating, and tends to be concerned with the other as well as the self—perhaps because otherwise there will be no agreement. (Cohen 1980, Fisher et al. 1991, Hawkins & Hudson 1990, Jandt 1985, Thomas & Kilmann 1974)

The extremes of competition and cooperation (sometimes labelled 'collaboration') can handle any variations on style. I agree with Fang's view that negotiating "behavior can be viewed as any form of human action" that influences the transaction, but not with his view of behaviour and style as synonymous (1999: 8). Style is always about pattern but behaviour can be random.

It is helpful to see style at two levels that apply to individuals and teams in domestic and international transactions. First is the broad tendency to operate towards a given end of the continuum over an entire transaction, as a calculated strategy or for non-strategic reasons, such as personality; second, multiple tactical or impulsive movements along the continuum. Thus, at some point a player might become briefly combative as a tactic, but have a collaborative profile overall. The *strategy* at macro level and the *tactics* at micro level are manifestations of tension management. They are about efforts at control. In explaining the way a negotiator controls or tries to control a transaction, the analyst would lose meaning by not distinguishing between levels of style, and by not separating deliberate management of negotiating style from more general patterns of behaviour. I will return to that point at the end of the chapter but in the meantime, to make it easier to discuss the literature, I equate style with the standard terms 'competition' and 'cooperation' or 'collaboration'.

Some authors identify more than the collaborative and competitive style categories. The nature of a third category diagnosed by Richards and Walsh (1990) throws light on the relationship between negotiating style and tension management. They say problems or dilemmas (the text shows they mean disputes) under negotiation are approached with one of three basic styles: competitive, collaborative or subordinative. The competitive negotiator tries to win and make the opponent lose; the collaborative negotiator finds and focuses on common interest rather than a predetermined position, and seeks a mutually beneficial agreement. So far, so good.

The subordinative negotiator plays to lose, hoping the other party or parties will have mercy. Like a dog that hopes to avoid a kick from an intruder or cruel owner, this negotiator is said to roll over in a situation perceived as hopeless. The subordinative negotiator should not be confused with the excellent negotiator who knows when to say 'No!' and walk away (Kozicki 1993: 184, 189). According to Richards and Walsh, the subordinative negotiator rejects the competitive style, with its rigidity and determination to win, in favour of concession.

There are degrees of loss, and anyone who is negotiating is at least attempting to cut losses. Anyone playing to lose *everything* is not really negotiating. If negotiation is taking place at all, the intention of the subordinative stylist is to *minimise* loss, with the approval of the antagonist. Because subordination is designed to reduce loss, and is very short on competition, the style is at the collaborative extreme of *competition ↔ collaboration* (to stay with the style labels of Richards and Walsh). However craven the negotiator may be, subordination is a tactic for managing the tension—to induce the persecutor to take a less competitive approach (i.e. in the jargon, more win-win than win-lose). The subordinative negotiator manages the tension in the sense that he or she attempts to manoeuvre the other party away from competitiveness along the continuum towards collaboration. Thus, I see subordination as a strategy or pattern of tactics designed to influence another party's style. Like most tension management, it is an attempt to change the influence and balance of an enduring tension, not an attempt to eliminate it.

Variations on the subordination technique are found in many cultural settings. For example, March (1988) says "If you ask Japanese businessmen to describe the most typical Japanese method of resolving or avoiding disputes, they will most frequently answer '*naniwabushi*'"(22). The strategy is a melodramatic plea for concession, based on the structure of ballads dating back to the Edo period (1600–1868). You recount the general background to your current difficult circumstances, then detail critical events that illustrate your deteriorating lot; you then conclude

> with an anguished plea for leniency, embroidered with the dire consequences [for everyone] should the request be denied.... *Naniwabushi* is artful, premeditated, calculated—and in Japan it works. The more tragic and moving the story, the easier it is for Japanese listeners to forget contracts or commitments. Indeed, listeners who do not compromise or show compassion in such circumstances would be condemned as being cold-hearted or mercenary. (March 1988: 23)

A real estate agent with the upper hand in a tight market can be forced to concede ground for fear of damage to personal and professional reputation. This is subordination employed as a tension management technique to manoeuvre the other party towards collaboration, away from the competitive pole of the style tension. The dog might roll over but it will bite if you kick it anyway.

Mulder's Placator (anything for a quiet life) is similar to the subordinative negotiator and opposed to the competitive, belligerent Bully (1992:

45-47). He sees them as extremes on a scale. By inference from earlier discussion of subordination as a technique, the Placator is a stylist who tries to manage the transaction—to increase the chances of desired outcomes—so that all players collaborate more.

Although Richards and Walsh (1990) tend to segregate their three basic styles, the typical writer defines two styles as extremes but not clear alternatives. The extremes reflect the competitive and collaborative styles of Richards and Walsh.

Rose locates style on a competitive–collaborative continuum (1989: 82); Hawkins and Hudson present a competitive–cooperative "negotiation style dimension" (1990: 14). Kozicki's Quick and Deliberate extremes are about competing and cooperating (1993: 7–9). He advocates thinking about style as "a continuum allowing you flexibility depending upon which style you are using at any given time" (1993: 7). Mulder, an international veteran, uses different labels but clearly understands the point:

> Between the Placator and the Bully lies a myriad of negotiating styles. Professional negotiators can usually move up and down the scale from Placator to Bully depending on what's needed in a particular negotiation and upon their own personal philosophy. They are able to attune their response to the different styles they come into contact with. (Mulder 1992: 45)

Such calculated choice and use of style variations from Quick to Deliberate, or Bully to Placator, is tension management at strategic and tactical levels.

To illustrate the stylistic tension and its management in a real negotiation scenario, take formal debate. This activity involves an extreme form of the competitive negotiating style, where opponents take predetermined, contrasting positions and fight for them without conceding ground. At strategic and tactical levels, they strive to be competitive in style. The idea is to win the debate and defeat the opponent. The transaction involves tension, where two contrasting positions are in competition; they are also complementary because one cannot exist without the other: *affirmative position ↔ negative position*. The poles are like teams in a tug-of-war, with oscillating advantage; but each adversary strives to win, and usually one does. Competitiveness is a feature of Australian Federal and State parliamentary sessions, where Government and opposition debate under two chief negotiators, with minor parties and independents usually backing one major team or the other. The tension might be expressed as *government ↔ opposition*. Although government almost always wins, through strength of numbers if not quality of argument, the conflict is real, as it might be in regular chess games between a grand master and a novice who always loses.

While noting appropriate but limited tactical uses of competitiveness, Richards and Walsh (1990) applaud the collaborative style, which starts with a search for a common interest. Most writers call the style win-win; Herb Cohen calls it "collaborative Win-Win" (1980: 150). Rose calls it "Blue ... the peaceful colour" as opposed to "Red, the warning colour.... The Blue style is typified by attitudes such as 'I will win only if you win too;' 'I will cooperate to find the common ground between us where we can both get some of our wants' " (Rose 1989: 81, 84). Thus, win-win and win-lose, synonymous with integrative and distributive, are labels for both styles and results.

From their experience of the Harvard Negotiation Project, Fisher et al. (1991) advocate a search for common interest as the basis of successful (i.e. to them, win-win) negotiating. In relation to China in particular, Blackman thinks this point of view reflects an American preference for a friendly atmosphere, rather than a grasp of the reality of negotiating (1997: 53). She says Chinese are emotional and dictatorial when they negotiate with *Chinese* outsiders within Chinese society as well as with foreigners (1997). Shue Lam Yip says Chinese believe negotiation is warfare and so there is always a winner and loser; they rely on dishonesty and other sharp tactics intended to bewilder, disorient, frustrate and demoralise foreign negotiators (1995: 182–183). To the contrary, Chen Ming-Jer says Chinese negotiators "strive to maintain smooth interpersonal relations throughout all phases of negotiation, and often expect their Western counterparts to do the same" (2001: 145). US trade negotiator Charlene Barshefsky, mulling over her bouts with Chinese Trade Minister Wu, would probably agree with Blackman and Shue rather than Chen on the approach to foreigners (Walsh 1996; Cooper, Davis & Johnson 1999). If so, she would find support in Fang (1999).

Jim Camp, one of the most experienced business negotiation coaches in the USA, says the win-win game is a trap set for naïve players by people who advocate it but do not use it themselves: "Those smooth-talking negotiators *don't* compromise, but they demand that you do" (2002: 6). No matter how strong or weak the win-win idea may be, my concern is that the search—naïve or otherwise—for a common interest expected to deliver win-win is a form of tension management designed to head off the actual or potential conflict inherent in all negotiations.

One tension identified in writing on style involves a trade-off between dominant personal style and the stylistic demands of the situation: *personal style ↔ situational style*. Rose says most people overcome the individual tendencies prompted by their attitudes and experience, so that a standard Red or Blue style is unconsciously adopted for a given type of situation (Rose 1989: 83). His examples suggest he advocates more flexibility, so that a person who normally uses a Red style might be better off settling on a Blue one. I would add that the expert does not see the two styles as exclusive, and knows when and how to move backwards and forwards along the continuum of Red–Blue (*Red ↔ Blue*) to cope with the changing context of a particular negotiation.

Bartos implicitly equates individualism with win-lose and collectivism with win-win when he identifies a tension-based link between style and conflicting motivations:

the individual (competitive) desire to maximize one's own utility *and* the collectivistic (cooperative) desire to reach a fair solution. In fact, we believe that negotiations proceed smoothly only as long as they are guided by the collectivistic desire for fairness; that problems arise whenever the individualistic motivations take over. (Bartos 1977: 13)

The sentiment is commendable, but to correlate smoothness and fairness is dubious. Negotiation involving Mulder's extreme types of Placator and Bully may be smooth but not fair. But this does not detract from the importance of Bartos's concept of motivational conflict as an example of a tension, in need of constant management, located within the individual negotiator — *individualist desire ↔ collectivistic desire*.

*Yin ↔ yang* is at the core of Fang (1999), who says outsiders (read 'Westerners') cannot hope to understand Chinese negotiating style — which he defines to the point of non-defining by saying it includes any behaviour at all — without delving into the complex cultural and other influences on the balance of competitive and cooperative behaviour.[2] He includes many Chinese examples of tension-based thinking. Kanayama (1996) is a Japanese study of style-related tensions generated by cultural differences between Japanese and Chinese negotiators about the nature of harmony and conflict, and about the relationship between them. Tensions apparent in differing views on correct behaviour in public and private situations, by insiders opposed to outsiders, further complicate Sino-Japanese negotiations. Kanayama also alludes to a tension (my term, not his) between the ideals that Japanese and Chinese people espouse and the way they behave. An analyst who identifies difficulties caused by a negotiator's failure to take into account the relationship between espousal and behaviour might express this tension as *ideals ↔ actions* — ideals compete with patterns of incongruous behaviour for influence over the negotiators, and tend to lose the battle. Kanayama's paper could be encapsulated in a set of tensions rich with meaning to a negotiator who must manage or advise on a Sino-Japanese transaction.

Managing style-related tensions is a ploy to maximise control of the negotiation. Such management is complex: you manoeuvre your own style along the continuum; through self-manoeuvring and other tactics, you try to manipulate the stylistic behaviour of other players; you use stylistic variation (your own and others') to create an ambience, for the overall negotiation, that improves your chances of agreement. That is, adept negotiators manage style to improve their chances of success in managing other tensions. Some experts know how to move their own and other players' styles back and forth along the continuum between competition and cooperation

---

2. Fang does not say the Chinese should consider delving into the complexities of other people. Chen Ming-Jer, in a book that often confuses ideals with behaviour (*ideals ↔ actions*), presents Chinese negotiators as so naturally sensitive and astute that they have no trouble understanding crude Westerners, who do not have the same capacity to understand the culture-rich Chinese (2001: 143).

to match or create contextual changes (Blackman 1997: 53; Kozicki 1993: 7; Mulder 1992: 45).

To finish my survey of the tension in academic literature on negotiation, I want to discuss the single work that best supports my argument for a refined knowledge of the tension and tension management. Mnookin, Peppet and Tulumello (1996) say negotiation "characteristically involves the management of three different tensions" (217). I have already discussed two of them: the first is the Lax and Sebenius tension between competition and cooperation; the second is between the interests of agent and principal. The third, the subject of the paper, is between empathy and assertiveness: "By assertiveness, we mean the capacity to express and advocate for one's own interests. By empathy, we mean the capacity to demonstrate an accurate non-judgmental understanding of another person's concerns and perspective" (218).[3] They say the tension exists because many negotiators wrongly assume assertiveness and empathy are incompatible "polar opposites" along a single continuum. There is stalemate at the midpoint: "In short, many negotiators feel stuck" (218). The authors "propose that empathy and assertiveness do not represent polar opposites along a single dimension and that rather they should be conceptualised as two independent dimensions of negotiation behavior" (218). Like Hegel, they seem to think a real tension must have incompatible poles. They also seem to think one pole must lose absolute as well as relative influence as the other gains strength. This limited concept leads the authors to a debatable view of negotiating styles and the way empathy and assertiveness relate to them.

The tension exists if people perceive it, no matter whether or not they *should* see empathy and assertiveness as incompatible polar opposites. But if it does not make sense for negotiators to see them as such, one approach to managing the mistake is to explain the tension's false premises, as Mnookin et al. proceed to do. They say an effective negotiator is empathetic and assertive as required. To make their case they create a two-dimensional figure with empathy on the vertical axis and assertiveness on the other, and call it "Two Independent Dimensions" (222). To create a second graphic called "Negotiation Styles" (see Figure 3.1 below) they add elements of the dual concerns model, so that high empathy associates with an accommodating style and high assertiveness with a competing style. An avoiding style, located where the axes meet, "consists of low levels of empathy and assertiveness" (224). (They say the framework "measures" assertiveness and empathy, which is contentious.)

---

3. It would be more logical to say "the capacity to form" rather than "demonstrate", as you can have empathy without demonstrating it to the satisfaction of an observer. A mute quadriplegic might be empathetic but unable to demonstrate it. I prefer Reber's definition: "Assuming, in one's mind, the role of another person [and] taking on [their] perspective" (1985: 238).

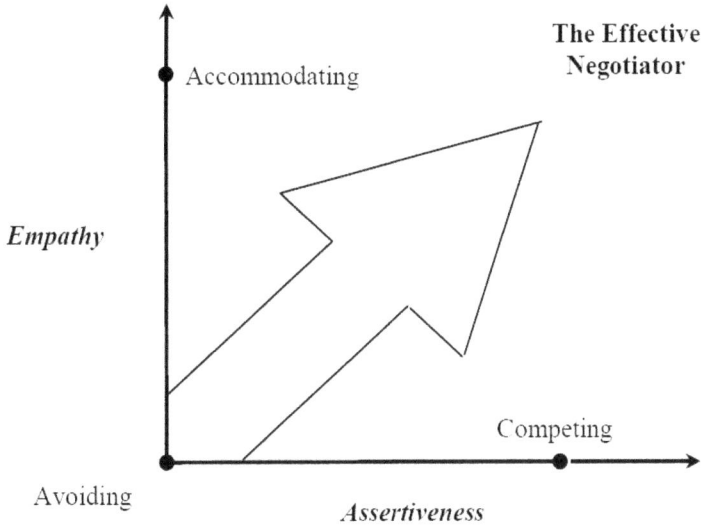

**Figure 3.1:** Negotiation Styles
Source: *Mnookin et al, 1996: 223*
'The tension between empathy and assertiveness.' *Negotiation Journal*, 12(3), 217–230.
© Reproduced with permission.

The authors say "the normative [i.e. prescribed] task is to manage the tension between empathy and assertiveness by moving to the 'northeast' on [the] graph ... and by helping design a process that permits the other side to do so as well" (226). They locate the "Effective Negotiator" in the far northeast where both empathy and assertiveness are high. The figure also seems to prescribe a style half-way between accommodating and competing, but this does not recognise the strong, empathetic tactician's ability to move either way as needed.

The attempt to argue for better understanding of the relationship between empathy and assertiveness is admirable, but the authors create conceptual problems by separating the two and matching them to negotiating styles. It does not make sense to propose two independent dimensions and then show how they intimately complement one another. Moreover, the framework seems to generate an oversimplified concept of style. For example: "A competitive style consists of substantial assertion but little empathy" (223). This belies the virtuoso negotiator's ability to empathise with other players, and then apply a great deal of assertion as a timely and informed tactic, perhaps to restart a stalled negotiation or to force concessions in a one-sided encounter with bullies. An 'avoiding' negotiator may be so because deep insights into the other party have led to a decision to back off, at least temporarily. This stylist may have low assertiveness at a given time, or over time, but not necessarily low empathy.

Their figure does not seem to represent the tension between empathy and assertiveness; rather, it is used to help explain that the tension should not exist because the poles are really independent and compatible. For that purpose the graphic is useful even though it is muddled a little by dubious definitions and placement of particular styles. But the paper says empathy and assertiveness *are* in tension for many negotiators, which means they are *inter*dependent according to my tension definition: 'two complementary phenomena that compete for influence over the perceiver's mental and other behaviour'. Like Mnookin et al. I believe the two are compatible, but the tension between them does exist nonetheless for many negotiators. Unlike those authors, I do not see why high levels of empathy cannot be associated with any given style, so that an extreme competitor could use insights gained through empathy to get a bigger slice of the pie than a less assertive counterpart.

Although Mnookin et al. do not give much evidence, they are probably correct when they say many negotiators see empathy and assertiveness in tension because they *seem* incompatible. But the authors seem to think that because empathy and assertiveness are compatible, and not distinct opposites, they are not really in tension. This tension concept is too limited, as poles do not necessarily represent dichotomies or any other type of incompatible or conceptually opposite phenomena.[4] It is possible for assertiveness and empathy to be compatible and not clear opposites, yet compete for influence over negotiators who happen to think the two are incompatible.

If empathy and assertiveness are assessed for negotiators in real transactions, the analyst might help the players to understand and manage their apparent inclination to succumb to the influence of one *or* the other, or to fall back on a stalemate. For the practitioner, the point is not to explain away the tension, but to recognise it in oneself and others, and find a way of managing it so that it does not hinder negotiation.

I have looked at the paper by Mnookin et al. in some detail because it has given me an opportunity to argue for a more refined grasp of tensions in general. Even though the authors do not recognise a generic construct, and do not compare tensions for relative weight or other traits, the paper is valuable because it recognises rich tensions at the core of negotiation and spurs us to analyse them. It implicitly supports my theory of negotiation as tension management. The authors do not say how a negotiator who sees *empathy* ↔ *assertiveness* in a counterpart would apply an understanding of its origins and effects; but I do not think they need to do so as it is reasonable to assume a better-informed practitioner will make better use of the standard range of skills to tackle problems caused by misunderstanding in the context of a specific negotiation.

---

4. See Jacoby (2008) for an amusing polemic on the 'scholarly' fad of attacking any analytical framework based on "binary thinking". Objectors seem to think that anyone who produces such a framework is a "reductionist"—the ultimate academic insult—who sees only rigid dichotomies that deserve scholarly deconstruction by sharper minds. Osama bin Laden is a promising client: "I tell them that these events have divided the world into two camps, the camp of the faithful and the camp of the infidels" (2001).

Across the beach between academic and creative writing, Francis Walder in *The Negotiators* (1960) and Frederick Forsyth in *The Negotiator* (1989) capture the negotiation process in different ways. The former novel reflects on the nature of the diplomatic mind and temperament; the latter is about hostage negotiation and is more a novel of action.

My specific interest is in a quotation from Walder that brings home the way the individual negotiator embodies complex tensions. The narrator describes Monsieur de Mélynes, the chief negotiator for the Huguenots, who seek religious and political autonomy within 16th century France: "You would think, as I did, that there were at least two persons there and the contrast between those two, so different, characters provoked the fancy that he had a whole range of others, intermediate, with whom you would have to reckon" (31). Just as *evil* ↔ *good* encapsulates Stevenson's Jekyll and Hyde, *combat* ↔ *collaboration* embodies the style of de Mélynes, albeit a more benign character than Stevenson's creation and notable more for manoeuvring himself and other players back and forth along the tension continuum than for parking himself, or allowing others to park themselves, at one extreme or the other. Walder's creation reminds analysts to search for tensions defining the individual negotiator's behaviour, which in turn influences the calculated and spontaneous behaviour of other players.

Overall, the literature seems to invite negotiators to assess and manage their own and others' sense of context—to heed the blend of contextual forces and tensions in specific situations. The literature also conveys a persistent message that figurative barricades associated with context, including the issues under negotiation, hinder communication. Understanding and heeding the blend suggests *sensitivity* ↔ *insensitivity* in the individual negotiator and within a group. The arrow is a clear continuum, as no one is entirely sensitive or insensitive, and everyone's sensitivity is changeable.

In summary, explicit and implicit tensions, and examples of tension management, pervade studies of negotiation process and content by diverse writers of different cultural origins. Explicit concepts of the tension do tend to be shallow, and no one recognises the tension and tension management for their power as generic constructs that represent a pervasive way of thinking in a wide range of intellectual, aesthetic and other human activity, including negotiation. Yet the representation of a thing is not the thing itself, but a new 'thing'.[5] Therefore it would be a step too far to say that all or any individuals, in any place at any time, use a tension model to think, or that they experience only what the tension construct represents. Moreover, other analytical models can claim to represent reality: "This clear tendency towards dual systems [of thought and organisation] ought not, however, to blind us to the occurrence of other patterns" (Bateson 1973: 15). On the other hand, for negotiation in particular it is enlightening

---

5. This seems to be the main point of Magritte's annotated painting of a pipe: "Ceci n'est pas une pipe."

to break down complex structures into the sets of related tensions that comprise the 'scenario' in the model proposed in the next chapter.

In the negotiation literature, the problem with the tension construct is its constrained and piecemeal use in an area of intercourse that is a smorgasbord of tensions, not least because it is founded on actual or potential conflict. Yet, in these influential works where tensions abound, there is no recognition of the tension as a construct to be defined, studied and applied to negotiations in general. The main purpose of this book is to foster better analysis, and perhaps practice, by way of a tension-based model of context that supports my understanding of negotiation as tension management. Rather than incidental use of the tension concept, I advocate a deliberate and central place founded on the training of analysts to identify tensions and their nuances as a matter of course in specific negotiations, and to describe and explain how the players manage those tensions. I bring out the complexity and nuances of the tension, and show how this illuminates negotiation. In the literature, the many ad hoc examples suggest merit in a tension-based model of context and action.

## A SURVEY OF NEGOTIATION DEFINITIONS: NEGOTIATION REDEFINED

If I advocate the tension as a generic construct for analysts, beyond the limited usage ascribed to authors already discussed, my stance has implications for defining negotiation. If tensions and tension management are at the core of negotiation I should have misgivings about definitions that do not refer explicitly to tensions. An apt definition should highlight them.

Existing definitions tend to evoke tensions, in part because negotiators are in a relationship of actual or potential conflict, whether all players use a collaborative style, all are combative, or style varies. It even makes sense to say two negotiators are in conflict when they both struggle to gain advantage by using a collaborative style. Definitions from diverse academic and other literature always embody conflict that is explicit or implicit, actual or latent. Here is a cross-section: "a process whereby a compromise is reached by parties whose interests are in conflict" (Bartos 1977: 23); "a field of knowledge and endeavor that focuses on gaining the favor of people from whom we want something" (Cohen 1980: 15); "the art of reaching an agreement by resolving differences" (Kozicki 1993: xiii); "a combination of searching, dividing, game-playing and fraud" (Cross 1977: 35); "a back-and-forth communication designed to reach an agreement when you and the other side have some interests that are shared and others that are opposed" (Fisher et al. 1991: xiii); "the process whereby parties within the conflict seek to settle or resolve their conflicts" (Miall, Ramsbotham & Woodhouse 1999); "a process whereby parties with conflicting aims establish the terms on which they will cooperate" (Hawkins & Hudson 1990: 6–7); "the art of getting what you want by convincing others that they will benefit from association with you in business or personally" (Mulder 1992: 8); "settling conflict [by] reaching a mutually satisfactory agreement with people" (Rose 1989: xiii); "win-win situations such as those that occur when parties are trying to find a mutually acceptable solution to a complex conflict" (Lewicki et al. 2006: 3).

At least one author is unsure about explicit conflict: negotiation is "the process of discussion by which two or more parties aim to reach a mutually acceptable agreement" and "the process by which two or more parties meet to try to reach agreement regarding conflicting interests" (Deresky 2006: 153, 467). Two definitions by Pruitt and Carnevale (1993) imply existing conflict, at least over content. Negotiation is "a discussion between two or more parties aimed at resolving incompatible goals" (xv), (which does not consider the need to negotiate ways to achieve compatible goals); and a few pages later: "a discussion between two or more parties with the apparent aim of resolving a divergence of interest and thus escaping social conflict" (2).

The presence or absence of explicit reference to conflict may reflect the experience, roles and research specialisations of the definers. They bring personal frames to the idea of negotiation and to practice. For example, Bartos is an academic concerned with strategic arms control; Cross seems to be a negotiation cynic; Miall, Ramsbotham and Woodhouse are specialist writers on deadly international conflicts; Cohen's interests are manifold. As one would expect from lexicographers, there is a graceful definition in the Oxford English Dictionary: to negotiate is "to confer for the purpose of arranging some matter by mutual agreement; to discuss a matter with a view to a settlement or compromise" (Oxford English Dictionary 1980: 1393).

Most definitions assume conflict is overt from the start. If not, it is close to the surface, according to labour disputes veteran Ted Kheel: "Since agreement is usually the stated objective of both sides in a negotiation, the possibility of disagreement is always present" (1999: 28). For instance, parties with identical or compatible intentions may wish to negotiate ways to achieve them, and so the transaction may be largely about conflict avoidance rather than resolution. Although the possibility of conflict is ever-present, several of the definitions quoted above are defective because they assume negotiators start out with conflicting aims and possibly rigid positions.[6] In fact, current or likely allies with common aims or interests—a joint venture, for example—may wish to clarify those aims or interests and negotiate ways of achieving them. Amicable, undisputed trade-off is a negotiation process: 'We like your suggestion that you take 55 per cent of the equity, and our people fill 60 per cent of management positions.'

---

6. In many works advocating congeniality that makes everyone a winner, apparent slips of the pen reveal an underlying view of negotiation as adversarial. A glaring example is in a popular win-win 'toolkit' book by Roger Volkema—a subheading is "Scout Your Opponent" (1999:169).

Weiss's definition of international business negotiation does not assume a current dispute: "the deliberate interaction of two or more social units ... originating from different nations, that are attempting to define or redefine the terms of their interdependence in a business matter" (1993: 270). Phatak and Habib do not mention a dispute: "a process whereby two or more parties ... interact in developing potential agreements to provide guidance and regulation of future behavior" (1996: 30). Iklé (1964: 2) says: "Without common interest there is nothing to negotiate for, without conflict nothing to negotiate about"; but he also says the necessary conflict is based on a diplomatic definition of negotiation that requires "confrontation of explicit proposals ... where conflicting interests are present" (3–4). He says these elements are essential to "negotiation (as here defined)" and so allows for other definitions in other realms.

Any definition evokes tensions because they are at the heart of actual or *potential* conflict over positions, interests and elements of process, including style and tactics, in an activity designed to maximise gain and minimise loss for one or more parties. They communicate because they must manage these tensions to reach agreement. Therefore, I define negotiation in general as 'consultation between two or more parties that involves the management of tensions associated with attempts to seek an agreement'. This definition is compatible with any I have found so far, and does not assume negotiation is *only* about tension management. Add 'across national borders' after 'agreement' and the definition adapts to international negotiation. It accommodates both the content and process of the transaction, is compatible with any negotiation type (e.g. one-to-one, multilateral) and suits any realm, including diplomacy, business and hostage negotiation.

The definition recognises that people of the same nationality and culture might represent different nations, or sub-groups or individuals from different nations. For instance, Australians of common cultural background represented both Australia and Papua New Guinea in the Torres Strait Treaty negotiations, according to informant Malcolm Lyon, Australia's team leader. Even so, international negotiations do tend to have cross-cultural complications: "... negotiating is a social process that is embedded in a much larger context. This context increases in complexity when more than one culture is involved, making international negotiation a highly complicated process...." (Lewicki et al., 2006: 405).

Earlier in this chapter I said I would later specify my use of negotiation 'style' because the literature is inconsistent. When some writers discuss 'competition' and 'cooperation [collaboration]' as styles they seem to confound a broad strategic approach with the specifics of negotiator tactics and incidental behaviour. For instance, some writers on the dual concerns model say 'strategy' when they mean style in the latter sense (e.g. Miall et al. 1999). When they allude to individual behaviour as calculated 'strategy' they are referring really to lower-level tactics, perhaps designed deliberately to match an umbrella strategy.

To writers in the tradition of Lax and Sebenius the umbrella strategy—co-opetition—is designed to create a bigger pie and share it well.

The formula is for negotiators to compete for their fair share while cooperating with counterparts to swell the pie. Ideally the minutiae of negotiator style would match the umbrella strategy, but tactics and incidental behaviour are not so simple. A good example is a variation on the black hat, white hat tactic. A negotiation team with a broad strategy of co-opetition may tame a born-to-rule counterpart by having one combative member unsettle her, then retreat; a milder member takes over and assuages the pompous counterpart in the hope that her future behaviour will not undermine the broad strategy. No one has deviated from the strategy; the tactics that may not seem to match the strategy are calculated to foster it.

I prefer to separate broad strategy from specific tactical and incidental behaviour, rather than lump them together as competitive and cooperative styles. To clarify my usage from here on: *competition* ↔ *cooperation* refers to the negotiation strategy; it is about the big picture. For that tension I will refer to 'strategy' not 'style'. Strategy is a broad, calculated pattern of negotiating behaviour in relation to the tension between competition and collaboration. *Combat* ↔ *collaboration* refers to tactical and incidental behaviour at micro-level, at a given time and in patterns over time, intended to support strategy but not necessarily doing so. I use 'style' only for that tension. Writers who mean micro-behaviour when they refer to a competitive style (belligerence, aggression, demand, dominance) mean what I mean by 'combat'; to the same writers, a cooperative or collaborative style (composed, reserved, harmonious, and so on) equates with my 'collaboration'. The big picture and detailed behaviour are so important to analysis of negotiation that I assume both the strategy and style tensions are always present.

From here on, I assume tensions are significant in every negotiation.

↔ ↔ ↔

# Part II

**《 Poles and Arrows 》**

**International Negotiation as Tension Management**

# « Poles and Arrows »

## International Negotiation as Tension Management

*When I took a decision, or adopted an alternative, it was after studying every rel-evant—and many an irrelevant—factor. Geography, tribal structure, religion, so-cial customs, language, appetites, standards—all were at my finger-ends.*
T. E. Lawrence [of Arabia], *letter to B. Liddell Hart*, 1933

*The flavours are only five in number but their blends are so various that one cannot taste them all. In battle there are only the normal and extraordinary forces, but their combinations are limitless; none can comprehend them all.*
Sun Tzu, *The Art of War*, c. 400 BC

## *Preamble*

Tension-based analysis is one way of interpreting human behaviour and cannot be proven right at the expense of other frameworks, no matter how credible it seems to be. Nor do I claim that negotiators should or can think only about tensions. On the other hand, it is reasonable to assume from the coverage in Part One that because negotiators are people they will tend to see or sense tensions in a negotiation and try to manage them. If so, much of their negotiating behaviour can be explained as tension management in a context inordinately rich in tensions. I propose that we can improve analysis through a systematic search for significant tensions, and that we can better analyse negotiations if we refine our understanding of tension types and dynamics, and the forces that generate tensions.

Chapter 4 restates the tension-based definition of international negotiation to set the scene for a model of negotiation context, interpreted as an open system of forces and the tensions they create. This model transcends others by linking infinite contextual forces with tensions, and presents a generic tension construct that subsumes ad hoc tensions in the negotiation literature. 'Scenarios' are sub-sets of tensions; they are frames distilled from the broader context to epitomise a given negotiation. At this stage I treat the model of context as a tool for independent analysts and do not prescribe it for negotiators. Chapter 10 explores its value to analysts who are also practitioners.

Culture tends to be a strong force in international negotiations, and in this model it is prominent but not necessarily the most powerful. I outline my culture concept and relate it to others in the negotiation literature. My overall focus is international but the model also applies to domestic transactions, in which culture may often be more significant than in the international arena. Few Israelis or Sri Lankans would disagree.

'Tension management' is defined to match the negotiation concept. Tension categories, properties and conditions are explained and organised in the detail needed to define scenarios and distinguish negotiation as tension management. Chapter 5 describes the process of defining and redefining scenarios.

Readers who are shy of theory and have a taste for fine literature should now discard this book and get a copy of Francis Walder's *The Negotiators* (1960).

# Chapter 4

## « The Negotiation Context »

### Forces, Tensions and Scenarios

This chapter explores the finer points of an international negotiation model with tension management at its heart. International negotiation is 'consultation between two or more parties that involves the management of tensions associated with attempts to seek an agreement across national borders'. The definition calls for a model of context and practice that exploits the tension construct, organises the relationship between tensions and their origins, and serves as a framework for independent research. As cultural differences tend to typify and complicate international transactions, it should pay attention to culture within a system of other influences.

## ELEMENTS OF THE NEGOTIATION CONTEXT

In this model the negotiation context comprises tensions and the forces that generate them. Tensions express the actual or potential influence of contextual forces on the content and process of negotiation. Analysts using the model (perhaps to complement other analytical tools) identify what they believe to be significant tensions and their origins, and consider the way negotiators are managing, have managed or might manage those tensions. By 'significant' I mean tensions that do or may influence negotiators to think and act in ways that do or may affect the path to agreement, and the nature of the agreement itself. The effect may be positive, negative, or somewhere in between. By 'origins' I mean the contextual forces that generate tensions. For example, forces giving rise to the ethical tension *personal ethics* ↔ *corporate practice* (described in Chapter 1) include endemic corruption, corporate ethics, and the negotiator's personal code.

Consistent with most textbook models of managerial context or environment (usage tends to be synonymous) my model places the forces in one of two categories according to whether they are specific to the transaction or more distant, more general, and clearly beyond the control of the players. In my model the first category is 'immediate' and the second 'macrocosmic'.

In the realm of negotiation, my two categories owe something to the model in Phatak and Habib's 1996 paper 'The dynamics of international business negotiations'. With significant forces in mind, the authors divide the international negotiation context into the 'environmental context' and the 'immediate context' (Figure 4.1). The former comprises macro forces that are beyond the control of the negotiators, and influence the negotiation process and outcomes. Macro forces are uncontrollable in the sense that negotiators cannot dispose of them or modify them in any absolute way, but should try to manage their influence. Such forces include culture, law, government, bureaucracy, ideology, and external stakeholders who have an interest in results but are not involved directly in the negotiation.

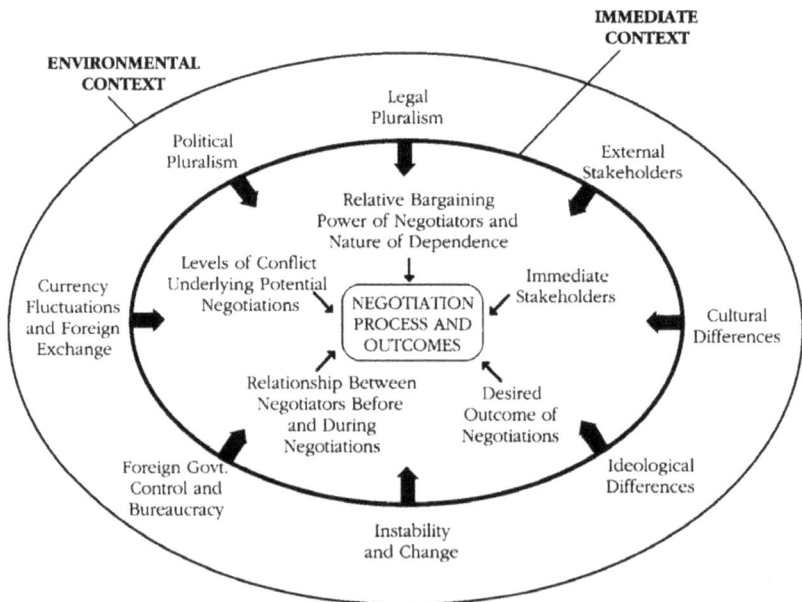

**Figure 4.1:** Phatak & Habib's Contexts of International Negotiations
*Source: Phatak & Habib (1996: 31)*
'The dynamics of international business negotiations'. *Business Horizons*, 39(3), 30–38.
© Reproduced with permission.

To Phatak and Habib's macro forces I add globalisation, history, geography, ecology, terrorism, corruption, communications, technology, and so on. The list is not definitive but open in order to reflect the complex and ever-changing system of interactive forces from which the negotiator must distil manageable order, without respite. They are abstracted from the system and labelled so that we can discuss that system and human behaviour within it. The forces interact and many overlap; for instance, political and economic forces are interdependent and not mutually exclusive. Macrocosmic forces tend to be of global, international, regional and national magnitude—for example, the economic boom in Asia during the early 1990s, then the sudden and widespread economic decline of 1997. Of the forces giving rise to *personal ethics ↔ corporate practice*, discussed in Chapter 1, endemic corruption is macrocosmic because the negotiator cannot avoid it or influence it in any absolute sense.

Phatak and Habib's immediate context comprises "factors [forces] over which the negotiators have influence and some measure of control" (30). The forces include relative bargaining power, levels of conflict, the negotiators' relationship, desired outcomes, and the specific cultural and other personal characteristics of the immediate stakeholders (the negotiators and their constituents). These characteristics include negotiating strategy, style and tactics. (I will explain later how my model includes strategic and stylistic tensions created by differences between the parties). I include the substantive issues, positions and interests because, as elements of negotiation content, they connect with the desired outcomes. As with macro forces, the list is open, the forces interact, and some overlap. With *personal ethics ↔ corporate practice*, the negotiator's personal code and the company's practice are immediate forces because the negotiator might have significant control over them.

My model substitutes 'macrocosmic forces' for Phatak and Habib's 'environmental context', and 'immediate forces' for 'immediate context'. I restrict 'context' to the totality of forces and the tensions they generate. (Moreover, 'environmental context' seems tautological.) Adding the tensions as an element of context is a step beyond Phatak and Habib and other authors who see context or environment only as forces (factors, influences), usually in immediate and more distant sets.

Phatak and Habib's list of immediate forces appears to be inspired by a view of a negotiation as an ad hoc organisation. The forces I add to their list are consistent with this impression. Just as the internal forces of an organisation are not the organisation itself, but are housed within it, the immediate forces in a negotiation are not the negotiation itself but are located there. For this reason I house the two types of contextual forces in the 'locus', which comprises two zones: the immediate zone is the negotiation proper, and the macrocosm is everywhere beyond the immediate zone. In Figure 4.2, which summarises my model of the negotiation locus and context, the immediate zone is separated from the macrocosm by a broken line to symbolise the somewhat arbitrary separation of the negotiation proper from the macrocosm.

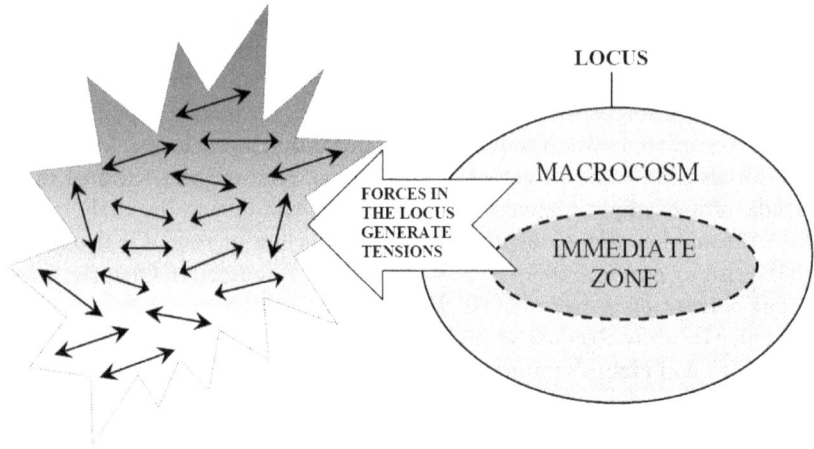

**Figure 4.2:** The Negotiation Context

Apart from the much too limited and conventional range of forces that other authors identify, I find no serious fault with the mainstream managerial models of context or with Phatak and Habib's negotiation model. Rather, I see an opportunity to build upon them by expressing the influence of contextual forces as sets of tensions. The step from context as internal and external forces to context as forces and tensions is prompted by much of the discussion in earlier chapters about implicit and explicit tensions in my research data and in literature on negotiation and other topics.

## THE NEGOTIATION SCENARIO

Forces in the locus are changeable. As an open system it generates an infinite number and configuration of tensions. As symbolised in Figure 4.3, the 'scenario' is a sub-set of tensions selected because the analyst thinks they are highly significant for a specific negotiation. The scenario is a framing device for excising relevant tensions from the broader context and expressing them in manageable order for an explicit purpose—to clarify the issues and other forces that ought to be taken into account when negotiators try to agree. Contextual information is chaotic until the analyst identifies, selects, defines and organises tensions as a scenario to reflect an underlying order that is otherwise obscure. The rich meaning of each tension is specific to a case, even though the model prescribes some tensions for every negotiation, and others that are not prescribed may be detected in more than one negotiation. I will return to these points later in this chapter and in Chapter 5, when I explain the technique for defining tensions and creating scenarios, and relate the scenario to academic literature on framing.

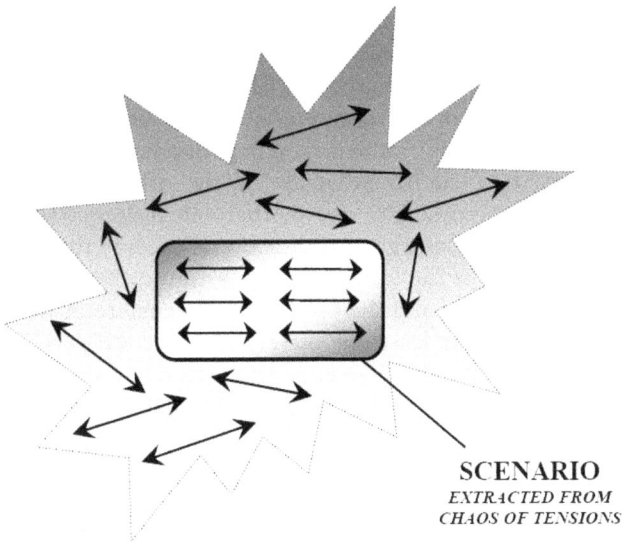

SCENARIO
*EXTRACTED FROM*
*CHAOS OF TENSIONS*

**Figure 4.3:** The Negotiation Scenario

## TENSION MANAGEMENT AND CLEAR CONTEXT

A clear view of context is crucial to the analyst and depends not only on credible linkages between forces and tensions, but also on a refined and structured grasp of the tension itself. It is not enough just to identify tensions. It is also necessary to study polar types and tension dynamics as they have implications for understanding how the negotiator reacts to tensions—the negotiator-as-manager can modify some; others influence the way the negotiator behaves but cannot be modified readily, if at all.

There are categories and properties that the analyst must understand in order to identify and record individual tensions and scenarios. To found analysis on such categories and properties is consistent with my concept of international negotiation: 'Consultation between two or more parties that involves the management of tensions associated with attempts to seek an agreement across national borders.'

I need to restate the tension basics, drawn from previous chapters, to set the scene for the finer detail of categories, properties, tension management and scenario definition. The generic tension is 'two complementary phenomena that compete for influence over the perceiver's mental and other behaviour'. The generic tension subsumes all types of binary relationship that involve competition and complementarity, including the dilemma, options, alternatives, quandary, ambiguity, paradox, contradiction, and opposition. In a figurative sense, the tension poles compete for influence over the negotiator as perceiver. A passive dyad—a simple pairing—is not a tension.

The relationship between the poles is expressed as a double-headed arrow (↔) to provide a parsimonious and manageable reflection of tension-based thinking. The poles have arbitrary labels with rich meaning to people who define a given tension and scenario. 'Compete' means the poles represent phenomena that vie for influence on negotiators; the influence of one pole determines the relative influence of the other. 'Complementary' means the poles give meaning to one another; one makes no sense without the other in the context of a given transaction. Forces in the macrocosmic and immediate zones of the locus generate tensions; the negotiation context comprises the forces and the tensions they generate. A tension exists in a negotiation only if at least one player experiences it personally and is influenced by it. A player may detect a tension in other players, and it may influence his tactical and other behaviour, including a decision *not* to change his strategy, tactics or style.

## OPERATIONAL DEFINITION OF TENSION MANAGEMENT IN NEGOTIATION

Any negotiator manages tensions without necessarily being conscious of them, but here my interest lies in an operational definition of tension management as a deliberate guide to analysis by observers of a transaction, rather than players in the transaction. The analyst looks for evidence of tension management as: (a) implicit or explicit identification of relevant tensions by one or more negotiators, (b) any action that alters the influence of one or more tensions on outcomes and negotiator behaviour; and (c) any attempt to avoid action that would modify tensions and their influence.

Part (c) of the definition is a reminder that not all tensions are malleable, and that it may be unwise or even futile for a negotiator to try to change some of them, rationally or otherwise. However, managing tensions includes reacting to them without trying to eliminate them or change the relative influence of the poles.

Rather than try to explain parts (a), (b) and (c) of tension management in abstract detail, I will ground them in two cases in Part Three: Some Players and Their Acts. In the meantime, two tension categories, four tension properties and eleven conditions are prescribed to ensure the analyst defines and records scenarios consistently.

## FINER POINTS OF THE TENSION

### Tension Categories

As analysts tend to think about *what* is negotiated and *how* negotiators go about it, there are two categories of tension—*content* (expressing issues being negotiated, positions, interests, and desired outcomes) and *process* (expressing style, strategy, tactics, attitudes, and other non-content factors that influence communication). The division is specific to negotiation and might not be suitable for tensions in general, although it is likely to suit most situations in which people define and manage problems.

Negotiation tensions are not in separate macrocosmic or immediate categories that correspond to the zones in the locus (Figure 4.2) because forces from both zones may generate a single tension. To return to the example of a negotiator who knows a bribe to a corrupt official would revive a stalled negotiation with a potential ally: the CEO tells the negotiator to pay like his predecessors in similar situations so that the company's stake is not in jeopardy; but to do so would breach the negotiator's ethics. The negotiator must deal with *corporate ethics ↔ personal ethics*, generated by endemic corruption in the macrocosm and by forces in the immediate zone—the negotiator's ethics, company attitudes, and shareholder pressure for the CEO to show a profit from the alliance.

Tensions are listed as either 'content' or 'process' when a scenario is defined. For example, in a hostage negotiation a ransom demand, in the immediate zone, generates *no payment ↔ full payment*, which is listed under 'content' because it is about the amount to be negotiated. Also in the immediate zone, the negotiators' relationship and relative bargaining power generate *negotiator control ↔ kidnapper control*, which directly concerns conduct and is therefore in the 'process' list. If the hostage negotiator tries to take control too soon and annoys the kidnapper, the former may not be able to reduce the ransom, so that poor tactics and style (process) jeopardise the desired outcome (content).

Every scenario includes *content ↔ process* to flag this type of interplay, which is perhaps most obvious when a negotiator's combative style (process) jeopardises one or more desired outcomes (content)—for example, a collaborative rather than combative tendency is likely to be more successful if we negotiate a business alliance, a peace treaty or a prenuptial agreement, especially if we are the weaker party. Or is a hard-headed focus on content causing problems with process? This tension also alerts us to variations in the way negotiators interpret content and therefore try to manage it—if I think your expected outcomes are based on a distorted view of history, I might decide to calmly educate you as a first step, but then introduce 'noise' by getting angry if you refuse to consider my view of the facts that bear on the negotiation content. This tension is also a reminder that I might see negotiable content where you do not, or we might both see it but in different ways; you alone might think we should do something about it, or we might agree that action is needed but disagree on method.

In comparative studies of Chinese and Caucasian students, Peng and Nisbett (1999) and Nisbett et al. (2001) found culture-related differences in cognitive style that also warn analysts not to approach negotiation as if content and process are separate concerns. In a broad sense, culture—however we might define this elusive concept (see Avruch 2000)—moulds and integrates the way we interpret and manage our world. Content and process are in tension at least to the extent that content may distract negotiators from the need to act in a manner that fosters communication, whereas too much concern with process may impede agreement by distracting negotiators from content.

Obviously *content* ↔ *process* cannot be a member of either of the two lists; rather, it subsumes and links them. The basic relationship is shown in Figure 4.4, the template used to record scenarios. It elaborates the scenario excised from the chaos of tensions in Figure 4.3.

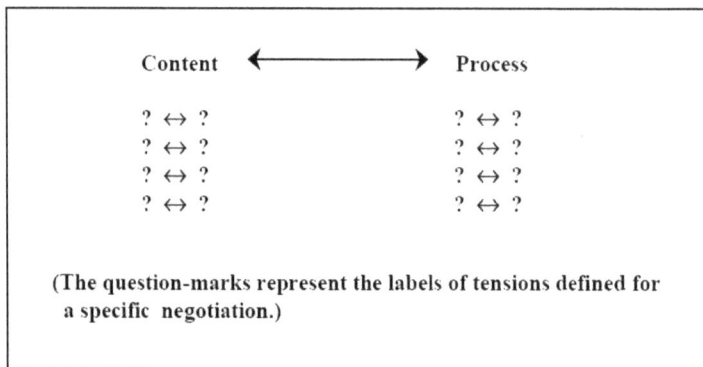

---

Content ◄————————► Process

| ? ↔ ? | ? ↔ ? |
| ? ↔ ? | ? ↔ ? |
| ? ↔ ? | ? ↔ ? |
| ? ↔ ? | ? ↔ ? |

(The question-marks represent the labels of tensions defined for a specific negotiation.)

---

**Figure 4.4:** Relationship Between Content and Process Tensions

## Properties of the Tension

Inductive and deductive reasoning from my cases and the sweeping coverage in previous chapters indicates that four properties capture the generic tension and the rich meaning of each tension in a particular scenario. The first of the four has two conditions; each of the other three properties has three conditions (Figure 4.5). The analyst selects one condition for each of the four properties to describe a particular tension. The first three properties concern the relationship between the poles, and the fourth is about the relative significance of particular tensions in a particular transaction. These finer points encourage thinking beyond simplistic black-white and either-or concepts of tension as the analyst delves into the influence of contextual forces on negotiations.

The letters after the conditions in Figure 4.5 are used to encode tensions when scenarios are created, so that each tension is assigned four letters to denote one condition for each of the four properties. Broad codes are preferred over scales that would suggest unrealistic precision rather than informed speculation about context as an open system of forces and tensions. The condition codes are assessed as the 'average' for all players over the entire negotiation or for a narrower period of interest. (The assessment procedure is explained in detail in Chapter 5.) The analyst describes and explains how the conditions move around the average during the play.

| PROPERTY | Condition | | |
|---|---|---|---|
| 1. **Conceptual Affinity** | Symmetrical (S) | Asymmetrical (A) | — |
| 2. **Balance** | Biased Left (L) | Equal (E) | Biased Right (R) |
| 3. **Balance Tendency** | Move Left (F) | Stable (Y)/Oscillate (O) | Move Right (T) |
| 4. **Intensity** | High (H) | Medium (M) | Low (W) |

**Figure 4.5:** Properties of the Tension

My main purpose in the next few pages is to clarify the concepts of property and condition that apply to tensions in negotiation; but the concepts apply to tensions in any situation, so I draw on a wider range of examples. There may be other properties and conditions of the tension but the ones included in this scheme are adequate and manageable for negotiation analysis.

## 1. Conceptual Affinity

If the poles are clear conceptual opposites they are *symmetrical* (S), and *asymmetrical* (A) if they are not clear opposites. My tension concept, unlike most examples from the literature, does not restrict the poles to conceptual opposition, but some are symmetric in that sense—for example *yin ↔ yang, left ↔ right, negotiator control ↔ kidnapper control, individualism ↔ collectivism*; if the law requires a company to hire a local citizen as manager, despite shareholder pressure to hire a foreigner, the arrow separates two opposite concepts in *local ↔ expatriate*. Other tensions are asymmetric because they are not conceptual opposites (e.g. *study loan ↔ new car*, from the case of the scholarly petrol-head; or, from Crystal's work, *intelligibility ↔ identity*; also *empathy ↔ assertiveness*, after Mnookin et al., 1996).

Whether the poles are *conceptually* symmetrical or asymmetrical, it may not be easy or even possible to separate them clearly when analysing the way they play out in actual behaviour. The poles are clearly discrete in *local ↔ expatriate* in the last paragraph, but where *individualism ↔ collectivism* is at play the two phenomena tend to phase into and out of one another, and it is implausible to say a player is—or can be—a discrete individualist or collectivist, which is not to deny either a clear tendency one way or an irregular pattern.[1] The same applies to groups, even though many people tend to separate Asians and Westerners as if they have two discrete ways of looking at human relationships, at all times and in all places. In psychology, some theorists reject the poles of the personality dimension *extraversion ↔ introversion* as valid opposites "since many persons exhibit aspects of both and may increase in their display of behaviors reflective of one pole without necessarily diminishing display of behaviors reflective of the other" (Reber 1985: 262). To the contrary, whether or not a pure exhibition

---

1. Critics who object to binary categories sometimes commit 'type fallacy': "Assuming a discontinuity between extremes and intermediate cases" (Reading 1977).

exists, the poles are *conceptual* opposites that represent two sets of extreme forces vying for influence over a person's behaviour. Change in the strength and relative weight of the poles as they manifest in an individual has nothing to do with their conceptual opposition.

The double-headed arrow represents transition in *sensitivity* ↔ *insensitivity*—for example, in a marriage where each partner needs to consider the other's emotional needs—as the poles are not absolutes and no person is wholly sensitive or insensitive, at a given time or over time. In *self* ↔ *other* the concepts are discrete but the tension refers to a sometimes cloudy blend of negotiators' concerns for their own and others' interests. As discussed in Chapter 1, we might agree that life and death are discrete concepts but argue about the point at which the struggle between the two is won or lost and a person is either alive or dead. On the other hand, I know from a near miss at Kuta Beach inBali that the difference between the two poles of *life* ↔ *death* may be absolute to someone trying not to drown.

## 2. Balance

Balance represents the *relative* strengths of the poles. For process tensions, 'strength' means influence on the behaviour of individual negotiators or a sub-group or all the players at a given time or over time. For a content tension, the 'strength' of a pole means the likelihood that outcomes will be more or less associated with it, relative to the other pole. For instance, if an observer thinks a hostage negotiator is likely to free the victim without having to make any payment, or by paying only a small proportion of the original demand, the right pole of *full ransom* ↔ *no ransom* is seen to be stronger than the left. Because tensions are about the relative strength of poles competing for influence on behaviour, the poles of all tensions are on a power continuum that reflects infinite blends of influence, regardless of the conceptual affinity of the poles and whether they are clearly discrete phenomena or phase into and out of one another.[2]

The poles may have *equal* weight (E) or one may outweigh the other—(L) for a *left bias*, or (R) for a *right bias*, which means the weight may be anywhere between perfect balance and one extreme or the other. Take *individualism* ↔ *collectivism*, one of the values dimensions (which I see as tensions) in Hofstede's scheme—in America, the former pole tends to have a stronger influence on behaviour; the latter pole tends to be stronger in Japan, and in Israel the balance is about even (Hofstede 1994: 54). The weight is never likely to be at a pure extreme for any person from these countries.

There are many implicit and explicit examples of the balance concept in the negotiation literature covered in Chapter 3. Mnookin et al. (1996) say

---

2. If the poles represent phenomena that phase into and out of one another (e.g. *individualism* ↔ *collectivism*), there is a power continuum and a conceptual continuum—which does not need to be categorised as a property in its own right for negotiation analysis.

the false assumption that empathy and assertiveness are incompatible generates a tension between the two in many negotiators (*empathy ↔ assertiveness*). Some are influenced more by assertiveness and think they cannot be empathetic, while others who tend to be empathetic think they cannot be assertive. Using my codes, the balance is either (L) or (R), but usually the latter, according to the authors, who prescribe an equal balance (E) as the ideal for an Effective Negotiator—oriented 'north-east' in Figure 3.1. (In Chapter 3, I disagree with their prescription but that is not pertinent here.)

Another good example is balance on the agent-principal continuum of negotiator role in Cutcher-Gershenfeld and Watkins (1999). They see the 'pure' agent at one extreme as an ideal type who acts wholly in someone else's interests. That is, the agent's role is to act only for a principal who does not play a direct part in the negotiation. *Agent ↔ principal* is a process tension experienced by the negotiator, and her (I retain the authors' gender bias) behaviour is influenced more by the idea of being solely an agent for someone else's interests than by self-interest. The balance is (L). At the other extreme, if the negotiator sees that her role is to represent her own interests and so works as a de facto principal, the balance is (R). The extremes are tempered by a continuum. In the middle "we find parties who are legitimately representing their own interests—effectively acting as principals—while at the same time representing others—effectively acting as agents. The result is a mixed set of interests being represented, with the consequent tensions [i.e. stress, ill-feeling] and complexities" (28). Each pole has about equal influence on such people, so balance is (E).

### 3. Balance Tendency

When the polar balance is assessed for a specific time or period it may be stable (Y) or there may be a tendency for the influence of one pole to increase consistently, so that the balance is shifting towards the left (F) or the right (T). The balance may be very fluid and influence on behaviour may continually oscillate (O) between the left and right poles.

Take *combat ↔ collaboration*, the style tension. Your normal style may be assessed as 'collaboration' at a given time; but as a deliberate tactic, or through inadvertent change, the balance seems to be shifting towards 'combat' as a stronger influence on your behaviour. The analyst records the trend as (T). A pushy negotiator who makes cultural, political or procedural gaffes may be biased to the right (R) in *empathy ↔ assertiveness*, but she might reduce the problem as she learns from her mistakes and reacts to pressure for more sensitive behaviour—for her the balance tendency is (F). Of course, if she repeats her gaffes she may reverse along the continuum and cause the tension to get an (R) code later from an analyst who is watching her behaviour.

A stable rating (Y) for Balance Tendency should not be confused with a Balance of Equal (E), which denotes an even balance of polar influence on behaviour. A Balance of Biased Left (L), for example, might not show any sign of change and is therefore rated 'stable' (Y) for Tendency. If the nego-tiator mentioned in the previous paragraph is incurably insensitive she is rated (RY).

Some tensions seem to have an inexorable shift in balance from one pole to another (either F or T) and reversal or equilibrium is judged to be im-probable if not impossible. An example from the modern history of In-donesia would be *Dutch control ↔ independence*. By the late 1940s, reversal from (RT) was unlikely if not impossible as Sukarno's declared independ-ence became fact in spite of Dutch opposition. From my international business research, *transformation ↔ conservation*, insofar as it concerns an overall trend towards globalisation of business, is (LF) and will be that way for the foreseeable future (English 1995).

Some tensions may show a trend one way or another at a given time but oscillate over time in the relative strengths of the poles. This condition is present in the theme of *The East-West Pendulum* (Lloyd George 1992), dis-cussed in Chapter 2. Since the 17th century the dominant strength in tech-nology and international trade has moved from East to West but is now moving from West to East. By inference, the pendulum is likely to swing again in the opposite direction. China is said to be moving from economic closure to openness; Lloyd George predicts a return to closure. An example from my research in Thailand is a tension generated by the macrocosmic force of pressure to localise staff (*expatriate recruitment ↔ localisation*), where a company has moved from high expatriate numbers at managerial level to a lower expatriate presence, then back to a higher one as more pro-jects have become available without local managers and technical people to run them.

Another example of an oscillating tension is the second of the "seven fundamental valuing processes without which wealth-creating organiza-tions could not exist" (Hampden-Turner & Trompenaars 1994: 6):

> *Constructing and Deconstructing.* Only an alternating mental and physical pro-cess of breaking down and reintegration can keep an enterprise and its products in a constant state of renewal and refinement. This generates the di-lemma [tension] *Analysing vs Integrating.*[3] Is it better management practice to break phenomena down into parts (facts, tasks, numbers etc.) or to integ-rate and configure such parts into whole patterns, relationships and wider contexts?

This 'dilemma', expressed as *analysing ↔ integrating* or *constructing ↔ decon-structing*, does more than illustrate oscillation. It also suggests the process of scenario definition and the narrower process of deconstructing and re-constructing individual tensions as we create the scenario.

'Tendency' hints at the energy in tension and the potential for change in any negotiation, or in any other situation where at least one tension is found. The policy of nuclear deterrence espoused by major players during

---

3. The authors use 'dilemma' loosely. A real dilemma is a double bind that "offers a choice between two eminently undesirable alternatives" (Chambers Dictionary 2006).

the Cold War suggests a stalemate based on equal balance and stability (EY) of firepower; but there was always a fear (tension in another sense) of the consequences if the balance were to change.

Imagine an agent influenced by *agent ↔ principal* who begins a negotiation with others' interests at heart. She detects an opportunity to make hay; she then advances her independent interests during the negotiation. The role balance moves to the right along the continuum. If the transition were to continue, in the end the agent would become her own principal, completely neglecting the interests of her formal principal. The tendency is (T) as the negotiator gives increasing weight to her role as someone who acts for herself in her own interests. She is managing the tension to suit herself.

## 4. Intensity

'Intensity' codes apply only to *content* tensions. Depending on whether the negotiation is past, ongoing or future, the code denotes the analyst's assessment of the actual or expected degree of difficulty in reaching agreement on matters associated with the tension. Ratings are high (H), medium (M) and low (W). For example, the content tension *no payment ↔ full payment* is very difficult to manage early in most ransom negotiations because the negotiator usually does not understand the kidnapper, and knows the hostage might die if the negotiator and kidnapper cannot agree on payment. The intensity rating is therefore (H). In contrast, it might not be very difficult to negotiate other content, such as keeping the electricity on so that hostages and kidnapper can use heaters and not freeze overnight (*electricity ↔ no electricity*). This is obviously significant content but if the analyst thinks it is, was or will be easy to negotiate the intensity rating for the associated tension is low (W).

I considered having an intensity rating for *process* tensions to record their level of influence on negotiator communication and other behaviour. (Do not confuse 'intensity' with 'balance', which is about the *relative* influence of the two poles in a given tension). After testing the idea on several cases and discussing it with appropriate people, I concluded that all process tensions included in a negotiation analysis have high intensity or they are not significant. In the case of the disloyal agent described earlier, the intensity level of *agent ↔ principal* is always high because the negotiator's changing role has momentous implications for her ability to communicate in a way that will foster agreement. Constant 'highness' does not mean all significant process tensions have the same influence on the negotiation, just that the analyst is concerned only with tensions that do have a strong influence on process. I also considered ratings of high, very high and extremely high but found they did not add anything to the analysis except the smog of over-analysis for its own sake. I then tried to redefine intensity for process tensions but could not see any sense in getting away from their fundamental significance as influences on negotiator communication and associated behaviour. Process tensions do not have intensity codes because they do not need them.

Negotiation gets nowhere if the parties bog down in either content or process instead of balancing and integrating them. Therefore the umbrella tension *content ↔ process* is always highly significant and does not need an intensity code.

Intensity level for *content* tensions may vary during a negotiation through managerial or other influence, including changes in the contextual forces that generate tensions. A hostage negotiator might appease a kidnapper by agreeing to a demand for food, and the latter might react by offering to discuss the ransom figure. If the negotiator finds it easier to reduce the ransom demand, the intensity rating for *no payment ↔ full payment* might fall to (M) or even (W).

Although I have decided not to give an intensity code to process tensions, this does not mean they all have equal or static significance. For example, the intensity of probably the most important tension in any hostage negotiation, *negotiator control ↔ kidnapper control*, might diminish as the kidnapper concedes more control to the negotiator, who becomes more confident of success. The chances of this tension hindering constructive communication and other behaviour has diminished but the tension is so crucial and influential that intensity is always high. The same tension might become an even more intense influence if a third party, such as the media, manages to contact the kidnapper and interfere in a way that thwarts the negotiator's efforts to communicate.

So, process tensions have different degrees of 'highness', which may change for some or all of them during the transaction. This avoids the troubling sense of stasis and uniform significance that detracts from other tensions in the literature—for example, Hofstede's values dimensions, which I have argued (Chapter 2) become more powerful if we see them as tensions with complementary poles competing for influence on behaviour in a given situation.

## OPTIONS & MANAGEABILITY

Managing tensions rarely means the negotiator can or should choose one pole over another as if they are simple options, even though choice may be possible in some cases, such as *study loan ↔ new car*, or as an extreme strategic choice in *competition ↔ cooperation*. In a subtler and more likely example, a Dane realises a negotiation in Japan is stagnating because he is too self-centred, and because he wants to negotiate content right away. He decides to pay more attention to the group interests of himself and his Japanese counterparts, thereby changing the balance of *individualism ↔ collectivism* in the relationship, without trying naively to choose collectivism as a simple alternative to his individualistic bent. His action should also reduce intensity from high to medium or low, so that at least one element of cultural difference becomes less troublesome and perhaps advantageous if he continues to manage it well.

The Dane in Japan demonstrates the negotiator's managerial influence on the effects of cultural and other forces in the *immediate* context. In contrast, *macrocosmic* forces are uncontrollable in the sense that we cannot dispose of them or modify them in any significant way, but a negotiator who manipulates the balance and intensity of tensions generated by them is managing their micro-influence.

Some tensions may be unmanageable in the sense that a negotiator cannot manipulate their balance or intensity. In other cases he or she may be able to manage the effects of their intensity, by diverting attention from them (if they are negative) or broaching them (if they are positive). A Taiwanese negotiating a technology deal with officials in Beijing cannot hope to change the balance of *independence* ↔ *reunification* (SRY), generated by geopolitics, history and ideology. Sovereignty is not under negotiation, so this tension, which is always the dozing dragon in the room when Chinese and Taiwanese negotiate anything at all, is in the process category because it may have a negative influence on negotiator behaviour. To reduce its potential to kill the negotiation, the parties may find a way to push this tension into the background; that is, to divert attention from it in order to improve discussion of matters that *are* being negotiated. Yet its intensity is always high because of the constant and powerful influence of the tension on the players, even if they never mention it.

Not all tensions can or should be changed deliberately for balance or intensity, but the negotiator will try to manage all content tensions because they embody the reasons for the negotiation. In keeping with part (c) of tension management as defined above, some process tensions might be manageable in balance and intensity but are best left alone because they are thought to be constructive as they stand, or too dangerous to meddle with. For example, if large power distance dominates a power-related tension, and a person who expects deference from everyone makes offers that suit a counterpart negotiator who prefers low power distance relationships, it makes sense for the latter person to accept the current balance. Or take *independence* ↔ *reunification*: if Taiwanese and Chinese negotiate a business deal no astute player will try to change anyone else's mind about the status of Taiwan. The analysts should see that a negotiator who leaves these tensions alone is a good tension manager.

## THE VERSATILE SCENARIO

I have depicted the tension scenario as a sub-set extracted from the infinite array of tensions generated by macrocosmic and immediate forces. It is a carefully excised segment of context; a frame that epitomises the main content and process elements of a transaction. Negotiation is the main concern of this book, but the basic negotiation scenario, with its interactive content and process categories for tensions, is a suitable frame for any managerial situation that requires people to work together to define problems, analyse them and make decisions.[4] This is consistent with the idea of negotiator-as-manager. Simpler scenarios that do not distinguish between content and process tensions are implicit in some of the listings of positions and interests cited in the negotiation literature (Chapter 3).

'Simpler' does not mean 'simplistic'. Sets of tensions may look too spare but this is deceptive as they embody rich meaning for whoever compiles them, and for others if the scenario is explained to them. Take Figure 4.6, a summary of John Naisbitt's best-seller of the mid-1990s, when the Asia frenzy was at its peak and foreign investors were obsessed with getting a piece of the pie. His "eight Asian megatrends" are tensions (he does not call them that) in which the right-hand pole is more powerful than the left one; some are symmetrical concepts, others asymmetrical; balance varies; all have a 'balance tendency' of (T). ('Intensity' as defined earlier applies only to negotiation scenarios.)

As a summary of the content and structure of the book, this scenario represents the order that Naisbitt has extracted from the complex forces influencing his perception of the Asian business context in 1995, two years before the Asian economic crisis dampened the frenzy. Anyone who has read the book could readily use this scenario as a mnemonic to explain Naisbitt's ideas in detail. I will not elaborate on the tensions as their meaning is clear enough for my purpose, which is to say that the scenario is a versatile device, and not at all esoteric. The negotiation scenario is a specialised form of the device.

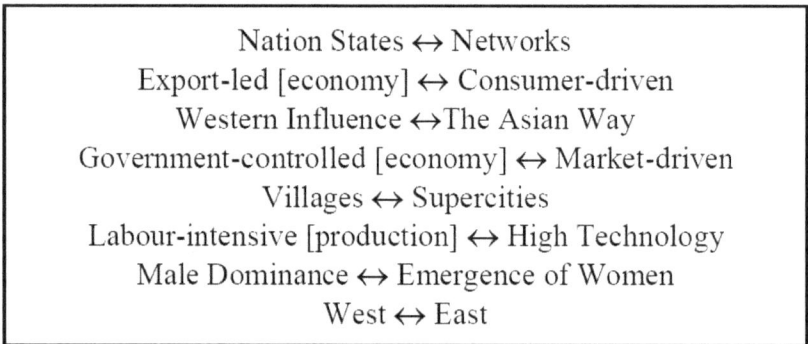

Nation States ↔ Networks
Export-led [economy] ↔ Consumer-driven
Western Influence ↔The Asian Way
Government-controlled [economy] ↔ Market-driven
Villages ↔ Supercities
Labour-intensive [production] ↔ High Technology
Male Dominance ↔ Emergence of Women
West ↔ East

**Figure 4.6:** Scenario for Naisbitt's Eight Asian Megatrends
*Adapted from Naisbitt (1995)*

---

4. Vines and Naismith (2005) prefer my approach to contextual analysis (English 2001) over Snowden's well-known model (2002), mainly because mine makes a stronger link between theory, analysis and decision-making in diverse situations. A war trauma psychologist in Melbourne asked me for permission to train counsellors to use the model for case analysis. A clinical psychologist told me he distributed English (2001) to colleagues at a Harvard teaching hospital. A Chinese management consultant with a renowned international firm told me she heard about my model in Hong Kong.

## CULTURE AS A CONTEXTUAL FORCE IN NEGOTIATION

Analysts creating scenarios should consider culture at macrocosmic and immediate levels. It generates tensions, and influences the way negotiators see and react to them. As Weiss says: "strategies that do not consider cultural factors are naïve or misconceived" (1994: 53). On the other hand, culture does not stand alone, nor is it always a dominant or even significant force. The anthropologist Roger Keesing says "cultural explanations are too often non-explanations or seductive disguises" promoted by education providers with culture mania (1991: 50). You can make a lot of money by convincing people they are insensitive, then offering to sensitise them, and so cure them of 'culture shock' which may be less about culture than stress associated with the traffic nightmare and miasma of places like Bangkok and Manila.

Phatak and Habib (1996) do not detail their concept of culture, perhaps because their main concern is a broad model of context. They might think the concept is too controversial and elusive to tackle in a brief paper. As I have more space than they have, I will outline the controversy in the field of negotiation, and explain how I think the culture concept can help and hinder negotiation analysts and practitioners.

The extremes of opinion in the negotiation literature about the significance of culture are captured in two articles in *Culture and Negotiation: The Resolution of Water Disputes* (Faure & Rubin 1993). William Zartman argues for the negative in 'A skeptic's view' (17–21) and Raymond Cohen for the positive in 'An advocate's view' (22–27).

Zartman does not hold back: "Like the particular type of breakfast the negotiators ate, culture is cited primarily for its *negative* effects.... Like power, class and quarks, we know that culture exists but are uncertain about its precise definition, its referent group, and other more specific attributes" (17, 20). He is probably correct on the first point, as we do hear a lot about inscrutable Chinese negotiators, and crass Westerners whose individualist culture primes them to attack sensitive, collectivist non-Westerners. Zartman also says some analysts interpret negotiation primarily in terms of structural relationships between the players; others focus on cultural influences on their interaction. He says the discussion of cultural influence is tautological because social structure is claimed to be an independent variable that determines aspects of culture, "but social structure is a cultural trait and hence determined by culture, of which it is part" (18). Faure and Rubin think he confuses tautology with complexity and dynamism: "[Culture] is both a dependent variable, reflecting the impact of diverse considerations, and an independent variable, with determining effects on negotiating behavior and outcomes" (225).

Zartman ends his sortie by dismissing culture as epiphenomenal because negotiation results are heavily influenced by many other variables associated with structure and process. Faure and Rubin agree with him about other variables but chide him for confusing subtlety with irrelevance: "Culture's effect on negotiation is subtle and easily explained away in terms of other, more prominent and noisy considerations. This ... does not eliminate the importance of culture, nor does it relegate the concept to secondary or derivative status" (229).

Zartman typifies the avoiders who think culture is too difficult to relate to cause and effect, and so want to ignore it. At the other extreme, Cohen (1993) makes a conventional case for the "often powerful effects of culture on negotiation. [He argues] that culture not only affects the negotiating behavior of individual actors ... but also that cross-cultural antinomies between the parties may affect the course and outcome of negotiations" (22). He does say culture is one of many influences but seems to think it includes almost every prejudice, political stance, and historical annoyance. He focuses on dissonance and incompatibility; for example, behaviour is individualist *or* collectivist, which is at odds with my tension-based view of the relationship. Moreover, he does not mention that common experience, such as diplomacy or development work, may minimise or even neutralise broader differences. In a paper based on his MBA project supervised by me, Rammal confirms my guess that the military background of many Pakistani managers is likely to influence their approach to negotiation (2005: 138). Non-Pakistanis with a military background may find productive common ground with such managers. Some well-known authors refer to the interplay between 'national' culture and corporate, organisational or professional culture during negotiations (e.g. Faure 2002, Kalé 1999, Lang 1993).

Like Hofstede, Cohen sees culture as variations on software programmed into common hardware. The software moulds our perceptions and frames our ideas: "It shapes our actions, defining the rules of interaction for meeting, parting, bestowing hospitality, trading begging, giving—and negotiating" (1993: 24). He seems to confound influence and determinism.

In summary, the skeptic wants to avoid culture because its nature and influence are too hard to pin down and measure, while the advocate wants to make it pervasive, deterministic and antagonistic. The first approach is whistling in the dark; the second sees people as cultural puppets in monochrome and is too broad to be useful.

As the culture concept is elusive, it would be a relief to be like an economist whose neat model is threatened by a variable that nags for recognition but is difficult to measure or define. That is, decide to ignore it, assume it is null, or deny its relevance. But 'culture' is a tenacious concept, so I must say what it means to me, even if I add to the confusion. Culture is a management and communication system—a pattern of evolving meanings and associated behaviours, including tension management, that derive from complex experience, and *tend* to be shared and reinforced by groups of people who identify as Sardinian, Singhalese, Masai, Japanese, Uighur, Yolngu, Gururumba, and so on. 'Evolving' indicates an open system that includes contradiction and inconsistency as drivers of change, which is not necessarily progressive; nor is change always the cancer decried by insiders and outsiders who see culture as a living museum piece with intrinsic value that we must not challenge.

'Tend to be shared' is crucial. In negotiation, mere tendency limits the value of the culture concept to broad forecasting of patterned behaviour that might or might not occur consistently, or at all. For example, rigorous research and long experience might tell me Arab negotiators tend to be reticent and Italians voluble because they are raised to behave according to cultural norms, so I can reasonably but guardedly expect them to approach the norm. If they do, I can manoeuvre them and myself to suit it. But forecasting is about possibility and probability, not certainty, so astute negotiators will not cripple their negotiating technique by locking it to tenuous forecasts (let alone predictions) of group-level behaviour or to the 'ecological fallacy' that attributes group norms to individuals. The values norms in Hofstede's framework are a point of reference—a place to start, not finish.

Culture is distributed, interpreted and played out unevenly within a given group according to the individual's experience, psychology, and mix of social roles (Avruch 1998, 2000). Therefore culture cannot be homogenous, static or concrete; nor is it simply an active force on passive people. This view of culture is at the core of the method (explained in Chapter 5) for defining tension scenarios; it heeds Zartman's warnings about the culture concept's limited value, and Cohen's advice that we should not dismiss cultural influences just because they are hard to pin down. Nor should we avoid approaches like Hofstede's because they are broad. They can provide a way into an understanding of culture-driven behaviour of individuals, as long as we remember that no one is normal—which is not to say an assessment of different eggs should ignore the common chicken that produced them. Griffiths has apt advice on the significance of culture for hostage negotiators trying to assess the psychological state of the captors, but the principle is universal:

> The ability to empathize psychologically with the individual captor in control of his side of a hostage incident is the corollary to cultural awareness.... [The] general perception of a person's culture can be used safely as a starting point, but only a starting point, in arriving at the psychological make-up of the particular individual with whom the negotiator is dealing. (2003: 149)

Perhaps we should invoke culture if behaviour tends to match forecast patterns, but rely less on cultural interpretations when specific negotiators deviate from norms for their group or sub-group. To pursue cultural explanations might cramp a search of the locus—especially the immediate zone—for significant forces in a given negotiation. We need to see the trees and the forest. The culture concept may be valuable to negotiators only to the extent that they can use knowledge of group tendencies to forecast and steer group behaviour when no one seems to markedly defy norms.

There is always more than culture to group and individual behaviour but it does not make sense to avoid cultural factors just because they are knotty. It does make sense to seek them out because we are likely to *need* them. I will return to this point when I discuss the attributes of veteran negotiators in Part Four.

A problem with some negotiation literature is that it seems to assume culture matters only in negotiations across international borders. My model places culture in the context of other local and international influences, but this is not to say culture-related tensions—for example, about power—are irrelevant to intra-cultural negotiations. Cultural influence does not become null because negotiators have common or similar cultural origins, which may sometimes make negotiation more difficult because of traditional rank (e.g. caste) and other factors. Moreover, analysts should consider culture-related tensions in multicultural negotiations within a single country.

The point is that an international context *tends* to complicate negotiations because there are cultural, political and other influences that are likely to be less familiar and perhaps less manageable than they are to players in domestic transactions, even very complex ones (e.g. in Israel, Rwanda, or India). The strong negotiator does not necessarily see these influences as negative, but Zartman is right when he says negotiation writers tend to see culture as a hindrance (Faure & Rubin 1993: 17). Some undergraduate textbooks and other literature assume the hindrance is caused by cross-cultural ignorance between the parties to a negotiation or other transaction; learn to understand one another and all will be cosy. Having lived in Sri Lanka for several years, I know that the Singhalese and Tamil zealots are no mutual mystery. To the contrary, they understand one another's culture and associated aspirations very well, which is the nub of their feud. The same may apply to Serbs and Croats, to Tutsi and Hutu, and to Palestinians and Israeli Jews.

I have deviated to show the versatility of the scenario beyond negotiations, and to suggest a judicious diagnosis of cultural influence; but my main concerns in this chapter have been, first, to move from the wide-ranging discussion in Part One to a model of negotiation that systematically links contextual forces with tensions and scenarios; second, to show that analysis of negotiation as tension management relies on a refined insight into the tension construct. The next chapter describes the technique for defining the scenario as an analytical device.

↔ ↔ ↔

# Chapter 5

## « Defining Tension Scenarios »

The last chapter explored the finer points of an international negotiation model with tension management at its heart. Lewicki, Saunders and Barry (2006) commend "models [of context] such as Phatak and Habib's (1996) [as] very good devices for guiding our thinking about global negotiations" (413). With its tension scenario, my device as presented in Chapter 4 is an even better guide to thought and action. It admits more contextual forces, and the process of defining and grouping tensions compels the analyst to use a more systematic method to identify and assess the most significant forces in each transaction. That process is the main business of this chapter.

### THE INTERNATIONAL NEGOTIATION SCENARIO: FORM AND SUBSTANCE

To reiterate from Chapter 4, a scenario is a sub-set of tensions selected because they are significant to a specific negotiation in the sense that at least one player experiences them, consciously or otherwise, and that they influence or are likely to influence the process and results of the negotiation. Tensions do not exist unless someone experiences them. If they are detectable, but weak and unlikely to influence the negotiation, they are not included in the scenario.

The scenario is a negotiation frame extracted from the infinite array of tensions generated by macro and immediate forces. Figure 5.1 is the template for international scenarios; as justified in Chapter 4, it lists the tensions by content and process, and depicts the relationship between the two. Even though some tensions are prescribed for every international negotiation, the rich meaning of each tension is specific to a case. Others that are not prescribed may be detected in more than one negotiation; again, the rich meaning of the polar labels and relationship is case specific. The question-marks represent the labels of non-standard tensions defined for a particular negotiation. The numbers before each tension are to make discussion easier and do not mean there can be neither more nor less than four content and ten process tensions. Therefore the numbers before the process tensions may change, depending on the number of content tensions. There is a structural need to have *content ↔ process* first, then the content tensions, but the listing in the template is not necessarily in order of significance. On the other hand, because the significance of any tension is likely to shift during a negotiation, through managerial action or changes in contextual forces, the analyst might want to organise and reorganise the lists in order of intensity for different stages of the negotiation. As explained in Chapter 4, the intensity of a process tension may change and may vary from one tension to another, but is always high (which means there is no need to record a code); likewise, the intensity of *content ↔ process* is always high.

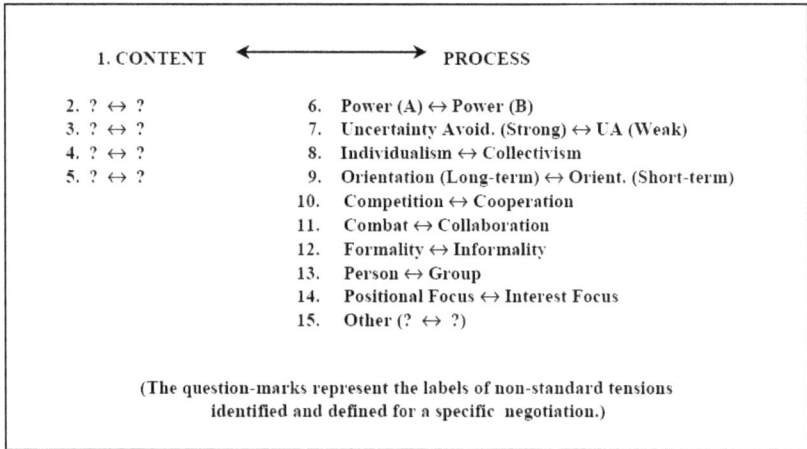

---

1. CONTENT ⟷ PROCESS

| | |
|---|---|
| 2. ? ↔ ? | 6. Power (A) ↔ Power (B) |
| 3. ? ↔ ? | 7. Uncertainty Avoid. (Strong) ↔ UA (Weak) |
| 4. ? ↔ ? | 8. Individualism ↔ Collectivism |
| 5. ? ↔ ? | 9. Orientation (Long-term) ↔ Orient. (Short-term) |
| | 10. Competition ↔ Cooperation |
| | 11. Combat ↔ Collaboration |
| | 12. Formality ↔ Informality |
| | 13. Person ↔ Group |
| | 14. Positional Focus ↔ Interest Focus |
| | 15. Other (? ↔ ?) |

(The question-marks represent the labels of non-standard tensions identified and defined for a specific negotiation.)

---

**Figure 5.1:** Template for an International Negotiation Scenario

Content tensions 2–5 are about *what* is being negotiated, and process tensions 6–15 are about *how* the players negotiate. Tensions 1 and 6–14 are prescribed primarily because they are prominent and consistent in the interview transcripts and notes. As indicated by the blank, *potential* fifteenth tension, the list is not definitive; nor is it entirely arbitrary as these tensions are strong in my interview transcripts and other data. Moreover, the discussion in Chapter 3 shows they are sometimes explicit and sometimes implicit in the negotiation literature. I have explained most of the ten pre-scribed tensions (1, 6–14) in previous chapters, so I will define them only briefly here. In every tension the double-headed arrow contains meaning about the interplay of the poles and their relative influence on negotiator behaviour. Where I draw on Hofstede's values dimensions I do not claim to use them exactly as he intended. Rather, I treat them as dynamic ten-sions that people experience or observe, not as scales that pinpoint mean national traits.

## The Ten Standard Tensions Plus One

### *1. Content ↔ Process*

This is about the things we negotiate and how we negotiate them; how the type of content and our understanding of it influences the process; how the chances of achieving desired outcomes are influenced by the way we nego-tiate, and how we interpret and react to one another's approach to process.

(2–5 are content tensions with labels created anew for each negotiation.)

### *6. Power (A) ↔ Power (B)*

Building on Hofstede's power distance dimension to include other factors as well as cultural values, this tension is generated by all the internal and ex-ternal power relationships that influence the process of negotiation, in-cluding negotiator experience and rank, and disparities in the personal au-thority vested in the negotiators by their principals. 'A' represents one ne-gotiator or team, and 'B' a counterpart individual or team.

### *7. Uncertainty Avoidance (Strong) ↔ Uncertainty Avoidance (Weak)*

Again after Hofstede, this tension is about the extent of the players' inclin-ation to follow fixed rules and procedures, cope with ambiguity, and adjust to contextual change—particularly if it is unexpected.

### *8. Individualism ↔ Collectivism*

This is the third of the tensions based at least in part on Hofstede's dimen-sions. In negotiation it represents the tendency of individual players and teams, and the players overall, to either focus on content without much concern for the niceties of relationship development (i.e. behaviour associ-ated with individualism), or to focus on developing relationships as a route to getting agreement (i.e. behaviour associated with group-oriented col-lectivist societies, in which smooth relationships and consensus have a strong influence on decision-making). As discussed in Chapter 3, this ten-sion absorbs Edward Hall's communication dimension, which locates cultural groups on a continuum that denotes, at the individualist extreme, their preference for low-context communication (explicit, verbal, direct); or, at the collectivist extreme, for high-context communication (implicit, non-verbal, reserved).

### 9. Orientation (Long-term) ↔ Orientation (Short-term)

Based on another Hofstede dimension, this tension contrasts concern for (a) patience and perseverance to achieve lasting, significant outcomes, with (b) quick agreement and immediate gain of some sort. This tension applies beyond the Western and Chinese comparison that gave rise to the dimension.

### 10. Competition ↔ Cooperation

This is the strategy tension. It is about the negotiator's broad plan of action to achieve outcomes that might or might not benefit the other party. It refers to the combination of competition and cooperation that underpins the broad approach of individuals and teams to a specific negotiation. This tension embodies the dual concerns model to the extent that it helps describe the broad spirit of the negotiators' strategy, jointly and severally. This tension is about the big picture, not the minute detail of negotiator style and tactics; but, of course, it makes no sense unless it is played out as tactical behaviour guided by the broad strategy, just as a military strategy is useful only to the extent that soldiers apply it with intelligence and purpose in the micro-skirmishes that comprise the battle.

### 11. Combat ↔ Collaboration

This is the style tension. It concerns the patterned detail of how negotiators behave as they try to carry out their strategic plan. It contrasts demanding, domineering behaviour, both tactical and incidental, with a milder style characterised by efforts to draw negotiators together rather than push them apart. Behaviour that is in essence demanding and domineering can be overtly polite, as with the friendly person in a black-hat and white-hat pair. This tension embodies the dual concerns model to the extent that it helps describe tactical and incidental behaviour, and aspects of Hofstede's *masculinity* ↔ *femininity* dimension that distinguish rough, aggressive play from warm and fuzzy concern for others. The style tension includes subordination, seen here as a tactic to induce collaborative behaviour in others who tend to be combative.

### 12. Formality ↔ Informality

This expresses the players' tendency to prefer or be required to accept a formal or informal process, or something between the extremes. Formal negotiations tend to have a fixed agenda and rigid procedures, whereas informal negotiations might be so casual that they do not even have an agenda or specified procedures. Preferences or requirements may be cultural, as pointed out by Weiss (1994), but this tension also includes those based on factors such as rank, role and negotiation content.

### 13. Person ↔ Group

This tension relates to *individualism* ↔ *collectivism*, which is about the degree of negotiator concern for group interests, consensus and relationship building; but the two tensions must not be conflated. At one extreme, *person* ↔ *group* is about negotiator tendency to differentiate between and focus on individual players, and at the other extreme to ignore the idiosyncrasies of the individual and focus negotiating behaviour on the group; or, in negotiations where the counterpart is not in a team, to fall for the 'ecological fallacy' and see that person as a typical member of a group—that is, to see a cultural or other stereotype (an Indonesian, a Maori, a politician, a terrorist) and try to negotiate accordingly. Personal traits and experience, including internalised culture, temper the macrocosmic and immediate forces of cultural difference and can be managed by others to benefit [or work against?] individuals and groups in negotiation as well as other settings (Smith and Berg 1997). Even if one or more teams are negotiating, the process is primarily about individuals dealing with other individuals: "In a sense, it must be admitted that the group is an abstraction, a mental construct, and that the reality is indeed a complex series of person-to-person interactions" (Boulding 1962: 171). As a negotiation proceeds, astute practitioners try to understand individuals better in order to work out how best to deal with them. This has nothing to do with liking or disliking someone who becomes better understood as an individual. A hostage negotiator who studies *this* kidnapper might find him to be the most despicable ever encountered.

### 14. Positional Focus ↔ Interest Focus

At the extremes, this tension contrasts a focus on positions with a focus on deeper interests. Provis (1996) flags ambiguity and inconsistency in the literature about what the terms mean and how they relate to one another. In my model, positions are explicit statements or inferences drawn about what a party will accept, or would prefer if not in a position to reject offers or decisions by the other party. Interests are the explicit or implicit advantage to be gained by the party from an agreement on positions (which might not be the only positions that could satisfy the same interests and perhaps additional ones). For example, a military negotiator's position might be a demand for a ceasefire in the interest of his soldiers' survival. Positions might or might not be founded rationally on interests, which might be misunderstood, distorted, or not even recognised. The mainstream literature and training programs tend to encourage negotiators to see positions and interests as alternatives, and to move the focus away from positions towards underlying interests. To attempt such a move may be naïve and destructive because rigid positions often have ancient roots and are inseparable from fears of humiliation, loss of dignity, and loss of power, as in the Israel-Palestine question.[1] This model does not assume that a negotiator's focus on interests is necessarily a more productive approach than a focus on positions; nor that a focus on both positions and interests is irrational.

### 15. Other (? ↔ ?)

This *potential* process tension is always included to remind negotiators and observers (a) that no scenario is definitive at a given time, (b) that context changes, and (c) to consider additions that cannot be absorbed by tensions already recorded.[2]

## THE SCRIPT

When negotiations begin and at any point thereafter, the blend of influence of all significant tensions on the negotiators, as individuals and as a group, is a script that defines their understanding of what should happen and guides their part in the play, including the way they react to other negotiators' scripts. The script includes cultural influences as discussed by Weiss (1994) but goes beyond culture to include any political, historical, power, experiential or other macrocosmic and immediate influences carried by the players. The scenario comprises tensions that reflect such influences. As the negotiation proceeds, new information, a different grasp of old information, new external events, a change of attitude and other factors may alter the script for one or more players. In a sense, negotiators are actors with some individual and collective control over some of the script, like jazz players in a jam session.

## SENSITIVITY AND EMPATHY

I used *sensitivity* ↔ *insensitivity* towards the end of Chapter 3 to summarise the need, suggested by the literature overall, for negotiators to assess and

---

1. See Pizer (1998) for a study of how negotiation theory helps clarify aspects of psychoanalytic technique for dealing with the link between patients' rigid positions, fear of change, and reluctance to participate.

2. One academic told me: " 'Other?' is not particularly helpful to me and its openness stands in stark contrast to the precision of the [other tensions]." In fact, 'Other?' is not a tension until its question-marks become labels. I retain it to reflect the caprice of negotiation, to encourage open-mindedness, and perhaps to challenge aversion to uncertainty.

respond to their own and other players' sense of context; to heed the blend of contextual forces and tensions in specific situations, relying largely on empathy—the inclination and ability to project oneself into other people's shoes. The cultural elements of the script are likely to influence the way a negotiator reads and responds to the tensions, and sees and interprets other people's sensitivity. As already discussed, even though culture is probably significant in most cases it does not always dominate international or domestic negotiations. For instance, I inferred from the transcript of my interview with Terry Waite that non-cultural elements of power seemed to eclipse all others when he dealt with President Kaddafi of Libya, whose air of royalty and grandeur seemed to issue more from personal fantasy than Arabic culture.

As *sensitivity* ↔ *insensitivity* seems to encompass all other tensions it would be illogical to list it in under content or process. Analysts might want to include it within the scenario as an umbrella tension but I prefer to simply rate the players' apparent grasp of context at any given time as high, medium or low. (A high-low empathy tension or a separate rating is not needed as empathy is intrinsic to contextual sensitivity.) The rating must be fairly arbitrary. It is tempting to suggest a scale of 1 to 10 but such a measure would foster a bogus sense of precision.

## TIMEFRAME, TIMING AND UNIT OF ANALYSIS

The analyst must decide on the timeframe (The whole negotiation or a limited period of it?), the timing of the analysis (Does it take place before, during or after the negotiation?), and the unit of analysis (All players or a selection?). The decisions depend on what is possible and on the analyst's purpose, which may be to understand what has happened, or is still happening, or might happen, or all three for a negotiation in progress; and to focus on the part played in the negotiation by an individual or some individuals, or to focus more on teams or other sub-groups, or the group overall.

For any unit of analysis, the actual or forecast scenario for the *whole* of a negotiation, whether it is finished, under way, or impending, includes all tensions thought to affect one or more players significantly at any stage of the transaction. The scenario for a *limited period* of the negotiation always includes all current and prior tensions (plus forecast tensions if the period in question is yet to occur). The scenario for part of a negotiation always includes prior tensions because the period of play selected for scrutiny cannot be fathomed without considering the influences that moulded it.

All credible scenarios are diachronic. This applies if the *timeframe* is the whole of a negotiation, or a narrow or broad period anywhere between the beginning and end. Even if the timeframe is very narrow—say a five minute period of table-thumping and splutter—a scenario makes sense only if the analyst tries to describe and explain its origins and actual or expected unfolding. The history of a negotiation is obviously crucial to a post mortem, and to the analysis of an ongoing negotiation, and to the forecast of paths it might take. An analyst who is also a practitioner, or adviser to a practitioner, needs to understand the development of an ongoing or impending negotiation in order to have some influence over its course. Forecasting in particular demands outstanding contextual insight, which implies a self-critical mind that never closes.

The broader the timeframe, the more complete will be the list of tensions in the draft scenario. For example, the players or their principals may introduce new issues and objectives during a negotiation and discard, play down or modify others. This could mean a content tension in a scenario for the overall negotiation does not exist in the early stages and is therefore not in a scenario limited to the early timeframe. If a new content or process tension comes into play because of changes in macrocosmic or immediate forces, such a tension will be in the broad scenario for the overall negotiation but obviously not in the scenario for a timeframe that precedes the changes. This would be so if there were later additions to an agenda agreed or negotiated at the outset. In the Hong Kong Handover Ceremony case analysed in Part Three, many issues were clear to both parties at the outset but other significant items were added along the way, the last only twenty minutes before negotiations concluded after two years.

*Timing* is a straightforward idea: the analysis happens before, during or after a negotiation. The cases in Part Three are both post mortem as they are based on informant reportage of times past.

To avoid unnecessary complication, the analyst creates scenarios for the play in general, not for individuals or sub-groups; but the general scenario can be analysed to highlight the role of an individual or sub-group as *unit of analysis* (UOA). For an individual, this does not mean the analyst looks only at a single person isolated from the overall play—that would not make sense because there is no negotiation unless two or more people communicate.[3] Rather, one person is under the spotlight as he or she deals with one or more players. A sub-group (or sets of sub-groups) as UOA may be from within any party or across parties. The analyst might be interested in how the leaders of two teams deal with one another, or with their own teams; or how people of different ethnic backgrounds relate to one another within a team. If the UOA is plenary, the analyst wants a very broad overview of the negotiation and is not very interested in individuals or sub-groups.

The plenary UOA may be the most sterile if it veils real people and the idiosyncrasies that influence the play, but it may help analysts to see broad principles of negotiating behaviour. The three types are not quarantined from one another and it is hard to imagine an analyst even trying to rely entirely on one or two of the three basic types. The UOA is about emphasis, not exclusion.

---

3. I leave to philosophy and psychology, and perhaps psychiatry, the matter of negotiation with oneself, which may be real but does not concern me here.

In the first case in Part Three the main UOA is an individual, the leader of the British team negotiating aspects of the Hong Kong Handover; the Chinese negotiators are prominent but less exposed to my spotlight, and the other members of the British team are almost absent. In the second case the main UOA is an Australian negotiator and his dealings with one Indonesian official, but other officials move between background and foreground as the two negotiate an exit visa for an immigration fugitive dying of AIDS.

If research is based squarely on one player's account, as in both cases in Part Three, the main UOA is usually but not always that individual, even though it is reasonable to draw inferences about other players from what the informant says about them, and from archival or other sources. At the other extreme, an analyst who has free access to all or most players in a large-scale negotiation, and can get data on the negotiation proper and the byplay, is in an ideal position to choose a sub-group or plenary UOA and report a broad but finely nuanced story about many individuals and their interaction. That ideal position is unlikely to arise, and may be unmanageable if it does; but more limited access to the play should not discourage analysts from choosing the second and third types of UOA if a bird's-eye view is preferred. Within reason, all negotiation analysts must speculate to fill gaps.

Any scenario, for any UOA, might include tensions that are not experienced directly by all or even most players. It is not necessary for *all* players to experience directly or even notice a given tension for it to be significant. It is significant if only one player experiences it and it leads to behaviour that influences the relationship with one or more other players. If I know my job is on the line should a negotiation fail, and no other negotiator knows about that threat, I alone will carry *salary* ↔ *penury*, but it may influence my concentration and style, which in turn will influence the way the other players deal with me.

## Implications for Coding Tensions

To choose an individual or sub-group as UOA does not affect coding because scenarios comprise all significant tensions identified for the entire cast of players for a given timeframe, and codes are estimated averages for that cast for that timeframe. But tension conditions, and therefore coding, may vary by timeframe. For example, if the timeframe is the first full day of a negotiation, the broad 'average' codes for all conditions (apart from the first—conceptual affinity) for that period may differ a lot from what they will be if the analyst reassesses them a week later, focusing on the entire period of negotiation. The conceptual affinity of the poles does not change. Once a tension is labelled it is either symmetrical (S) or asymmetrical (A), and logic says it must stay that way. The conditions of the other three properties (balance, balance tendency, intensity) can change during a negotiation (within limits for intensity, stated earlier for process tensions—for them the code is always (H) ). This is unsurprising for an open system, whether or not the players deliberately or inadvertently respond to tensions and the contextual forces that generate them.

Timing bears on coding. The codes that are forecast for a future timeframe are unlikely to be a perfect match with those for the same timeframe coded with hindsight.

## HOW TO DEFINE SCENARIOS

The analyst uses the template (Figure 5.1 above) to define scenarios, exploring the meaning of every standard tension for the specific negotiation. The ten standard process tensions are usually adequate, but no scenario is definitive, so *Other (? ↔ ?)* is always there to remind the analyst to consider additions that cannot be absorbed by those already on record.

A single tension cannot convey the kaleidoscope of negotiation, while fifty would be unwieldy. My experience is that the standard tensions, plus four or five created for the specific negotiation, capture the event. The non-standard tensions are usually under 'content' but sometimes a few are added to the standard ten under 'process': for example, *negotiator control* ↔ *kidnapper control* in a hostage negotiation.

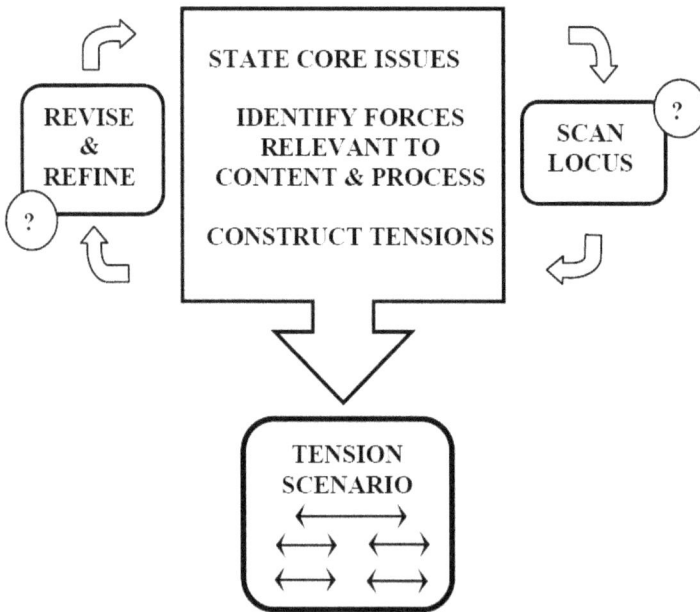

**Figure 5.2:** The Process of Scenario Definition

I have trained people from diverse cultures to extract tension scenarios from complex cases. Figure 5.2 represents the process used to create scenarios for simulations or actual negotiations. When learners describe the way they went about extracting and defining the tensions embedded in case studies, they almost invariably agree that Figure 5.2 represents their method. Individual analysts can produce excellent scenarios with practice but I have observed pairs or small groups building well on one another's ideas and questions, with or without experts enlisted to help explore issues and identify relevant forces. The process can be used to try to forecast the content and process of a future negotiation, to analyse a current negotiation, or to conduct a post-mortem. The sources may include verbatim records of the formal sessions, transcripts of interviews with players, books or articles written by players or observers, and direct observations or previous forecasts by one or more analysts.

I sometimes ask learners to explore a tennis analogy to dissuade them from overestimating their ability to forecast (let alone predict) the precise content, course or results of a negotiation.[4] A professional tennis match is played according to fairly standard international rules, on a standard grid painted on a flat surface of natural grass, fake grass, clay, or a range of hard surfaces—usually a shade of blue, green or red. You score by hitting the ball over or around the net so that it lands on or inside specified lines on the other side and bounces twice before your opponent can return it into your court. The linesmen, umpire and referee are fallible in their decisions. Some tournaments have electronic checks on line-calls but a player must see a reason for a genuine or bogus challenge and then make it. By making an unwarranted challenge, knowing it will fail, a player might try to distract the opponent and stop his or her momentum, or stall for time to catch breath or calm down or fire up. In singles matches, men play men and women play women. There are doubles matches between men and men; there are mixed doubles.

Already you must consider many variables if you are forecasting the broad result without even specifying the score-line. There are many more. Is it a day or night match? Will it start in daylight and finish in artificial light? Indoor or outdoor? Temperature, humidity and wind affect the balls, the rackets and the players. What is the record of these players under these conditions? Who has the superior backhand, forehand, first serve, second serve, return, lob, overhead, volley, smash, pick-up and drop-shot? Is the match early in the tournament or midway? Or towards the end when the best players clash? Is it the final? What is the seeding of these players? What is their relative experience? What are their records when the heat is on? Have they played one another before? If so, what have been the results? Are they in their home country? Is the crowd large, partisan, boisterous? Is coaching allowed? How old are the players? Are 'tennis parents' there to frown or cheer or threaten? Is any player carrying an injury or trying to fight off a bellyache with medication that might dull the senses and

---

4. Some people with advanced degrees have trouble understanding my assertion that uncertain, unmeasurable variables constrain our ability to forecast (and certainly predict) with much accuracy. Intelligent people without degrees tend to be quicker to see my point, whether or not they agree with me.

reflexes? Blisters? Will anyone get hurt? Has a player's boyfriend just dumped her? Are any players betting against themselves?

There are other variables but those already raised are usually enough to convince even diehard statisticians that they cannot hope to do much better than forecast the winner and loser, and only if the players are obviously mismatched. Otherwise a coin-toss or simple guess will do just as well. When it comes to more precise, reasoned forecasts—not guesses—about the course of the match and the result, the chances of accuracy are slim. How many sets will be needed for a win? What will be the scores within each set? What will be the scores for each game? How long will the match last? How long will each set last? Each game? How many deuces will there be? How many forced and unforced errors will each player make? Forehand and backhand winners? How many times will the players hit the ball? Will something happen that is beyond even the most fertile imagination? And so on.

Some learners might argue for predictions and forecasts based on distributions compiled from many previous matches, and might find it difficult to accept my point that probability based on accumulated statistics—even for matches between these players alone, on this court—would tell me nothing definitive about *this* match's final score-line, and how and why it will happen. Even a 'forecast' that turns out to be perfect is still only a more or less informed guess. The influence of known variables and their interaction in this open system is not known yet; the forecaster cannot be privy to some existing variables; others do not yet exist. Someone is likely to accuse me of saying results are accidental (or something similar), in which case I say accident might be a questionable idea as there are always causes and effects.[5] However, the problem of trying to identify and map them to explain results *after* a tennis match is hard enough, let alone before or even during a match—at least until it is almost over.

Whether or not the learners stand by the statisticians, they always agree that variables influencing all but the simplest negotiations are less patent, more numerous and more complex than for a tennis match; and that analysing negotiation process and outcomes with hindsight, let alone forecasting them, is much shakier than for tennis. If I then describe my non-career path to learners they can make sense of it with hindsight but agree that it would have been impossible to forecast, let alone predict. There have been too many crucial surprises, such as the Asian economic crisis and a contract arising from a job advertisement, long closed, in an old newspaper which my wife asked me to throw out. My point with this exercise is to get learners to see that any scenario created with hindsight is likely to be far from perfect but more accurate than one for a future negotiation. The scenario is a way in; it is a malleable guide—analysts and players must be ready to revise it to reflect new or developing insight into what has

---

5. In 1996, an MBA student about to graduate from a reputable school said: "If you think like that you should believe in a Creator."

happened, is happening, or might happen under the influence of the players themselves and external factors. Learners from business are quick to see the connection with problems caused by a rigid SWOT analysis and an associated strategic plan. Military people recount tales of tragedy caused by imperious generals with cast-iron battle plans.

From here on I will assume there is more than one analyst working on a case in a training program or in the 'real world' of negotiation. The first step is to state the core issues in plain language to everyone's satisfaction: for example, 'sovereignty and water supply' or 'localisation of managerial positions held by expatriates in Indonesia'. Disciplined brainstorming is a good way to launch the process, especially if the analysts are not familiar with the core issues. They scan the locus to identify forces associated with the issues, which may themselves be treated as contextual forces that generate content tensions. There is no definitive list of forces but the analysis must relate identified forces to the macrocosm and the immediate zone. A macro force in the former may have a micro counterpart in the latter: for instance, cultural differences.

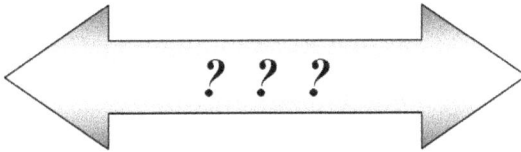

**Figure 5.3:** Questioning the Arrow

The analysts choose timeframe, unit of analysis and timing, and formulate and reformulate tensions as they refine their grasp of the contextual forces. The labels of the standard process tensions do not change but their meaning for the specific transaction is explored. The method spurs the analysts to question their own and others' assumptions about the case and negotiation in general. The question-marks in Figure 5.3 are there to encourage the questioning habit; to remind the analysts that the meaning of the arrow varies for each tension according to the relationship between the poles, and that it can change during negotiation because the contextual forces that generate tensions are changing or likely to change. The probing raises questions about more than the appropriateness of each tension to a given scenario. In addition, analysts constructing and reconstructing tensions should question the polar concepts and labels.

When the analysts agree on a basic scenario they code the tensions for conceptual affinity, balance, balance tendency, and intensity. The first is largely a matter of intellectual interest, and has little bearing on analysis of the negotiation, unlike the other three properties. The second expresses the relative influence of the poles on one or more players (balance); the third tells us whether or not that balance of influence is stable or changeable (tendency). For intensity, the analysts must keep in mind the different meanings of intensity for content and process tensions: again, for a content tension it is the degree of expected difficulty in reaching agreement on matters associated with the tension; for a process tension, intensity is the (always high) level of influence on negotiator communication and other behaviour.

As stated in Chapter 4, negotiation gets nowhere if the parties bog down in either content or process instead of balancing and integrating them. Therefore the umbrella tension *content ↔ process* is always highly significant and does not need an intensity code, but is coded for balance and balance tendency.

It takes only a few minutes to learn the codes but a lot longer to apply them well as a means to an end. For analysts who are also practitioners or advisers to practitioners, encoding is valuable because it forces them to study the tensions and scenario in minute detail with a view to devising, reviewing or assessing strategies and tactics. As the tensions are abstractions from an open system, the analysts must remember that any managerial action by the players will almost certainly relate to more than one tension.

When defining a scenario the analysts should look for tensions generated or fired up deliberately, by a negotiator or some other arsonist, for strategic or tactical reasons. For example, a managing director of a prosperous business wants to shed staff to cut costs and please shareholders (however brief their pleasure might be). She spreads word of her plan, and so generates the content tension *termination ↔ retention* throughout the staff, who have felt secure because the business has been doing well. A few days later, she invites them to negotiate redundancy packages that will be more generous than the payout to people fired later. Most workers rush to take the package, thereby making the negotiations and the firings easier in logistics and law. On the other hand, consider a manager who wants to raise productivity and pass on a share of extra profit to the workers. He might offer a contractual choice to work at their current pace without a pay increase, or to work for 90 per cent of their current pay plus a monthly bonus as a proportion of profit from increased personal output. This engineered tension could be recorded as *current wage ↔ new package*.

The search for tension properties and their conditions helps analysts appreciate the complexities of the negotiation scenario and the keen judgment and intellectual flexibility required of a good negotiator. This is evident in the cases in Part Three, when Hugh Davies and Peter Settler negotiate across borders. They seem to sense and react to the properties and conditions of a particular set of tensions, whether or not those tensions are explicit to them.

Finally, the analysts end up with a scenario recorded as a list of tensions under *content ↔ process*. Owing to the way it was created, the list is a mnemonic aid with deep meaning, especially when augmented by notes made during and after the exploratory sessions.

Like negotiation itself, the process of defining scenarios is not strictly logical or linear; both are more art than science. Nor is it like building a brick house from the bottom up. It is more like sculpting with clay, moulding, remoulding and balancing the entire form to clarify concepts as well as express them. The analysts reshape each tension and the set until they think the rational-intuitive exercise has created a scenario that represents reality. The process involves reformulation of ideas and perceptions, as a team or individual effort, until the analysts decide they have scanned the locus enough to grasp the context of a particular negotiation for a particular time or period. The exercise goes on, within time limits dictated by common sense, until the analysts identify and label a convincing, accessible set of tensions. 'Accessible' usually means up to about twenty tensions for a complex scenario; more is cumbersome. In the end, the sculpture is only as good as its creators, who must ask the right questions about the right issues.

In complex cases, scenario definition by groups can bog down as individuals and sub-groups argue for the minutiae of their own creation. Where more than one person is doing the analysis it is rarely possible to define a single scenario that suits everyone in every detail. Rather, within a specified period some responsible person must induce the team to develop a scenario acceptable to everyone as a working summary of the case.

People who try the procedure almost always say their grasp of the core issues becomes much more systematic and accurate. Problems that seem clear and familiar are reformulated, often radically, as assumptions are questioned and the scenario takes shape. A psychologist might explain scenario definition as framing and reframing (concepts to which I will return towards the end of this chapter). Moreover, the learners come to understand that a well-formulated problem does not guarantee successful action. Yet, it is "through the non-technical process of framing the problematic situation that we may organize and clarify both the ends to be achieved and the possible means of achieving them" (Schön, 1983: 41). This is a good enough reason to proffer scenario definition as a tool for analysts trying to understand the complexities of a transaction as the players seek an agreement. In particular, this applies to international transactions. This is not to say culture-related tensions (e.g. about power) are irrelevant to intra-cultural negotiations, as cultures do not cease to exist because negotiators have common cultural origins. These tensions are also found in multicultural negotiations within a country. The point is that an international context tends to complicate negotiations because it injects cultural, political and other influences that are likely to be more familiar to all players in even very complex domestic transactions.

The tension-based model of context does not cast any negotiation in concrete. Every scenario extracts order from chaos for a given timeframe but still embodies the dynamism of an open system. If I had observed both of the Part Three cases from start to finish I might have forecast a broad scenario at the outset but revised it several times to track changes in the transaction and its context. Using the type of thinking summarised in Figure 5.2, the analyst should review scenarios in the spirit of Phatak and Habib (1996: 37): "[Our] model should be treated dynamically. Any changes in the environmental and immediate contexts will bring subsequent changes in the negotiation process and outcome." The 'average' codes are a reference point for analytical discussion about how and why they changed or did not change. Some analysts might choose to draw up revised scenarios with recoded tensions to reflect different points in the negotiation, but discussion of change around the original averages is probably rich enough in most cases.

If the analysts are forecasting for a complex negotiation it would make sense to create several scenarios to cover various paths it might take, and later to produce a hybrid or completely new scenario if none of the originals turns out to be accurate enough. That exercise has great value because it forces the analysts to delve into context to understand change or to correct earlier misunderstandings of the forces at work.

To define the scenario is one thing; to analyse the way a negotiator manages it is another. At the risk of being accused of not knowing how to guide analysts on the latter, the best advice I can offer is to wait for the Part Three cases, for which I define scenarios and explore them for evidence of the negotiator as tension manager. There I dispel any suspicion that tensions are deterministic; that the negotiator is at the mercy of tensions. The player may decide to act in ways that modify one or more tensions—to influence the forces that generate such tensions. Action will depend on many factors, including the extent to which politics and other forces permit any action at all, and in many cases the personal skills and experience of the individual may be crucial. In addition, the extent of the negotiator's explicit insight into the dynamics of tensions, or implicit sense of those dynamics, is likely to influence the quality of response.

Analysts sometimes drift away from the idea that tensions exist whether or not the negotiator formally identifies them—he or she may influence them, and be influenced by them, without explicit awareness and intention. Informants do not talk about generic constructs, but tensions and de facto tension management are apparent in the cases that combined with my interests and experience to give rise to the model of context.

## SCENARIOS, FRAMES AND CHECKLISTS

The idea of idiosyncratic and changeable scenarios links scenario definition and tension management to frame theory. Frames are "fields of vision or frames of reference that help [negotiators] construct meaning or make sense of the situation" (Putnam & Holmer 1992: 128). Reframing is revision of the frame due to experience, new information or some other development associated with the negotiation. Such development would include what I call tension management.

Scholars define the concepts in various ways, but "both [framing and reframing] ... refer to the way negotiators come to understand their situation" (Putnam & Holmer 1992: 128). Scenario definition is a framing procedure that analysts use to make sense of content and process, with particular concern for the influence of the negotiator as tension manager. Any framing model is about abstracting phenomena from context to make sense of them in a formal way, to apply analytical order to negotiators' conscious and subconscious ideas—informal frames—about what the negotiation is for, and how it should be conducted. The negotiator script discussed earlier in this chapter is such an informal frame.

From an academic point of view, Putnam and Holmer (1992) identify three main approaches to framing in the negotiation literature: cognitive heuristics, frame category, and issue development. The *cognitive heuristics* approach is about the way negotiators base their frames on perception of risk and potential gains or losses, and on familiar ways of making rational decisions that will deliver agreement. Familiarity breeds bias; reframing is about correcting biases in order to reach agreement through rational negotiation. There is at least one link with scenario definition, which requires the analyst to identify biases (and any later adjustment to them) in the way the parties see the transaction. To presume all players are biased is part of the informal frame for defining scenarios.

*Frame category* research uses bargaining behaviour and linguistic patterns to classify frames according to aspects of content, process, interests and outcomes. The categories represent a system of influences and seem to organise immediate forces that roughly match those in the model of Phatak and Habib (1996). The tension scenario does much more than classify such forces: it identifies and organises the significant tensions they generate; it treats interests and possible outcomes as forces that generate content tensions; it integrates content and process (*content ↔ process*).

In the frame category approach, negotiators are seen to use a variety of frames. Associated misunderstanding between the parties "may lead to escalation and stalemate or, conversely, may promote reframing", better understanding, and therefore conflict resolution (Putnam & Holmer 1992: 136). The approach is suspect because "it inadvertently conflates mutual understanding with agreement" (1992: 137). Scenario definition does not do so. If analysts working for both parties in a bilateral negotiation were to create a common tension scenario, or set of scenarios, they might have an ideal foundation for negotiating an agreement; but the parties still might not agree, perhaps because of social, political, constituent or other forces beyond their control.

In *issue development* "a frame refers to the definition, meaning and conceptualization of an issue" (Putnam & Holmer 1992: 138). Lewicki et al. (2006) cite many studies that show how negotiations are influenced by differences in the players' frames, including variations in concepts of fundamental issues. For example, is conflict in the Middle East *primarily* about security, sovereignty, or historical rights? (411) Negotiators bring their particular understanding of agenda items to the table, and as they discuss the agenda the interaction leads to joint construction of the frames that define the issues. The assumptions that underpin the frames are challenged: "reframing refers to the transformation of a problem or the way each party develops a qualitatively different field of vision for understanding an agenda item" (Putnam & Holmer 1992: 140). Ideally, contest gives way to joint problem-solving.

Scenario definition is consistent with several aspects of issue development. First, analysts review core issues as they work alone or with others to create or redefine a scenario. If they were to use the formal procedure together they might achieve a common view of issues; if the analysts also happened to be players they might achieve a problem-solving focus and a cooperative style. Second, the scenario records content (including issues) and process separately but stresses their interaction, like issue development research. Third, this type of research tries to track changes in issues. This could be achieved by expressing issues as content tensions, then explaining changes in balance and intensity, and even changes in the tension labels. New tensions could be added as new issues are identified or created. Finally, the tension scenario overcomes two flaws in issue development theory: the suggestion that negotiators do not have frames until they start negotiating, and the failure to directly assess negotiator predispositions as an element of framing and reframing (Putnam & Holmer 1992: 141).

Scenario definition embraces many aspects of the three familiar approaches to framing. It compensates for some of their conceptual limitations and may provide a better grasp of content and process because the analyst pays attention to minute detail and the dynamic whole. As a research tool, the model may go some way towards integrating the three familiar approaches while giving more weight to negotiator bias and to negotiation as an open system. Yet the tension model may be more than a research guide: it may also guide negotiators as they define and manipulate frames to engineer agreements. Moreover, the significant control of one's own and others' behaviour is not feasible without insight into the frames brought to the transaction by oneself and the other players.

The analyst defining a scenario develops a personal frame that takes other frames into account. However, like any preconceived framework for research or practice, the tension model will contribute to bias in the way the analyst sees a transaction. With or without using a formal framework, different people may perceive problems and context in very dissimilar ways, depending on experience, motivation and other personal traits. International negotiations in particular are often complicated by individual and group tendencies to see, interpret and manage tensions in culture-specific ways (Peng & Nisbett 1999; Nisbett et al. 2001). Analysts are just as susceptible as negotiators. Yet such differences do not make the tension model less reliable than other scanning and framing devices, including analytical charts (Fisher et al. 1994, 1997), context models (Phatak & Habib 1996), and SWOT analysis, which identifies and assesses an organisation's internal strengths and weaknesses, and scans the external environment for opportunities and threats.

A colleague pointed out that a checklist of questions for the negotiator about aspects of content and process is another scanning device that invites comparison with the tension scenario. The latter may be similar to generic checklists insofar as it includes standard tensions, but there are fundamental differences. Take the checklists of Salacuse (1991) and Winham (1979). The former comprises 68 questions under four broad headings: Prenegotiation and Preparation, Opening Moves, Negotiating Dynamics, and End Game. Winham spreads 27 questions across three negotiation phases. A "task" heads each phase, which is divided into "external considerations related to the foreign government(s) and internal considerations related to the home government (and negotiating team)" (133). These lists exist at the outset of any negotiation and do not change during the transaction. In the tension scenario all content tensions and perhaps some process tensions are created for each case. The scenario might *then* be treated as a checklist that can be refined as the negotiation proceeds, whereas the other checklists are like a shopping list that never changes. Like them, the tension scenario calls for a grasp of contextual forces, but unlike them it suits any type of negotiation: Salacuse is concerned only with business negotiation and Winham only with diplomacy. In addition, the scenario has different purposes: it is designed primarily for analysts, not practitioners; it has a theoretical bent in that it brings tensions and their management to the heart of negotiation, and urges the analyst to examine the interplay of content and process. Some questions in the Salacuse and Winham checklists might help someone defining a scenario to focus on aspects of past, current and potential cases. For that purpose the checklist complements the scenario, a terse but rich mnemonic for those who create it.

The scenario and generic checklists may be complementary but one drawback of the latter is their reliance on stage models of negotiation that may not match reality, especially if we assume a rigid sequence; and they may have "a strong Western bias" (Weiss 1996: 220). The tension scenario is not at odds with broad stages but it does call for more empathy with nonlinear ways of thinking about content and process.

In summary, Chapters 2 and 3 argued that the tension-based approach is consistent with research in anthropology and other fields—including negotiation—that reveals a human tendency to use binary relationships to order and manage information and ideas. The associated model of negotiation outlined in Chapters 4 and 5 induces analysts to explore different points of view and to refine their grasp of tension types, balance and intensity as they create parsimonious, dynamic scenarios with rich meaning. The scenario is not a catch-all frame but a consciously defined statement of tensions that analysts identify and refine as they try to account for biases and other influences on negotiation. Scenario definition creates a base for serial extraction of manageable order from chaos, based on observed change and better understanding of things that have not changed. The approach itself is more important than whether we accept the standard process tensions for international transactions, whether scenarios should be consistent from one analyst to another, and whether tensions can and should be measured. Perhaps what matters most is that the model subsumes and builds on other authors' more limited concepts of tension, specifies tension properties and conditions, and brings tension analysis to centre stage as a tool for researchers and possibly practitioners.

I do not assume a champion pole-vaulter has a theoretical grasp of leverage, sports psychology and the mechanics of the human body. In similar vein, I frame negotiation scenarios as sets of tensions, but I do not assume a given negotiator—even a great negotiator—has an explicit grasp of the tension concept. Tension management is *my* theory about what negotiators do. A good negotiator might be even better with an explicit, systematic grasp of tension theory, but that is a matter to be canvassed in the final chapter. For the moment my task is to set the scene for (a) scenario definition of cases I have researched, and (b) analysis that shows how the concept of tension adds meaning to my veterans' descriptions of how they negotiate.

The cases in Part Three are about negotiators who were not conscious tension managers. The importance of the cases lies in their cross-cultural and other complexity, and in the suggestion that an analyst who defines and reviews a scenario can connect negotiator perception and action with tensions. In these cases the action is within the repertoire of any good negotiator who must deal with the forces specified in more conventional models, such as Phatak and Habib's.

↔ ↔ ↔

# Part III

《 Some Players and Their Acts 》

## « Some Players and Their Acts »

*Words are rough, like ill-cut blocks of thought. Most shades of meaning, and all continuity, escape them. How much of these colourful characters overflowing with warm life and full of movement, whom I saw, will you grasp from a few motionless features I have presented?*

Francis Walder, *The Negotiators,* 1960

*The facts speak only when the historian calls on them: it is he who decides to which facts to give the floor, and in what order or context. It was, I think, one of Pirandello's characters who said that a fact is like a sack—it won't stand up till you've put something in it.*

E. H. Carr, *What is History?* 1961

## *Preamble*

Entertainment and education are desirable allies, so a case intended to illuminate theory and practice should be interesting as well.[1] With that in mind, this section has two main purposes. The first is to retell one of the veterans' stories about international negotiation, and reproduce another in the player's own words. In each case an editor is at work as there are languid periods in most negotiations and plodding sections in all research interviews, no matter how articulate may be the diplomat or other professional talker. The second purpose is to use the stories to show the presence of tensions and their management in international negotiation. That is, to use the model of context and tension management, inspired by previous studies and this one, to extract a form of order, meaning and management.

The stories are faithful to my interview transcripts and notes, and other knowledge of the cases, but on the other hand my fixation on the tension concept dominates the meaning I give to the story.[2] In any field from hard science to art, this is in keeping with being human. For example, when Gauguin painted *Riders on the Beach* he was influenced by his deep interest in two equine works by Edgar Dégas and Albrecht Dürer (Dening 1998: 12). If Gauguin had not kept prints of these works on display in his studio at Atuona, on the Marquesan island of Hiva Oa, he would have created the beach scene in a different way, or might not have bothered to paint that scene at all. If I had not ridden my tension hobby-horse into this study, I would see my interview data in some other way; or I might not have bothered to collect them. Another analyst with little or no concern for tension theory—perhaps a linguist interested in phraseology, or a narrative analyst interested in how people create a plot from past events—would produce a much different piece of work from the same transcripts. The reader will find more in the stories than I cover in my analysis, and would find a lot more in the transcripts.

In the Introduction I discussed my judgment sample of informants and will add here a few points about my research method for this study. Refer to English (1995) for a detailed account of my approach to research, based on judgement samples and semi-structured interviews.

---

1. I use 'case' loosely, as I do not always follow the standard business school formula, which decrees that problem situations first be presented as raw narrative, then analysed.

2. Academics rarely admit to fixation and tend to chide others for being 'theory-laden'. Yet some delegates ride to conferences on new hobby-horses that they expect everyone to mount. Depending on what is in vogue with funding agencies, promotion panels and journal editors, some riders leap from one theoretical steed to another like Wells Fargo despatch riders. Business schools teem with former accounting and human resources experts who are now strategy specialists. Terrorism is a hot topic in politics departments. A friend has just discovered Karl Popper and would like me to ride tandem, thirty-five years too late.

Hoping to meet twelve people with experience that I could transfer to my university course in international business, I wrote to twenty-five potential informants, some famous, some obscure, but all selected with care, and in most cases recommended to me by people with a thorough knowledge of at least one of the three realms included in this study: diplomacy, hostage release and business. There were men and women of many nations—Australia, the United States, Britain, Malaysia, Singapore and China. No one from the last three countries would participate. An Australian Chinese man took part but all other informants were of Western origin. Chinese nationals ignored me. This was no great surprise, as Chinese tend to be reluctant to deal with outside researchers, whether or not they plan to tote a tape-recorder (Fang 1999: 12). This may be through fear of losing face under scrutiny. There is also the matter of distrust generated by an intrusive political system, and disdain issuing from the assumption that Chinese culture is too ancient, deep and complex to be accessible to barbarian outsiders.

I researched the background of each addressee before writing. With each letter I sent a brief discussion guideline that would encourage the informant to talk about international negotiation in general while paying some attention to a single transaction—issues, problems, solutions, strategies, tactics, styles, environmental influences, successes, failures, how things might have been, and so on. Several people ignored my original and follow-up letters. The grapevine told me why two diplomats did so but I will keep my counsel in the spirit of diplomatic decorum. The most amusing rebuff was from a former diplomat who said it would be impossible to meet me because he was about to move from one office (i.e. room) to another and did not know what the future held.

A veteran negotiator in Malaysia, Trade Minister Rafidah Aziz, entertained me with her steadfast reluctance to decline as she set and reset meeting dates in the apparent hope that her obvious tactic would bore me sooner than it did. I withdrew from the game after playing it for a few weeks, disappointed but knowing her brush-off would not ruin the project. In China a trade official with a formidable reputation was pursued for me by a Chinese friend who drew too much attention for his own good. In a disquieting email he said: "I have rung several times to the relevant offices. They told me that many numbers were secret and cannot be connected. This is the first time I know that." He was raising his profile to an unhealthy level so I asked him to give up the chase. Several other Asian veterans declined to meet me.

The hostage negotiation industry is secretive, but only one quarry did not want to get involved. Most business managers were enthusiastic but a couple seemed to fear scrutiny. Two well-known CEOs withdrew at the last minute to deal with unforeseen crises but this was to be expected—the higher up the ladder one seeks interviews, the greater the chances of sudden rescheduling or cancellation. In international research, the anxiety generated by this uncertainty compounds with fears of personal illness, late or cancelled flights, lost address books, visa problems, traffic jams, a jammed recorder, lost tapes, seized tapes, jet-lag, and faxes that do not get through. "Why do you do this to yourself?" the head of my university department often asks. At times, but not for long, I am tempted by his cosy cognac-and-computer approach to research.

In the end, without having to move to my reserve list, I interviewed thirteen people in Australia, the United States, England and Belgium to supplement two cases already collected during earlier research in Indonesia.[3] Overall, there were three chief executive officers and one technical adviser in business, five diplomats, two advisers in unofficial diplomacy, and four 'personal security' negotiators. There is overlap, as international hostage negotiation is a business activity as well as a diplomatic or humanitarian one.[4] In the introduction to the single case selected for detailed exposition in two realms—diplomacy and hostage release—I say more about my dealings with individuals, doing my best to preserve the anonymity of people who asked for it or seemed to need it anyway to protect themselves and their colleagues or families. Where I have tried to protect them I have ensured the case is no less authentic.

The interviews and informal meetings were fruitful. All informants were well focused despite pleas from some for me to pardon them because they had not had time to prepare, or had forgotten to do so. Veteran negotiators prepare well for any meeting even if they protest otherwise. One retired Australian diplomat refreshed his memory by doing me the honour of visiting the capital to study official files he had not seen for many years. I rarely had to intervene to keep the discussions on track; hence my voice is heard far less than would be expected on one-hour and two-hour tapes. My approach was based on Dowsett's advice:

> In the semistructured interview you're not there to express yourself—you can be discursive, offer opinions, but these are all subsidiary—you're there to listen.... You get a sense of where people are coming from. It's good because it takes account of exceptions. You can uncover something unexpected and take off and follow it. (Dowsett 1987: 31)

Bernard says much the same about semistructured interviewing:

> [It] works very well in projects in which you are dealing with high-level bureaucrats and elite members of a community—people who are accustomed to efficient use of their time.... It shows that you are prepared and competent but that you are not trying to exercise excessive control over the informant. (Bernard 2002: 205)

When I speak on the tapes it is usually to steer the interview back on track or to hear more about a gem that does not seem valuable to the informant but interests me. Overall, I let the interviews run freely as I did not want to corrupt them by herding the informants towards examples of tensions and tension management "that [would] serve to strengthen an attractive

---

3. See English (2001) for elements of one of the cases collected earlier.

4. See Prochnau (1998) for an excellent journalistic piece on what he calls "the ransom trade".

developing hypothesis or bolster a cherished world view" (Levy & Hollan 1998: 348).

Although we had agreed earlier that I could use a tape-recorder, several people feared the device at first through memory of burns inflicted by journalists wielding this variation on the flame-thrower. Two people accepted my offer of transcripts. No one asked me not to tape the meetings, nor did anyone take up my suggestion (as far as I know) to make a simultaneous tape with their own recorder. In my many research interviews over several years, the only informants to take up the suggestion overtly have been three Catholic nuns and the Philippines Ambassador to Australia. I assume some people in some places will make clandestine tapes.

Through diverse experience with 'elites' before this project, I was aware of the reluctance of many people, especially in the business world, to grant interviews to academics. One deterrent is the one-way street. Some academics assume the 'target' will feel privileged to be selected by a mastermind and will not expect any other return. Maccoby's experience with corporate managers applies also to other elite groups: "The corporate manager must fit the visitor into a carefully budgeted schedule and he must be convinced that he will get something more than a pleasant conversation out of the meeting" (1978: 10).[5] Some people plead time constraints to mask fear of scrutiny by an independent researcher who might not defer to them or might find chinks in their armour. They know an experienced interviewer can lead people out of their comfort zone, so that even the empress herself may come to realise too late that she is not wearing new clothes.

To reduce the risk of rejection, I think about non-academic elites in various realms as a range of species with some of the characteristics attributed to ethnic groups by Barth (1969). In particular, there are boundaries that outsiders may cross if permitted by insiders who expect to benefit from the visit in some tangible or intangible way. I therefore offer genuine respect to potential informants; I tell them they seem to have experience and ideas that I covet; I will try to give them useful reports from the project if they will allow me to cross the boundary. I also tell them I have spent most of my working life as an international manager, which seems to help me gain access.

I often wonder how my informants see me. All the anthropologists I met in Indonesia, the Gilbert Islands (now Kiribati), the Philippines and Papua New Guinea assumed they had high status with 'their' local people—inducted into the clan, and so on; but a few were seen as clownish nuisances and sometimes fed nonsense as a form of sport. This was how the villagers of Lesu village in New Ireland coped with Hortense Powdermaker in the 1930s (Powdermaker 1933). An old man scoffed when I mentioned her at Lesu (now called Lossu) in 1971: "If we went for a shit in the bush she

---

5. As Maccoby was an academic, perhaps his university (Harvard) had to reconstruct him for writing 'he' rather than 'she' or 'they'. In academia, generic use of 'he' is acceptable only if negative (e.g. 'When someone plans a murder, he etc.'). It is common to hear 'she' for God but not for the Devil. Chairman is out; taxman is okay.

would find us and write in her notebook. One day I was throwing stones in the sea with some other boys and she asked why. We told her a bullshit story. She asked a lot of questions and wrote our lies in her notebook." I hope I have not been a duped nuisance or a clown.

Over the years, several people have agreed to interviews only because they have not seen me as a career academic. Whatever the case may be, I know the taste of rebuff but have usually managed to disembark from the ship, cross the beach to the village, and return to the vessel with data, on credit. The data are on credit while I try to extract and report on meaning that is significant to the suppliers, to me, to funding sources, and to at least one publisher; and, with this project, to at least some international negotiation analysts who might or might not be professional negotiators. To extract meaning I search interview transcripts and notes for themes: "Analysis is the search for patterns in data and for ideas that help explain why those patterns are there in the first place" (Bernard 2002: 429). I think of this search for order in chaos as 'fossicking'; Turner calls it "botanising" (1988: 109).

To claim resolute open-mindedness as I went about this project would be to don the objectivist mask. Rather, from the outset I searched for evidence of tensions and their management, concepts that emerged unexpectedly from the earlier project but were brought to this one with unequivocal purpose. On the other hand, as I used the standard process (Figure 5.2) to search for significant tensions, another part of me fossicked for other patterns and found a lode. After a great deal of reading and rereading, formulation and reformulation, coding and recoding, I labelled and linked these patterns as seven attributes of the veteran international negotiator.[6] There was also a pattern of meaning in their relationship to tension management, with its elements of behaviour manipulation and 'boundary play'. In this section of the book I concentrate on tensions; in Part Four, I will describe the seven attributes and boundary play, and link them to tension management in a broader framework.

In Part Three, I demonstrate two different ways of relating a scenario to a case. At the beginning of Chapters 6 and 7, I describe the realms of diplomacy and hostage release to the extent needed to position the cases. In a prologue I say something about the veteran's background and our encounter, and then present the two cases 'in the raw'. The first is a verbatim transcript of my interview with the main player and the second is my narrative of events as I understand them. There is no interpretation until I present the graphic scenario and ponder each tension, embedding points

---

6. To support my reliability as sole coder, I encoded three transcripts after my system had fully evolved, and then encoded a clean set of the same transcripts almost a month later. There were no differences that mattered. Anyway, there is no hard evidence that multiple coders are more reliable than a sole coder, as their consistency may mask common biases and distortions associated with coder training and culture (Druckman 2002: 289, Hopmann 2002: 71).

about the players' tension management in those mini-analyses.[7] I chose the two cases because they are interesting and fertile, and because I had much more detail about them than informants gave me for most of the others.

I could not reproduce some cases because the detail would have unmasked people who wanted anonymity for legal, family, diplomatic, commercial or security reasons. I wanted to include an international business case but only one was full enough in its detail. The informant, who is CEO of a large and complex company, preferred anonymity and it would have been impossible to recount much of the case without revealing his identity. Anyway, this book is about a way of analysing negotiation and is not meant to be a collection of case studies across the board. I use some of his ideas in Chapter 8, where I call him Robin Talbot.

Doug Anderson of P & O Ports described his experience in negotiating a port development in China, but even if there had been enough detail I might not have used it as a case in its own right, as recent books and journals have binged ad nauseam on business in that country. As with Robin, I reserve Doug's experience to illustrate aspects of Chapter 8. Geoff Goon, a Chinese-Australian who came to grief in Asia but has prospered in the Middle East, did not have much to say about any single case; but he gave me astute comparisons of business dealings in diverse countries. He also features in Chapter 8.

I know my informants are proficient and therefore do not represent all negotiators, many of whom are incompetent and short-lived in the role. Some veterans did admit to occasional minor mistakes but most were like surgeons who prefer to dwell on success, which by reputation and my direct knowledge is the norm for the practitioners in this study. All I can do is work with the best information available to me, from the veterans and other sources, as I apply a generalising model that also brings out the uniqueness of each case.

I rely a lot on 'controlled speculation' because I am yet to see a negotiation case analysed well without it. More scientific (or pseudo-scientific) analysis, especially in game theory research, tends to convert complex reality into fanciful neatness and to squash roundish characters into flat ones.

---

7. By "no interpretation" I mean there is no explicit identification and analysis of tensions. Of course, any 'history' (for example, the informant's narrative in the first case, and my story of the second case) is interpretive in a more general sense because, piloted by hindsight, it imposes sequence, coherence and other order on information selected from the chaos of past events. Someone with different hindsight might make a different selection and impose different order.

# Chapter 6

## « Diplomacy »

### Borders, Trade, Gases and the End of Empire

## THE REALM

The story told in this chapter is in Track 1 diplomacy, which includes bilateral or multilateral negotiations involving players who are career diplomats or other official representatives of governments and international organisations, such as the United Nations or the World Bank. Five of my veterans were in this category: Malcolm Lyon, a retired diplomat who was Australia's lead negotiator for the Torres Strait Treaty with Papua New Guinea, and later Australian Ambassador to South Africa; Don Kenyon, Australian Ambassador to Benelux and the European Community, and former GATT representative; Meg McDonald, Australia's Deputy Ambassador to the United States, and former lead negotiator for the Kyoto Protocol on greenhouse gases; Sir Alan Donald, retired British Ambassador to China, Indonesia and a few other places; and Hugh Davies, Executive Director of the Prudential Corporation (Asia), and former lead British negotiator for the Hong Kong handover to China.[1]

---

1. Sir Alan Donald asked me to keep some points off the record. This request was proper but it has locked up interesting and often comic material about diplomatic negotiations and associated intrigue.

I interviewed a few people in Track 2 diplomacy, in which representatives of churches and other non-government organisations attempt to manage some form of international conflict.[2] Terry Waite fits into this category as well as hostage negotiation because he has vast experience in negotiating international conflict that has not involved hostages. My other two
informants were senior advisers to former President Jimmy Carter, whom
an Atlanta barman called 'The President Who Won't Lie Down'. At the
Carter Center in Atlanta I interviewed Steven Hochman, Director of Research and Assistant to President Carter; and Kirk Wolcott, Coordinator
of the Conflict Resolution Program, who brought along a German intern
with a French name—André.

There are major differences between Track 1 and Track 2 diplomacy.
The latter tends to involve conflict settlement or resolution that has
eluded Track 1 diplomacy, or cannot be tackled officially for political reasons, or requires contacts and methods unavailable to governments or other
official bodies. Steve Hochman said of Jimmy Carter: "The US government
doesn't recognise North Korea. We don't have diplomatic relations. But
President Carter as a representative of an NGO can go there and talk to
the 'Great Leader'.[3] He can talk to bad guys that the US, with its very mor-
alistic approach, doesn't talk to." Another difference is that Track 2 diplomats are more likely to act as mediators or facilitators when other parties
need to negotiate with one another.[4] That is, in principle the Track 2
diplomat-as-mediator is a third, neutral party who may negotiate the details of the negotiation process and the content agenda with the conflicting
parties, but ideally not the content itself.

Track 1 diplomacy may also involve mediation of other parties' negotiations. During his presidency, Jimmy Carter used the 'single text' approach
to mediate between Anwar Sadat and Menachim Begin at Camp David in
1978 as they negotiated frameworks for a peace treaty between Israel and
Egypt:

> President Carter thought he was going to get Begin and Sadat to be buddies.
> They just weren't going to be buddies. So he kept them apart, and he was the
> go-between.... He had a text which he controlled as mediator, and he would
> give it to the Israelis and they would work out what they could accept.
> [Carter] would sort of negotiate [with the Israelis] on behalf of the Egyp-
> tians, and then he'd take it to the Egyptians and say 'This is what the Israelis
> are willing to do.' And he'd work back and forth with them instead of having
> them face-to-face. (Steven Hochmann, Carter Center)

---

2. Miall, Ramsbotham & Woodhouse (1999: 19) say that Track 3 should be added to
   Tracks 1 and 2 to take into account and encourage a wider range of "third party in-
   terventions" with "increased emphasis on ... indigenous resources and local actors."

3. An NGO is a Non-Government Organisation.

4. 'Pure' mediation is an ideal, and its meaning varies among academics and practitioners. Some academic shades of meaning may be a little too shaded. See the introduction to Miall et al. (1999) for a range of definitions that tries to minimise
   confusion about terminology in conflict resolution and related activities.

Purists might argue that Carter was not mediating but negotiating as a broker or agent for two principals. (Jimmy Carter as double-agent?) Because of his power as US President, his role might best be described as "mediation with muscle" (Miall et al., 1999: 22). Others might say he was a 'facilitator' or 'conciliator' because he was an intermediary encouraging the parties to negotiate. Maybe he was really a 'problem-solver' because he tried to get Sadat and Begin to "reconceptualize the conflict with a view to finding creative, win-win outcomes"; or maybe he was into 'reconciliation', "a longer-term process of overcoming hostility and mistrust between divided peoples" (21–22).

Most Track 2 diplomats prefer to bypass government and operate independently of Track 1 diplomats, who may give them unofficial encouragement and other support that would not be approved by their governments. Some Track 2 diplomats who have had political or civil service careers offer their skills openly to government, or at least seek its blessing before going ahead, usually after an invitation by the parties in conflict. At the same time it is crucial for the parties to see Track 2 diplomats as independent of government, otherwise there is not enough trust. For obvious reasons, former president Jimmy Carter has a hotline to Washington and can gain the attention of the parties because of his status. However, in the words of Steve Hochman:

> President Carter makes it clear that [the Carter Center] is an NGO, and he is a *former* President. He is a citizen, and he has access to the President of the United States and the US government. But when he goes out he's not representing them. We have been successful in keeping that separation. But President Carter does have the ability to have access ... so sometimes we say he is Track One-and-a-Half, because he's sort of in the middle.

For this chapter's case I have chosen Hugh Davies' sometimes hilarious Track 1 account of how he and others negotiated the details of the Hong Kong Handover Ceremony in the context of the broader and longer negotiation for the Handover itself. Occasional absurdity and pique intruded, but the parties negotiated in a proper, formal manner that would have earned praise from Sir Harold Nicolson, the doyen of British diplomacy, whose writings lament the passing of the old-school style (Nicolson 1963).[5]

The Hong Kong case is engaging for many reasons. One is that it shows negotiation is not always a staid performance by solemn players, especially if they are British diplomats. Sir Alan Donald also brought home the point with his account of trying to negotiate with tiers of Indonesian officials for invitations, meetings, costs, and itinerary for separate visits to Jakarta by the Lord Mayor of London (who wondered if he should wear his mayoral cocked hat, chains and red robes) and Prime Minister Margaret Thatcher.

---

5. If Sir Harold had survived into the 21st century, the negotiating tactics applied to poor countries by the EU, USA and Japan during the World Trade Organization's Cancún and Doha meetings would have killed him off. See Buckman (2005) for well-documented examples of sometimes vicious "debt relief/aid/preferential trade bribery" (70).

She wanted to host a lunch for Indonesia's economic leaders, who happened to be many and not all on good terms. There was deep interest in Mrs Thatcher but not much in the Lord Mayor because the Indonesians decided he did not have much political or economic clout.

I heard an anecdote about Sir Alan which reinforced my view that although diplomacy is usually plodding and routine it may be unorthodox and droll, especially when diplomats need to cope with the naivety of their political masters.[6] He was acting British Chargé d'Affaires in Beijing for a few weeks in 1965 when Harold Wilson was Prime Minister. In a telegram to major British missions throughout the world, the Foreign Office said Wilson was sending a special envoy to Hanoi to try to head off the impending outbreak of full-scale hostilities between the USA and North Vietnam. Heads of mission were to contact, at the highest possible level, the government to which they were accredited and warn of Wilson's impending announcement. The telegram was coded 'Flash', which meant the recipient had to act on it and report back to the Foreign Office within two hours. The proposed envoy was unknown to Sir Alan, who was obliged to carry out the instruction even though he guessed the visit to Hanoi would be ineffectual. He telephoned the Chinese Foreign Ministry just after normal working hours to say he had an important message from the British Prime Minister and that the Chinese Foreign Minister should receive it right away. The person who picked up the phone told Sir Alan, who spoke Mandarin, that no significant person was there and that he should call the next morning at 9 o'clock. Sir Alan had someone type a diplomatic note and went to the Ministry anyway. Only a startled cleaner was there. He confirmed he was working for the Foreign Ministry, so Sir Alan gave him the note and asked him to give it to a responsible official for delivery to the Foreign Minister. Sir Alan went back to his office and sent a 'flash' telegram to London: "Action taken."

The Hong Kong case has more than entertainment value. For instance, like some of Sir Alan Donald's own anecdotes about China and Indonesia, it gives lie to the assumption in most definitions, especially outside the business realm, that negotiation tackles existing conflict. When negotiations for the handover ceremony began there were no apparent conflicts to resolve but a lot to avoid. Moreover, the case is apposite because it is rich in tension management and sense of changing context. After all, the ceremony was about the end of Empire for the British and a step in the building (or rebuilding) of another for the Chinese.

---

6. There are variations on the anecdote. Sir Alan's unpublished memoirs confirm this version.

## CASE ONE: THE UNITED KINGDOM VERSUS THE MIDDLE KINGDOM — THE HONG KONG HANDOVER CEREMONY

*There had been kilted pipers and massed bands, drenching rain, cheering crowds, a banquet for the mighty and the not so mighty, a goose-stepping Chinese honour guard, a president and a prince, speeches, flags, pride and tears.*

Chris Patten, East and West, 1998

### Prologue

On 30 June 1997 I watched a direct broadcast of the ceremonial handover of Hong Kong by Britain to China; or, from the Chinese point of view, the recovery of Hong Kong by China after 150 years of British occupation. Foul weather concluded "the Empire story of the most humane and well-intentioned of the colonial powers...." (Patten 1998: 6); which is not to say the British were *always* humane and well-intentioned. As one of the youngest of the old colonials, I can speak with minor but balanced authority on that matter.

In the mid-1970s I worked for the British Foreign and Commonwealth Office (FCO) as a District Officer in the Gilbert Islands Colony, after a few years in a similar role with the Australian administration in Papua New Guinea. As I watched the Hong Kong ceremony, I remembered British colleagues in the Gilberts who had worked in Hong Kong or wanted to work there. The former dreamed of their past, the latter of their hope. They would speak of Hong Kong as Muslims speak of Mecca. To evoke the mood, substitute 'Hong Kong' for 'ivory' in my favourite quotation from Joseph Conrad's *Heart of Darkness*: "The word 'ivory' rang in the air, was whispered, was sighed. You would think they were praying to it" (1902: 75). I liked and respected most of the dreamers, isolated on a string of dry atolls, deserts in the ocean; but there were a few prats, private schoolboys forever, some of whom received mail with 'BA (Hons) (Oxon.)' or '(Cantab.)' after their name on the envelope. Unlike most of my colleagues waiting for their brass handshake from the British Government, these twits role-played superior Britons and liked to tell one another they did not suffer fools, a fool being anyone who disagreed with them or did not see them as they saw themselves. If you were not one of them they would smirk ever-so-slightly, half-close their eyes in cultivated ptosis and look over your shoulder as you spoke to them. If they did strain themselves to speak to an inferior British or other creature they would sound constipated and bored. Some of these Hong Kong dreamers and other colleagues wanted the commanding officer of a visiting British Navy ordnance disposal unit to come to dinner without his six enlisted men. He always declined, which led one miffed cynic to tell me the officer was afraid his team of explosives experts would otherwise arrange an accident for him. I managed their visit to the Gilberts as the 'Disposals Coordinator for Unexploded

World War Two Ordnance'. The only houses the team dined at during their four-week visit to Tarawa were the Governor's and mine. His Excellency threw a dinner party for them because he was a decent and unpretentious man, with a name to match—John Smith.[7] They dined at my house several times and very much liked my wife because she let them dance on the table if they took off their shoes. The officer stayed shod and did not dance.

As I watched the Hong Kong handover ceremony, I thought it would be interesting to interview a couple of the Britons who had spent so many years negotiating the transition. Their knowledge might transfer to my business students, for whom I was setting up negotiation simulations based on the experience of veterans in business and other realms. On the other hand, if the players in Hong Kong's final act were like some of the cast in the Gilberts who had worked in Hong Kong or hoped to work there, I might not enjoy the experience. I put the idea on the shelf for a few years but took it off again after reading this passage from *East and West*, by Christopher Patten, the last Governor of Hong Kong: "Hardly a week went by without British and Hong Kong negotiators—led by the affable and polished diplomat Hugh Davies—heading for the trenches in Hong Kong's Kennedy Road, where the talks with China usually took place" (1998: 79). With such tribute from a man who is scorned by some career diplomats in the United Kingdom and Australia, perhaps because he does not tug his forelock to them, how could I not try to meet Hugh Davies? I asked someone in Hong Kong to find out if Davies was still there. "No, he's in London. Yes, I'm told he's very affable and not full of himself."

I wrote to Mr Davies, Companion of the Order of St Michael and St George, at the FCO after researching his background and finding it to be excellent for my purposes. True, he went to Rugby School and Cambridge, but this did not worry me as Patten's words and my brother's assurances told me Davies was neither prig nor prat. He joined the British Diplomatic Service in 1965. Over the next thirty-four years he served in Hong Kong, Beijing, Singapore, Bonn, Paris and London. He spent about fifteen of those years in the Far East. About ten of his years in London were in the FCO's Far Eastern Department, which he led from 1990 until 1993, when he went to Hong Kong as British Senior Representative (Ambassador) to the Sino-British Joint Liaison Group; that is, Britain's lead negotiator for the Hong Kong handover.

Just before I met Mr Davies I heard he had left the FCO and joined the Prudential Corporation as Executive Director for Asia. This move made

---

7. The Governor asked me to organise the party at the Residence: "Please come with your wife but it won't be necessary to invite anyone else." He later agreed that I also invite ten Gilbertese nurses and their female British trainer as chaperone. After a jovial dinner the Governor's charming wife invited the barefoot nurses and the other women to retire to the drawing-room. The assorted gentlemen stayed at the dining table to pass port to the left and toast Her Majesty the Queen. A year later one of the enlisted men returned to Tarawa to marry one of the nurses.

him even more important to me because I had won my research funding with an argument that my students' grasp of business negotiation skills could be improved by drawing on the experience of non-business practitioners.[8]

I met Mr Davies at his home in Pimlico after a saga whereby his response took three months to reach me by surface mail, and I had to postpone my fieldwork because I was ill. Through my aversion to the chill of London breezes in winter, the meeting did not start well. I arrived a little early; Hugh Davies was a little late. As he did not answer his door-bell, and I could not get into the lobby of the apartment block until he let me in, I walked to and fro in front of the doorway, feeling as if I were being stabbed by icicles. A courier entered to deliver a parcel to another apartment so I slipped into the lobby behind him to thaw out. Ten minutes later, alone in the lobby and feeling thawed but criminal, I decided to go outside again. I opened the door as a gentleman was putting his key into it. "Err... Err... Are you Mr Davies?" "Err... Yes." "I'm Tony English." "Who let *you* in?" "No one." "Pardon?" "It was cold outside." Silence. He did not look affable. This Englishman's communal lobby seemed to be part of his private castle. I offered my hand. He took it with a fumble, forgetting his was full of keys. I grinned in spite of the pain but he did not grin back and seemed far too distant for an interview. "Would you like me to come back later?" "No. It's fine. Come in."

We stood in the kitchen as Mr Davies searched his briefcase for notes. He took out a book I had just read—Patrick French's *Younghusband: The Last Great Imperial Adventurer* (1995). My body had thawed but now I needed a social icebreaker, so I drew him into a chat about the book while he made mugs of coffee. It took me only a couple of minutes to realise he was witty, indeed affable, and had a touch of self-deprecation. We moved to armchairs in the living-room to find out a bit about one another before the interview proper. As part of my summing him up I supposed women would see him as handsome, urbane and so on. He was eight years my senior but looked five years my junior and much fitter.

We chatted about my stint with the FCO as District Officer in the Gilbert Islands. He and the FCO parted early in 1999 when they could not see eye-to-eye on a long-term role for him: "After the Hong Kong experience it seemed like an anticlimax to become an ambassador somewhere." In the eighteen months after Hong Kong he led an enquiry into British trade with China and coordinated FCO relations with China, Hong Kong and Taiwan. He visited China with Prime Minister Tony Blair. He examined the Australian experience of amalgamating the departmental functions of trade and foreign affairs, when the British government was thinking about a similar structure. There was a talking point here as my PhD research many years earlier had unearthed sensitive material on 'destreaming'

8. Another former diplomat, Sir Alan Donald, has served on several company boards as a non-executive director.

problems associated with the Australian model. For instance, a few career diplomats resisted attempts to open their club to mere mortals from trade offices or business, just as the elite political corps had resisted when the US Foreign Service tried to destream in the late 1920s (Schulzinger 1975).

After two hours I had taped a story rich in the enticing twists and turns of human relationships that suffuse the best qualitative research. Given the hang-dog television images of Governor Patten, Prince Charles and Prime Minister Blair suffering through the deluge of the British farewell cere-mony (as distinct from the joint handover ceremony), I was intrigued by the comic element underlying this confrontation between the colonial power wanting to die with dignity and the Middle Kingdom wanting to or-chestrate the funeral. In our discussion, Hugh Davies relived the role of joint funeral director with good humour and impious animation.

After the interview, we prepared to leave the apartment together as he was going to dinner at the House of Commons where his older brother was Clerk of Parliaments. Hugh went downstairs to another room while I waited just inside the front door, congratulating myself on being the master puppeteer who had just recorded an outstanding interview. The door opened and Mrs Davies walked in. "Err... Hello. I'm Tony English. Err..." I do not think she was expecting to find a bumbling stranger in her living-room but she handled the surprise with British cheer and composure: "Hello there!" She did not stab my hand with her keys.

Hugh Davies is entertaining, rollicking at times, eloquent and a clear thinker. Therefore it makes sense to let him speak for himself with minor editorial help to eliminate occasional grammatical glitches and repetition. My condolences go to mainstream case-writers who frown because I repro-duce a verbatim interview rather than a narrative with quotations here and there. My comments and questions are included (in italics) only when they add meaning to the discussion.

**The Story**

[Hugh Davies]: There's a lot of context to the Hong Kong handover—the historical context, and the immediate political context, by which I mean the differences between Chris Patten and the Chinese. All that coloured how we went about the negotiations, particularly in the last four and a half years when I was there. Most people might have thought the handover ce-remony was just a minor negotiation to put the icing on the cake at the end. In fact it was a subject which to our surprise—perhaps we shouldn't have been surprised—took two years to get an agreement.

As far as I remember the matter was first touched on, as a subject that we should discuss in the Joint Liaison Group, by Foreign Secretary Douglas Hurd, in some meeting with the Chinese Foreign Minister in the summer of 1995. Hurd suggested we set up a sub-group of the Joint Liaison Group. Because of the importance of getting the ceremony right the sub-group should be headed not by deputies but by the heads of delegation on each side. Eventually that is what came about. I don't think we began any substantive talks until 5-6 months later and by this time we had a new Foreign Secretary, Malcolm Rifkind.

We began talks in Hong Kong between myself, with a small team, and the Chinese Ambassador and his small team. We had done quite of lot thinking about the parameters for a ceremony that we would think acceptable and appropriate for the occasion. I cannot recall exactly at what point these parameters were provisionally established but there were a number of things which we always aimed at, and they were also relevant to the whole political context in which we saw the process of transition.

One of the principal drivers for our view was that we should ensure the handover ceremony involved the broader international community. In the last few years of the transition, it had certainly been the policy of the British government, the policy of Chris Patten, that we should internationalise the Hong Kong issue. This was much resented by the Chinese and we used to be constantly accused of internationalising an issue which was in fact a bilateral one based on a resolution between the two sides.

*Did the Chinese want a secret negotiation process?*

They regarded this matter as simply a colonial issue left over from history for us to resolve with the Chinese. What they did not like was that we might expose some of the problems to people like the Americans, Australians, and Canadians, who were likely to be friendly to our point of view. So that was fundamental for us, to internationalise the thing, and to give it components of a certain dignity and ceremonial nature. Some of the most obvious things would be the pulling down of the Union flag and raising of the Chinese flag, and some sort of military guards of honour. There would be some sort of civilian transfer, and some sort of ceremonial conducted by leaders on the two sides. This should be witnessed in public by invited guests not limited to Britain, China and Hong Kong but embracing as many international figures who had the time to come there. That was our scenario.

Before we brought it down to detail, we had drawn on experience of transfer of sovereignty in former British Colonies. We looked at Zimbabwe and one or two other places to see how these things had been done. There tended to be some sort of a ceremony, very often in a large stadium. It tended to be at midnight of the day in question, with one flag going up, the other flag going down, national anthems and so on. So we regarded that as the model we should be looking at. We put these ideas to the Chinese, around the turn of the year 1995-1996. At this remove I don't quite remember their immediate reaction, but when we re-engaged later it became clear that our concept of the ceremony and their concept were poles apart. They came up with a model that would have used the Hong Kong City Hall, a pretty run-down 1960s building. No doubt in the 1960s it was quite grand, but it was now used for urban council activities. Frankly, by Hong Kong's really rather superior standards it was a pretty inferior building. It only held four or five hundred people and had a small stage. Their idea was that there would be some British participants and some Chinese participants, and once the flags had been raised and lowered the Chinese participants would see the Brits off the premises and that would be that.

We said to the Chinese "Well, that's very interesting, but in our view it doesn't really do justice to the significance of this moment. For one thing, that venue is hopelessly out of date and doesn't hold the number of people who would certainly want to come there. We think that we should both take pride in the fact that this is an example of a peaceful resolution of a historical problem." I was trying to use some of the Chinese phraseology— 'leftover of history' or whatever the phrase is. We quipped how Deng Xiaoping thought this was all a wonderful thing, and we should therefore demonstrate that this was something the world should note and use as an exemplar, as it were. "So we can't possibly do it all in that place!" Our proposal was to have it out of doors on an area of land which by that time would be reclaimed. Stands could be erected, and so on. We suggested a few activities that should govern that ceremony. This went on for months, and the Chinese said "No, that's quite inappropriate. We certainly couldn't have it outside." They were very worried about security, and of course the weather. They were right about the weather.

So, this was getting nowhere. The discussion went on for several weeks. Of course, we were only meeting once every three or four weeks to discuss that matter. We were dealing with twenty-five other subjects at the same time. Eventually we came to the conclusion—and we conveyed this to our masters back in London—that it was quite conceivable that this argument would go on to the last weeks. If so, it would be impossible to arrange a satisfactory ceremony in whatever time the Chinese deigned to allow us. They might just talk it out of time. So we took a decision that we would have a farewell ceremony. Once we had established what we were going to do with that, we would then be ready to continue talking to the Chinese about a handover ceremony. We would make it clear to them that if we could not reach a satisfactory outcome, too bad. We would just have a farewell ceremony and get on the Britannia and leave. That became quite a significant lever.

So, with the support of the Foreign Office and the administration in Hong Kong, we worked up our farewell ceremony. At the same time we began to work out a minimalist view of what we wanted to achieve with the handover ceremony. We decided the only way to tie the Chinese down was to negotiate a bit of paper. So we negotiated an agreed minute, which is in the public domain.[9] It didn't take much time—probably three or four weeks, maybe a bit longer, in the summer of 1996. The agreed minute set out the parameters for the handover ceremony, and was eventually finalised at a meeting between the two Foreign Ministers in the margins of the UN General Assembly Meeting in September 1996.

---

9. See Joint Liaison Group (1996). An agreed minute is a brief record of decisions reached by diplomatic parties. It is sometimes an administrative annex to a main agreement.

But there were some pretty sticky bits as we went through that document. I can't remember them all just now. I should have reminded myself, but one in particular does stick with me and that was the question of the provision of security for the handover. It took a great deal of negotiation to persuade the Chinese that the full responsibility—the *full* responsibility—for the security of the event, and of the participants and VIP guests from all over the world, should be left with the Hong Kong Police. We absolutely insisted. At various stages in negotiation it was really a breaking point because the Chinese were giving a very strong impression that this was not acceptable to them and that *they* wanted to take responsibility for security. Presumably they expected us to take responsibility for security until midnight and then they would take it over.

*Did they say they were reluctant to accept what the British Government wanted, or did they just make a statement saying "We don't want it that way"?*

Oh, no, no! It went on for a long time. It was "How can you expect our leaders to be reassured about security provided by your *British* Hong Kong Police?" We said "Look, these guys are going to be the police for the SAR.[10] At midnight they will be changing badges. These people are loyal to the SAR, as it will be. They are loyal to Hong Kong now." And so on.

*And, they understand Hong Kong.*

And they understand Hong Kong. We were absolutely determined that we wouldn't have the Ministry of State Security crawling all over the place. So that was a major issue. There were one or two other major issues in the negotiation, but then as usual there was the question of finding some weasel words to save face, to allow the minute to be agreed. But certainly the Chinese got quite agitated during that period. It was probably some of the tensest period of discussion, because we actually took a leaf out of the Chinese book. Normally, in their negotiating strategies they like to establish what they call 'principles' before moving into detail. On this occasion, in a sense, we took that Chinese model. We established the agreed minute which laid out the principles within which we would establish the format of the handover ceremony.

It was pretty tense at times. From time to time our Ambassador in Beijing would be told that Mr Davies was behaving intolerably, by saying that the British would not attend the handover ceremony. What sort of provocation was that? But eventually it all came right and very often with a deal of bluff. You learn to bluff and stamp your feet. And we got the agreed minute and then we all sighed with relief. We thought we were there. But, far from it. The discussions went on about various aspects of the handover ceremony until, I kid you not, twenty minutes before we actually handed over. When we were finding it difficult to get the agreement, there were cartoons in the Hong Kong Press showing the Chinese having a handover

10. Hong Kong's post-handover designation as a Special Administrative Region of China. Macao, a former Portuguese territory handed over in 1999, is China's other SAR.

ceremony in China and the British still talking about it. The view was that we were never going to get there.

Anyway, we then got into the next stage, during 1996 and into the first six months of 1997. We got into increasingly detailed discussions about the arrangements. We made the concession that we would have the ceremony indoors, provided the Chinese made various concessions to us, which included policing. So, one of the problems was we didn't have anywhere to have it indoors. Until the thing was built, we were all betting on the fact that this amazing new Convention and Exhibition Centre would be ready in time for the handover ceremony. It was a close run thing but that's where we aimed to have it. It was still a shell while we were negotiating all this, and the Chinese of course got pretty agitated about whether it was going to be ready and we were beginning to get a bit worried ourselves.

*Were you accused of deliberately delaying the construction so that it wouldn't be ready?*

No, we weren't accused of that. *They* had managed to delay some of the other construction projects in Hong Kong over that period, like the airport. So, we then had to start deciding on details, such who was going to be invited. By this time they had accepted that this wasn't simply a bilateral event. That was part of their concession. It was going to be an international event, and of course once they had accepted that, they became very enthusiastic about it and began to think of all the people—like Yassir Arafat—who should be invited. The guest list became quite an argument, because our initial bid, perhaps over-optimistic, was that we should aim to have members of ASEAN, members of the European Union, and countries which had very strong trading links with Hong Kong. Of course, we included Australia and New Zealand.

*Not Taiwan?*

Not Taiwan! Taiwan became an interesting side thing. There were always some little side things going on.

*I can understand that. I've had Taiwanese and Hong Kong and mainland students in the same MBA seminar group.*

Right! Anyway, that was one argument which went on and on. Then just planning the layout of the handover ceremony was in itself very problematic. We were driven largely by the advice of media consultants. We were looking to have a ceremony which could be reasonably media friendly—in terms of presentation on television and so on—where all the main participants and main events would be in one place and reasonably photogenic.

*Accessible to direct broadcasts, throughout the world?*

Exactly. We had to build our own stage because the one in the room we were going to use was facing the wrong way and was rather small. We decided it would be very good to have a stage on which small honour guards could parade. There would be space for the chief participant on each side to stand and make a speech, and there would be a flag pole. Or four flag poles—that in itself became an argument. We were absolutely insistent there should be Hong Kong flags there, to start with, but the Chinese said

"No, no. no!" But in the end it was agreed. And that there should be on the stage a group on each side, as witnesses, as backdrop. However, they didn't like our plan at all and we were given some appalling rewrites of that. Those of us who had served in China recognised the sort of scenario that they produced. It was a very, very Chinese scenario. I mean it was very communist-looking, unattractive.

*Grandiose?*

Yes, a fascist sort of style. And we had some real humdingers of arguments with these guys. I was the leader on our side, and my opposite number was Ambassador Zhao, on their side. They brought in a guy from Beijing who was their expert from their protocol department. He kept on pooh-poohing our ideas, saying "You guys don't understand protocol. I've been doing it for 25 years." So, we didn't have much time for him. He was extremely aggressive, extremely unpleasant, and we all got very pissed off with him. By the end though, when everything was finally settled, he became a pussy-cat, and we managed to achieve things in the short period towards the end which we wouldn't have dreamed we could achieve, judging by his performance earlier. I think a lot of it was nervousness about what he could say to his directors, and he had to show that he had fought the good fight.

*So they needed to show the masters in Beijing that they hadn't capitulated?*

Yes—to the cunning Brits. It became pretty tense at times, and we had to break for various cooling-off periods. In a way, it's a story in itself, which, if one had recorded it at the time, could have been a very good tale. No doubt in thirty years time someone will go through the files.

*Or when you start to write your book?*

Maybe it will come back if I do that. And so it went on. Then other things ancillary to the main handover ceremony also became involved. The backdrop was unpromising, because over the six months of the negotiating period the Chinese had established the Provisional Legislative Council, which met in Shenzhen, just across the border. It was purported to be the legitimate legislature for the SAR. Of course, that became very awkward, although we gave it absolutely no scope to claim any legitimacy. Nevertheless, the PLC was being seen increasingly as the future legislature. So that was going on in the background. And Tung Chee-hwa had been elected at the turn of the year as the new Chief Executive of Hong Kong, so there was a certain amount of attention being paid to all that.

Then, in the very last four to six weeks before the handover, the Chinese suddenly came up with a demand that was totally out of the blue. Rather than the People's Liberation Army arriving after mid-night, they wanted a substantial contingent in Hong Kong *before* the handover. This was presented to us as absolutely normal and natural and, of course, had we ever thought they could have possibly considered anything else? But, it had been quite clear in our earlier discussion that they had not even considered the possibility. We would have regarded it as inappropriate to have their military in British territory beforehand. But something had changed. It was pretty clear that some in the leadership became very nervous that unless there were some of their own boys in khaki there, things might go wrong. They were very mistrustful of the Hong Kong population.

*So it came back to the security issue that was raised in the early stages of discussion?*

Yes, that's right. So all that added to the tension. There were separate negotiations going on about that. Then, in the last six weeks before the handover, something happened in the UK that had an effect on many of these things. That is, we had a new government, six weeks before the handover. It was the middle of May, and there was a new government which did not have the baggage of eighteen years of negotiations with the Chinese over the transition. While inheriting a lot of the general views in principle about how the matter should be handled, the new government was not necessarily attached to all the detail that had become part and parcel of the discussion over the years. That also had some effect on the final period. So, there was quite a lot going on outside.

Meanwhile the handover ceremony itself was beginning to come together. Eventually, the Chinese almost entirely accepted our version of the stage layout. They agreed with the numbers for the guards of honour that we wanted to fit onto the stage. They agreed that there should be four flag poles—two tall ones for the two national flags and two smaller ones for the Hong Kong pre-1997 flag and the SAR flag. They liked the brilliant mechanism we came up with for making the flags blow inside. We had fans installed inside hollow poles right at the bottom, underneath the stage, and holes near the top of the stage. As the flags went up, just as they reached the apogee, as it were, they began to blow out. It was rather dramatic.

*They liked your guest list?*

Well, the guest list was pretty farcical by the end. The problem was that the Chinese, being Oriental hosts, didn't like to turn people down. We kept pointing out to them "Well, you know, if you let Bloggins in, how are you going to tell the other guy that he can't come unless you have established criteria?"[11] And, you know, we should agree on the criteria for who should be invited." "Oh, but if people want to come we should welcome them because that indicates friendship." That's all very well. There were X number of people from Thailand—princesses and so on—who all insisted on coming, and we had to keep batting them into the long grass![12]

*Once they all knew the television cameras were going to be there, I suppose they were even more interested.*

Indeed. But the final thing was all right. In the last period, they became pussy-cats and things began to fall into place. When we actually got down

---

11. 'Bloggins' is an offhand British version of the American 'John [Jane] Doe'.

12. A cricketing term which means to belt the ball outside the arena. This disheartens the bowlers and so destroys their attack.

to the dress rehearsals, we could only use the building about a week beforehand. We got the PLA to send their guard of honour down, and the protocol people were there, two or three days before.[13] All sorts of senior Chinese from Vice-Ministerial rank began to show up and rehearsals were held.

I remember one particular thing that was quite interesting because it indicated the Chinese readiness to take our views into account. I went to one of these rehearsals—probably not a dress rehearsal, a rehearsal before that—when the PLA and the British military guards of honour were doing their first practice together. The PLA are incredibly polished when they do these guards of honour. It puts the Grenadier Guards to shame. The PLA select very slim people for this role, all the same size, and all wearing white gloves. And they glister! To the Western eye this is not attractive because we all associate it with the Nazis.

*I can imagine them marching past the synagogue in Hong Kong.*

Well, that's right. Anyway, so there they are doing their little goose-steps on the stage. Incredibly precise. [*Mr Davies stands up, stomps his feet, swings his arms, and calls out 'left-right-left-right!'*] And our poor old soldiers were looking somewhat shoddy beside them, because they're not the Guards anyway—they're just some guys off the navy ships and a few RAF people. Not really drilled to the same extent. But if you ever see a Chinese guard of honour doing its thing, wherever it is, in Tienanmen Square or wherever [*more sham marching by Mr Davies*], you will see that the final thing is to deshoulder arms, put them to the charge and, with bayonets fixed, go off with one of those martial yells that Orientals use. So you get this "[*obscure shriek by Mr Davies*]!"

*A Chinese version of 'banzai!'?*

That sort of thing. So, what they were proposing to do in this ceremony was to do that [*more marching sounds*] on the stage, come to the edge of the stage, down the steps and then charge off into the wings going "[*an unintelligible yell by Mr Davies*]!"

Exactly! [*Mr Davies sits down again.*] So I took the protocol man with whom I'd had these rows over the years, and said to him "Look, I know this is entirely an internal matter. It's your decision. I accept that you may well regard this as interference in your domestic affairs, but I just want to tell you that if the soldiers leave the stage that way on the night, the foreign media and the Hong Kong people are going to be shocked. It will look as though your military—as you know, there's a great controversy about whether they should be here at all—are going out into Hong Kong with bayonets fixed!"

*You can just imagine the photographers waiting for that one. Front page of every newspaper.*

Right. To my amazement, the next time I saw the rehearsal, that bit had been dropped.

---

13. The PLA is China's People's Liberation Army.

*They accepted the problem as obvious, once you pointed it out?*

Yes. Except, the point is that I was told this was how they finish off normally, and I've seen it done subsequently when I was with Tony Blair in China last October. They did a march-past for him. The protocol man said "They're supposed to be showing respect to the leaders by doing this." They are probably saying something like "On parade!" I don't really know but it sounded very martial. So we ended up with a series of events that evening. It started with our own farewell ceremony, to which no Chinese officials came.

*Were they invited?*

They were invited but we didn't invite them formally. We said to them —I was always the channel—"We are having this event, and we would be delighted if any of your Chinese leaders would like to attend. Please let us know." We were then told politely a bit later "Thank you very much, but they will not be there."

Well, they were concerned that there might be parts of it that they wouldn't want to be associated with. What we wanted to ensure was that at least part of the handover would be totally within our control, where we would not be beholden to any agreement with the Chinese about how the event should be handled. That's why we insisted on having the British farewell ceremony in addition to the joint handover ceremony. As it happened, the farewell got rained on very hard, which was a great shame. It was always going to be a risk and we missed by 24 hours. The weather the night before was perfect for the dress rehearsal, then it rained every day for a month.

*Is that unusual for Hong Kong?*

Rain for a whole month is unusual. Everyone said the skies were weeping for the handover. Immediately after that, there was a meeting between Tony Blair and Robin Cook and the Chinese leadership.[14] The latter had been skulking in their tents, as it were, in a hotel on the other side of the harbour, which was rather inconvenient. They had been provided with this accommodation by Mr Li Ka-shing, who had just built a new hotel. Blair and Cook, who were anxious to establish relations with China as the new British Government, elected to go over and have a meeting with them on their premises.[15] In protocol terms that was correct, because President Jiang Zemin was there.

So they did that, then came back across the harbour to the Convention and Exhibition Centre. We had this huge dinner with a reception before the joint handover ceremony. The senior Chinese who came to the dinner was the Foreign Minister, but Jiang Zemin and Premier Li Peng stayed over in their hotel. In order to get round the problem that the Chinese might not come to our dinner, given by the government of Hong Kong, the dinner was formally hosted by Robin Cook, although it was all funded by

---

14. Robin Cook, British Foreign Secretary.

15. Li Ka-shing is Hong Kong's richest magnate.

the Hong Kong government. Some of the negotiations were internal to the British. We had to decide how we were going to resolve some of these problems, trying to get the best out of the event. So we had this huge dinner, and 3500 people sat down in a restaurant that hadn't been there a week before, which wasn't a bad effort.

So after this dinner Jiang Zemin and Li Peng came across to the Convention Centre and then came one of the more curious parts of the evening—the meeting between the Chinese President and the Prince of Wales. The Chinese got a bit muddled up. They would insist on calling him the "Prince *of* Charles". We always referred to him from then on as the "Prince of Charles". Trying to agree on the format of this meeting was where the negotiation went on and on and on until twenty minutes before we were due to start. It was right that the two principals should meet before the actual ceremony, where they would be formally on stage together, but it was a question of how that should be orchestrated. The problem was that the Chinese had their head of state there, but ours wasn't there. If our head of state [the Queen] had been there, it would have been only right and proper for the Chinese head of state to pay a call on our head of state. The Chinese therefore made the point that since he was only the Prince of Charles he should go and call on the Chinese President. We said "No way. We are in charge of this place until midnight. We're not going to have our Prince of Charles calling on your Jiang Zemin."

So, we had to start again. Where do we go from here? Well, let's meet on neutral territory. So it was agreed we would meet in an anteroom of the Convention Centre. How do we actually orchestrate that? Who is going to sit on the right? Whoever sits on the right is clearly the guest, so we can't have the Prince of Charles sitting on the right of the President. And the President wouldn't sit on the Prince of Charles's right because it would indicate that the President was junior, so we're back to the drawing board.

*There weren't many choices, were there?*

This was wonderful—it went on and on. I kept sending off my guys to negotiate at some junior level and come back with messages. Actually in the last few hours I was just clearing what parameters the Prime Minister and so on thought were acceptable. Anyway, we ended up with a classic diplomatic solution. In the Convention Centre there was a long, thin, and slightly curved room. It was right on the apex of the building looking out to the harbour, and it had, conveniently, a door at each end. So we agreed that the best thing would be to bring in one delegation from one door and the other delegation from the other door, and we would meet in the middle.

*Arriving in the middle at exactly the same time!*

Yes. The problem was that each side had five principals. In our case there was the Prince of Charles, the Prime Minister, the Foreign Secretary, Governor Chris Patten and the Chief of the Defence Staff. The Chinese had Jiang Zemin, Li Peng, the Foreign Minister, Tung Chee-hwa—the new Chief Executive—and the head of the PLA. So there were five on each side. The problem is that under British protocol, you send your junior person of the delegation in first and the last person coming in is the senior, so

Prince Charles comes last. In the Chinese system, the senior person comes in first and the junior person comes in last. How are you going to resolve that?

*[Almost uncontrollable laughter by the interviewer.]*

Oh, well, all right, let's split them. So we put the three juniors on each side, already in the room. There will only be two left to enter and it won't look so obvious that one is senior to the other. Well, you've still got problems. Who's going to sit on the left and who's going to sit on the right? Well, they'll have to sit opposite. So we eventually got five seats on one side, five seats on the other, and our small triumph was that we took the south-facing seats, which in the Chinese system is the imperial seat. So we ended up with the Prince of Charles looking south and the Chinese President looking north. Anyway, this lovely little bit of drama took place. Only those participating really ever heard about that, because it took place literally fifteen or twenty minutes before the beginning of the formal handover ceremony. It was a pretty extraordinary occasion. I was sort of standing inside, having orchestrated it all, watching it all, and the conversation was remarkably stilted, as you can imagine. The British lined up on one side and the Chinese on the other, and someone taking photographs, and the television cameras. Of course they would have to send the footage off for broadcasting, but by the time it was ready to be broadcast they were into the live coverage of the handover ceremony. So although that footage must be in someone's television archive, as far as I know it's never been shown.

*It's a pity isn't it? It would be like Monty Python.*

It was awfully good! So then we all trooped out of that room, and by this time 4000 people had been seated in the main hall. The two delegations of British and Chinese then made their way up onto the stage. There were other people sitting behind them. Now, *that*—who was going to be seated up there—was of course a matter of considerable discussion. We said "It's entirely up to us who we bring" and the Chinese tried initially to argue X, Y and Z should be there.

*On the British side?*

Yes. They said certain people should be there, and we said "No, no, no." In fact, of course, they had much more of a problem than we did in selecting their people because there were an infinite number of Chinese who wanted to be there, whereas in fact we found it quite difficult to find people of significance. It even meant flying a hell of a lot of people out from London—former Foreign Secretaries and people like that. Our team included the lovely Patten girls, which I think the Chinese thought was a bit off.

*The rest of the world enjoyed it.*

Indeed! So there we were. We all went up on the stage and then the ceremony took place. Having been so intimately involved in planning it all, I was in a slight daze when it was going on. Two things struck me as being slightly out of place. The first concerned the bands. The two sides had their own bands there—the Chinese and British military bands. We had agreed, when we negotiated at great length, that they would take it in turns to play a little piece. On the night I was surprised, I don't know why, that people applauded after each piece was played, and suddenly the whole thing came to life because people were actually applauding in the audience. That added a little more activity than I had expected somehow.

Another thing which had been quite interesting in the negotiation was the way in which the Chinese eventually accepted that a commercial organiser would coordinate the event. Their acceptance surprised me because they were not used to that idea. Such things were always handled by their protocol officials. And although it was of course planned by their protocol officials and our officials, eventually we put ourselves in the hands of an event co-ordinator from a commercial company. The co-ordinator was there with microphones and so on to keep the whole thing up to speed.

*This was a British co-ordinator?*

Well it certainly wasn't Chinese. It was a company which was, I think, originally British and just taken over by an American company. The people who were actually on the spot doing it were a mixture of Americans and Brits, mainly Brits. Some of them have since been engaged by the Portuguese to do the handover ceremony in Macao, using a lot of the expertise they built up in Hong Kong.

Anyway, right in the middle of the audience there was a little booth from which things were controlled by the event co-ordinator. Each side had a master of ceremonies. Ours was the Hong Kong Director of Protocol, who had a fine, resonant British voice, and the Chinese had someone from their side speaking in Mandarin. What was agreed was that, before midnight, all the directions should be given first in English and then repeated in Chinese, and after midnight the other way round. That went fine. Except that we had tried to cut down on the stage directions. The Chinese had insisted on an incredibly staged, directed event with lots of statements, because they love doing that. They say "Now the banquet will begin!", "Now the banquet is ended!" — that sort of stuff, which isn't at all something we're used to, so we cut back a lot. In the end, of course, they were right at one point, because the Prince of Charles got it wrong. He hadn't read his brief properly. Towards the end, after he had made his speech, the final thing was the speech by Jiang Zemin. Having made his speech, Jiang Zemin came back to his seat in the row established for the principals. At that point, had the Prince of Charles read his brief, he would have stood up, shaken hands with Jiang Zemin and then begun the process of walking down the front of the stage and peeling off. But he just sat there. And Jiang Zemin decided he'd better sit down because the Prince of Charles was sitting. So he sat down, and there was a moment of "What happens next?" Fortunately the Chinese master of ceremonies was pretty quick, and he said in the same voice he had used throughout, "Would President Jiang Zemin and Prince Charles please stand up and shake hands." He said it in Chinese. The event co-ordinator in her little booth in the middle of the floor, I heard subsequently, said frantically to the British MC, "Repeat what he said!" The British MC, who couldn't speak Chinese, said "I don't know what he said!" But that had the right effect because Jiang Zemin stood up and walked across to Prince Charles and said his piece quite clearly. He said, "I think we're supposed to shake hands now." "Oh, is that right?" So the Prince of Charles stood up and shook hands.

*"Is that so! Haven't read my brief!"*

And that was it. So they then escorted each other to the front of the stage, and they peeled off. Then the final event, of course, of the British evening, was the departure of the Britannia with the Governor and the Prince of Charles. I got a bit involved in that because I had made myself responsible to make sure Mrs Patten and the three girls would be taken quickly off the stage so they didn't get caught up with everyone else. I had to get them around the back and into the limo. We got them down to the quayside where there were all sorts of farewell ceremonies which were pretty ad hoc and lasted for about twenty minutes, with the Governor saying goodbye to all of his friends and to his staff and to people like myself.

*It was really quite poignant. I watched the entire process, and there were quite emotive reactions.*

Yes. Well, it was a marvellously staged event, wasn't it, in the end?

*Yes, it was.*

By this time, of course, Hong Kong was Chinese territory. The Chinese had sent a small delegation led by the Vice Foreign Minister. There were four of them, and there they were standing around rather forlornly in a little line, and just before Patten stepped onto the brow of the ship I took him by the hand, and I said "Look, the Chinese are here to say farewell."[16] So we took him over and he shook hands with them. Considering all the background, each was very courteous to the other. And that was it! He went onto the ship, the Chinese officials peeled off back to the Convention Centre, and off he went.

After the handover ceremony there was the sort of Chinese equivalent of our farewell ceremony. They sort of mirrored ours. It was outside our negotiation, but we of course were aware of how things were developing. Starting about 1.30 a.m., as far as I remember, they had the swearing-in ceremony for the various senior officials from the Chief Executive to the various judges to the Legislative Council and so on. It was interesting because the Hong Kong Government had spent a great deal of money building the stage in this other room, which really should have been used for other events as well. The Chinese refused to have anything to do with it, and spent something like three million pounds on building another one upstairs. The event was in the Chinese style that we had rejected for the handover ceremony. So that was the final event of that night, and it was an event which was deliberately boycotted by the Americans and the British. Other than myself, curiously. I was sent along, together with my colleague who was going to be the Consul-General there, to demonstrate that on an official level we certainly intended to maintain our business links with the

---

16. 'Brow' is a naval word for 'gangway'.

new administration. The reason it was boycotted was because of the swearing-in of the Provisional Legislature, about which we had all expressed reservations. We had at one point expected that people like the Australians and Canadians would also decide not to go but they decided that their relationship with Beijing was important enough for that small issue not to interfere.

*The Australians would have been thinking of the Australian Business Council and other trade-related constituencies at home.*

So that was about it. Then there were various celebrations the next day, but that was the handover. Now, what I've told you is very much a narrative, so if you want now to try and dig out of that any particular issues that you want to talk through, I'll try and do that.

*Mr Davies, just as the tape switched off on the other side you said you noticed two remarkable things on the evening itself, during the ceremony.*

Well, the first one was simply the way in which the audience reacted, and the other one was the fact that it went wrong in the sense that the Prince of Charles got it wrong at one point. Otherwise everything went entirely according to script and nothing went seriously wrong. I think most people who saw it found it to be a very cold ceremony, rather bleak, and some people on the British side who had not been Pattenites said "Oh what a missed opportunity. We could have made a great thing of it." But I don't think we would ever have achieved a ceremony which was full of happiness and verve, which the two sides could have associated themselves with. One phrase in our agreed minute, that governed a lot of our discussions, was that the ceremony should be solemn and dignified.[17] We wanted to make certain that neither side would do anything provocative or unacceptable to the other, because it was not beyond the bounds of possibility that one side might have said something in a speech, for example, that the other side wouldn't have liked.

*Did each side see the speeches beforehand?*

As far as I remember, speeches were exchanged beforehand, yes.

*With that idea in mind?*

Yes. Certainly on our side we wanted to maintain our principles while ensuring that what was said was not going to be so offensive to the Chinese that it would cause difficulties on a night which everybody wanted to go smoothly for the sake of Hong Kong. So, I think it went well but it was undoubtedly a fairly bleak occasion. Taken together with the farewell ceremony, which was so well covered by media, the two things together made it a rather sad event. Now, the farewell ceremony, had it not been rained on, might have been a much jollier occasion. In part it was supposed to celebrate Hong Kong's development over the one hundred and fifty years, and an occasion of some pomp and circumstance with the final military events.

---

17. Section 1(1)1 of the agreed minute says "A solemn and dignified ceremony will be held jointly by the two Governments around midnight on 30 June 1997 in Hong Kong" (Joint Liaison Group 1996).

I think it worked quite well, but no doubt it was spoilt by the weather. Oddly enough, I think those who watched it on television found the raininess quite moving, although those of us who were sitting in that rain were pissed off. Excuse my language. It was very, very wet. One of the problems was that, when we had been looking at having it outdoors, I had strongly advocated with the Governor that if we were going to do so we should hold it in the stadium, which has lots of covered space. But he didn't want that. He wanted to have it in the middle of Hong Kong. I can see why, with the skyline and all that sort of thing. Brilliant to have it there, on this bit of re-claimed land.

*To demonstrate positive British influence on the development of Hong Kong?*

Well, I think it was just to make it a great event in the centre of Hong Kong, which would be a good media event. In a stadium it could be almost anywhere in the world. But there he was, surrounded by the great skyscrapers of Hong Kong, by the harbour and with Britannia there as the backdrop. So it was a splendid place. The difficulty was making it watertight. We knew from the beginning that it was a major risk doing it from there, but the cost of putting up stands was something absolutely horrific. I don't think any of us, until we got around to planning it, had any idea how much it would cost to put up temporary stands of reasonable solidity. When we investigated putting a roof on these stands, it doubled the cost. We are talking about millions of pounds. So it was not justifiable. Instead, an order was put in to accommodate 60,000 or 20,000, I forget how many. I think only 10,000 were allowed to sit down. And umbrellas. Everyone was issued with an umbrella, rather a nice souvenir—specially printed umbrellas. They are great for a light shower when you are standing up, but when you were sitting down for an hour and half, and it was not a light shower, the umbrella simply kept your head dry. But all the rest of you got wet because everybody else's umbrella poured into your lap. It *poured* into your lap so we were all absolutely soaked. It was quite awful. Those who were sensible had come prepared with a sort of plastic coat. Those people survived. The rest of us got soaked. Other than the Prince of Charles, who was fortunate to go to the Britannia and change, most of us went straight on from that into the Convention and Exhibition Centre for the reception prior to the dinner. In soaked clothes we went from a hot, steamy wetness outside, into a strongly airconditioned building. Why we didn't all get pneumonia I don't know. Within about two and half hours we were all bone dry again, just from being in the airconditioning. You can imagine what that does to you health.

*Yes, I'm sure. I can remember at the time thinking that the 'Prince of Charles' was forlorn for most of that ceremony. Maybe it had something to do with the rain.*

He did very well, didn't he? He stood up when the rain decided to come down, not just as it had before in streams, but in bucket-loads. Nobody could but admire what he did. He stood there without an umbrella and read out his speech, which must have almost been reduced to pulp as the rain came down in sheets. Of course, it also had the same effect on the poor old honour guards down below. I think the band struck up the royal anthem just as the rain went completely mad. What was so sad was that you could see light in the sky, only three miles away to the west, while we had the deluge on top of us. So everything conspired against us. We were very unfortunate.

So, 'the best laid plans, etcetera'. The Chinese were actually right in saying that it was not wise to hold a ceremony in the open air at that time of year, but they were also extremely concerned about security. They were paranoid. They are always, as far as the elite are concerned. We got questioned about whether high-powered rifles could hit people from the other side of the harbour, about two miles away. The security for the occasion was amazingly stringent, and because the Chinese had been so slow in agreeing on the list of those who should attend the events, the issuing of tickets almost fell into complete chaos. There was something called the Handover Ceremony Co-ordination Office. In the last week they were working 24 hours a day. Some people were only getting an odd two hours sleep every couple of days, just going through these 4000 invitations, making certain that each one got a different colour co-ordinated stamp on their pass, indicating which part of the ceremony to go to.

*Was that entirely co-ordinated by the British side?*

That was all eventually co-ordinated by the Handover Ceremony Co-ordination Office. It was a nightmare. It was all right on the night, as it happened, but frankly it was a damned close thing. From the British side, when our VIPs started arriving, most of the stuff had not been settled, two and half days before the event. We had to send down our own team of people from the British offices there to take control of the British part and make certain that we got all the tickets for our people. In the Danish Consulate, a friend of mine said that on the day before he had been down in that office for six hours trying to identify his guests. It was extraordinary that it came together, considering all the complications. The Chinese are very bad at making decisions other than at the last minute. Had we got all their names and details two weeks before, it would have been all right, but when it's up to the last week it was a recipe for disaster. On the whole, I don't think there were many mistakes. We had one or two dropped catches.[18] It was only the next day that the Thai baht went into nose-dive, bringing the whole of Asia around its ears. It was ironic that one of the few VIPs who got lost at the banquet—he complained afterwards—was the Thai Foreign Minister.

*Mr Davies, could we use a variation on a Chinese expression to finish off? Let's take a 'great leap sideways' rather than a 'great leap forward'. If the Prudential board were to say to you "We have some people who want to understand how to negotiate with Chinese from a business perspective", what lessons could you draw from your experience with the handover ceremony, or other aspects of the handover, that would help business negotiators?*

---

18. Another cricketing analogy, meaning to make a mistake.

Sure. People very often ask whether there are lessons I can draw from negotiating with Chinese. I think that a lot of the things one says about negotiating with the Chinese probably apply to negotiating with a lot of other counterparts. A lot of them are obvious, but one thing is clear—the Chinese are very tough negotiators. They may be that way because they haven't got anywhere to go when they start negotiations, and they are simply stone-walling to make you reveal more of your own position than you want to reveal. Or maybe they are tough negotiators because they have already decided what they want to achieve and are going to press you to the wall. I don't know. Very often I think it's a case of *not* having fully prepared themselves, and being given firm instructions not to move, and then deploying a whole series of delaying devices. So I think one has to be prepared for protracted negotiations, unless one has a lot of flexibility and knows that the Chinese are the *demandeurs* and themselves want a rapid resolution. If one is the *demandeur*, one has to expect a long, drawn-out event. So, the obvious first quality you've got to display is considerable patience and readiness to take it reasonably slowly.

The next thing, and this would apply to almost any negotiations, is that you really need to think through your overall objectives in advance, pretty clearly. You need to have some idea of where you can move back from those objectives, and some sort of room for manoeuvre. At all points you must remind yourselves consistently of where you are trying to go, and not be diverted from that. If you find you are not going to achieve your objectives, then the answer is to take stock and decide whether you are going to continue with them or move back.

There is a lot to be said for hanging tough at various points. Sometimes you achieve things by making clear that you're not going to go anywhere in that direction, that you will take an entirely different course. We saw that when we made clear to the Chinese that unless we had a ceremony that we could live with we would not continue the negotiations, and would not be at that ceremony.

There were a number of similar examples in other negotiations that we conducted. You just have to decide that it is not necessarily in your own interest to continue down a certain line. In this case we thought a handover ceremony was desirable but not essential. So if it is something the other side wants very much then you are in a stronger position to achieve the main objective that you set yourself in the beginning. Those are the sort of general lessons that one can apply to virtually any negotiations with the Chinese.

*In what ways if any, did you consciously modify your strategies and tactics as the negotiations proceeded?*

I think one does modify inevitably because one of the parameters with which one always operates is that one is not the final arbiter of the policy. The policy is determined on the basis of considerable inter-departmental discussion. In our case, not only within our office, where we could try and explain what we thought was achievable in the negotiator framework, but also we were fundamentally driven by the wishes of the Governor. Also by the instructions that emerged from discussions between the Governor and the Foreign and Commonwealth Office. So the instructions we worked within were not necessarily of our making. We didn't therefore have the manoeuvrability within our operating framework to make many modifications.

But, on the other hand, having exhausted what we thought we could achieve, within the negotiating framework, we were then at liberty to re-turn to the decision-making forum and say "This is as far as we have got. We believe that we can get to there, possibly" or "We don't think we can get any further. What shall we do next?" We would then re-establish the next step and move forward from there. From time to time things were therefore modified. As I indicated, our original wish had been to have this ceremony outdoors, but as part of a deal which encapsulated their readi-ness to have international participation, their readiness to do various other things, we would move from outside to inside. Actually by that time we had all reached the conclusion that it was a good idea anyway because of the weather. It was a form of bartering. You don't play your readiness to con-cede on one of those issues until that last minute. The negotiation of the agreed minute was very much on that basis. So you end up inside with an agreed minute. We were the first to draft, then we would get a counter-draft from them, and then we would try to narrow down the differences. You end up with square brackets and you trade one square bracket against another, and eventually it's sorted out by the two Foreign Ministers. Rath-er bizarre that it has to go up as far as that, but that's how things were in those days. By that time there were only a couple of limited issues to do with security. So, definitely one does modify. Some of the modifications are made on the spot. They may be very minor things, and you think "Oh, that's not a bad idea. Okay, we go along with that." It might be something that did not occur to you previously. You do have some flexibility. Again, you have to consider, when you are discussing the matters with the other side, whether you demonstrate that flexibility then or whether you use your readiness to be flexible as a lever to get something out of them. So there is always a judgement there. As you can see from what I described, we had really quite an extended time in which to make these moves, al-though in the end it was right up to the wire.

*Did you ever have any doubts about the authority of the people with whom you were negotiating any aspect of the joint handover ceremony? A point that is often raised by people in business is that a negotiator who claims to have the authority to make decisions will in fact not be the person who carries authority. Major delays can be associated with that person hanging in there while somebody else is working it all out behind the scenes with somebody who does have real authority. Is that an exaggeration?*

No, I don't think that's exaggerated. In the Chinese context it is a very common problem because of the labyrinthine systems they operate under. But in this instance there was a formally established channel of communication on all things to do with transition in Hong Kong, and that channel was the Joint Liaison Group. I was the British leader and the Chinese Ambassador was the Chinese leader. All matters relating to the handover ceremony were to be handled through that channel, so we had no problem about that. Of course, that doesn't mean that their position might not be changed by someone coming in at a higher level. But normally we weren't exposed to that because the Chinese position was usually ultra-cautious at the ambassadorial level, and it meant that we had to negotiate and to explain at great length where our position did not meet their expectations. We had to explain very clearly what we were looking for. It might take some weeks before we got a response because they had to put it through their system. So, we were definitely using the right channel, but the decision-making process was often ponderous. That's why we had some pretty tense discussions when, frankly, we began to lose our temper with some of these guys, who were just not prepared to move. But one knows that they were unable to make those sorts of decisions.

*So it's not just a ploy to stall to gain advantage over you? There's more to it than that?*

Well, I think that varies. I think they have genuine problems getting decisions out of their decision-makers. We all have those problems in any bureaucracy. I gather it got even worse in London than it used to be, with the new Foreign Secretary refusing to read papers and so on. But I'm even more aware of it now that I'm working in the private sector. It may be that those of us in government roles who have dealt with the Chinese have underestimated the problems their officials have in working their way through the system to get decisions. When you're in the private sector you see clearly that it is very difficult for the Chinese people you are dealing with to produce the answers, however full of goodwill they are. They have to play so many different parts of the system to get sometimes inconsistent answers.

*Other negotiations are going on behind the scenes?*

Indeed. I keep in touch with my old colleagues in the Hong Kong Administration. I was told by some senior people there that they are extremely happy about the way in which the authorities up in Beijing have kept their hands off Hong Kong, and on the whole have been impeccable in their performance since the handover. Nevertheless, there are things on which the SAR authorities need to get answers, and they have found it very difficult to find their way through the Chinese system. They have had to learn the labyrinthine routes that Chinese officials have grown up with. So you need to take time to learn the lobbying routes to get through to the right people.

*Which ties in very closely with the patience factor you alluded to earlier.*

Quite. Yes. Yes.

*I can imagine there are problems for people who must find their way through that system from a business perspective. Shareholders and people in headquarters often don't understand that context, but want evidence of short-term progress, which many international managers find impossible to achieve.*

Yes, I think that's right. The classic case is always that the chief executive shows up and is wined and dined and has very good relationships with some of the senior people on the Chinese side, and he says to the local manager "Well, that's all okay, isn't it? Sorted it all out." Six months later there still hasn't been any progress because the guy on the ground has to work his way through all this appalling sort of mix-up.

*I feel we've got very rich material here.*

I do feel that I've skated over a lot, because I hadn't reminded myself of a lot of the detail. It's quite interesting that I've forgotten so much of it. I thought I'd never forget it!

*(End of interview)*

## The Scenario

The main unit of analysis for the scenario at Figure 6.1 is Hugh Davies, and the timeframe is from the beginning of his involvement in the negotiation until the very end.[19] The codes are estimated 'averages' for the overall play for the complete negotiation. As with the case to follow in Chapter 7, not all content tensions in this scenario correspond explicitly to the minutiae of the negotiation agenda. It would be possible to record a tension for every issue negotiated, large and small, but that would be overkill. Rather, these tensions tend to reflect the interplay of British and Chinese interests and desired results at a broader and more significant level. Much of Hugh Davies' commentary suggests a cardinal tension based on content that is not debated by the players but is the elephant—or dragon—in the room: *British Sovereignty* ↔ *Chinese Sovereignty* (tension 2). The British seemed to treat the handover ceremony as a tribute to historic power and glory and as the noble last gasp of Empire. They were determined to assert sovereignty over Hong Kong until midnight on 30 June 1997, whereas the Chinese wanted to control the format, choice of venue, guest-list and security arrangements before the formal transfer at the agreed time. This theme pervades the scenario.

---

19. My focus on Hugh Davies should not be construed as a claim by me or him that he resolved the issues as an individual. He told me "This was by definition a team effort and I was simply the guy at the prow of the vessel, taking some of the spray and hoping to battle through. If I gave the impression ... that it was all down to me, that was wrong, and many others involved would be justifiably miffed. At the end of it all, those of us most involved indulged ourselves in an emotional and very collective hugging session."

1. CONTENT

PROCESS [AEO]

2. British Sovereignty ↔ Chinese Sovereignty [SLYH]
3. International Ceremony ↔ Domestic Ceremony [SLYH]
4. British Security ↔ PLA Security [SLFM]
5. Free Mode ↔ Communist Mode [SLFW]

6. Power (Davies) ↔ Power (Chinese) [SEY]
7. Uncertainty Avoidance (Strong) ↔ Uncertainty Avoidance (Weak) [SLY]
8. Individualism ↔ Collectivism [SRYH]
9. Orientation (Long-term) ↔ Orientation (Short-term) [SEY]
10. Competition ↔ Cooperation [SLY]
11. Combat ↔ Collaboration [SLY]
12. Formality ↔ Informality [SLY]
13. Person ↔ Group [SLO]
14. Positional Focus ↔ Interest Focus [AEO]
15. Other (? ↔ ?)

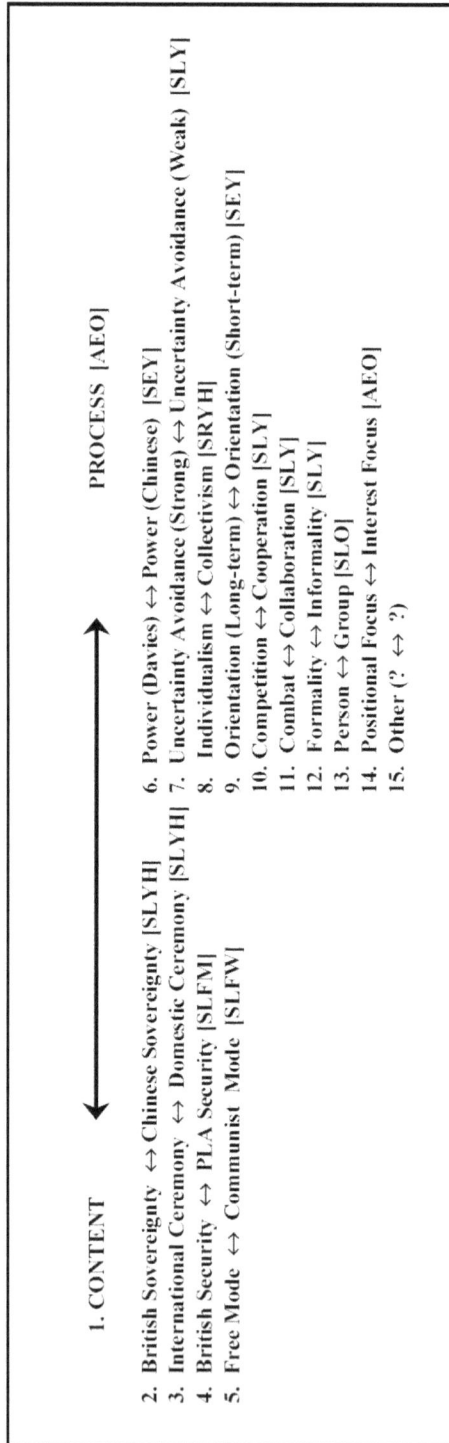

**Figure 6.1:** Scenario for the Hong Kong Handover Ceremony Negotiations

The discussion focuses on the handover ceremony but brings in Hugh Davies' other associated activities and opinion because they shed light on the specific negotiation within a broader set of negotiations about the handover. I have reproduced the entire transcript because Davies' comments on the broader context are important for understanding the sub-transaction.

For this scenario and the next one (Chapter 7) I do not always define the general meaning of the tensions, so anyone who has forgotten the definitions or the codes should refer back to Chapter 4.

Although the tensions described below are extracted from and explained in relation to a specific case, they will be recognised in other cases where similar forces are at work.

### Content ↔ Process

1. *Content ↔ Process* [AEO]: The leitmotif of content is Britain's struggle to control the ceremony so that she can bow out with dignity. To allow the Chinese to dominate the negotiation process would make Davies the ever-weakening party and therefore undermine his chances of protecting Britain's dignity while achieving her associated objectives. As one would expect of a negotiator with his experience, Davies seems always aware of the danger of paying too much attention to the British team's desired outcomes and not enough to the way of negotiating them. He has content in mind whenever he manipulates process.

In the transcript there is a constant sense of his focusing on tactics to achieve long-range objectives, then bringing the focus back to content, then reversing according to need. For example, he says he relied on "a [drawn-out] form of bartering" to negotiate the detail of the agreed minute, holding off as long as possible on revealing the desired detail in order to force the Chinese to agree under pressure of time: "You don't play your readiness to concede on one of those issues until [you approach the end]." Despite the Chinese use of principal-agent protocol to manoeuvre content and process, or inadvertent stalemate caused by that protocol, there is usually a sense of Davies presiding over the interplay or regaining control if it should drift away from him. There is almost constant oscillation (O) for the negotiation overall but the balance evens out (E). Davies and the Chinese sustain their attempts to orchestrate content and process.

### Content Tensions

2. *British Sovereignty ↔ Chinese Sovereignty* [SLYH]: I considered labelling this tension *British control ↔ Chinese control* but decided to go with *sovereignty* because the label has deeper meaning that subsumes the immediate struggle for 'control' of the detail and conduct of the handover ceremony. There are occasional worries, especially when the handover is about to happen, but Davies does not stray from confidence in his team's ability to

protect Britain's right to hold sovereign control of Hong Kong, including reasonable authority over the ceremony, until midnight on 30 June. To be confident is not to play down difficulty, and even though a form of agreement is never in serious jeopardy, intensity is rated high (H) to reflect "the degree of actual ... difficulty [for both parties] in reaching agreement [throughout the negotiation] on matters associated with the tension" (definition of intensity for content tensions, from Chapter 4).

For a content tension, the 'strength' of a pole means the likelihood that outcomes will be more or less associated with it, relative to the other pole. As it seems likely for most of the negotiation that Davies and his team will have the skill to engineer an agreement allowing Britain to retain the trappings of formal sovereignty of Hong Kong until midnight, balance is biased left (L) and balance tendency is stable (Y).

Western imperial history from different points of view is the main macrocosmic force generating this tension. China has long seen itself as a victim of Western imperialism, and in the mid-1990s the reviving Middle Kingdom was about to evict the United Kingdom, the most powerful usurper of all, from its last relic of Empire in Asia. Although Davies does not say so, it is no secret that China needed (and still needs) to counter the Century of Shame that followed the Treaty of Nanjing, signed in 1842 after China lost the First Opium War (1839–42)—in essence a Sino-British clash over trade and sovereignty.[20] Under the terms of the treaty, China ceded Hong Kong Island to Britain. Eighteen years later, after the Second Opium War (1856–60), China ceded the Kowloon Peninsula, and in 1898 leased the New Territories and 235 adjacent islands to Britain for 99 years from 1 July—hence the 'recovery' time of midnight on 30 June 1997. Although Britain was not legally obliged to return Hong Kong Island and the Kowloon Peninsula, she agreed to do so after paying lip-service to Chinese arguments about the unfairness of the treaties. Much more persuasive was the ceded land's dependence on the New Territories for food and water. A new lease was not feasible; nor a British outpost at the mercy of a Chinese tap controller.

In the negotiation, the tacit Chinese plaint about dubious transfer of sovereignty by the treaties is countered by the British view that Hong Kong is British territory and will remain so until the formal handover. This attitude to the endgame of sovereignty underpins Davies' report of British determination to control the essentials of the handover ceremony, within reason, and not to have one at all if the Chinese insist on doing it their own

---

20. The Treaty of Nanjing was the first in a series known as the Unequal Treaties, forced upon China during the 19th and early 20th centuries by European imperial powers and Japan. The treaties ceded Chinese territory and control over foreigners and trade, at first in the five prosperous Treaty Ports and later in many other parts of the country. Caricatures populate Robert Standish's novel *Gentleman of China* (1949) but it conveys a strong sense of the British swagger and Chinese pique that grew out of the treaties.

way. As Davies says, his team's default position is to hold only a British farewell ceremony with or without Chinese approval.[21]

As well as the specific history of Hong Kong and associated treaties and leases, a macrocosmic force that generates this tension is the change in relative roles of China and the United Kingdom in geopolitics and the international economy. Britain is waning in both respects; China is burgeoning. The Chinese negotiators seem to think Britain will bow to the rising power of China, just like the rest of the world, even down to control of the handover ceremony. Part of Davies' agenda is to get them to see otherwise, which is why 'sovereignty', albeit fleeting for the British, is a broad negotiation item hovering above the more specific items expressed in the other content tensions. Undeterred by the trend towards role reversal in the wider world, Britain wants China to accept, and be seen to accept, British sovereignty over this vestige of Empire until there is no choice but to relinquish. There is muscular symbolism in the use of English translated into Mandarin before midnight and vice versa after midnight.

The international image desired by both parties is another macrocosmic force driving this tension. The international media are watching. Among other things, the future of trade between China and the rest of the world depends in part on confidence in China's new image. The British want to exit with dignity and goodwill; the Chinese need to present as a benign, accommodating power that looks outward rather than inward as it engages with the world. China must assert itself as the rightful owner of Hong Kong without scaring the people of Hong Kong or causing the British to lose face. On the other hand, Davies points to Chinese fear of losing face if the ceremony content and format contradict China's claims to de facto sovereignty, reinforced by evicting the colonial tenant.

Also at macrocosmic level, the difference between Britain's liberal democracy—applied to Hong Kong's economy if not to the political system—and China's command structure help create this tension because the Chinese authorities are programmed to assert absolute Party control over Chinese territory, which to them has always included Hong Kong.[22]

In the immediate zone of the negotiation proper, the most obvious force contributing to creation of this tension is the relative power of the negotiators. At first glance the Chinese team seems to take much more power into the formal and incidental negotiation sessions than Davies and his team. The Chinese are in the box seat—Britain is on the way out, with

---

21. In American negotiation jargon, the default position is the BATNA—Best Alternative to a Negotiated Agreement (Fisher et al. 1991: 101-111).

22. To be fair to the British (at least for the period after about 1970), political democracy was withheld largely because it was thought to be incompatible with Chinese communism and would therefore bring more grief than benefit to the people of Hong Kong. "Treat Hong Kong like other British colonies, senior Chinese officials including premier Zhou Enlai warned, and the territory may be deluded into thinking that it will one day share their destiny and achieve independence" (Patten 1998: 25).

no choice in the matter. On the other hand, Davies knows China's local and international image is at stake, so he makes demands about the ceremony and digs in his heels on the assumption that China will compromise to avoid the stain of belligerence.

Even though there are minor concessions, such as the fortunate indoor rather than outdoor venue for the handover ceremony, Davies seems to gain and hold the upper hand as he protects the remnants of British sovereignty over Hong Kong. The negotiations are slow, sometimes unpleasant, and precarious to the end, but he and his team work doggedly for a ceremony that will not cause Britain or China to lose face.

3. *International Ceremony* ↔ *Domestic Ceremony* [SLYH]: I will not go into lengthy detail about the macrocosmic and immediate forces that create this tension, or the next two content tensions. To do so would be to cover much the same ground as for *British sovereignty* ↔ *Chinese sovereignty*. Tensions 3, 4 and 5 are more specific reflections of negotiated content but they are also largely about claiming sovereignty. For Tension 3 in particular, the need for image control is a macro force that causes the Chinese to look inward and the British—who seem to be more confident of their international prestige—to look outward as they encourage the world to watch and judge.

Early in the negotiation, Davies sees polar conflict when he presents the British proposal for an international ceremony: "We put these ideas to the Chinese, around the turn of the year 1995-1996. At this remove I don't quite remember their immediate reaction, but when we re-engaged later it became clear that our concept of the ceremony and their concept were poles apart." Soon after Davies starts to work on the Chinese, an international ceremony seems more likely than a domestic one; the left pole (L) dominates the overall play consistently (Y) despite the influence of the right pole—with its messages of Chinese control, lower risk and less scrutiny—on the attitude of the Chinese negotiators. Intensity is (H) because negotiating the finer detail is usually difficult and drawn out, even though the players negotiate broad acceptance of an international ceremony without great difficulty.

The Chinese negotiators stonewall under the influence of their country's inclination to turn in on itself as a command society that does not like external media or other scrutiny, and decries it as interference in internal affairs. Because Hong Kong has always been Chinese soil to them, they see the recovery as a domestic matter to be sorted out between Britain and China alone. Any dissent or grievances that Hong Kong residents might want to show at the time are also a domestic matter, and should not be encouraged by the exposure of an international ceremony broadcast to the world. In the Party tradition, they prefer a domestic ceremony, controllable in itself and its by-products: private rather than public, closed rather than open, low-key rather than high-key, small rather than large, Chinese rather than cosmopolitan. In contrast, the British want an international handover ceremony, with an international guest-list and full media exposure, to demonstrate the benefits of their rule over Hong Kong, and to make people confident that an international eye will discourage China from reneging on promises about minimal interference in the new SAR.

Davies manoeuvres the Chinese negotiators and their principals towards the left pole by convincing them they have nothing to lose and a lot to gain from an international ceremony. Although they accept it fairly early, the initial Chinese preference for a more controllable domestic show stays in Davies' and the Chinese negotiators' heads as they react to proposals and counter-proposals. With patience, logic, minor concessions and some digging-in of heels, Davies consolidates the broad manoeuvre to the left pole by convincing the Chinese to accept finer detail appropriate to an international ceremony.

4. *British Security* ↔ *PLA Security* [SLFM]: Apart from the obvious association with issues of sovereignty, this tension issues from the ideological and practical disparities between a liberal society and one based on command. Davies knows the Chinese do not to trust security provided by others, and that they fear international scorn if visiting dignitaries are endangered or worse; hence the pressure from the Chinese negotiators to use the People's Liberation Army, countered by British insistence on using the Hong Kong Police — still under sovereign British control.

When the Chinese make their security demands well into the negotiation, Davies convinces them that the psychological effects on local people of a forbidding military force, compared with more familiar but equally effective police, would intrude on the ceremony and work against China's desired international image. They do not put up much resistance to Davies' argument that it is in their best interests to go with the Hong Kong Police as the main security force, with small PLA and British military guards of honour for the ceremony proper, and with no finale of bayonets or blood-chilling shrieks.

Overall, the benefit of British-controlled security arrangements leading up to midnight appears to be an increasingly stronger influence on the players' stance than the PLA alternative; hence the (LF) coding. The players had much less difficulty reaching agreement on this tension than the previous one, so the intensity is medium (M).

5. *Free Mode* ↔ *Communist Mode* [SLFW]: The main forces creating the previous content tensions also contribute to this one. More specific macro forces are aesthetics and ideological symbolism. The Chinese want a ceremony in communist mode, with uniforms, high formality, rigid structure and timing, and a focus on hierarchy — of course, with the Politburo at the apex. A ceremony in this style would be more about fortifying Chinese power over Hong Kong than celebrating an important international event that depends on sustained cooperation between the parties.

Apart from questions about the aesthetic suitability of Chinese Communist kitsch for an international event, Davies seems to rebuff Chinese preferences because, in the interests of Hong Kong's composure and Britain's image, the British do not want communist ideology and displays of centralised power to hijack the ceremony. He compromises throughout the negotiation, as negotiators do, but he never gives ground where even a hint of ideology or sovereignty is at stake.

Ceremonial 'free mode' (L) tends to be the expected outcome for most of the negotiation, and the pole gets consistently stronger as Davies argues his case; hence the balance tendency is left (F). In spite of ongoing Chinese disquiet, and irritation caused by the protocol expert, the negotiators have less trouble agreeing on the 'mode' issue than any other, so the intensity is low (W). Of course, 'less trouble' does not mean 'no trouble'.

Faced with continual but not very strong pressure from the Chinese negotiators, Davies engineers a more casual and populist ceremonial style—focusing on Hong Kong and its people—that suits both the British and the Chinese. His method of reaching compromise on contradictory protocol, especially for the meeting of the main British and Chinese dignitaries before the main ceremony, is at once astute and droll, in the spirit of good diplomacy and Monty Python. He negotiates seating to neutralise opposing Chinese and British concepts of the relative status of left and right, and delights at "the small triumph" of taking the south-facing seats for the British delegation, so that "the Prince of Charles" sits in the traditional Chinese emperor's position while the Chinese Premier faces north.[23] Apart from aesthetics and quirky one-upmanship, the origins and management of this 'mode' tension ooze matters of history, sovereignty and ideology.

### Process Tensions

6. *Power (Davies)* ↔ *Power (Chinese)* [SEY]: As explained in Chapter 5, the power tension includes but is not limited to the cultural attitudes to authority that define Hofstede's power distance dimension. The tension is generated by all the internal and external power relationships that influence the process of negotiation, including negotiator experience and rank, and disparities in the personal authority vested in the negotiators by their principals. This and all other process tensions are about influence on the communication and other negotiating behaviour of the players.

The main contextual force underpinning this tension is macrocosmic—the relative power of the two countries in the 21st century compared with what it was for most of the 19th and 20th. The Chinese are adamant about their expectations for much of the negotiation, seeming to think it is their turn to dominate, to take back what was taken from them; to turn the tables. Davies' account suggests the Chinese see a large power disparity between the two countries, and therefore the negotiators, in the context of

---

23. See Chapter 2 for discussion of the cultural significance of *left* ↔ *right*.

this negotiation, and so expect the British to accept China as dominant and so defer to her. To the contrary, the British people are proud of their imperial history and disinclined to defer to anyone, which is obvious in the gusto with which the audience sings *Rule, Britannia* on the last night of the Proms each year at Royal Albert Hall in London.[24] As a product of this ethos, Davies does not defer to the Chinese view of their relative power and tends to send that message to the Chinese negotiators when they push unacceptable demands, expecting to prevail because they are in the box seat at this stage of Hong Kong's history.

Another power-related influence on behaviour is the elitist tradition of the British Foreign and Commonwealth Office. Davies is of the right stock for steady promotion and eventual appointment to leadership of this prestigious negotiating team. The force is macrocosmic in the sense that it relates to a centuries-old organisational culture and image founded on British imperial power, and immediate in the sense that Davies carries his status, skill and associated confidence into the negotiation. His experience in dealing with diplomats and bureaucrats in many countries over many years boosts his authority.

As a macrocosmic and immediate force, culture—tempered by politics and bureaucracy—also generates this tension. While the Chinese and British teams are agents for principals in Beijing on the one hand, and London and Hong Kong on the other, the Chinese negotiators appear to have less authority to compromise and make decisions, even though China's team leader, Ambassador Zhao, is a senior official. There is a 'command' political and bureaucratic structure at work here but the Chinese cultural preference for high power distance is probably a related factor. The Chinese obligation to continually consult higher authority causes long delays that frustrate Davies, who does not have carte blanche from the FCO or Governor Patten and "[does not] therefore have the manoeuvrability ... to make many modifications.... You end up with square brackets and you trade one square bracket against another, and eventually it's sorted out by the two Foreign Ministers." Nevertheless, he does have more freedom to give and take within his brief, which is to be expected of an agent for a nation with much lower power distance than China. He understands the different cultural, political and bureaucratic demands on the Chinese and behaves accordingly, knowing when to hold back and when to assert himself in the negotiation proper and on its fringes.

---

24. Sir Henry Wood Promenade Concerts, sponsored by the BBC. I like to play Elgar to British guests as they swill gin-tonic. *Land of Hope and Glory*, the theme of the first of his five *Pomp and Circumstance Marches (Opus 39)*, usually swells breasts. *Rule, Britannia* was popular in 1982 with my British friends in Sri Lanka, Britain's former colony of Ceylon, while Mrs Thatcher was recapturing the Falklands from Argentina. "Thatcher" or "that bloody woman" became "Our Maggie". Lest anyone think I am an Anglophobe, I advise that in 1978 I founded the Somerset Maugham Club of Bali. The other members were an American aid worker, an English chef (Martin Heap, now a sausage magnate, and star of the BBC's *Blood on the Carpet: The Sausage Wars)*; and a Balinese barman.

For the overall negotiation the right and left poles have much the same influence over the negotiating behaviour of both parties, as there is never a sense of one party consistently overpowering the other. When the Chinese try to draw the power balance their way, Davies is forced to assert himself in order to maintain equality (E), where the balance hovers for most of the negotiation (Y). Davies might be accused of whistling in the dark to some extent, but he knows the reality of Britain's situation and the place of this negotiation in a withdrawal procedure. He sees no value in trying to be seen to dominate—to draw the power balance away from centre to 'his' pole—when he does not need to do so to get what Britain wants. In this negotiation, this tension it is probably the most sensitive and influential of the process tensions because it always threatens to fortify communication barriers.

7. *Uncertainty Avoidance (Strong)* ↔ *Uncertainty Avoidance (Weak)* [SLY]: As with the power tension, cultural difference tempered by contrasting politico-bureaucratic systems is a strong macrocosmic force. It sets the entrenched Chinese pattern of always consulting the pinnacle against the British way, which is far less hierarchical and encourages the agent to be more flexible than the Chinese at the point of engagement. This is not to say there is a tradition of British officials having complete autonomy and Chinese having to refer always to the Politburo; rather, it is a matter of relativity.

It is clear from Davies' account that the Chinese find it more difficult than he does to deviate from normal rules and procedures, in keeping with their strong uncertainty avoidance. They are uncomfortable when they cannot follow instructions to the letter as usual, and when the unexpected comes up they may tread water for weeks while they wait for orders to come back from the Beijing labyrinth. Even though the circumstances of the negotiation are far from routine, the Chinese doggedness in following routine is no surprise. On the other hand, Davies has no trouble adjusting to the way of the Chinese—which is not *his* normal way—to improve his chances of getting what his principals want from the negotiation:

> We actually took a leaf out of the Chinese book. Normally ... they like to establish what they call 'principles' before moving into detail. On this occasion, in a sense, we took that Chinese model. We established the agreed minute which laid out the principles within which we would establish the format of the handover ceremony.

Because he tends to adjust to their way more than they adjust to his, even though he does not always go along with them, the overall balance is (L)—that is, strong rather than weak uncertainty avoidance by the Chinese consistently drives *all* players' actions and reactions throughout the negotiation (Y).

As a macro force, different concepts of negotiation also contribute to this tension. For the Chinese team, negotiation tends to be a series of meetings where the players' routine is to deliver decisions made elsewhere;

for the British, it is more about flexible decision-making within the constraints of a brief.

Perhaps more than any other tension, this one elucidates *content* ↔ *process*. People with strong uncertainty avoidance tend to have qualms about unpredictable results of their decisions, in this case for fear of tarnishing the desired international image of the Middle Kingdom. Even though the Chinese change their stance towards the end, for most of the time they negotiate in a way that shows they are uncomfortable with compromise on some issues, including security arrangements, ceremony format, and an international rather than domestic guest-list.

A powerful immediate force is Hugh Davies' personality as much as his cultural-political background and relative autonomy. None of the Chinese negotiators seems low on uncertainty avoidance, but in contrast Davies is very confident and inordinately willing to play by ear, by both British and Chinese standards. He says he was ready to apply planned or spontaneous pressure to get what his team and his principals wanted, within reason, even to the point of not having a handover ceremony. He has occasional doubts about outcomes but right to the last minute he is a long way from fearing the unpredictable. The Chinese negotiators are cautious as counterpoint to his spontaneity, so he uses great skill to move them his way when necessary, always coming up with arguments that suggest a debacle if they insist on their 'safe' way of designing and running the ceremony. He knows they do not like uncertainty, so he convinces them that his way will reduce risk for both parties to the handover. He is a nimble tension manager. (He would have looked a little less nimble if he had not traded an outside ceremony for international participation away from the rain.)

8. *Individualism* ↔ *Collectivism* [SRY]: People from collectivist cultures, including the Chinese, are said to be more oriented than people from individualist cultures (such as the British) towards "strong, cohesive ingroups [that offer protection] in exchange for unquestioning loyalty" (Hofstede 1994: 260). Cultural values theory holds that collectivism correlates with a need for comfortable and harmonious relationships. This may play out as a tendency for negotiators from a collectivist background to have a strong interest in building relationships as a prelude and route to agreement, whereas negotiators of individualist origins may focus more on content and less on relationship development. In the Hong Kong negotiation, Davies' awareness of collectivist culture as a macrocosmic and immediate force may influence the way he relates to the Chinese, but culture does not stand alone. In this case he manages *individualism* ↔ *collectivism* with an eye on Chinese politico-bureaucratic forces as well as Chinese culture. A form of professional collectivism also influences relationships 'across the table' as the Chinese simultaneously deal with Davies and Beijing.

In the extreme case of China's command society, collectivism in the negotiators' workplace may be about ancient cultural values but it is also about maintaining good relationships through instruction and compliance.

The link with power distance and other elements of the 'power' tension (no. 6) is obvious. The Chinese players are officials in a negotiating team with little authority in its own right, and they will not risk disturbing the established relationship with their principals, who are very senior in this case because of the handover's importance. It would be facile to argue that this reflects only an ancient Chinese cultural trait based on consensus and subordination to the group in the social, economic and other interests of that group. The need for a smooth relationship with Beijing is also about command structure, and about the fear of penalty at least as much as the promise of protection in the collectivist bosom.

Davies' awareness of the Chinese negotiators' greater need to consult their masters, for structural and probably cultural reasons, induces him and his team to stay calm and patient despite getting "pissed off" behind the scenes from time to time. If he pushes too hard for quick and favourable decisions, the Chinese imperative to maintain their relationship with their masters will become even stronger, and friction may come to dominate the fairly harmonious relationship developing between the British and Chinese teams. Davies knows he has less chance of getting what he wants if he allows the delays, or difficult individuals like the Chinese protocol expert, to detract from the way he projects himself as a worker for the collective good of both parties. At the same time, he leaves no one in doubt that he is fair but not a soft touch. He is congenial and helpful but will not be bulldozed into conceding very much of what he and his team want from the negotiation. He knows good relationships are essential to success but is prepared to risk them if necessary to protect Britain's interests.

The reserved forcefulness and urge to get things done right away as time runs out are immediate forces that Davies brings to the negotiation as an 'individualist' Englishman and as a senior official who is used to being in charge. At the same time, he knows he must maintain smooth relationships in the face of procedural and personal annoyances that could easily cause bitterness in a less astute practitioner than himself. The left pole in this tension therefore pulls at him constantly but he knows success depends on behaviour influenced by collectivism as represented by the right pole. The form of collectivism influencing his negotiation is cultural to the extent that he understands and works around Chinese values, and professional in the sense that he strives for an agreement conducive to smooth diplomatic relationships now and later.

As allowed in Chapters 3 and 5, Hall's (1976) communication style dimension (*low context* ↔ *high context*) is embedded in *individualism* ↔ *collectivism*. British people tend to be culturally individualist in Hofstede's system, and to prefer low context communication (roughly, direct and literal messages). Chinese people tend to be culturally collectivist and to prefer high context communication (indirect, less explicit messages). Yet both parties in this negotiation tend to prefer low context communication about the details of the ceremony itself, while messages in both directions are always high context about the elephant in the room—sovereignty.

Unlike the specifics that reflect the sovereignty issue, the issue itself is too sensitive to broach directly for fear of damaging relationships and jeopardising the ceremony. In keeping with practice detected by Kalé (1999) in negotiations between professionals, the players' common diplomatic culture seems to steer them towards high context communication on the sovereignty issue. The same diplomatic culture may guide Davies as he neutralises the imperious protocol expert from Beijing, whose behaviour is diplomatically aberrant but consistent with Blackman's claim (discussed in Chapter 3) that Chinese negotiators take more care to develop smooth relationships with group insiders than with outsiders, especially foreigners.

Davies is a strong tension manager. He works intelligently to ensure the influence of the individualism pole does not undermine collectivist relationships as a route to an agreement that suits the British. For the overall negotiation, with only occasional aberration, patterns of behaviour associated with collectivism rather than individualism are paramount for all players; hence the codes (R) and (Y).


9. *Orientation (Long-term)* ↔ *Orientation (Short-term)* [SEY]: Much the same macrocosmic forces generate the sovereignty tension (no. 2) as this one. The players' obligation to harmonise specific details and long-term consequences is a noteworthy immediate force. For both parties, 'long-term orientation' is as much about the past as the future: past glory is to be maintained or recovered, and this must be kept in mind by the players as they haggle over the minutiae of the ceremony. Its long-term significance does seem always present as the parties negotiate the detail; hence their short-term and long-term orientations are never exclusive.

Each party wants the ceremonial particulars to exalt rather than mar the immediate and long-term international image of its country. The British want to bow out with a ceremony that celebrates the effects of Empire on Hong Kong and elsewhere but does not ruffle the Chinese in a way that will damage business prospects or diplomacy, the modern twins. The Chinese want the ceremony to celebrate the recovery of Hong Kong and confirm modern China as the potent but benign Middle Kingdom with burgeoning global influence.

For the overall negotiation, each pole has strong influence that does not flag; balance is even (E) and tends to be stable (Y). Davies knows everything he says and does must induce the Chinese to agree to here-and-now ceremonial detail that will do much good and no harm to Hong Kong, Britain or China proper, now or long term. Davies' account indicates the Chinese think the same way, overall, about the immediate and long-term implications of their behaviour towards the British negotiators, notwithstanding a demanding attitude from time to time—especially in the early stages—and friction caused by the protocol man from Beijing.

For this tension I do not see much value in cultural explanations for the patience and perseverance that Hofstede and others associate with long-term orientation. The need to consider the big picture causes Davies to be patient but tenacious with the Chinese as he engineers the here-and-now with an eye on the future. The Chinese are patient and tenacious for much the same reasons as Davies, but in addition their patience is forced by a lack of choice about waiting for the Beijing labyrinth to disgorge reactions to issues they have fed into it. This in turn forces Davies to be stalwart and calm as, in his words, the negotiations go "down to the wire".

10. *Competition* ↔ *Cooperation* [SLY]: This broad strategy tension is the backbone of every negotiation. Are the players inclined to compete for a win at the expense of the other party? At the other extreme, are the parties so obsessed with cooperating that they pay little attention to their own immediate and long-term interests? Does one party plan only to win while the other party (or parties) plans to give and take, and bake a bigger pie along the way? For much of the negotiation Davies is forced to work hard to move the Chinese away from their favoured competitive pole as he tries to apply his broad strategy of classic 'co-opetition': he believes everyone will gain most from Britain's preferred ceremony and must convince the Chinese it will make them look better than their preference.[25] His strategy succeeds eventually and the handover ceremony is bigger and better than either party envisaged.

Although the eventual outcome suits both parties, the dominant strategic influence on the behaviour of all players for most of the negotiation is competition (L)—the Chinese are relentless in their competitive approach and Davies spends most of his time countering it. At the outset and for most of the negotiation the Chinese push their demands very hard without much evidence of concern for British interests. As time runs short, and there is a serious threat of the British not participating in the ceremony, the Chinese realise they must become less demanding and rigid. Under Davies' influence their strategy moves belatedly along the continuum from left to right until the 'co-opetition' balance is achieved; there is some oscillation but the balance has a stable (Y) bias towards competition for most of the negotiation.

Davies is well aware of what his principals want him to achieve but he also knows he must help satisfy Beijing. If he cannot do so the handover itself, not only the ceremony, may turn sour. Hong Kong may suffer because China may be less inclined to stick to agreements made in parallel negotiations about such things as post-handover elections and the legal system. Chinese pique may undermine British business interests in Hong Kong and on the mainland.

Apart from the future of British business interests, macro causes of this tension include the sovereignty factor and the international image of the parties. Strong immediate forces are the Chinese and British briefs, which oblige the players to try to include in the ceremony whatever will flatter their countries in international eyes; but they must not concede anything

---

25. We are stuck with 'co-opetition'. The cliché is ugly but it does have rich meaning.

to the detriment of their principals. The Chinese try to meet their inflexible and apparently unrefined brief through competition; Davies' brief is a bit more flexible, making it easier for him to opt for a refined strategy that blends competition and cooperation. Perhaps the Chinese, like many business negotiators, lack a refined strategy because they have not prepared a clear and flexible brief or extracted one from their principals.

One of the most interesting messages in Hugh Davies' account is that chumminess is not always essential to constructive relationships and good results. It is possible for negotiators to be less than affectionate to one another but still achieve strategic 'co-opetition' in the end if the stakes are high enough for everyone.

11. *Combat* ↔ *Collaboration* [SLY]: Again, the dominant macro force is the loaded issue of sovereignty, which determines much of each party's script. As with macro forces in general, the negotiators cannot control the nature or presence of the issue but as tension managers they can have some control over its positive and negative influence. Immediate forces include differences in international experience, concepts of diplomatic negotiation, and attitudes to diplomatic etiquette. By Davies' account, he is usually collaborative as decorum demands; eventually so are the Chinese, apart from the belligerent protocol man, who maintains combat almost to the end and creates a tense atmosphere that works against good communication and normal diplomatic etiquette.

The Chinese combative style matches their competitive strategy for most of the negotiation and dominates the play—the balance is (L). To counter the Chinese style and match his strategy of co-opetition, Davies tries consistently to use a collaborative style tempered with occasional combativeness. For instance, he knows when to be combative as a tactic:

> From time to time our Ambassador in Beijing would be told that Mr Davies was behaving intolerably, by saying that the British would not attend the handover ceremony [and would have just a British farewell ceremony]. What sort of provocation was that? But eventually it all came right and very often with a deal of bluff. You learn to bluff and stamp your feet.

A collaborative style overall does not preclude tactical or incidental combativeness, which may involve digging in one's heels with impeccable politeness.

The effects on style of the immediate forces of experience, personality and intelligence are difficult to separate in Davies, as with most people, and it would distort reality to try to create neat sets of dependent and independent variables. We know only what he tells us about himself in that negotiation, but he does present as someone whose diplomatic experience has taught him how to feel and express annoyance—to be combative—without fist-shaking. He handles the protocol man and his negative influence with aplomb:

> And we had some real humdingers of arguments with these guys.... [The protocol expert] was extremely aggressive, extremely unpleasant, and we all got

very pissed off with him. By the end though, when everything was finally settled, he became a pussy-cat, and we managed to achieve things in the short period towards the end which we wouldn't have dreamed we could achieve, judging by his performance earlier. I think a lot of it was nervousness about what he could say to his directors, and he had to show that he had fought the good fight.

Perhaps the protocol expert, who seems not to be a diplomat, has a 'normal' Chinese style when combative and has not tempered it with diplomatic savvy. It would be interesting to interview him to find out if he is usually a pussy-cat but knows how and when to use combativeness as a tactic — to throw his black hat into the ring. On the other hand, Davies would surely recognise the tactic in a counterpart, but in this case he puts it down to a bullying personality and the arrogance of rank; to incidental rather than tactical style. Whatever might be the case, Davies used his empathy and tension management skills to turn a tiger into a kitten.

If the timeframe were narrower there might be phases where the code for the balance trend would be (O) for oscillation between combat and collaboration; but (Y) for 'stable' fits the overall timeframe because communication tends to be influenced much more by combativeness — tactical and occasional by Davies, perhaps tactical and certainly relentless by the Chinese until they become collaborative late in the negotiation. Throughout the negotiation the style of the Chinese heavily influences everyone's communication and other 'cross-border' behaviour — they are combative and Davies must manage his behaviour to cope with that reality.

The best display of collaboration in this case is use of the single-text method, as employed by Jimmy Carter to encourage a common cooperative strategy and collaborative style between Sadat and Begin at Camp David. Davies introduces it in the endgame: "We decided the only way to tie the Chinese down was to negotiate a bit of paper." The single-text tactic encourages orchestrated give and take and demonstrates Davies' skill as a tension manager. He knows draft and counter-draft will move things along in a decisive but transparent and even-handed way. He also knows the Chinese feel more comfortable with a document than without one, which seems at odds with the 'high context' rating of Chinese people on Hall's communication dimension. In reality, the use of text is a matter of timing and precedent, not about using it either always or never. Doubtless the Chinese are familiar with the agreed minute in diplomacy, and the eventual need to document all important agreements in diplomacy as in business. Davies and his team know when the time is right.

12. *Formality* ↔ *Informality* [SLY]: The main macro force here seems to be the culture of international diplomacy. Its main game of formal procedures and documents is supplemented by informal meetings at the periphery, unscheduled and casual, to strike deals that are later proposed at centre stage for formal discussion and ratification. Each negotiation finds its own blend. As much as by any other factor, the tension is generated by the experienced practitioner's knowledge that pretty well all negotiation involves

judgements about when to be formal and when to be informal, and what the balance should be.

This negotiation is very formal despite Davies' need to sort out misunderstandings and other problems in occasional asides, away from the main game. There is a sense throughout the interview that Davies would have preferred less formality but had to accept the highly formal Chinese approach. The balance is therefore (L) and stable (Y) for the duration. As with the style tension, the balance trend might be oscillating (O) if the timeframe were narrow, perhaps focused on a phase during which Davies goes to and from the table more frequently than he does for the overall negotiation.

A great deal of communication and other behaviour is determined by formal diplomatic procedure. Davies seems to realise there is no escape from dominant formality, and one of his ways of reacting to the tension—of managing it to advantage—is to reinforce the influence of the left pole by introducing the single-text method in order to produce an agreed minute in the tradition of the formal diplomacy, preferred by the Chinese and familiar to the British.

Associated macro forces contributing to the tension are the less formal British approach to authority and decision-making compared with the Chinese, who must stick to instructions and deviate only after approval from Beijing. In most negotiations that I have witnessed or conducted, the less authority the negotiators have in their own right, for cultural or other reasons, the more likely they are to see negotiation as a formal activity with a timetable, a rigid agenda and strict rules of procedure. The British have little choice but to go along with the Chinese, and are perhaps more formal than they would like to be because the sovereignty factor requires both parties to stand their ground, a situation that does not foster informality. This umbrella issue, albeit unvoiced, suggests that the gravity of negotiation content may influence the balance of procedural formality and informality. Purchasing a refrigerator is not the same as passing a colony, several million people and huge fixed assets from one country to another. In addition, the use of interpreters may be an immediate force that reduces spontaneity and so draws Davies and others away from informality towards formality.

13. *Person ↔ Group* [SLO]: This tension relates to *individualism ↔ collectivism*, which concerns the degree of negotiator subordination to group interests, consensus and relationship building; but the two tensions are not to be conflated. At one extreme, *person ↔ group* is about negotiator tendency to differentiate between and focus on individual players, and at the other extreme to ignore the idiosyncrasies of the individual and to focus negotiating behaviour on the group; or, in negotiations where the counterpart is not in a team, to see that person as a typical member of a group—that is, to see a stereotype (an Indonesian, a Maori, a politician, a terrorist) and try to negotiate accordingly.

Macrocosmic forces may include culture. I could speculate on whether a person from a collectivist society is more likely to focus on the group, and a person from an individualist society to focus on isolated players. As there seems to be no published research on that point, I will go no further than to say the veteran negotiators I have met are all very good at digging into the characteristics of both the individual and the group, and at orchestrating their own and others' behaviour in response to their findings. Apart from studying counterparts, they are good at assessing themselves and their own team (if there is one), and their role within it.

There is some evidence that different British and communist Chinese concepts of diplomatic negotiation are a macrocosmic influence. The totalitarian concept may cause the Chinese team to look and feel like a homogeneous group in the sense that they are dominated as one by their principals and may not do much more than report the stance of obscure controllers (Davies says "directors") behind the scenes.[26] In contrast, the British negotiation concept, at least for this case, is more about a team with a visible leader who is not autonomous but does have substantial authority and flexibility.

Immediate forces generating this tension are difficult to suggest, apart from the experience of Davies and the other British players in dealing with Chinese negotiators, and the Chinese experience in dealing with British teams and their relatively powerful lead negotiators. Intelligence and other aspects of individual psychology must also play a part, but this assumption should be tested with scientific research. For instance, how empathetic are the players? Does a negotiator tend to be a 'lumper' or a 'splitter' when analysing and learning to deal with new information and unfamiliar people, and is culture an influence on whether one lumps or splits? Hugh Davies seems to be empathetic, very intelligent, and to lump and split as required.

There would be little point in Davies dwelling on the idiosyncrasies of each Chinese negotiator unless it would help him to get individuals to sway decisions within the Chinese team or curry favour for the British in Beijing. For cultural, bureaucratic and historical reasons his chances would be slim: for a start, the Chinese team is collectivist and favours high power distance, and the ambassador and his team have little authority in their own right. For most of the transcript Davies pays minor attention to the range of Chinese individuals (he almost always refers to "the Chinese"), including the team leader, but he does home in on one player—he scrutinises the troublesome protocol expert and uses patience, timely withdrawal and shrewd combativeness to reduce the man's negative influence on communication, across and beyond the table. Davies shifts his focus away from the group to that person in order to bring him on side, or at least to neutralise

26. Sir Alan Donald made that point to me about his dealings with Chinese negotiators in Guandong many years earlier. There were problems with breaches of the China-Hong Kong border, "whereby immigrants who had entered Hong Kong illegally ... were captured and returned to China". He found out only much later who had been in charge of the Chinese team, from the man himself.

him so that he has a less destructive influence on the Chinese team's approach to the British. This is excellent tension management in response to problems that develop as the undiplomatic ring-in exacerbates the plodding, formal and not very affable relationship between the parties. Like any good negotiator, Davies sees the particular and the general, and the way they relate to one another.

There is a strong sense of 'British team and principals versus Chinese team and principals', but the bias for this tension is towards 'person' (L) rather than 'group' because both parties' must react continually to the protocol expert as he influences communication between the teams (and, by inference, within the Chinese team). Overall, the balance tendency is oscillating (O) to reflect the players' frequent need to focus on the protocol man, take his demeanour and arguments into account, then refocus on inter-group negotiation. His idiosyncrasies constantly hinder communication at group level.

14. *Positional Focus* ↔ *Interest Focus* [AEO]: It is primarily the historical, political, ideological and future economic interests of the parties at macrocosmic level that beget this tension, even if the principals and negotiators seem to decide on some or all of their positions before being clear about the interests from which they derive. Positions do not crystallise in a vacuum; rather, they express a formulated or developing grasp of interests.

Even though positions may lead to clearer and perhaps adjusted interests, in essence the latter generate the former, rationally or otherwise. Davies' strength as a tension manager is apparent in the way he induces the Chinese to refine their grasp of China's immediate and long-term interests and so modify their positions. He has a keen sense of the intimate relationship between the poles.

The fundamental interest that generates British positions on the handover ceremony is the need for dignity and international approval as the Empire closes down. With an eye on the future, other interests include the stability and calm of Hong Kong on the day of the handover and beyond, and British business prospects in Hong Kong and China. As part of their deep-seated need for dignity and self-esteem, the British are determined to retain and demonstrate sovereignty until midnight on 30 June 1997. That position is clear and non-negotiable, and dominates all other positions linked with the content tensions.

The essential Chinese interest is to recover sovereignty of Hong Kong without tarnishing the image of the rejuvenating Middle Kingdom at home and abroad. Their original positions, modified to some extent during the negotiations, all issue from that fundamental interest. Given that interest, sometimes the Chinese positions seem irrational. For example, the Chinese want a large PLA contingent in Hong Kong well before the handover to provide security for the ceremony even though it is obvious to Davies (who convinces the Chinese to change their position on that point as it would work against their interests) that the people of Hong Kong will feel very uncomfortable. Anyway, Davies will not agree because that security arrangement would subvert British sovereignty before the time appointed to relinquish it. His arguments to the Chinese integrate British positions and interests; contrary to what the literature tends to prescribe, he does not sideline positions in favour of interests.[27] By focusing on the connection he gets the Chinese to see how the arrangement they want would work against their interests on the day and in the long run. The same applies to the Chinese plan to have an honour guard with a finale of fixed bayonets and blood-curdling yells.

Davies focuses on positions and interests when he decides what he can and cannot concede. When he does concede a position there is never a threat to the fundamental British interest. For example, he agrees to have the ceremony inside instead of outside, knowing the change can do no harm to British interests. In contrast, he maintains his position on having an international ceremony rather than a 'domestic' one, as he wants the world to applaud the British legacy in Hong Kong while making sure the Chinese are under international pressure to maintain it. His non-negotiable position expresses he interests of Hong Kong and Britain, and probably China as a whole.

Communication revolves around relentless pressure on all parties to juggle positions and interests, with constant fear—by the Chinese in particular—of undermining their interests by giving ground on rigid and sometimes naïve positions. The unyielding positional demands (and otherwise boorish behaviour) of the Chinese protocol man may be determined by fear of Beijing and a shallow grasp of Chinese interests. Whatever the case, his view of positions and interests may be the single most powerful influence on communication between the teams. This man forces much of Davies' manoeuvring.

The balance between positions and interests is equal (E) because there is always a sense of the players trying to deal with the complementary relationship between them. Throughout the negotiation the focus of discussion oscillates (O) between the poles.

15. $? \leftrightarrow ?$: As with all scenarios, the set of tensions is not definitive. The analyst's task is to identify and select tensions that represent significant content and process, and the relationship between the two, and to mull over the negotiators' tension management. In the Hong Kong case, I considered adding *agent* $\leftrightarrow$ *principal* as a process tension but decided the discussion of other tensions conveyed enough about the way the players

---

27. See Provis (1996) for a critique of prevailing opinion. Most advertising for courses on negotiation and mediation skills says participants will learn how to focus on interests, not positions. It might be better to learn to focus on their tight relationship. The literature tends to assume the focus on interests should involve deep and open discussion of them, but this could undermine some negotiations. For example, it is certain the Chinese would have been taken aback by explicit British claims to sovereignty until midnight.

understood and managed the quite different relationships between the Chinese team and Beijing, and Davies and his masters in Hong Kong and Britain. Another tension might have been *British principals ↔ Chinese principals* to reflect the relationship between the two governments and the influence on negotiator behaviour, but I have said enough about that matter in discussing the sovereignty factor as it relates to other tensions. *Xenophobia ↔ xenophilia* and *obstinacy ↔ flexibility* would be possibilities for analysts wanting to apply Lucien Pye's abductive reasoning to the case: "Chinese negotiators, behind their reserved and poker-faced approaches, are highly susceptible to mercurial sentiments that are easily provoked merely by interactions with foreigners.[28] Many American executives spoke about the sudden changes in attitudes.... Chinese negotiators [probably often respond] to their own internal tensions between liking and disliking the foreigner" (1992: 95). The protocol expert comes to mind.

↔ ↔ ↔

---

28. Perhaps as evident from much of my analysis, 'abductive reasoning' is reasoning that might make sense but cannot be proven.

# Chapter 7

## « Duress, Extortion and Deliverance »

### THE REALM

The common factors in personal security cases are the holding or coercion of people, and an overt or implied offer by a captor or extortionist to release them from danger or duress in return for money or some other consideration—for example, a political decision, release of a prisoner, or media publicity for terrorists. Most political, religious and other high-minded excuses for detaining or coercing people are attempts to camouflage the real purpose, which is to make money from other people's misery.[1] 'People in danger or under duress' includes but is not limited to kidnap victims, owners of stolen paintings or other treasures, vendors who hear their stock has been laced with poison, people being blackmailed, potential victims of a bomb, passengers on a hijacked plane, threatened targets of computer hackers, and fugitive or arrested sojourners who are de facto hostages because they cannot leave a country unless they bribe an immigration official, a magistrate or a policeman. The case in this chapter is in the last category, which is not mentioned in any study I have seen. It is nonetheless about hostage release, defined broadly, because the most plausible interpretation

---

1. For detailed commentary on this point and hostage-taking in general, see Kidnap and Ransom (1999), Auerbach (1998), Clutterbuck (1987), Crelinsten and Szabo (1976), Moorehead (1980), and Prochnau (1998).

of events is that immigration officials in Indonesia would keep the police at bay and allow an ill fugitive to leave the country if he were to pay the right bribe to the right people under the right circumstances. Otherwise, he would go to gaol and die there within a few days.

It is now normal in domestic and international cases for specialist practitioners to negotiate 'relief', 'release', 'recovery' or 'retrieval' from danger or duress. Depending on the case, the negotiator may be a police officer, a soldier, a diplomat, a non-government emissary like Terry Waite, a private operator working alone, or an employee of a consultancy such as Britain's Control Risks Group or the USA's Ackerman Group, Kroll Associates, the Steele Foundation or Pinkerton. *Troubleshooters* is an association of freelancers with US military experience. The specialist companies also offer security advice, investigate fraud and embezzlement, and trace suspects throughout the world. They usually employ multilingual negotiators with police, commando or intelligence backgrounds. Mossad, MI-5 and the CIA are rich sources, the latter in particular since the end of the Cold War.

Hostage-taking and release is an integrated business that tends to make money for everyone except the victim (although there are staged kidnappings), unless the latter sells the story to the media or writes a popular book. Multinational insurance companies offer coverage for threats to people or property for huge fees that vary a great deal by country. These policies are called KRE, short for 'kidnap, ransom and extortion'. For instance, Chubb has a policy called Executive Protection Portfolio Kidnap/ Ransom and Extortion Insurance, which includes coverage for ransom delivery: "Chubb's policy insures the money or other consideration used to pay a ransom or extortion demand while it is being delivered" (Chubb 2007). Like some other insurance companies they pay a retainer to a 'recovery consultancy', in their case to Ackerman. Lloyd's of London, who created the KRE business, favours Control Risks but also uses Ackerman. The hostage-takers make money because the insurance companies and their agents expect and intend to pay a reduced ransom, usually negotiated down to less than 20 per cent of the original demand. Depending on other policies written by KRE insurers or their affiliates for a given hostage, a cynic might argue that it usually costs less to fund a ransom than pay out a life policy. A flat fee for service seems to be the norm but I have heard of bonuses as a percentage of the amount by which the negotiator reduces the original demand.

In most countries it is illegal to pay a ransom but prosecution is rare, often because it is difficult to trace the money if hostage-takers and police collude in hotspots where kidnapping is a national sport, such as Colombia, Venezuela, Brazil, Mexico and Yemen. Unless the police can be trusted, the professional negotiators may try to keep the kidnap secret from them, or try to work independently of them if they do know about it. The insurance companies and their agents want hostage release and do not always worry about compromising police investigations or funding a hostage-taker's escape. Honest police want hostage release but they also want an arrest and conviction. Therefore the professional negotiator's task may become more difficult if the police get involved, especially if they are impatient and untrained in hostage negotiation. On the other hand, reliable and cooperative police intent on an arrest are an asset because they subject the offender to pressure that a negotiator can exploit, and they can usually induce the media to maintain the pressure by controlling their reports or not reporting at all (Clutterbuck 1987). Uncooperative media may hinder the negotiator by confounding coverage and interference (Feldmann 1989).

Beeston and Farrell (2004) say kidnapping has increased in Iraq because governments and companies pay up routinely. *Alibaba*—thieves, bandits, carjackers—take cash and valuables from victims who are then handed over to political or Islamist groups for a reward. Canon Andrew White, successor to Terry Waite as the Archbishop of Canterbury's negotiation agent, says "selling up the chain" is a lucrative business that has made it more difficult to negotiate hostage release in the Middle East, in part because it is difficult to know who holds the hostage at a given time (ABC 2004).

To pay or not to pay, that is the question. In cases where a ransom is demanded, or a bribe expected, the pragmatic answer is that you pay if you can, especially where lives are in danger. The negotiator's job is to agree to pay as little as possible to quash the danger. This is crucial if the payer does not have an insurance policy or enough cash to cover the demand. Apart from ability to pay there is the ethical matter of putting other people in danger or under duress because paying sets a precedent or reinforces an existing pattern. This issue arises not only when insurance companies, expensive negotiators and big business are involved. The release of the hostage-as-fugitive in this chapter's case study was arranged by a generalist negotiator, not a hostage specialist, who manoeuvred for several days to set the scene for an affordable bribe. The otherwise certain death of the fugitive outweighed any ethical qualms the negotiator might have had about future victims, just as it seems to do when big people and big money are involved. Perhaps in such cases it is reasonable to act against an espoused code of ethics.

Hostage release does not always rely on ransom payment or other solutions that may be illegal or contentious. Terry Waite, the Archbishop of Canterbury's negotiation agent, told me he "would not enter into any unfair exchange of any commodity for the release of innocent people. Some people said 'But that puts you at a distinct disadvantage, because what have you got to offer?' The only thing you have to offer is an effective resolution to the problem, because it is a problem for them to hold hostages." In 1984 he went to see President Kaddafi of Libya to seek the release of three British businessmen detained for no clear reason by young Islamic radicals who were modelling themselves on the Revolutionary Guards of Iran. After roundabout discussion, Waite concluded Kaddafi was in a double bind: the West was now taking an even dimmer view of him, even though he had been trying to improve his image; but "He couldn't say 'Release them' because that would have alienated him from his radicals and given him political problems in his own country."

Waite then met the leader of the radical group, who said the problem was that the police and other authorities in Britain were harassing Libyan citizens after a policewoman was killed, allegedly by a shot fired from the Libyan Embassy in London. Waite thought the harassment claim was exaggerated but "there was probably some truth in it". Back in London, Waite met Libyan leaders who confirmed the claim. "So then I devised a plan whereby we set up a telephone network run through the churches, so that any Libyans who felt they weren't treated fairly could dial a number and get an immediate response. The matter would then be investigated." That assurance was enough for the radicals to release the hostages. No ransom was paid. The agreement "got Kaddafi off the hook [internationally] because he could say 'I've let them go' [and] it got him off the hook with the radicals".

Like Terry Waite, the negotiator in the next story deals directly with the decision-makers, unlike many negotiation agents for insurance companies and other big businesses. Even if they are fluent in the local language, these specialists often negotiate indirectly. They instruct frontline spokesmen who have better contextual knowledge and may stand a better chance of calming captors and heading off precipitous behaviour. Guided by the specialists, who may be sitting beside them and writing instructions in a flurry, the spokesmen can also stall for time and apply psychological pressure by claiming they cannot make decisions and must confer with higher authority.

Like so many other good negotiators, whether or not the negotiation is direct or through a spokesman, the practitioner in this chapter's case shows how painstaking analysis of the immediate and broader context may guide the nature, and determine the effects, of more formal sessions across the table or over the telephone. Ted Kheel, an expert of vast experience in another realm (labour disputes), says "Negotiations can be conducted through express, implied or even tacit exchanges" (1999: 24). The Bali case shows how studying context as an open system may help a negotiator to succeed without explicit or even roundabout mention of crucial issues and desired outcomes. The case itself and its subsequent analysis also show that the players' motivations, perceptions and purposes, and the reasons for particular negotiation outcomes, may be ambiguous even in the brightest beam of hindsight. You might know the outcomes after the game is over but the path to them might never be much better than hazy. This is the reality of many negotiations.

## CASE TWO: AIDS AND BRIBERY IN BALI—ACROSS THE BEACH AND BACK AGAIN

*Men come very easily under the spell of small islands.*

Robert Standish, *Bonin*, 1943

### Prologue

This story concerns three days of negotiation to obtain an exit permit for an ill Australian, stranded in Indonesia and on the run from the Department of Immigration (Imigrasi). I classify him as a hostage because it was obvious to immigration officials that he would soon die if they were to carry out their plan to imprison him at Denpasar, Bali, rather than let him fly home to Australia and survive a little longer. The negotiation content revolves around bureaucracy, culture, sovereignty, sexuality, deception, and corruption—'bribe' is a variation on 'ransom' in Indonesia.

Gregory Goggin, aged thirty-five, painter of exotic pastorals and male nudes, lived in a cabin on the coast of eastern Bali for about two years.[2] He had advanced AIDS, and lapsed into mild dementia from time to time. He consumed only lentils, yoghurt and tea for sustenance, and marijuana to distract him from physical pain and mental anguish.

Just as Gregory's much-renewed tourist visa was about to expire he ran short of money and therefore could not pay the visa renewal fee and normal bribe. His contact in the Imigrasi told him he would have to refinance the visa immediately or go to gaol. He evaded police and immigration officials for several weeks before Peter Settler arrived at Denpasar airport. He knew Gregory but had not seen him for several years. Gregory's family had heard of his plight and had asked Settler, an international veteran with many years of experience in Indonesia and other Asian countries, to find Gregory and take him to Australia. The family finances were scant.

Many years earlier, Settler had induced Indonesian security officials not to arrest and deport an Australian aid consultant for entering a forbidden area of West Timor where there was support for the guerrilla arm of Fretilin, East Timor's separatist movement. During two high-context discussions in an office behind cordons of barbed-wire, Settler led the regional head of security to infer that pursuit of the matter might cause a diplomatic rift between Australia and Indonesia, and therefore jeopardise the aid project which nourished so many officials and their cronies. The Indonesians agreed to let the matter drop with a warning because the culprit was an academic and therefore too naïve to know what he was doing. Settler had kept him out of the way because he was likely to create and try to win an argument about where he had and had not been. Settler said the man had apologised for the nuisance and would stay under voluntary house

---

2. 'Gregory Goggin' is a pseudonym; so too is 'Peter Settler' in the next paragraph.

arrest for a week or so. The project manager, who was away at the time, would be asked to tighten control of his foreign staff. The Timor experience prompted Settler's high-context approach to the immigration officials dealing with Gregory Goggin in Bali.

The Goggin case is true to Settler's story in fine detail.[3] Because I speculate on motivations, attitudes, and so on, perhaps I dilute the case's 'empiricism'—a social science buzzword, often misconstrued. Not to speculate would gut the incident, which would also happen if I were to crop out everything except the negotiation proper. As with all protracted negotiation, Settler's success had a lot to do with manoeuvres made well away from face-to-face discussion between the parties.

## The Story

Peter Settler finished other business in Jakarta and flew to Bali via Surabaya late on a Wednesday afternoon to search for Gregory. Settler had sent a note to him one week earlier, not really expecting the letter to find him at his address in eastern Bali. Settler certainly did not expect Gregory to meet him at the airport. While Settler was waiting for his baggage, a Balinese man sidled up to him and whispered in English: "Are you Peter?"

"Why do you ask?"

"Gregory asked me to find you and take you to meet him."

"Where is he?"

"It's not far."

Based on his experience of such assurances, Settler expected a two-hour drive to eastern Bali. Instead, his guide took him to a pillar near the airport entrance and then walked off without a word. Behind the pillar was Gregory, gaunt, dazed, frightened and almost too frail to stand, with shoulder-length hair like unravelled rope. Clothes that once had fitted him were now several sizes too large. He said nothing, but winced and then sniggered when Settler shook his hand.

Settler found a taxi and took Gregory to a bar in Kuta, three kilometres from the airport and five from Denpasar, the provincial capital. As soon as the taxi had gone, Settler sauntered and Gregory staggered three hundred metres to a quiet restaurant, well away from the main road. The journey took twenty minutes, not because Settler was carrying a suitcase but because Gregory had to stop many times. While they sat at the rear of the restaurant and drank tea, Settler quizzed him.

The owner of Gregory's cabin in eastern Bali had sent his son on a long drive to deliver Settler's note to Gregory at a cheap guesthouse on the Kuta-Legian tourist strip, temporary home to a few thousand lotus-eaters, mainly from continental Europe and Australia. Several times, in eastern Bali, the police had interrogated the cabin-owner and his family, who

---

3. For reasons that will become obvious as the tale proceeds, it would not have been a good idea to try to track down the Imigrasi officials and ask for an interview to discuss their version of events.

pleaded ignorance of Gregory's whereabouts. In great pain, Gregory had already gone to Denpasar to collect money expected from his mother in Australia. He said she had not remitted the money; therefore he could not pay for his visa renewal and bribe in Denpasar, nor could he buy a ticket to Singapore to arrange the renewal there if Imigrasi insisted on following black-letter regulations. He did not have enough cash to pay his doctor, so had not seen him for several months. He had a small supply of marijuana but had run out of his other medication. For three of the last four weeks he had been living on credit at the guesthouse and had been confined to bed for most of the two weeks prior to his trip to the airport, for which he used his last cash to pay the taxi-driver. As far as he knew there had been no en-quiry to the guesthouse proprietor in Kuta by police or immigration officers.

At dusk, Settler took the room-key from Gregory, told him to wait at the restaurant and invited him to order food and add it to the bill for the tea. Lugging his suitcase, Settler found his way to the guesthouse and went to Gregory's room without challenge. He packed Gregory's belongings—a small rucksack, a few clothes, a novel, a sketchbook and toiletries—and went to the proprietor, who accepted a small payment to let him see the re-gister of guests. Gregory's name was not there, but a match against the room number revealed the name used by Gregory, who later told Settler he had bribed the woman to enter a false name and bogus passport details. Settler guessed a bribe had been paid on check-in as he knew Indonesian law required guesthouses to record correct names, matched against pass-port details for foreigners. Settler handed over the key and paid one third of Gregory's bill. He told the proprietor he would pay the rest a few days later, with a bonus. In the meantime, the proprietor should assure any in-quisitive government official that no one fitting the guest's description or Settler had been there. Settler expected the proprietor to comply as she would be in trouble if the police knew she had not recorded the guest's cor-rect name and passport details.

On the way back to the restaurant, Settler searched for a guesthouse where he could book two adjacent rooms. On the third try he found one about half a kilometre from Gregory's former lodgings. For a small com-mission and three days advance payment for both rooms, the clerk re-gistered only Settler's details and one room. Settler unpacked his bag in the room booked in his name, changed into shorts, t-shirt and sandals, then donned Gregory's rucksack and walked back to the restaurant. Gregory was almost asleep on a bench in the corner, ignored by the crowd that now filled the restaurant. A waiter gave Settler the bill for the tea and for yoghurt eaten by Gregory while Settler was away.

Gregory was too weak to walk far, so they took a taxi to a bar about one hundred metres from their guesthouse, waited outside until the taxi had gone, then went straight to their rooms. The night-guard was uninterested in them. Settler told Gregory they would go to the Australian Consulate next morning and that he must not to leave the room until Settler called for him.

Early next morning, Thursday, Settler took tea and yoghurt to Gregory, who sipped some of the tea but could not eat. They went about eight kilometres by taxi to the consulate. On the way, Settler stopped at a travel agency to book a seat for Gregory on his own flight, leaving for Brisbane on the Sunday. No seat was available.

The consul and vice-consul agreed to a meeting as soon as they saw Gregory's condition. The vice-consul tried to book Gregory on the full flight. After two calls, he had a seat. At Settler's suggestion, the consul telephoned the Sydney clinic that had diagnosed Gregory's AIDS. They said they would confirm the diagnosis by fax if they had Gregory's permission in writing. Settler wrote a note and Gregory signed it. One hour later, the consul received a fax confirming Gregory's condition.

While awaiting the fax from Sydney, the vice-consul got Gregory to agree to co-operate with any strategy worked out between Settler and the consulate to get him out of the country on the Sunday. Gregory then dozed on a chair in a corner of the waiting-room.

The consul and vice-consul told Settler they could not gloss over the reality of Gregory's illegal immigration status, and had no doubt about Imigrasi's official obligation to detain him while they took several weeks to arrange deportation. The vice-consul would contact Imigrasi to test the water. He agreed with Settler that Gregory seemed to be dying and would not last more than a day or so in the local prison at Kerobokan. Settler asked the vice-consul to consider presenting the case as a consular problem that could be solved by Gregory's immediate departure, otherwise the consulate would have to deal with the political and administrative complications of a body. That is, the vice-consul needed Imigrasi's help and vice versa. The vice-consul seemed to absorb the advice but did not comment on it. He agreed with Settler that it would not be wise to employ a lawyer to deal with Imigrasi as this would provoke an even more complex and drawn-out conflict than the one they expected to face anyway.

'Compassion' was the only official reason the consulate could invoke to ask Imigrasi not to arrest Gregory. The consulate would give Imigrasi a guarantee of Settler's intention to stay with him until Sunday and fly out with him. The vice-consul was sure Imigrasi would not make an explicit commitment to let Gregory go, and would insist on interviewing him to assert their authority: "They do have more leeway than they ever let on. They'll insist on going through the full bureaucratic process, even though a favourable decision *might* be made very early."

"If they think I'll pay a bribe?"

"Well, I can't give any opinion along those lines, but you've spent more time in Indonesia than I have. Anyway, you can't avoid a meeting with Imigrasi." The vice-consul would call Imigrasi then contact Settler to discuss the next step. Meanwhile, Settler should buy Gregory's ticket and take it to the inevitable meeting as a show of good faith.

While the vice-consul arranged an official car, Settler asked Gregory if he wanted to see his doctor, warning him that the police might have told the doctor to contact them if Gregory showed up. Gregory declined and insisted he would not go to any other doctor.

On the way to the travel agency, Settler helped Gregory into the bank to see if a remittance had arrived from Australia. The money had been there for several weeks. Settler had to tell Gregory to keep quiet when he loudly accused the clerk of lying to him on his earlier visit. As they went back to the car with the money, which was barely enough for an airfare and nowhere near enough to cover the sort of bribe Settler thought he might have to pay, Settler told Gregory, who was still agitated, that he would continue to help him only if he were to keep his mouth shut in public and let Settler do the talking. Settler would not get into the car until Gregory agreed.

At the travel agency Settler told Gregory to stay in the car. There were five clerks at the counter and about six customers in each queue. Settler asked for the ticket and its price. He put an extra banknote with the payment but the clerk gave him the correct change, so Settler put a larger note in Gregory's passport when the clerk asked to see it. He opened only the first page to get the number and the note, and did not look for a valid visa. As they were about to leave, the clerk asked where Gregory was staying. Caught unaware, but without faltering, Settler named a guesthouse he had seen near the airport.

They were back at their guesthouse by midday. Gregory wanted to sleep for an hour before deciding whether or not to have lunch, and Settler also decided to doze. In the background he could hear someone sweeping the courtyard with a rough broom. Half an hour later he heard Gregory abusing the sweeper in English: "You're deliberately doing that, you prick! You know I can't breathe when you're doing that! Fucking piss off!" By the time Settler opened his own door, two other staff were coming to watch the entertainment. Gregory obeyed Settler's order to retreat into the room. Settler apologised to the sweeper, and asked him not to sweep for the next hour. He said he would talk to him again later and compensate him for the abuse caused by Gregory's conspicuous ill-health and excessive drinking. Gregory did not drink much but Settler lied to curtail the chat and reduce the chances of questions and conjecture about the nature of the illness. Owing to the binge-drinking of many Australians in Kuta, he hoped the sweeper and his colleagues would see Gregory as a soak, and link the alcohol and ill-health as cause and effect.

After the strife, Gregory collapsed on his bed and started to snore. Settler ate at a nearby restaurant and took yoghurt back to Gregory, who was sitting in front of his room drinking tea and chatting to the sweeper, by now his friend. Gregory told Settler: "You shouldn't have worried. This guy knows me because I've stayed here a few times." Settler went out immediately and booked two adjacent rooms at another guesthouse, using the same technique he had used the day before. When he came back he named the place and asked Gregory if he had ever stayed there. "I don't think so." An hour later, Settler took Gregory to the new guesthouse then came back to check out of the current residence, not asking for the return of his advance payment. There was still no message from the vice-consul, so Settler called him from the front desk of the new lodgings to tell him about the change of address. The vice-consul was still waiting for a return call from Imigrasi. Settler went for a walk. When he returned, Gregory said he had taken a call intended for Settler from the vice-consul, who would pick Settler up at 8.30 the next morning, Friday, to go to Imigrasi. The vice-consul had told Gregory to stay at the guesthouse.

In the morning, Settler dressed in a business suit and went sweating to Imigrasi with the vice-consul. Gregory agreed to stay in his room at the guesthouse. The two men spent three hours at Imigrasi—one hour waiting, one hour with the Head and Deputy Head and a man introduced as "the interrogator"; then an hour with him alone in an adjacent office, watched through a glass partition by the more senior men. All three officials spoke basic English. With the senior men present, the vice-consul did most of the talking; Settler listened for the first half-hour, and then got more involved. Everyone agreed that Gregory was at fault despite the illness verified by the fax from the Sydney clinic. The head asked if the visitors had noticed a beautiful, fit "white" girl in the outer office: "She is French. She *says* she has AIDS also. Visa have expired."

Discussion with the senior officials and later with the interrogator alone was tranquil, but the vice-consul could not get permission for Gregory to fly home, no matter how obvious it was that he had to go soon or everyone would be dealing with a body. The deputy head clearly disliked the vice-consul and insisted ad nauseam, always directing his point to him, that Imigrasi would "interrogate" Gregory according to regulations. The head, who seemed to have no interest in the discussion and fiddled with paperwork throughout, eventually concurred. Settler and the vice-consul therefore agreed to bring Gregory the next morning for interrogation even though his arrest was likely. Settler's request for himself and the vice-consul to attend the session was granted by the head on the grounds that Gregory was too weak to travel alone and might not understand the questions because of his dementia. Settler thought Gregory's current condition, compared with his last visit to Imigrasi several weeks earlier, would horrify the officials as they all said they knew him by sight. Compassion might avert an arrest, even though no such assurance was requested or offered. The deputy head still seemed hostile.

The officials all inspected Settler's passport and asked him a few questions about his visit to Indonesia, but he could not understand why no one asked where he and Gregory were staying. Did they already know? As they were about to finish their private meeting with the interrogator, the deputy head came into the room and demanded Gregory's ticket. He asked the interrogator to follow him as he took it into another room. He did not bother to speak quietly, perhaps because he knew the vice-consul's Indonesian was limited and Settler had not showed any sign of knowing the language. Settler had decided not to use his Indonesian yet, even though it was almost fluent. He heard the deputy say he preferred to ask the travel agent, not Settler or the vice-consul, where Gregory was staying. One of Settler's reasons for moving house the day before was his fear that someone at Gregory's first guesthouse might have seen the two men check into the place where the hapless sweeper worked, and might tell policemen or immigration officials checking accommodation as they searched for Gregory. On the other hand, Settler knew that the police would find Gregory before long if they really wanted to, despite the thousands of foreigners in the Kuta-Legian area. He was unsure about the deputy head, but he suspected that the interrogator did not want to know where Gregory was staying as an arrest would complicate matters and reduce the chances of a bribe, some of which would find its way to the policeman in charge of the search. But he would continue to change guesthouses as the deputy head, a curt man who seemed to be more than a little xenophobic, might push the police to arrest Gregory because a bribe was unlikely now that Settler had involved the Australian Consulate. The head's indifference, perhaps feigned, might have the same cause.

Settler thought the officials did not seem to know just who he was. For a start, he was dressed more formally than the vice-consul, who deferred to him as he gradually took over the negotiation according to plan. The vice-consul had told Settler he preferred to act as official observer rather than negotiator. Moreover, he said he was sure Settler's experience of Indonesia suited him better for the role.

Twenty minutes into the plenary meeting a clerk had brought a file to the deputy head, who had looked through it for a couple of minutes. A quick comment in Indonesian to the other officials suggested he now knew Settler had been on an official Australian passport several years earlier. They did not ask him or the vice-consul for an explanation, so none was offered. The officials also seemed to think the organisation named on Settler's business card was a government office. Settler did not clarify the confusion; the vice-consul did not seem to notice it in the first place, as with the reference to the earlier passport.

The visitors reassured the interrogator of their plan to bring Gregory to Imigrasi the next morning, and again stood up to leave after retrieving the plane ticket from the interrogator. The deputy head came back into the room and said the fax from Sydney was not enough to satisfy him of Gregory's diagnosis. He shoved the original at Settler, who offered to take Gregory to a local doctor for a report that would support the fax. They would bring the report the next morning when they came to see the interrogator. The vice-consul nodded in approval. The deputy head walked away without a word. The interrogator nodded and smiled. At this point Settler revised his speculations on the deputy head's game and decided he might in fact be playing for a bribe by showing that he, not the head, was in control and would decide Gregory's fate. If so, Settler also concluded that part of the interrogator's role was to negotiate and collect the payout.

The vice-consul took Settler to the Kuta Clinic where he knew there was a doctor who had experience with AIDS patients. They met her for about fifteen minutes. She spoke excellent English, learned during postgraduate study in the United States. She would examine Gregory but was unhappy with the consulate for ignoring her complaints, during the term of the previous consul, about the malpractice of a doctor whose name had been in the Australian headlines. In the press 'a clinic in Kuta' had become "the Kuta Clinic" even though the infamous doctor was not associated with the latter. The protest worried Settler as he needed this woman to cooperate. The vice-consul read the situation well, expressed due shock at the inadvertent slight against the clinic and agreed to set the record straight in Australia. She was delighted.

The scene was well set for Gregory's examination, so Settler walked a kilometre back to the guesthouse to get him. The vice-consul went his own way, and would expect an afternoon call from Settler to discuss the doctor's report and arrange transport for the Saturday meeting at Imigrasi. The vice-consul was sure there would be no arrest before the next meeting, owing to his stated plan to accompany Settler and Gregory: "But what happens during and after the meeting will depend on Gregory's attitude. For a start, he *must* admit fault."

"Right, but let's leave it up to me to decide when he should lapse into deep contrition, beg for mercy, etcetera."

"Agreed. Let's hope he doesn't get stroppy."

"Yes. The deputy would love it."

"He certainly would."

Gregory was weak and became agitated when Settler told him they would have to visit the Kuta Clinic. He preferred his own male doctor in Denpasar but could not tell Settler who the man was or how to find him. Gregory had no prescription or other relevant document with him. He agreed to go to the clinic after Settler guaranteed they would fly out on the Sunday if they had the doctor's report to back up the fax from Sydney. Settler did not mention the impending 'interrogation' or the possibility of arrest. He told Gregory to rest for half an hour, and then went out to find a more comfortable place to stay. Using a new set of names and passport details, he came to an understanding with the reception clerk at a nearby hotel surrounded by a stone fence, and booked two rooms for one night.

Back at the guesthouse, they packed and walked to the hotel without checking out of the former. On the way, Gregory asked Settler to buy him some biscuits and papaya from a small store. Settler washed and sliced the papaya, made tea for Gregory, then went to the hotel restaurant for his own lunch. After placing his order, he went to the front desk and rang the clinic to confirm the 3 p.m. appointment.

Settler went back to collect Gregory, who had eaten some of the papaya, drunk the tea and was puffing on a tiny reefer. Intending to seize and get rid of Gregory's cache, Settler said he wanted to roll one for himself before they went to the clinic. Gregory said he was smoking the last of it. When Gregory had finished, Settler washed the butt and ash down the bathroom basin. He picked up a small plastic bag and the rest of the cigarette papers from the table, wrapped them in toilet paper and flushed them.

Gregory went to sleep in the back seat of the metered taxi on the way to the clinic. The driver decided to take a short cut and got caught on a one-way street, going the wrong way. Gregory woke up and yelled "We're going away from fucking Kuta! Peter, you don't know what the fuck you're doing! The prick's ripping you off!" He reached between the front seats, punched the meter, turned it off, then fell back exhausted. As the driver braked he cursed his passengers and withdrew a lump of wood from under his seat. In rapid Indonesian, Settler told him not to worry, to keep going, that Gregory was insane, that Settler would control him, that there would be a large tip if the driver could get to the clinic by 3 p.m. He put the club back under the seat.

At the clinic there were no other patients. The doctor greeted Gregory with great warmth and invited him into the examination room. Fifteen minutes later she helped him out to the waiting room, where he sat on a chair next to Settler and went to sleep. The doctor invited Settler into her office, where she told him Gregory would survive only a few days even if he were now in hospital in Australia. There was no suitable medication for him in Bali. Settler managed to get a report with the right wording after much discussion with the doctor. She wanted to write, in English, that Gregory should leave "as soon as possible" for treatment in Brisbane. Settler wanted her to write "immediately/urgently" in Indonesian—*penting/segera*—explaining that her phrasing would be open to unhelpful interpretation by Imigrasi, depending on their attitude to Gregory when they met. She was reluctant to make the change but did so after Settler said he was impressed by her skills and compassion and would therefore pay an abnormal fee for her services. The doctor woke Gregory and helped him to the taxi summoned by her receptionist.

Back at the hotel, Settler tried to call the vice-consul several times but could not get past his answering machine, and eventually left a message to say the trip to the doctor was a success and that he would meet the vice-consul at Imigrasi at 9 a.m. the next day—Saturday. He also gave the address and telephone number of the hotel. No one returned the call.

The next morning at 8 o'clock Settler tried to call the vice-consul but again had to leave a message on the answering machine, this time saying he would wait for him in the Imigrasi foyer. Gregory was agitated and insisted he would not go to Imigrasi without the vice-consul. Settler lied to Gregory, saying the vice-consul had to go to another meeting first and had told him to proceed with the Imigrasi meeting as it was a mere formality. Gregory was satisfied so they went by taxi to the office. They waited fifteen minutes for the vice-consul but Settler decided to proceed without him when Gregory started to get angry. While they were waiting, one of two German girls in swimming costumes and wisps of sarong asked loudly at the front desk, in Indonesian, if a certain official was there because they wanted to pay him to renew their visas.

Before Settler asked to see the interrogator, he again extracted a promise made earlier by Gregory to let Settler do most of the talking. If he was unsure of a question or what his response should be, he should feign bewilderment and seek Settler's counsel. The night before, Settler had thought about coaching Gregory for the meeting but decided it was not feasible.

The interrogator and his two superiors were shocked to see Gregory, who did not recognise any of them. They were far more compassionate and friendly than Settler had expected, especially the deputy head. The two senior men took the doctor's report after the interrogator had read it, and left him to do his work. There was a standard set of questions. The interrogator knew Gregory was trying to answer them but was too weak to stay awake; so, as the interrogator suggested, Settler took Gregory to a sofa just outside the door and told him to lie down and go to sleep while Settler responded to the questions for him. This development suited Settler's plan to ensure Gregory presented as a man who could die at any moment, thereby complicating everyone's weekend.

The interrogator was perplexed at the many repeat tourist visas in Gregory's passport. Settler knew Gregory had paid bribes, in Bali and Singapore, for the previous five. The perplexity seemed favourable to Settler as the interrogator would know bribes must have been paid and would not want the matter to be raised, especially with the consulate now involved. The interrogator took the passport to the department head's office. Settler watched through the glass partition as the head and his deputy studied the visas while the interrogator looked out the window. When the interrogator returned he said he would ignore all previous visas apart from the most recent one, as he did not want to complicate the meeting. To Settler, this seemed to be a major turning point in Gregory's favour.

Settler managed to dig into the interrogator's background. He was a former seaman on cruise ships, had travelled widely, was fond of Sydney, and spoke functional English. As etiquette demanded, Settler disagreed with the interrogator's assessment of his own English skills as "very weak". Settler helped him to translate some questions and responses, admitting to some small knowledge of the Indonesian language. Always subdued and deferential, Settler worked hard to develop an amicable relationship with the man without playing down the reality of the immigration regulations and procedures. To the contrary, Settler told the man he understood that it was an official's duty to implement them. When he told Settler he had several children who were costly to keep at a good school, Settler signalled the bribe by saying he knew how difficult it was, and that the two should talk about that common problem in the near future. The response was a slight grin. Settler did not mention that part of the encounter to the vice-consul.

At one point Gregory staggered into the office to contribute but could not sit without severe pain. "Gregory, Gregory" whispered the interrogator. "You can lie down outside. We will call if we need you." Gregory returned to the sofa. The deputy head, sullen, watched through the glass panel.

The interrogator asked how Gregory had contracted HIV. Settler lied: "From a woman in Australia. He has a child at home but he needs to be in Bali for spiritual reasons."

"Ah, good, good, good. Not homo? Okay." There was obvious relief that Gregory was unlikely to have had homosexual contact in Indonesia, where it is a crime. "Has he been with a woman in Bali?" Settler said Gregory had not had sex with anyone in Indonesia, tourist or local person. The interrogator said "We don't care about foreign women. We must protect only Indonesian women by finding out any contact with them." Settler said "Of course. I know it's your duty."

As the time seemed ripe, Settler said Gregory would admit fault in writing. Would the interrogator like him to do so now? "Yes, if he can do that." Settler went out alone to Gregory, woke him up, and told him to come into the office, where he must do whatever Settler told him to do without objecting. "Okay. I want to get away from these pricks."

"Do what I say, and only what I say, or you're going to end up wallowing in a shitty cell in Kerobokan."

"I bloody said okay, didn't I?"

"When you go back in there, you're going to write an apology. But first say you're sorry for not staying awake to help with the interrogation."

"The bloody what?"

"Interrogation."

"What bloody interrogation?"

"The one you just missed."

"Sorry I haven't helped with the interrogation," said Gregory to the interrogator, who invited him to sit down and pushed a pad and pen across the desk to him. He asked Gregory if he would like to make a written statement, then said he had to leave the room to talk to the deputy head. Settler assumed the latter would be told Gregory was not a homosexual deviate after all.

Settler dictated as Gregory wrote with substantial pain but no protest: "I am sorry to have caused administrative problems with my visa. I did not deliberately break immigration regulations but I know I am technically at fault." The deputy head and the interrogator watched through the panel. Gregory signed the paper. Settler pushed it to the other side of the desk, then retrieved it and put it in front of Gregory, telling him to write another sentence: "Please refer to my excellent record over many visits to Bali and to Imigrasi." The interrogator collected the statement, read it and took it into the head's office. He left the paper there and returned just as the vice-consul arrived. Gregory staggered back to the sofa.

After exchanging pleasantries with the vice-consul, Settler left him with the interrogator and went outside to join Gregory. In a nearby office, he could hear an aggressive Australian woman trying to argue her way out of a deportation order for overstaying her temporary residence visa. The racket she had been making for almost an hour had intruded on Settler's meeting with the interrogator. Settler had made sure the interrogator could sense his disapproval of the woman's conduct, and exaggerated his own style of subdued and dignified understanding of proper behaviour towards government officials. He had rolled his eyes as he described the two German girls in the foyer.

When the interrogator left his office after talking to the vice-consul for a few minutes, the latter came out and told Settler he had just been told about the noisy woman's case: "There are no compassionate or other grounds for us to argue on her behalf. All I can do is ask for a fair hearing, but she hasn't even been in touch with us. She hasn't got a leg to stand on, and it seems she won't admit fault. Anyway, I'm keeping away from it now as it might complicate Gregory's case. It's looking okay, by the way, but I wouldn't bet on it yet."

Gregory said he wanted to get some exercise, so Settler helped him into the foyer. The noisy woman came out there. When she saw Settler she accosted him: "Are you the new Australian Consul? You look official in your flash gear." He did not give away the vice-consul's presence. "No, but here's some free advice for you. Tone down your style, and accept blame for the problem." She didn't seem to hear him, and went back to her own interrogation. Later, while the officials were discussing Gregory's case in the head's office, the vice-consul and Settler were chatting near the sofa. The woman came out of another office and asked Settler how his case was going. "Quite well."

"Did you contact the consulate for help?"

"No, they're useless," said Settler. "I prefer to work without them. But leave a message on their answering machine if you are really desperate."

"Yeah, they're bloody useless," she agreed, then walked away. The vice-consul seemed to enjoy the joke.

An hour later, Gregory continued to sleep as the interrogator told Settler and the vice-consul of the decision. Imigrasi would hold the two tickets and Gregory's passport. Gregory and Settler must meet the interrogator at the airport the next night at 9 o'clock, an hour before the flight. He would bring the tickets and Gregory's passport. Settler said he and the vice-consul would like to thank the head and deputy, who were watching. The head accepted the thanks with grace but the deputy was churlish, possibly because he was not sure how much money Settler would pay for the tickets and Gregory's passport. On the way out the interrogator took Settler aside and told him not to worry about the police at the airport but to avoid them elsewhere. The deal was in place.

Settler and Gregory went back to the hotel at midday to snack and then doze for a couple of hours; then at 3.30 p.m. they selected enough of their belongings for an overnight stay elsewhere and left the rest in their rooms. At another hotel, Settler hired a car—chauffeured because he was too tired to drive—and they travelled two hours to Gregory's cabin in eastern Bali, arriving just on dark after a few stops to buy drinks. The owner of the cabin said the police had not been around for over two weeks, so Settler booked a neighbouring cabin for himself. The owner said that after dark the police rarely left their base, twenty-five kilometres away. Settler told Gregory not to stray from his cabin, and asked the owner to make sure Gregory's presence was not broadcast. The owner said his son would drive the men to the hotel at Kuta next day, so Settler paid off his own chauffeur, who departed right away. Settler realised, perhaps with a touch of paranoia, that it would have been smarter to keep the man with them rather than have him go back to Kuta where he might report their location to any policeman who asked what he had been doing that day; or perhaps he would tell a police-man if one waved him down for a bribe on the trip home.

Gregory was now alert and quite mobile. When Settler reminded him to stay put, Gregory said "I just want to sit on the veranda in the dark and listen to the sea. I won't get back here for a while." The cabin-owner and five of his family came to chat and laugh with Gregory. He seemed to be the family's mascot, their pet beachcomber. A middle-aged woman said "We will look after your things, Gregory. No one can stay in your cabin. You can pay when you come back." Settler had a self-enforced toughness of mind when he worked, but he found the scenario to be poignant, given Gregory's pending demise and the ongoing prospect, diminished some-what, that he could still die in Kerobokan Prison after being treated like a pariah for a few days.

At 8.30 p.m., when the family had gone and the streets of the hamlet were quiet, Settler asked Gregory if he knew of a nearby restaurant where the owner could be trusted to keep Gregory's presence to himself. Gregory led the way to a cosy bamboo restaurant where he surprised Settler by or-dering soup and rice for both of them. The other two diners were also eat-ing soup and rice. The waiter offered cold beer, so Settler ordered his first since leaving Jakarta. Gregory said "I don't know how you can drink that piss. I only drink tequila."

On the way back along the poorly lit street they took care not to tread on the many *banten*—offerings of rice, flowers and incense in small contain-ers woven from palm-fronds or other leaves. They appease the myriad Balinese deities, malevolent and otherwise. Gregory pointed to an offering on the bitumen: "My mother fell over on that spot when she was here six months ago. They still put an offering there every day."

The next morning Gregory was still cheerful and mobile. Settler urged him not to pack much for the trip to Australia as he did not want him to get agitated and unmanageable, which would happen if he picked up Set-tler's opinion that there would be no return. When Settler came back at 1 p.m. from a long walk, Gregory had eaten and was sitting on his veranda, ready to go to the airport. As the plane would not leave until 10 p.m., Set-tler said he would have lunch and then they would drive to Kuta to collect their gear from the hotel. When Gregory became abusive Settler walked away without a word.

By the time Settler returned from lunch at 2.30, Gregory had calmed down and was on the veranda inspecting his collection of curing seashells, sponges and coral. "When I come back all this stuff will still be where I left it. My suitcase is on the bed. I can't lift it off." Inside the cabin were a few books, an altar with offerings in the Balinese style, a few paintings and loose sketches, a sketchbook, artist's implements, and beachcomber's bric-a-brac—bottles, driftwood, more seashells, more coral. A mosquito net hanging over the bed was pushed to one side. The suitcase was light and Settler lifted it easily off the bed. Outside, he said: "I could see your ashtray wasn't used. No pot?"

"None."

"Are you sure you haven't left any inside?"

"None."

"Okay. Now, let's not screw around on this next point. If there's any pot in this suitcase or in your shoulder-bag, or anywhere else, get rid of it out now or we'll both get arrested here or in Brisbane."

"There's none, I fucking told you!"

At 3.30 p.m. the family came to say goodbye as the men prepared to leave. Settler paid for the cabins, including Gregory's overdue rent, and gave the owner a large tip for making his car and son available to take the men back to Kuta. By the time they reached their hotel at 5.30, Gregory was aggressive and had lapsed into dementia. Settler paid out what was necessary, and at 7 p.m. they went to the airport by taxi. Settler found it difficult to calm Gregory and was afraid the airline would refuse to take him. Apart from his behaviour, he looked so ill that he might not be allowed to board without a medical certificate to say he was fit to fly. Settler realised he should have asked for one at the Kuta Clinic.

The interrogator was standing just inside the departure lounge, holding the tickets and Gregory's passport. Settler shook his hand and said he would find a seat for Gregory elsewhere in the lounge, then come back. The porters and the baggage stayed with the interrogator, who was now in civilian clothes. Settler found a seat for Gregory and managed to get him to understand that he would not be allowed to board if he were loud or aggressive. Settler returned to the interrogator and handed over his own passport, asking him to handle the check-in with Garuda as Gregory needed to sit for an hour or so and should be watched constantly by Settler. The interrogator asked "Shall we talk first?" Settler said it would be better to talk after the check-in and immigration clearance. The interrogator hesitated but then agreed and went straight to the head of the long queue with the porters. The clerk stopped what she was doing, issued the boarding passes and checked the baggage through. The interrogator then went to the immigration hall. Ten minutes later he came back to the departure lounge and gave the tickets, boarding passes and passports to Settler. "Gregory is seated in the middle of two empty seats so he can lie down. Your seat is two away from him." Obviously the supposedly sold-out flight was less than full. Settler checked both passports to ensure exit had been approved.

In Indonesian, the interrogator said "I think you know that I have tried to help more than my job requires, and maybe more than other people in Imigrasi." Settler replied in Indonesian that he thought this was so: "Correct. Because of you, Gregory will see his family again. Family is very important to Australians, just like Indonesians. It's very crowded here." The interrogator agreed and suggested they talk further in the men's toilet. Settler told Gregory he would be back in a few minutes. Several people were in the toilet so the two men walked to a deserted corridor in a restricted area, with no challenge from the security guard. Settler handed over a sealed envelope filled with cash. "I know we didn't talk about exactly how much it costs to educate children but you will be happy with my estimate." On the envelope he had written "Children's school fees for [the interrogator's name]." The interrogator folded it and put it into the patch-pocket of his shirt. In English he said: "I have sometimes wonder, maybe you speak better *bahasa Indonesia* than my English."

Settler gave the interrogator a pen and asked him to write, on the ticket folder, the full name and address of a person of his choice. "I want to send a larger contribution to your children's education. If we get to Brisbane on this flight, I'll be in touch to work out how to send more." The interrogator was delighted to do so as no one else would know about the second tranche, so he would not have to share it. Then Settler said "As you have seen, Gregory is looking very ill and is aggressive. Even though the pass-ports are already stamped, we will have to join the queue to go through im-migration, then another queue to board the plane. This will annoy him. He will create a big problem and we might not be allowed to fly. If you can get us on board first, he's so tired he'll go straight to sleep and it won't matter how long it takes for the other passengers to board." The ground-staff, se-curity guards and Garuda cabin staff smiled at the interrogator as he led Settler and Gregory through the immigration area and onto the plane, fif-teen minutes before boarding time.

On board, Settler did not tell Gregory he had three seats as he would stretch out on them, and then abuse the cabin attendant who would ask him to sit up and secure his safety belt for take-off. In his sleep, Gregory groaned in pain as the plane took off. After the seatbelt sign went off, Set-tler removed Gregory's belt, raised the armrest between his seat and the one next to him, and lowered him onto his side. Apart from one toilet trip at 2 a.m., he stayed as he was, asleep, until an hour before the plane arrived in Brisbane at dawn. He and Settler stayed in their seats until almost all the other passengers had disembarked. Settler was tired as he had stayed awake all night watching Gregory and reading newspapers. As many of the passen-gers were young Japanese tourists, Settler was particularly interested in an article identifying them as the new drug couriers of Asia.

The two men went straight through immigration but in the customs hall a young male officer told Settler he had been selected for a complete bag-gage and body search. "Why me?"

"Because you're with him, and he's going to get one," nodding towards Gregory seated on a bench against a wall.

"Why him?"

"Because he looks the way he does."

"How does he look to you?"

"It's not a matter of how he looks to me. It's how he looks to my boss."

"Is that her over there?"

"Yeah, that's her."

"He's ill and weak. Tell her you'll kill him if you try to give him a body search because he'll freak out and have a seizure. Here's a business card for her." He was tempted to show the original fax from the Sydney clinic to the consulate in Denpasar, but decided it was an ace he should not use yet. It would have more strength if offered after the business card than at the same time.

When the officer went to speak to his boss about ten metres away, Settler went to Gregory, who was agitated and in serious pain. "Everyone else has gone. What the fuck's going on?" asked Gregory. Settler told him they wanted to know why he looked so ill. "Don't you bloody tell them I've got HIV. It's none of their fucking business!" Settler said he wouldn't tell them, then went back to the waiting customs officer, who said "She agrees you don't need a search but he does."

"If he ends up as a body, you're going to have a big problem, especially when you don't find anything. How many people did you decide to search from that flight?"

"Only you two."

"Well, when you end up with him as a body, and no drugs, you're going to be famous. And how will you explain the way you've just waved fifty young Japanese through the airport without even checking their baggage? Everyone knows they are the new couriers in the Asia-Pacific region."

"Look, I can see he's in bad shape, but she says he has to have a body search."

"He's not having one. Ask her if she wants a medical opinion." The officer talked to his boss, came back and asked Settler "Are you a doctor?" Settler looked behind him, where he could see Gregory dozing. "No. That's obvious from my card. But show her this." Settler gave him the fax. He read it, gave it back and said "You can take him through without the search. I'll worry about her. Grab your bags and go."

"Thanks. Here's another card. Get in touch with me if she makes trouble for you."

Settler woke Gregory, picked up their bags and went into the arrivals lounge, where Gregory collapsed into a chair. Settler asked him if he knew of an AIDS clinic in Brisbane. Gregory said "Wherever you like" and went back to sleep.

Settler went to a public phone, searched the directory for AIDS clinics and called one at random. When a woman answered, Settler explained the basics of Gregory's case but could not speak further. After about ten seconds she said "You don't have to say any more. I'll bet he's been giving you a really hard time. Just bring him here straight away. The address is in the phone-book."

At the clinic, the young woman to whom Settler had spoken took Gregory to the specialist, and then came back to Settler with coffee. "The doctor says Greg won't survive more than a few days. He certainly can't travel to his family in Melbourne. I've already booked him into the AIDS unit at Royal Brisbane Hospital. Will you take him over there?"

"Sure. Then I'm going to Sydney tonight."

When Gregory was admitted to the unit, he was mobile and in a jovial mood. Unlike Settler he was not bothered by the many gaunt men, some collapsed in armchairs, some unconscious in bed, others shuffling around attached to mobile drips. Two smiled at Gregory. He said "This place looks really nice. Thanks for bringing me here."

"Yep, it looks great." He said he would call Gregory's mother to give her his telephone number. "Then I'm off to Sydney."

"Okay. *Bon voyage.*"

## Postscript

A few days later, around the time Gregory should have died, he checked himself out of the hospital and went by train to a North Queensland beach community. He stayed for a few weeks then flew to his family in Melbourne, where the airline staff annoyed him by bringing a wheelchair to the plane. When I heard he was in a Victorian hospital said to turn a blind eye to marijuana, I bought 250 grams and drove 1500 kilometres to give it to him. He was lucid as he crumbled and sniffed a palmful with the relish of a connoisseur: "Pot doesn't kill pain, it just takes your mind off it. Mmmm. Let's have one." When I saw him again a few weeks later I asked if I could use his case for teaching and writing. He said "Sure. I guess it's quite interesting, really."

Gregory died six months after Settler negotiated the exit from Bali. In the meantime, he told anyone who would listen that Settler's confusion, lack of Indonesian language, and abrasive approach to Imigrasi had almost caused them both to be gaoled. Only Gregory's presence of mind, calmness under pressure, language skills, and so on, had salvaged them from the mire created by Settler. Most of Gregory's family and friends knew this was fantasy, but some still believe he spoke Indonesian; in fact he knew almost none, and always spoke English to Balinese people, few of whom could understand him.

Gregory was cremated with a fat reefer in his pocket. A few months later, his Balinese friends arranged for his eldest brother to scatter him ritually in the sea near his cabin, which is still decorated with some of his art—admired, deplored or ignored by the tourists who sleep there, with no inkling of the artist's dramatic exit from Bali and then his human form. Gregory's niece, who speaks fluent Indonesian, left a few pieces when she went to Bali to collect the personal effects Gregory had stored in the cabin at Settler's suggestion, expecting to return within a few weeks. Settler thought the guesthouse owner and his family had seen Gregory as a quirky mascot delivered to them from another dimension, so it was no surprise to hear they wanted a few pieces to be sure he was with them in spirit, as if he had come back across the beach or had never gone away.

## The Scenario

The scenario summarised at Figure 7.1 represents my post hoc analysis of the overall transaction. The main unit of analysis is Settler, as Gregory's agent, in direct negotiation with one immigration official in particular, and less directly with that person's colleagues as they move between background and foreground. The Australian vice-consul plays a passive but crucial supporting role to Settler. Like the Hong Kong case, this one is ana-lysed with hindsight, so the codes are an attempt to create a feel for the way the overall negotiation actually went, and do not suggest that if I had observed all the action from the start—an impossibility—I would have cre-ated even the same set of content tensions, let alone have coded them in the same way.

The content tension codes denote the 'average' strength of the poles for the negotiation overall, and the degree of difficulty in negotiating associ-ated issues and outcomes, given my understanding of the contextual forces at play. The process codes represent the way I see the relative influence of the poles on overall negotiator behaviour for most of the negotiation. The discussion attempts to justify the codes, and deals with implicit tension management by Settler in particular. As with any scenario, the tensions are not the only ones evident in the case. I have selected them as the most sig-nificant because they express the essence of the transaction in a manage-able set of fifteen.

### Content ↔ Process

1. *Content ↔ Process* [AEY]: Before the first formal meeting at Imigrasi it is unlikely that anyone other than Settler was thinking much about various ways of conducting the negotiation—if there was to be one at all. Indone-sia's record for bribery implies the Imigrasi officials would have expected to negotiate the amount and possibly the conditions, and to use their upper hand without much subtlety in such a desperate and therefore lucrative case. There would be harsh process and the threat of harsh outcomes. At that early stage, Settler knew the situation was about speed, survival and limited resources. His role would require much more than routine haggling to reach a 'price'. His finances and those of Gregory's family were too mea-gre for him to offer a bribe that he could get the officials to accept right away; he would need to work on them for at least a few days, and his offer might be too small for them to accept even after skilful negotiation. Settler could raise more money in Australia but it would take a week to reach him, and he would not be able to keep Gregory out of the gaol that would kill him before the higher amount could be paid for his release. A promise of more to come would not keep Gregory free. For Settler, an important part of the process would be to neutralise Gregory for fear that his aggressive style would upset the officials and therefore cause them to raise the poten-tial bribe or to apply the immigration rules, gaol him and refuse to accept any bribe at all.

The officials seemed to think there was an obvious link between con-tent and process: Gregory had breached laws on immigration and probably sexual practice, and they would sort out the matter on their terms with little room for compromise.

PROCESS [AEY]

6. Power (Imigrasi) ↔ Power (Settler) [SLY]
7. Uncertainty Avoidance (Strong) ↔ Uncertainty Avoidance (Weak) [SLF]
8. Individualism ↔ Collectivism [SRT]
9. Orientation (Long-term) ↔ Orientation (Short-term) [SRY]
10. Competition ↔ Cooperation [SLT]
11. Combat ↔ Collaboration [SLT]
12. Formality ↔ Informality [SLT]
13. Person ↔ Group [SLF]
14. Positional Focus ↔ Interest Focus [AEY]
15. Other (Honesty ↔ Deception) [SRY]

1. CONTENT

2. Prison ↔ Exit Visa [ALTM]
3. Slow Decision ↔ Fast Decision [SLYM]
4. Flexibility ↔ Rigidity [SRYM]
5. Large Bribe ↔ No Bribe [SLYH]

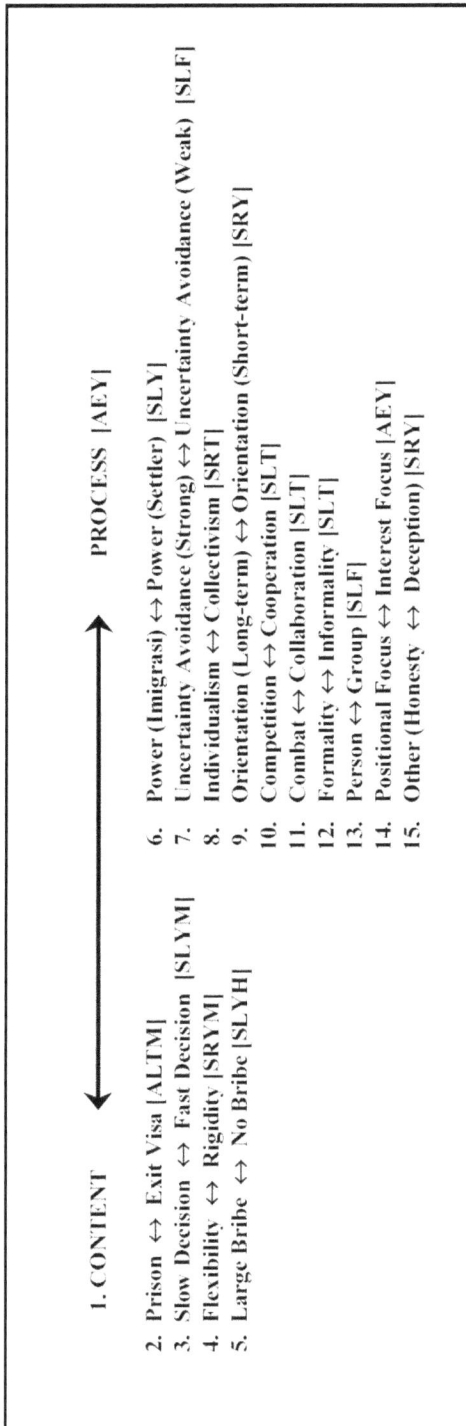

**Figure 7.1:** Scenario for the AIDS and Bribery Negotiation in Bali

199

As the sense of interdependence of content and process seemed consistent and strong for all players for most of the time, I rate the balance as equal and stable (EY). After the first meeting, Settler's sense of the need to orchestrate content and process was very strong. It stayed that way as he manoeuvred with great care, within and outside of the Imigrasi office and until the plane was airborne, for results that would keep Gregory out of custody and get him home alive. If Settler's approach to the transaction were not to the officials' liking there might be no agreement at all; the regulations would apply, and Gregory would die in gaol. Whatever might have been the exact outcomes desired by each of the Imigrasi officials, and whether or not they were playing a game of black hat and white hat, they always seemed intent on using an authoritarian process—at their chosen pace—that would force an appropriate bribe or lead to Gregory's gaoling.

### Content Tensions

2. *Prison* ↔ *Exit Visa* [ALTM]: The main macrocosmic force generating this tension is obvious: Indonesian immigration regulations and prescribed punishments for breaches. The tension embodies two clear alternatives. At the end of the first meeting the left pole dominated, and for most of the transaction (despite the eventual outcome) the prospect of prison was more likely than an exit visa—hence the balance code is (L). Owing to the attitude of the deputy head of Imigrasi, there was always a very strong chance that Gregory would go to prison, at least for a token day or two; but even that might be enough to kill him. The unvoiced idea of a bribe to get an immediate exit visa always hovered, but the deputy head's hostility suggested money might get Gregory out of prison but not stop him from going there. Until the potential problem of a body began to sink in, the chances of staying free were reduced by the deputy's annoyance at Gregory's ability to evade Imigrasi, apparently with Settler and the vice-consul conniving to help him. The immediate forces of Gregory's homosexuality and the Indonesian macro and immediate abhorrence of it also generated the demand for punishment at the heart of this tension.

Even though the balance was biased heavily towards prison (L) for all but the last day of the transaction, Settler's manoeuvres tended to move the balance by small increments away from certain imprisonment towards the prospect of an exit visa; hence a tendency for the balance to move right (T). The degree of difficulty in negotiating the visa is medium (M). This might seem incongruous with the life and death situation for Gregory, but the rating expresses my general impression about the difficulty of negotiating the outcome for the players *overall*. If the rating were for Settler alone the code would be (H); but the officials were confident in their supremacy and did not seem to be under anything like the same pressure as him to get a particular result. Overall, they behaved as if they did not think the negotiation was extremely difficult; nor as too easy to be true, largely because Settler had involved the Australian vice-consul.

3. *Slow Decision* ↔ *Fast Decision* [SLYM]: The main force generating this tension was Settler's immediate need to keep Gregory alive by getting him out of the country, which would require a fast and favourable decision. On the other hand, Indonesian cultural and bureaucratic style at macro and immediate levels made for slow decision-making. In addition, the immigration deputy head's annoyance and ego were immediate forces that seemed to dispose him to delay a clear decision just to assert his authority—he would delay because he could—or to apply pressure that would generate a bigger bribe. Settler did not want to behave in a way that might provoke a fast but unfavourable decision. Thus the left pole still dominated at the end of the first meeting, and for most of the transaction showed no signs of weakening in favour of the right (LY).

As for the previous tension, if the rating were for Settler alone the code would be (H); but the rating is an average (M) for the players overall because the officials were confident about being in control and did not seem to be under anything like the same pressure as Settler to get a particular result. Coming from their position of power, the matter of a fast or slow decision was very not very negotiable and therefore not very difficult for them—the intensity rating would be low (W) if it were for them alone.

4. *Flexibility* ↔ *Rigidity* [SRYM]: This tension was associated with the bureaucrat's precept in Indonesia (and a lot of other places) that if a regulation is in place you may choose to enforce it even if you do not have to, particularly where the people you are dealing with are vulnerable and cannot harm you. Indonesian officials tend to assume regulations will apply to the letter until they see a financial, social or career-related reason for becoming more flexible. The primary force generating the tension was organisational culture in general (macro zone), and as played out in the specifics of Bali's immigration office (immediate zone). From the start of the first meeting there was a minor chance of bureaucratic flexibility—some question of the degree and type of enforcement—because of the vice-consul's presence.

Later, the apparent compassion of at least one Indonesian official (the interrogator), or maybe just the prospect of having to deal with a body, seemed to move the Imigrasi stance away from rigidity, however slightly. Settler wanted the vice-consul as a witness to Imigrasi's approach, hoping he would be a disincentive to rigidity. On the other hand, involving the vice-consul seemed to annoy the deputy head, possibly because it seemed the sovereignty of an Indonesian office was being challenged by a foreign official. Again, in Indonesia it is possible to offset such problems with a bribe, so corruption is always in the air as a macro and immediate force. Even so, the right pole was firmly dominant (R) and the imbalance stable (Y) until the last day, primarily because of the deputy head's attitude and Settler's uncertainty about whether the man was playing for a large bribe. Settler's task was to negotiate extreme flexibility—to manage the influence of the forces that created the tension. For him the task was very difficult and uncertain but quite the opposite for the Indonesians; hence an 'average' rating of medium intensity (M).

5. *Large Bribe* ↔ *No Bribe* [SLYH]: Considering Settler's needs, tensions 2–4 were all biased the wrong way for most of his dealings with Imigrasi. At first glance the fifth content tension might also seem skewed against him, but this overlooks his knowledge that paying a bribe was probably the only way to reverse the balance of the other three tensions in the specific context of Gregory's case. The 'no bribe' pole played on Settler's emotions because he thought the only humane way for any official to treat Gregory was to get him out of the country right away; but this was Indonesia and he was realistic. While he did not *want* to pay a bribe he knew he would need to pay one soon to save a life (or at least prolong it for a few weeks). He must pay at the right time, to the right person, in the right place; and pay no more than he could access immediately.

Owing to Gregory's homosexuality, there is some sense of the officials' interest in protracting his suffering for emotive and possibly religious reasons, and perhaps in not pushing for a bribe at all despite having done so previously—attracting only small payouts for routine visa renewals when his circumstances were less dire and they knew less about him.

To manage the influences that created the previous three tensions and their bias, Settler first had to hint that he would pay a bribe, and then engineer just enough control over the negotiation to ensure a good result without upsetting the other party because they would feel a foreigner was trying to upstage them. It is clear from the detailed case that he managed the tension well, undeterred by relentless uncertainty about the real position of Imigrasi.

The way the Indonesians were managing the tension, right up to the time of payment, was difficult for Settler to see at the time, and is still so for me. On the one hand, they were expert at using fear of arrest to squeeze large bribes from travellers in trouble; on the other, their disdain for deviate foreigners like Gregory may have inspired them to stay rigid and put Gregory away permanently, whether or not he or his agent could pay an acceptable bribe. Despite the uncertainty, my experience tells me the Indonesians would not have passed up the opportunity to exploit fear to generate a payout, so I opt for the line that they were always more in favour of 'bribe' (preferably large) than 'no bribe' but had to demonstrate high moral ground as they negotiated a deal, combining subtle and unsubtle stagecraft.

As there was always a strong prospect of an eventual bribe of uncertain amount to keep Gregory out of gaol, or get him released if he were arrested, the bias was at least slightly towards the left pole (L) at the outset and tended to move slowly that way (F). Intensity for this tension was (H) for both parties for the whole negotiation. It was very difficult for Settler to move the balance to the left, and he could do so only in small increments without mentioning money until the endgame at the airport. The

Indonesians were always under pressure to save face, and never to mention cash but still extract an acceptable amount without pushing so hard that they would end up with no money and an inconvenient corpse.

### Process Tensions

6. *Power (Imigrasi)* ↔ *Power (Settler)* [SLY]: The tension had a stable left bias (LY) for almost the entire negotiation. The reality of power relationships and values within Indonesian organisations, and between bureaucrats and a submissive public, overwhelmed the amount of personal power, and the inclination to small power distance, that Settler might have carried into the transaction as a confident individual and as an Australian. His management of this tension was largely about accepting the reality of Indonesian power relationships in general and in this case, and keeping his own inclinations at bay without being a pushover.

Regardless of country and cultural milieu, with this case Settler would have been a vulnerable source of cash for decision-makers who could prolong Gregory's life or snuff it out within a few days. That said, a prominent macrocosmic force creating this tension was the power distance element of Indonesian culture, played out as an immediate force — the great power gap in the organisational setting between the bureaucrats and Settler. From my experience with Indonesian military officers and bureaucrats, I presume post-colonial sensibility about giving ground to foreigners was also a macrocosmic force.

In Indonesia, power is associated with decision-making in which the controller must present as a person who has a lot of authority and therefore does not need to hurry. The wishes of powerful people are paramount, and deliberate or incidental delays result from the necessity for those with less power to wait patiently until they know what the boss or some other powerful person wants. In negotiation, this often means until he decides counterpart players have had enough pressure and it is time to move to the next phase of a transaction. In the Bali case there is a strong link with the content tension *Slow Decision* ↔ *Fast Decision*.

Settler knew he did not have much overt personal power and therefore could not adopt a negotiating approach at odds with the norm for bureaucracies. He was low-key and humble because he knew any wrong move in the way he dealt with Imigrasi would amplify the power differential, hinder communication, delay or preclude an agreement, and therefore jeopardise Gregory's chances of getting out of the country alive. Settler's main reason for involving the vice-consul was to try to use his diplomatic cachet to narrow the gap, however slightly, helped along by the sense that he might be subordinate to Settler in some veiled way. Involving the vice-consul was therefore crucial to Settler's management of this tension, even though the Imigrasi power advantage was still on pointed display after the first meeting, in part because the deputy head did not seem to like the vice-consul. At no point did Settler or the vice-consul try to challenge the authority of the particular officials or Imigrasi as an institution. That is why Settler kept quarrelsome Gregory out of the way, bringing him forward only to acknowledge local authority by confessing guilt and apologising for his behaviour. In manoeuvring to manage this tension, Settler increased his relative negotiating power and improved communication between the parties while confirming the authority of Imigrasi. Although the interrogator might have been genuinely compassionate, Settler knew it would be futile and provocative to try to narrow the power gap by inducing him to resist or even question the hard-line approach of his immediate boss, the deputy head.[4]

This tension's influence on the communication and other behaviour of all players was very powerful from the start until close to the finish, when Settler's polite but assertive way of managing the payout at the airport, and his promise of a second tranche from Australia, reduced the power differential in his dealings with Imigrasi. The bagman was alone at the airport, away from his office and the gaze of his superiors and other colleagues.

7. *Uncertainty Avoidance (Strong)* ↔ *Uncertainty Avoidance (Weak)* [SLF]: At the end of the first meeting uncertainty avoidance was strong and trending stronger, which was the dominant pattern (LF) for most of the negotiation as Settler engineered subtle changes in the nature of the uncertainty that was to be avoided. This tension's influence on communication between the players was strong and relentless. Prominent forces included Indonesian organisational culture and Imigrasi regulations at macrocosmic level; in the immediate zone there was fear of being caught out and reluctance to deal with a corpse. For Settler as an individual, a powerful force in the immediate zone was his almost obsessive concern with ensuring he did nothing to dispel the Indonesian assumption that they were dominant and driving the transaction, as usual.

The Imigrasi officials were clearly in control of decision-making about Gregory's future, and it seemed to Settler that they might be intending to apply the regulations to the letter because the situation they faced was much more complicated than usual, and seemed to become more so as discussion proceeded. It might not be a routine bribe-generating exercise. The deputy head in particular seemed disinclined to bend the rules, and Settler could not be sure that the prospect of a bribe would change anyone's mind, perhaps because it would be too risky and uncomfortable to take a payout with the vice-consul on the case. Even though corruption is endemic in Indonesia, an associated element of organisational culture is a retreat to rigorous enforcement of official rules and regulations when the informal 'pay and approve' routine seems unsafe.

---

4. Compare this subordination with the young official's decision to wave Settler and Gregory through Customs in Brisbane, against his boss's instruction. In Australia, power distance tends to be much lower than in Indonesia.

For Settler, uncertainty avoidance was strong in the sense that he feared the repercussions of slips in etiquette, style and demeanour—which had to at least appear respectful to those with authority over him. He was inclined to use unorthodox methods and take risks in negotiation and other aspects of his life, but in this case he was worried constantly about making oral or other *faux pas* that might hinder communication and therefore sabotage any possible agreement for Gregory to leave immediately for the cost of a reasonable bribe.

Settler's main ploy for steering Imigrasi away from applying the rules to an abject lawbreaker, or playing for an excessive bribe, was to introduce the abnormal prospect of having to deal with a corpse if the players could not strike a quick agreement. He presented Gregory at the right time to show his desperate condition, showed the HIV diagnosis from Australia, backed it up on demand with a well-worded medical opinion from an impeccable local source, and brought in the vice-consul, whose role was to be passive while implying Australian diplomatic support for Settler, a man of some mystery to the Indonesians.

8. *Individualism* ↔ *Collectivism* [SRT]: The main driver of this tension was the Indonesian officials' sense of 'them and us', which had cultural, historical and bureaucratic origins at macrocosmic level, carried into the immediate zone and played out to the extreme. From an Indonesian cultural perspective, the association of collectivism and high power distance is strong in this scenario. The officials worked together closely with no hint of individual dissent by the interrogator, even though he seemed to have fleeting moments of compassion, unlike the deputy head. For reasons that might or might not be commendable from an outsider's point of view, the group solidarity of the Indonesian party on its own turf prevailed in the negotiation process. As collectivism is based on boundaries separating the in-group from others, the balance of this tension worked against a cooperative approach and good communication between both parties as they tackled a common problem, albeit from vastly different perspectives—one party wanted to enforce immigration regulations, at least until it knew there were good reasons (e.g. a suitable bribe) to relax them. Settler also presented as ad hoc collectivist, contrary to the broad individualism attributed to Australians under Hofstede's system. Rather than turn in on itself like the Indonesians, Settler made it clear that the Australian group was eager to cross the identity barrier and work with the Indonesians in everyone's interests to prolong a life, no matter how it had been lived so far. He managed this tension by trying to get the Indonesians to see that it was in both parties' interests to get Gregory out of Indonesia right away. That is, Settler was trying to create congenial relationships and a broader collectivism to include all players. To make productive communication possible, he had to break down the 'them-us' division that prevailed after the first meeting.

In Chapter 3 I noted and accepted, for the purposes of the tension model of context, the opinion of Gudykunst and Ting-Toomey (1988) that

Hofstede's individualism-collectivism dimension absorbs Hall's (1976) continuum of 'low context-high context' communication, associated with individualism (explicit, verbal, direct) at one extreme and collectivism (implicit, non-verbal, reserved) at the other. The Indonesian preference for high-context communication was apparent in the largely unvoiced messages from the officials about Gregory's sexuality and deserved fate. Settler recognised their communication approach on these matters, and used the same high-context style to suggest that no one wanted to deal with a body; that there would be a diplomatic fuss if Gregory were to die in Bali; and that a bribe would be available if the balance of the content tensions were to change. Some other points, such as Gregory's breach of immigration laws, were discussed by both parties towards the low-context end of the spectrum. Like the Indonesians, Settler knew when to lean towards one end or the other.

In summary, Settler's main way of managing this tension was to create an ad hoc collectivist sense of 'We're all in this together, albeit for different reasons, and whether or not we like or trust one another we need to reach an agreement that satisfies our respective sub-groups.' The forms of collectivism were various and evolving, and the right pole always prevailed (R). Its influence became even stronger (T) as Settler manipulated to cross the identity border to exploit the Indonesian collectivist tendency rather than struggle against it.


9. *Orientation (Long-term)* ↔ *Orientation (Short-term)* [SRY]: The overall balance of this tension during and after the first meeting was consistently 'short-term' (RY). The immediate forces creating the tension included Settler's preferred approach negotiation, his compassion for Gregory, and the unusual time demands of this transaction. On the one hand, Settler was drawn towards his normal patient and persevering approach—not treating time as a commodity, and consciously developing relationships that could have long-term benefit for him and others. On the other hand, the urgency drew him more towards doing whatever was necessary to evacuate Gregory immediately, and he did not dwell on the long-term implications for his own career or for future sojourners who could not negotiate as well as him, or could not pay the amount he intended to pay for a prompt decision in Gregory's favour. He wanted Gregory out of Indonesia so he would survive longer—obviously a long-term purpose—but adopted a decisively short-term orientation to the negotiation process by which he would get Gregory out. This situation shows the need for analysts to be wary of categorising negotiators as having *either* a short-term *or* a long-term orientation. Settler had both but his main orientation had to be here-and-now.

In the immediate zone, another major force generating the tension was the pressure felt by the Balinese regulators to apply the immigration regulations right away, or to bend them right away. Either way, their orientation was decisively short-term, even though the vice-consul's involvement applied some pressure for the decision-makers to be patient and careful so there would be no diplomatic incident that could damage their careers. Settler was careful to negotiate in a way that would maintain everyone's short-term orientation but engender flexibility through the prospect of a bribe and creating a sense of everyone's need, in various forms, to get Gregory out of the country.

10. *Competition* ↔ *Cooperation* [SLT]: This tension is about the strategic mix of competition and cooperation that characterises the overall negotiation. The main macrocosmic force was the top-down relationship, characterised by Hofstede's idea of large power distance, that is normal between the Indonesian bureaucracy and the public. Officials tell people what to do and they do not argue. Forces in the immediate zone included a great power discrepancy, differences between the parties about desirable results, the Indonesian officials' presumption of their right to a bribe, and their disdain for miscreants like Gregory. Settler could sympathise with the hard-line approach as the Imigrasi staff spent many of their working hours dealing with foreign nuisances.

During and after the first meeting the dominant strategic influence on the negotiating behaviour of both parties was the competitive approach (L) of Imigrasi, even though Settler tried by example to cultivate a more co-operative attitude in them. The officials were on home ground and there was little evidence, despite the polite demeanour of the head and the interrogator, that as a group they felt a need to do anything other than stand firm and dominate the weaker party. The deputy head clearly intended to get what *he* wanted, but doubt remains about whether he was planning to gaol Gregory without compromise, or use fear of death in gaol to play for a large bribe to keep him out; or have him arrested and then released for what Settler assumed would be a much higher amount.

Reciprocal competitiveness would have been futile, so Settler's cooperative strategy was forced upon him by the Imigrasi strategy; but he felt comfortable with his approach because he assumed Gregory had already inconvenienced the officials more than enough—they would want to avoid the burden of administrative and diplomatic problems that would follow his death as a fugitive or in custody. And they would not want to pass up a bribe. Although they would not want to deal with a body, the potential problem did not seem real enough by the end of the first meeting—before they knew how ill Gregory had become since they last saw him—to move the tension balance along the continuum towards cooperation.

For most of the negotiation, Imigrasi's extreme competitive strategy swamped Settler's efforts to temper competition with cooperation. However, during the second meeting there were signs of interest in the mutual benefit of a living Gregory, so the balance trend is code (T)—slight movement towards a balance with the right pole, maintained from the second meeting onwards. Over the next couple of days Settler generated a strategic change towards a mix of competition and cooperation, in that each party would work towards a win without trying to make the other party lose. He would try to instil a sense of interdependence.

It would be over-imaginative to depict the strategic ambience as one of competition converting to co-opetition towards the finale, as there was never a sense of anyone trying to produce a better deal for everyone involved. Settler's strategy was intended to get Imigrasi to recognise by increments the problems facing them if they were to deny Gregory an exit visa right away in the hope of attracting a very large bribe. From the information available, it may be inferred that the Imigrasi strategy was to take a hard line to secure the bribe through intimidation. The late trend towards begrudging cooperation was hardly the stuff of classic co-opetition.

11. *Combat* ↔ *Collaboration* [SLT]: This is the style tension: it is about the specifics of the players' deliberate tactics and incidental behaviour. The main forces generating the tension were in the immediate zone. They included bureaucratic authority, relative bargaining power, negotiator experience, personalities within Imigrasi, sexual mores, one party's sense of urgency, and differences about desired outcomes. Combativeness is about making it clear, with behaviour ranging from strident aggression to calm firmness, that you will apply pressure (reasonably or otherwise) to other players and will not be pushed around. A combative style can be subtle or blatant. In this case both parties were combative at the outset, with the overt behaviour pattern of the deputy head being more blatant and demanding than that of his colleagues or Settler. Imigrasi tempered their combative style with collaboration (LT) as Settler's manoeuvring led them to realise they would end up with a body, a diplomatic incident and no bribe if they did not adapt their strategy and style to match the reality of Gregory's condition and Settler's doggedness.

Settler's *strategy* (tension 10) was cooperative, even though his style was combative as he tried to manoeuvre Imigrasi away from a competitive *strategy* towards a more cooperative one. His combativeness was manifold but always reserved. He involved the vice-consul as a sort of watch-dog and diplomatic symbol to bring tactical pressure on Imigrasi to be more flexible. As a negotiating tactic on the periphery, Settler moved Gregory from one guesthouse to another to frustrate Imigrasi, hoping they would get tired of looking for him and give ground; but he knew he risked even greater annoyance. Settler dressed more formally than the vice-consul to create doubt about their relative status. This was combative because he was warning Imigrasi to be careful how they treated him. When his business card seemed to confuse them he took the unexpected opportunity let them think it might mean he was more powerful than he was; he asserted himself by not explaining away the doubt. When he intimated but never offered a bribe he was also playing for tactical control. Again, in that sense he was combative at the airport when he pressured the bagman not to renege on the deal as there might be another tranche, for him alone, if he and Gregory were to leave without a hitch. To the same end, Settler asserted himself at the airport by holding the cash until he had boarding passes and immigration clearance to leave the country.

Settler tempered his combative style with collaboration, sometimes with the same deliberate manoeuvre. Involving the vice-consul would help Imigrasi to grasp the problems that might follow Gregory's death. 'Offering' a bribe without a fuss had a collaborative message. Bringing Gregory to Imigrasi (but only when Settler decided the time was right) was collaborative in the sense that it was tactical 'subordination' and a statement of trust. His dress was collaborative because it showed respect for Imigrasi and empathy with them for having to deal with the rabble of underdressed foreigners who were so much unlike him. Also unlike the others, he was always polite and respectful in speech as part of his act. Overall, his combative bias and parallel deference to authority were intended to persuade Imigrasi to adopt a more cooperative *strategy* that would lead to an agreement. The dominant style of each party would logically become more collaborative, albeit in the negotiation endgame, to match the late-developing cooperative strategy. Along the way, he cultivated a congenial relationship with the interrogator as a foil to the deputy head's intransigence and so engendered a less antagonistic atmosphere overall.

Early in the negotiation Imigrasi's dominant combative style was evident in the 'our turf' attitude; in seizing the tickets and Gregory's passport; in demanding a local diagnosis to back up the fax from the Sydney AIDS clinic; in trying to find out where Settler was hiding Gregory; and in the terseness and contempt of the deputy head. Later signs of a transition towards a collaborative style included not arresting Gregory after Settler brought him to Imigrasi; deciding not to interrogate him; accepting his written confession; apparently telling the airport police to let Gregory leave; arranging extra seats for Gregory's comfort; clearing the pair through check-in, immigration and boarding procedures at the airport. Even the most linear of thinkers would find it difficult to link dependent and independent variables: to say how much the Imigrasi style change owed to genuine compassion; how much to Settler's demonstrated empathy and respect for authority; how much to the logistical, diplomatic and career nuisance of a body; and how much to the prospect of a bribe, and the offer of a second tranche to head off treachery (or argument about the amount of first payment) as the pair were about to board the plane. Causes and effects might not be distinct but the stylistic pattern was clear.

12. *Formality* ↔ *Informality* [SLT]: Formality in negotiation coincides with interpersonal distance and barriers associated with such factors as culture, bureaucracy, rank, and power. At the outset formality dominated the process at Imigrasi, with uniformed bureaucrats on one side of the table stating their case and Settler doing the same on the other side while the Australian Vice-Consul observed. Settler knew from prior experience that if he could steer punctilious politicians, bureaucrats, security officials, policemen and soldiers towards empathy for someone in trouble, or get them

to dwell on the size of a possible bribe, there tended to be a transition, however slight in some cases, towards more manageable informality associated with lowered barricades, reduced distance, less concern with enforcing regulations, and a more personal touch. Although formality prevailed as an influence on negotiating behaviour for the overall negotiation (L), Settler gave the right pole significant influence (T) by cultivating the interrogator in his evolving role as Imigrasi's point-man.

Notable forces creating this tension included the macrocosmic formality of Indonesian bureaucratic culture, played out in the immediate zone, and Settler's immediate need to cultivate personal relationships that tend to transcend formality if they are associated with shared conspiracy and humanitarianism. At macro and immediate levels, the Indonesian organisational preference for formal negotiation associated with large power distance and control was also in play. As with most negotiations, one-to-one discussions away from the mainstream were less formal and became more so; for instance, between Settler and the interrogator in the latter's office, and later at the airport. Settler tried to manage this tension by creating a sense of personal intimacy and interdependence—even friendship—that gradually separated him and the interrogator from the other players and the formality of the mainstream. The prospect of a bribe tends to have this effect when one deals with the person who will collect it, perhaps on behalf of others; and in this unusual case the interrogator's apparent compassion also fostered informality.

Settler always knew he would need to pay a bribe at some stage and it did occur to him that part of the game might be a 'formal black hat, informal white hat' role play by the deputy head and the interrogator, perhaps directed by the head from a dignified distance. Whatever the case, Settler speculated that Gregory's exit depended on an informal relationship with the interrogator that was a foil to the zealous formality of the deputy head in particular, but not so relaxed and intimate that Settler became too well-understood, too predictable and therefore the other party's puppet on their home ground. At the airport Settler further reduced the formality by offering a second tranche that would benefit the interrogator alone because the head and his deputy head would not know about it. By creating a conspiracy between himself and the interrogator, against his bosses in Imigrasi, Settler tried to consolidate the personal relationship and so lengthen the odds of last-minute treachery.

13. *Person* ↔ *Group* [SLF]: An early agreement seemed to depend not only on the prospect of a large bribe but also on getting Imigrasi to see Gregory as an individual in uncommon danger, and as someone whose gaoling and demise would complicate their management of the case and perhaps damage their careers by attracting international attention. When the first meeting began at Imigrasi the 'group' pole prevailed—the officials saw Gregory as just another visa-breaching, decadent foreigner with no respect for Indonesian law or values, and Settler as little better than an accomplice

who was getting in their way. The abnormal involvement of Settler as agent and the vice-consul as observer may have done as much as Gregory's nuisance value and reports of his bad health to nudge Imigrasi's mindset away from stereotyping towards a focus on the man.

As an implicit tension manager, Settler tried to steer the balance of influence towards the left pole, knowing he could not push it far in the first meeting. Despite high formality overall (tension 12), by the end of the meeting the officials were less aloof with Settler but their view of Gregory as 'typical' still seemed to dictate their generally authoritarian demeanour. Yet they were starting to refer to him as an individual, probably because he was likely to become an even bigger nuisance than most foreigners they had dealt with. Overall, there were signs of a tendency—minor at that stage—for the balance of influence on the behaviour of both parties to move left under Settler's management and through deeper Imigrasi insight into the case's ramifications.

After the officials saw Gregory's condition at the second meeting the influence of his individuality on the negotiation for an exit permit became stronger. The Imigrasi head remained distant and the deputy head was still formal and demanding; but as the interrogator took over the direct management of the case he became more relaxed and gave Settler confidence that an agreement was in sight. The interrogator's increasingly benign manner suggested he saw compassionate reasons for an immediate exit without arrest or penalty. Whether or not the subdued display of compassion was genuine, this was Indonesia and the unusual urgency made Settler vulnerable in negotiating the conditions of departure, working out an acceptable figure for the unvoiced bribe, and controlling the method, time and place of payment.

As described under *formality* ↔ *informality* there was another movement from 'group' to 'person' as Settler worked on his personal relationship with the interrogator, who was the best official to help him orchestrate an agreement and a snag-free exit. Settler elicited useful personal details about the interrogator while oozing empathy for the demands of his official role in handling Gregory's case. No matter who was puppeteer and who was puppet, the parallel changes in balance from 'group' to 'person' improved communication and made it easier for Settler and Imigrasi to reach an agreement—however tacit in some respects—to repatriate Gregory.

The individual nature of Gregory, the interrogator and Settler, rather than their identity as members of groups, seemed to influence the way the negotiation developed and concluded. The overall codes are therefore (L) and (F). Note that a focus on the person does not depend on a positive attitude to him or her, nor does it necessarily reduce formality (tension 12). The deputy head remained disdainful, obstructive and formal as he paid more attention to Gregory and Settler as exploitable individuals in a fearful situation. The head was always distant and formal even though it is certain that he would have come to understand and take into account the specifics of the Australians and their case.

The complex forces creating this tension and therefore influencing behaviour included negative attitudes—prevalent at macro level in Indonesia— to homosexuality, permissiveness, and defiance of bureaucratic authority. The players also carried xenophobia and other forms of stereotyping into the transaction (e.g. the officials' view of foreign tourists as decadent, and Settler's opinion of Indonesian bureaucrats as venal, unfeeling and incompetent).

14. *Positional Focus ↔ Interest Focus* [AEY]: In this model of negotiation, positions are explicit statements or inferences drawn about the decisions a party will accept, or would prefer if not in a position to reject the other party's decisions. The positions relate to the content tensions. Interests are the explicit or implicit advantage to be gained by the party from those decisions, which might not be the only ones that could satisfy those interests (and perhaps others). There was a bias towards positions as the focus of discussion throughout the first meeting, with Imigrasi calling the tune because of superior power founded on bureaucratic authority and home country advantage. Yet there were signs of Imigrasi considering deeper interests under the influence of Settler's hint that if they were to modify their positions both parties would benefit. He was focused more on everyone's interests than positions from the outset, always aware of the relationship between the two. For the negotiation overall, there was a roughly equal balance (E) of interests (usually implicit) and positions (both explicit and implicit) as influences on the players' communication and other behaviour. Even though Imigrasi were adamant on their positions for much of the time, the balance is rated steady (Y) throughout because implicit interests were always in play.

The most explicit of Imigrasi's positions was that Gregory must be arrested and punished under Indonesian law, and that there would be no immediate exit permit allowing him to bypass the penalty for overstaying. Another explicit position was that they would not reconsider Gregory's case quickly as due process took a long time and he did not deserve any favours ahead of other miscreants.

Based on precedent, Settler assumed Imigrasi's governing position was that a large bribe might cause a change of heart on the other positions; rigidity might give way to flexibility, and so on. Yet it might be unfair and perhaps wrong to say Imigrasi's main concern was to emphasise rigid positions and inflate bureaucratic hurdles in order to generate a large bribe. Their job was to enforce regulations in Indonesia's sovereign interest, and to discourage threats to Indonesians' health and moral fibre by punishing foreigners for bringing AIDS and homosexuality into the country. The deputy head's demand for an opinion from a local doctor on Gregory's condition, in spite of the diagnosis faxed from Australia to the consulate, might have been designed to maximise the bribe; but it might also have been about a post-colonial need, still strong in Indonesia, to assert sovereign control even in petty dealings with foreigners. Also, bribes in

Indonesia and other parts of Asia to officials at this level are not necessarily about greed and bastardry, unlike corruption by more powerful people who are already rich. At the lower end, an underlying interest is often the official's need to supplement a meagre salary so that his or her family can have a better diet, education and healthcare.

Settler assumed the officials *needed* the bribe, which they would not get if Gregory were to die in their custody. Therefore Settler felt that holding back on an explicit offer gave him tacit negotiating strength as soon as it dawned on the interrogator that payment would not be made or discussed until Gregory was at the airport and sure to leave without a hitch. Settler reduced the chances of treachery and thwarted interest by springing the surprise of a second payment that would go to the interrogator alone. Moreover, the interrogator was at the airport with a personalised envelope full of cash in his pocket, and Settler had the man's postal address in his own handwriting. Settler had created a pay-off arrangement that put pressure on the interrogator to keep in mind his career and family interests, which could be harmed by a last-minute, public fuss at the airport. By then the negotiation focus had moved decisively from positions to personal interests, with a waning influence of grander interests such as sovereignty, duty and public protection.

Prominent forces creating this tension included organisational culture and questions of sovereignty at national (macrocosmic) level, manifest in the immediate zone in the attitudes brought to the transaction by the Indonesian players. In the immediate zone, relative bargaining power and fixed ideas about desirable outcomes encouraged the officials to focus more on rigid positions than the deeper interests that underpinned the nature and expression of those positions. The positions and all of the interests except 'income enhancement'—eventually the strongest influence—became weaker influences on effective communication after Settler's manoeuvring raised doubts about an easy bribe. The most powerful force carried into the negotiation by Settler that helped create this tension was his deep interest in prolonging a life, and his hope to fulfil that interest primarily by taking a deliberately unclear position on the amount and method of paying a bribe.

15. *Honesty* ↔ *Deception* [SRY]: I selected this non-standard tension from several other possibilities (including *agent* ↔ *principal*) to make up my preferred limit of fifteen per scenario. It refers to Settler's deceptive tactics (immediate force), not the corruption (macrocosmic and immediate force) of the officials. He exploited their apparent uncertainty as to who he was, what game he might be playing, and how he might be playing it. Although the tension originated with Settler, his deceptions influenced the behaviour of all players throughout the negotiation—hence the codes of (R) and (Y).

'Deception' is not necessarily negative in this case if one accepts that sometimes the end justifies the means. Gregory might not have left Bali alive if Settler had not hidden him from Imigrasi and the police by moving him from guesthouse to guesthouse, checking him in and out illegally, and paying bribes to proprietors to deceive the authorities if necessary. Settler was usually honest and it bothered him that it was illegal and therefore dishonest of him to bribe officials in order to evade due process. However, hinting at a large but always unquantified bribe to kindle greed was a necessary ploy to keeping Gregory out of the gaol that would kill him within a couple of days. Diplomatic intervention would be unlikely and it would take too long anyway. If he were gaoled, it would not be possible to raise the extra money to pay extra people in time to get him out alive or in good enough shape to survive a flight home—assuming the airline would allow him to board.

Settler was also drawn to deceive rather than be honest—his ethical preference—when he told the interrogator that Gregory was not homosexual and had contracted AIDS from a woman in Australia. Perhaps this opportunistic lie did as much as any other factor, including the bribery game, to move the negotiation towards outcomes acceptable to both parties.[5]

↔ ↔ ↔

---

5. Since 15 February 1999 it has been illegal under the Bribery Act—extra-territorial provisions of the Commonwealth Criminal Code—for Australians to bribe foreign public officials in cash or kind. It still seems acceptable to bribe anyone else, so Australians must now try to camouflage bribes to public officials by directing payment through other people. The best trick is to make a bribe look like a 'facilitation payment', which is legal (and tax-deductible) because it is intended to speed up an inevitable decision rather than influence the decision itself. CAER (2006) summarises and discusses the law.

# Part IV

《 Marks, Boundary Play
and Contextual Intelligence 》

## « Marks, Boundary Play and Contextual Intelligence »

*I am not a man to boast of understanding the human mind and I laugh at those who believe themselves capable of it. They are madmen who think they can cut up into pieces an elusive mist that escapes them on every side.*

Francis Walder, The Negotiators, 1960

*These, then, are the qualities of my ideal diplomatist. Truth, accuracy, calm, patience, good temper, modesty and loyalty.... "But," the reader may object, "you have forgotten intelligence, knowledge, discernment, prudence, hospitality, charm, industry, courage and even tact." I have not forgotten them. I have taken them for granted.*

Harold Nicolson, Diplomacy, 1963

## Preamble

My main purpose in Parts One to Three has been to argue for a tension-based model of the international negotiation context that will help analysts to understand the forces that influence negotiator behaviour and to see how negotiators manage content and process. I assume the polar relationships represented by the tension construct are at the core of human life and are therefore present in negotiation. There is evidence across a range of human activity that the tension construct is a good way to represent our attempts to extract order from the chaos of influences on us, and that tension management is a reasonable way to represent our efforts to manage ourselves and our environment. Other writers recognise the tension construct in negotiation but few refer to it explicitly; no one else examines it in detail, considers its generic value, or comes even close to using it to create an analytical framework. Some might argue that the tension construct is differentiated in the negotiation literature and that neither a generic construct nor a framework is needed. My counter is that the tension construct is underexploited as a way of understanding negotiation in general, and the minutiae of specific cases. Its meagre use is ad hoc and fragmented rather than differentiated in any systematic or refined way, which is to be expected because the nature and pervasiveness of the tension are not noticed, let alone explored, in the negotiation literature. There is nothing about my construct and framework that detracts from any tension-based idea in the literature, but a lot about them that can bring ad hoc examples together and refine their meaning.

The case analyses in Part Three show how the tension pervades negotiation, and that the idea of tension management gives insight into the negotiator's use of tools familiar to anyone who practises negotiation or analyses it as an independent observer. That is, tension management is not a new or esoteric (let alone prescribed) way of negotiating, but a construct intended to help explain what negotiators already do. An inevitable question is whether the tension-based model of context and the concept of tension management can help negotiators to improve their practice. I think the answer is 'probably' rather than 'yes', not because I have serious doubts but because negotiation is so volatile and has so many variables that the claim might be untestable, which does not make it wrong. Chapter 10 suggests transfer of theory to practice without prescribing my model as the latest snake-oil remedy for struggling negotiators. Practitioners can judge for themselves.

Suggestions for practice are a relatively minor component of Part Four, which at first moves away from the model of context and tension management to draw out some of the personal traits of my veterans. In Chapter 8, I describe seven 'marks'—skills, inclinations and other traits—that seem to be stronger in my veteran negotiators than the rest of the field, and are evident in the cases and more general points made by my informants. In my scheme those marks make a good negotiator a good tension manager. I introduce the concept of 'boundary play' as an activity in which the veterans demonstrate prodigious skill as they employ the seven marks.

Chapter 9 links the seven marks, boundary play and tension management with my concept of contextual intelligence, which in turn links with Robert Sternberg's psychological theory of "successful intelligence" (1997, 2002). I make the connection to help analysts understand and express what negotiators do and why some do it better than others. The discussion sets the scene, in the first part of Chapter 10, for my advice to practitioners who might wish to apply tension theory and improve their contextual intelligence, and for negotiation trainers who might help them do so. For the negotiator, the only new skill I suggest is scenario definition as a foundation for more astute action based on a better grasp of negotiation in context.

# Chapter 8

## « Marks and Boundary Play »

A military veteran is someone who has experienced combat, however briefly, and may have tasted defeat but not victory. In contrast, the tag 'veteran' in this study denotes only the international negotiator of long experience and with a reputation for consistent success, perhaps with a smattering of failure (although they tend not to entertain that notion). These negotiators are veterans because they have been good enough to become veterans. What makes them stand out? Any response that tries to make definitive links between cause and effect is bound to be strained and simplistic. For a start, some people may have had the opportunity to become diplomatic negotiators because they had the right 'breeding' and went to the right private school. Therefore they were likely to be considered for the diplomatic corps, with its superb learning environment for international negotiation, ahead of others who, given the same luck or other opportunity, might also have become veterans. Yet there are attributes identified in this study that are common to the informants in their negotiation practice. I do not claim my veterans are successful practitioners simply because they have a particular set of distinguishing features; only that these marks, perhaps also found in strong measure among pilots and chefs, are prominent in the negotiation cases and observations gathered from my informants.

## THE SEVEN MARKS OF THE VETERAN

The seven interactive marks are *anticipation, diagnosis, drama, empathy, flexibility, opportunism* and *potency*. These nouns capture diverse skills and tendencies that I will define as I deal with them in turn. I favour 'mark' because it suggests distinctiveness more than 'skill', 'trait', and 'attribute', although I do use them for variety. The last reminds me that, in another sense of the word, I attribute these features to the players according to how I interpret what they say about their experience as international negotiators. Other analysts, including the players, might disagree with my list of attributions and their application to particular cases, but such risk goes with the territory of all qualitative and probably most quantitative research. All research generates arbitrary categories and labels that endure if they make more sense than others.

The dotted lines joining the cells in Figure 8.1 symbolise the overlap and interaction of the marks. I define them in alphabetical order because I do not want to suggest an ascending or descending order of general significance. Their weight varies from person to person and case to case, and there seems to be no pattern associated with personality traits such as introversion, extraversion, dourness, cheerfulness, flamboyance, and so on. For example, former Australian diplomat Malcolm Lyon is good-natured but serious, and conscious of his status, whereas Hugh Davies and Sir Alan Donald are hilarious and also conscious of their status. Meg McDonald is unassuming and good-humoured; she has outstanding intellectual power and a sense of authority that she wears well. In the business realm, Doug Anderson is reserved and incisive; Robin Talbot is animated and incisive; Geoff Goon is serene and inquisitive. All are outstanding negotiators.

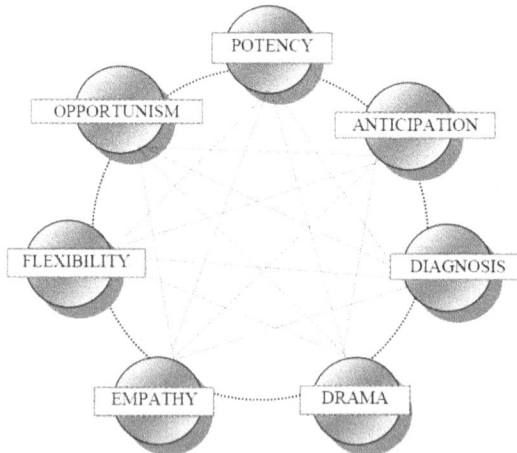

**Figure 8.1:** Seven Marks of the Veteran International Negotiator

**Anticipation** is the inclination to plan before and during a negotiation, based on foresight into the influences that might come into play and therefore the range of paths that a transaction might take. The astute negotiator prepares various strategies and tactics in advance, based on judgment rooted in experience and analytical skills. A good analogy with military planning can be drawn from principles in De Jomini's *Art of War*: "a general's science consists in providing for his side all the chances possible to be foreseen, and of course cannot extend to the caprices of destiny" and "a general should never move without arranging several courses of action for himself, based upon probable hypotheses" (1837: 43, 274); and from one sentence in Liddell Hart's *Strategy*: "In any problem where an opposing force exists, and cannot be regulated, one must foresee and provide for alternative courses" (1967: 343). Hostage negotiator Terry Waite thinks good players anticipate because they know it is foolhardy to predict negotiation process and outcomes in a formulaic or definitive way:

> For example, in the Beirut situation I was the only person to establish face-to-face contact with the kidnappers of the Western hostages, and was making limited progress. But it was completely shipwrecked by political intervention which was beyond my control. The Irangate and Oliver North business.[1] That can happen and does frequently happen in business dealings. You establish a relationship, you are moving ahead, maybe slowly, and you're scuppered!

There are too many uncontrollable forces at work, so anticipation should include a plan to abandon a negotiation if a destructive force, predictable or otherwise, comes into play.

Hostage negotiator Jacob Crowe anticipates limits to anticipation: "At any particular point in the negotiation we will draw up two, three, four, five possible scenarios, and we work with the communicator and one of the scenarios will be where they throw up a real wobbly, and something totally unexpected happens and you have to trim that off and yet retain control." He tries to work out in advance who might influence the negotiation. He calls them "participants" with whom "side negotiations" may be necessary:

> So whilst the main negotiation is going on and you are getting down from, say, a two million dollar demand to a couple of hundred thousand, you are dealing with a whole range of side issues that incorporate all these other participants. Part of our job is to try and anticipate where all these might be and the type of pressure that they can bring onto the case, either harmful or good, and either to see if you can harness what they can do, or if you could isolate

---

1. In 1986, while Waite was trying to negotiate the release of Americans held in Lebanon by Shi'ite terrorists with Iranian backing, the head of the US National Security Council secretly and illegally sold small missiles to Iran in the misguided hope that the hostages would then be released. Lieutenant Colonel Oliver North, the covert planner and money mule, intended to cloak the deal by leading Waite and the media to think Waite was the successful negotiator. Unfortunately for North the operation was exposed. Hewitt (1991) says Waite returned to Beirut in January 1987 to try to finish the job because his ego was bruised; the kidnappers now saw him as a US agent, kidnapped him and held him for four years. The ego barb may be unfair. Perhaps he simply wanted to finish a job that needed finishing.

them from the family or whoever is conducting the case so that they can't sidetrack things. The range of participants [can be] just enormous and you can never be quite sure where they are going to come from. You have to try and anticipate as many as you can. [You try] to identify them in advance.

'Anticipate but expect the unanticipated' with confidence in your ability to manage whatever arises is an attitude typical of my veterans.

**Diagnosis** is an inquisitive and analytical bent founded on high intellect and clear thinking, often applied after intuition has guided the veteran to a quick grasp of the essentials of a situation or problem, and possible ways of managing it. I prefer 'diagnosis' over 'analysis' because the former puts more emphasis on using knowledge and understanding to drive action, as in medicine. All of the veterans are dogged in their search for features that define the negotiation, and for ways to organise and react to whatever the search dredges up. As excavators they are like the most intelligent managers encountered in earlier research: always trying to dig beneath the surface, always trying to extract order from chaos, and always trying to respond to their discoveries with appropriate action.

The veterans are inquisitive and introspective; they are unflagging questioners of themselves and others as they search for the interests and other influences that underpin their own and others' negotiating positions. This is in keeping with Fisher's reference to "diagnosing mindsets", including one's own, in a comparative exercise: "One must remember that one's own point of view may constitute half or more of the reason for any breakdown that occurs" (1988: 74). Lowi and Rothman elaborate: "A reflexive analysis of conflict begins with the assumption that where one stands and who one is—one's context, identity, cultural norms, values and priorities—influences what one sees, how one perceives and interprets events and invests them with meaning" (1993: 166).

Consistent with Zartman's warning as discussed in Chapter 3, the veterans do not found their diagnosis routinely on cultural difference. When they do consider culture it is not as a narrow set of values—they are wary of focusing on value differences between large groups. The narrow focus would not match their inclination to dig out contextual factors such as individual background, personality, personal rivalries, power relationships, national history, politics, government structures, trade policy, internal race relations, and the links between government, the military and business. The veterans know that these factors, influenced by culture but broader than cultural values, are likely to affect the conduct and results of negotiations. Geoffrey Goon, an Australian Chinese exporter of vegetables and fruit to the Middle East, is always trying to both confirm and improve his grasp of the influences on his Arab counterparts: "I love dealing with the people over there. If a documentary comes out on anything about the Middle East, I like to see it. I like to familiarise myself, to recognise things I know about, and pick up something new."

'Diagnosis' implies skill at sifting information for its essentials and expressing them in a structured way so that the negotiator and colleagues can use the information to formulate strategies and tactics. British diplomat Sir Alan Donald says the best negotiators are excellent researchers: "Homework, homework, homework. You've got to think of the culture, think of the background, think of the organisation you are dealing with. Your homework is history, culture, religion, social background, concerns, and all that sort of thing." Sebenius (2002) agrees that if you are trying to influence an organisation through individual negotiators you have to know how it operates, who makes the decisions, and how decisions are made: "Who are the players? Who decides what? What are the normal influences that can make or break a deal?" (78). Based on the Davies and Settler cases, I would add 'abnormal influences'.

Sir Alan suggests training negotiators by giving them large amounts of chaotic information and putting them under pressure to produce a précis of about five essential points. He says the ability to do this is a hallmark of the best individual negotiators and support teams of any cultural or national origins: "It's a Churchillian virtue, in part, of hitting the nail right on the head. It's not an ethnic thing, it's an intelligence thing. It is a gift, it is a talent, and it's a minority who have it." He thought the talent could be honed by the right sort of education.

Sir Alan remembered a series of meetings in China with ever-more-senior officials, all the way up to Premier Deng Xiaoping:

> You would go with [the British Minister] to meet the Vice-Minister for Foreign Affairs and they would talk about Hong Kong or trade, or whatever it was. Then [the officials] would say "Oh, quick! In half an hour's time you have to go and see the Minister himself!" By the time we got in the cars and around to the next building, it was perfectly evident from the way the Minister was speaking that he had been fully briefed on the conversations that had happened in another building. [It was] use of the telephone by very competent minds who could précis a half-hour discussion into five minutes on the telephone, get it through to competent people on the other side, who then briefed the Minister. Then these conversations would be sifted. And then there would be a meeting with the Vice-Premier [and] he would be absolutely, totally, fully briefed on the two [earlier] conversations.

By the time they got to see Deng Xiaoping "it meant the conversations had been vetted all along and if it was going to be time-wasting for the big boy at the top, then the meeting never took place. You know, this quick briefing on the way up, and the vetting."

Meg McDonald, Australia's lead negotiator at Kyoto, maintained control by applying her intellect to sometimes complex matters that only technical specialists could understand:

> [One sub-] negotiation was totally arcane, and incomprehensible except to a very small group of people. [Specialists] are reporting to you in jargon and in very complex terms, and really being able to keep a handle on where that is in terms of interest really meant I had to apply a lot of resources to translating it and filtering it through. But in the end, to deliver an outcome like that, it came down to finding some very simple language, within a very short period of time.

She said the briefing had to make sense to the conference chairman and other people who were not at the centre of the sub-negotiation. It had to be put to them "in a way they could understand and which wasn't a fiddle". She has the diagnostic trait in abundance—she knows how to dig into the unknown, extract the essentials, then organise and impart them in a clear way for a clear purpose.

Former Australian diplomat Malcolm Lyon often refers to the importance of the negotiation "brief". It must be refined and ordered so that it is accessible to the players without oversimplifying the system of influences on the transaction. He talked about the Torres Strait negotiations between Australia and Papua New Guinea:

> The matters to be determined and agreed were extremely complex. I can't tell you how important this is to negotiators. The briefs for each meeting involved most careful consultation, usually with a number of Federal departments, and with the Queensland Premier, Mr Bjelke-Petersen, and his ministers and senior officials, and also with the Torres Strait Islands Chairman.[2]

The range of interests that Lyon and his team had to research and understand—in consultation with cartographers, fisheries experts, sea lawyers and other technical specialists, as well as politicians—is clear from the content and ramifications of the treaty: "It took five years before it was ratified, and that reflects the complexity that we faced in the negotiations."

The diplomatic negotiator's need for acute diagnostic skills is evident in Lyon's description of the search for key issues and the need to refine and subdivide them as the negotiation proceeds:

> I think both sides agreed early that it was logical and necessary to first tackle the question of sovereignty over certain islands in the Strait before working on the location of their territorial seas, and then the lines delimiting the division of rights over fisheries and seabed resources. So there was a clear, logical road to finding the first set of key contents for negotiation and then passing on again, to things that flowed from that.

Although a clear order for negotiating the key issues and sub-issues was moulded and agreed by both teams, the negotiators tended to move through the former in the agreed order but put sub-issues aside for later negotiation. This required a grasp of logical sequence at a broad level, and holistic insight into the fine detail of content that developed and changed as the negotiators worked their way through the main problems. Order was always being reordered.

Meg McDonald would not dispute Sir Alan Donald's plea for homework and more homework, nor Malcolm Lyon's meticulous search for order, but she warns against overkill: "If you sit worrying and waiting until you've got the complete picture, the bus will have left." The diagnostic trait in the veterans never seemed to lead them into paralysis, even though diplomatic negotiation, with its often lengthy timeframes and lack of urgency

---

2. Torres Strait separates Papua New Guinea and the Australian state of Queensland, which includes many islands in the strait.

compared with hostage and business negotiation, appears to offer scope for excessive homework.

**Drama**: This mark is a sense of negotiation as theatre, and an ability to perform according to a role that suits the transaction. Drama connotes meticulous preparation, a grasp of the broad plot, an eye for sub-plots and nuances, and a talent for persuasion. Griffiths says "The negotiator is like an actor who, while immersing himself in a role to carry conviction, must keep a part of himself sufficiently detached to exercise the stagecraft necessary to the mechanics of the play" (2003: 142). Jeffrey Rubin's paper 'The Actors in Negotiation' depicts the negotiator as a performer who becomes a different person between dressing room and footlights (2002). Perhaps the extreme negotiator-as-actor is the Japanese *naniwabushi* stylist described in Chapter 3.

Tactical adjustment of personal style is a feature of my veterans' repertoire. So too are role modification and extempore performance, reminiscent of musicians in a jam session. In keeping with the need to control rather than be controlled, the veteran attempts to direct the play as well as act in it. Script variation among actors may threaten such control; their performance may be unpredictable, and they may react against attempts to write or rewrite the script as the play proceeds. The negotiator as coordinator tries to manoeuvre all the players towards a common script:

> The very best negotiators … are game-changing entrepreneurs. They envision the most promising architecture and take action to bring it into being. These virtuoso negotiators not only play the game as given at the table, they are masters at setting it up and changing it away from the table to maximize the chances for better results. (Sebenius 2001: 95)

This theme was most powerful in the interviews with diplomats who talked about complex multilateral negotiations; namely, Don Kenyon on the Uruguay Round of GATT in Brussels in 1990, and Meg McDonald on Kyoto.[3] In these cases every country seemed to have its own script, plot and sub-plots that had to be understood and massaged to create collective bargaining by groups of small players who otherwise would be overwhelmed by the big powers.

Don Kenyon said "I guess it's like playing poker, isn't it?" As a Texas Hold'em player I can readily see his analogy.[4] Like negotiation as theatre,

---

3. The General Agreement on Tariffs and Trade (GATT) was signed in 1947 by 23 states that wanted to develop an international free trade system. GATT was the parent of the World Trade Organization, which started on 1 January 1995 as a result of the Uruguay Round (1986–94).

4. Texas Hold'em is the world's most popular poker game. Each player gets two private cards; three common cards are dealt face-up in the middle of the table, then another, and another, with betting rounds in between and at the end. When the betting is over, the winner is the 'live' player with the best five cards drawn from the five on the table and the two held close to the chest. For dramatic, statistical and other complications of the game, see the 2006 James Bond movie *Casino Royale*, Harlan (2006) and Purdy (2005).

poker is dramatic in obvious ways at one extreme and subtle ways at the other. 'Tells' are hints, either inadvertent or deliberately misleading, given by players about their hand, and signalled by their demeanour and the amount and structure of bets. Some cards are face-up on the table; others are held close to the chest. Some players fold; others should fold but play on. Some bluff. Some are noisy and bumptious, others reserved and polite. Some will make a bad bet to mislead others, to put them off guard as the deceiver draws them into creating a bigger pot for him to take through greater skill or because he and his backers have more money and can force the poorer players to withdraw as the risk grows. In these and other ways, negotiation and poker as drama are related in the process if not the broad objective, which is always win-lose in poker but not negotiation.

As Australian team leader at Kyoto, Meg McDonald was both actor and stage director, perhaps like a playing coach in a football team that has players with skills he must exploit and coordinate but may not have himself:

> I'd have people out there doing particular bits of the negotiation, and being able to keep all those things rolling on in a way which meant that you were coordinated and you understood how you were coming across. One [sub-transaction] was an incredibly complex negotiation that I couldn't participate in because it was all being done at a technical level, and just went on and on in a very tricky, very intense atmosphere. My role there was to influence the timing, the tempo of our participation, the sorts of suggestions that our proposals were putting into it.

She had to manage the entire negotiation without always being in the spotlight.

At one point McDonald combines images of sport and drama to explain the flow of negotiation:

> When you have a whole lot of issues running you have to decide what your key issues are, who are the main protagonists, co-protagonists and antagonists, but keep in mind that your overall position is very important. You have to keep running with all the other [lesser] issues [if you are] building support for the main game, and keeping it.

It makes sense to invoke drama and sport because both are about controlled performance and coordination by experts who direct the action with authority and some licence. Like McDonald, some other veterans who seem to equate negotiation with drama also draw analogies with sport, especially cricket. In Chapter 6, I flag the connection in footnotes to comments by Hugh Davies. Early in my discussion with Malcolm Lyon he relates aspects of negotiation to "Mr Steve Waugh and his cricket team".[5] Later he says:

> And once we had got the first two of those [issues] done, we then set about number three in the order of batting. It wasn't a Gilchrist flurry.[6] It was a

---

5. A former Australian cricket captain.

6. The Australian wicket-keeper. He is also a batsman who belts the ball hard and often into the long grass mentioned by Hugh Davies.

very tedious and slow scoring rate, to create a line that ran right away from where you met Indonesian waters right out into the Coral Sea.

In discussing border control negotiations between Hong Kong and China (long before the Handover), and the differences between British and Chinese negotiators attitudes to people who managed to sneak across, Sir Alan Donald refers to "a sort of British cricketing belief that if you could escape the notice of the umpire you could get through and touch base, and so you were okay."[7] In relation to the same case he says the cleverest thing he has noticed about Chinese negotiators "is that by their actions and by their words, they always leave a great deal of ambiguity. It's like *jujitsu* [or poker?]. You make the enemy's force destroy him by putting fear into the opponent's mind about what you could do." Never mind that *jujitsu* is a form of unarmed combat developed by the Japanese *samurai*. My interest is in Sir Alan's sense of negotiation as drama illuminated by sport and other games.

More than any other informant, Sir Alan uses adversarial, game-based language even though his negotiating experience and attitude, as described to me, tend not to be combative. He refers to "opponents" in an amicable way, as if negotiation is like a game of chess between friends who drink a bottle of wine or a flask of Chinese spirits while they stalk one another. In addition to the influence of games, Sir Alan may use such language because he is a student of military strategy and sees parallels between theatres of war and negotiation as drama. He studied Sun Tzu's *Art of War* in the 1950s, thirty-five years before the ancient text hit the airport bookshops during the Asia frenzy which preceded and perhaps created the crash of 1997. When he wants to make a point about negotiation he sometimes quotes Sun Tzu in the raised voice of an actor, with arm-sweeps to match.

Several years after our meeting, I asked Sir Alan to explain his allusion to metaphorical connections between negotiation strategy, warfare and the differences between the Western game of chess and the types played in China (*Wei Chi*) and Japan (*Go*). His response is worth quoting at length:

> The Japanese and Chinese games are really the same, so the contrast is only between the Western and Eastern types of chess strategy. Western chess is based on a strictly limited number of squares—64—on a board, with the pieces 'weighted'. The game ends with the death or capitulation of the King.

---

7. The veterans who included cricket in their repertoire of analogies all spent at least a couple of years at elite, male-only schools where sport may have much the same purpose as bromide in soldiers' tea. Hugh Davies went to Rugby and Sir Alan Donald finished secondary school as a scholarship boy at Fettes College in Edinburgh, where he was exposed to cricket but detested it. Like many Australian diplomats, Malcolm Lyon went to St Peter's College in Adelaide. If you went there, you are likely to say the school fine-tunes Adelaide's elite and fortifies their network; if you did not, you are likely to say the school panders to pretentious people by including delusions of grandeur in its curriculum. 'Old boys' were delighted when the current Mayor of Adelaide replaced a Chinese businessman. One reaction I heard was "Things should be fine now. A St Peter's boy [aged about 60] is in charge." When you meet even very old men who went to St Peter's they are likely to let you know within ten seconds.

It is a set piece battle-ground with rules and boundaries that suggest manoeuvring and out-manoeuvring the other side, with losses or exchanges of
pawns (little value) or heavier forces (knights, bishops or castles). Khrushchev
and Kennedy were playing a chess game over the Cuban missile crisis at the
end of which the Soviet side accepted defeat. The Soviet 'king' was dead in
that encounter. Both sides had tacitly accepted the Western 'rules' for the
encounter. *We Chi* has a huge board of squares suggesting the vast spaces of a
continent. Each opponent has a bowl of a very large number of beads, usually
black and white, all of equal value, as many as the intersections on the big
board. The players take turns to place a counter on the board. When one
player has encircled a group of his opponent's counters, he is entitled to remove all the 'enemy' beads within the encirclement from the board. The winner is the one with most captured territory under his control. It requires
great skill in choosing where to put your 'pawns' on the ground and in what
numbers, and also where to create threats in another part of the board. In my
opinion, the Americans were playing at Western chess in Vietnam—carpet
bombing and napalm and tanks, and so on (their heavily weighted
pieces)—while the Vietcong were playing a game of encirclement with an unlimited number of equal value pawns on the ground, and often underground.
The Oriental game arises from the condition of having vast populations and
large tracts of territory.

A few lines from De Jomini capture much but not all of Sir Alan's attitude
to diplomatic negotiation as a mix of pliable drama, simulated warfare, and
game-playing influenced by culture: "Among other things, combats may be
mentioned as often being quite independent of scientific combinations,
and they may become essentially dramatic, personal qualities and inspira-
tions and a thousand other things frequently being the controlling elements" (1837: 321).

Like victorious generals, elite athletes and great actors, top negotiators
have an extraordinary capacity to concentrate on their role, strategy and
purpose. Several informants made the point in one way or another but Malcolm Lyon said it best as an understatement: "I think it is known that concentration is a limited gift and different people have different powers of
concentration."

In keeping with the idea of negotiator-as-actor, about half of my veterans seemed to treat the interview as a performance, a much higher proportion than I had noticed in any other research project. Perhaps this was to
be expected from diplomats in particular because they spend much of their
lives as role-players for their governments and their profession. Occasional
requests for me to turn off the tape-recorder, or warnings that some statements already taped were off the record, were sometimes melodramatic. I
saw some of these events as messages about who was really in control of the
interview and others as attempts to get back to the veteran's script after
deviations that were casual or engineered by me. At times I felt as if I were
a negotiator, or an actor writing a dialogue with the other actor while we
were both trying to direct the play. Several informants seemed to have an
eye on the audience for any writing that might come from my research, just
as some of them seemed to think of their principals, constituents and the
international press as audiences during the performances they told me
about.

**Empathy:** Closely associated with the diagnosis mark, empathy is the inclination and ability to imagine the transaction accurately from the point of view of other players. Or, as Reber says: "Assuming, in one's mind, the role of another person [and] taking on [their] perspective" (1985: 238).[8] None of the veterans uses the word but the concept expressed in other ways is strong in the transcripts. To gain control the veteran tries to project into others' minds and emotions to get a more systematic and holistic understanding of the transaction and its context. Strategic and tactical moves, including style adjustments, may be made in response to this projection, which is crucial to working out what negotiating and how much of it the other players are prepared to do, and under what conditions. Griffiths makes the point well in his study of hostage negotiation; the principle applies to all realms:

> The negotiator's difficulty, like that of [a] carpet buyer, is in deciding what is the absolute sticking point, the minimum below which the negotiation will be broken off never to be resumed and, in the hostage case, that may result in the captor taking desperate measures. How well the negotiator makes this assessment depends more on how well he has got into the mind of the captor than on what he has to offer in exchange. (1993: 152)

Clutterbuck says "The art of negotiation with an extortionist lies in seeing the crisis through his eyes" (1987: 216). One hostage negotiator says he needs to understand the other's mind so he can get into it and change it: "...we sometimes want to create a thought process in a person's mind that we know we can convince the authorities to go along with; and therefore we are creating a demand *for* them, without telling them what it is" (Cambria et al. 2002: 336).

Getting into the minds of counterpart negotiators is about much more than working out the premises and logic of their positions. The veterans seem wary of the human tendency to assume people are rational and therefore predictable, even if we cannot quite crack the code. Hostage negotiators seem to be the most wary as illusions of order can cost lives: "One of the lessons to be learned in hostage situations is that as often as not hostage-takers do not behave logically" (Griffiths 2003: 129).[9] Much of what the veterans say about specific cases and negotiation in general suggests the negotiator's role is to engineer rational, functional agreements in irrational, chaotic situations without downplaying variations on what Lowi and Rothman call the "underlying visceral concerns" that cloud minds in water-related disputes in the Middle East (1993: 173).

---

8. To define empathy this way is not to reject outright the definition by Mnookin et al., discussed in Chapter 3, but I am uncomfortable with parts of it: "... the capacity to demonstrate [I prefer 'form'] an accurate non-judgmental understanding of another person's concerns and perspective" (1996: 218). Is "non-judgmental" realistic?

9. This reinforces my doubts about game theory as a framework for negotiation research. Unlike the veterans' analogies, formal game theory seems to be its own game. It assumes players are rational and predictable; it is too linear in its analysis; it conveys no sense of negotiation as an open system; it tells us little about real people in real situations.

At Kyoto, Meg McDonald saw how the reasons for others' rigidity and lack of cooperation could be emotional rather than rational. She had to deal with an American player who was suspicious of her and uncooperative because Australians had worked against him in a previous transaction:

> One US negotiator had had a similar idea [to the one Australia was now tabling] in an earlier negotiation where Australia had the high moral ground and consistently blocked [the US proposal]. So, there was now absolutely no sympathy for us when we pushed for it in much bigger negotiations because that negotiator just wasn't interested in listening to us. Let's say some pretty rough-house tactics had been used to push that whole US idea off the table, and that had not been appreciated.

As Walder says in *The Negotiators*, "In stirring up old deposits one releases acrid odours and unexpected fermentations" (1960: 149). Although Kyoto was not necessarily payback time, McDonald's motives were being questioned. After delving far enough into the mindsets of the Americans to realise the historical source of the problem, she had to tread carefully for several days rather than apply immediate pressure to bring them on side.

Other veterans could see how their counterparts' perceptions of history, at personal and broader levels, influenced behaviour at the table. Hugh Davies is exemplary in the Hong Kong case. Australian negotiator Malcolm Lyon understood the historical and cultural reasons for a belligerent outburst from his Papua New Guinean counterparts—former Australian colonial subjects—during the Torres Strait negotiation. Although they breached diplomatic etiquette, Lyon's empathy caused him to relax and suggest a break rather than jeopardise the negotiation by taking a stand on niceties. A less empathetic and more conceited diplomat might have protested, created a standoff and so stalled the negotiation. The Davies, McDonald and Lyon examples are but three of many that show how the veterans use empathy with patience to generate productive relationships with individuals and groups, including their own teams. Terry Waite, Peter Settler and Jacob Crowe are calm and patient as they dig into the minds and concrete conditions of captor and captive. Patience in that task is a key attribute of hostage negotiators in particular, according to Crelinsten and Szabo (1976: 51).

McDonald's experience with the slighted US negotiator suggests the value of strong empathy when you need to understand what negotiation means to a counterpart at a given time, and cope with that meaning, perhaps by changing it. At first the American sees negotiation as combat, at least when dealing with Australians at Kyoto; McDonald uses her social and intellectual skills to move him away from combativeness towards collaboration. Malcolm Lyon sees aberrant combativeness in his Papua New Guinean counterparts and backs off until they return to their collaborative norm.

Hugh Davies knows Beijing breathes steam down their necks of the Chinese negotiators, so he is patient and congenial because he knows they have little authority in their own right, unlike the British negotiators. Most veterans showed they could relate to the demands made by principals and other constituents on counterparts, in part through comparison with their own experience. McDonald says: "Understanding your constituency at home — you have to know exactly where they are coming from" and decide whether you think they are right or wrong, and work out how that will influence your negotiation role. Awareness of the influence of her own constituency on negotiation process and content induces her to project into the shoes of her counterparts, "digging into their positions and their motivations and their constituencies".

The empathy of the veterans who work in teams tends to have triple focus: introspective; on the counterparts; and on the informant's own team. McDonald is typical in her concern for team-building: "You really have to know who your individual negotiators are, and have a good relationship with each of them, as well as making sure there are reasonable relationships between them." Before and during the Kyoto negotiations she would observe meetings between team members "just to get a feel for how things were going, to make sure it was rolling along. I needed to get a feel for the dynamics, the personal politics." If any sort of difference, whether personal or about the negotiation, got in the way she would work to maintain a level of professionalism that required all of her players "to sublimate all that to the common objective".

Apart from McDonald, the hostage negotiators seemed to be the most empathetic of the veterans. Ears, fingers, lives and more money than necessary can be lost if the negotiator cannot use the captor's eyes to see the kidnap and negotiation. As a hostage negotiator and former policeman, Jacob Crowe is used to dealing with liars, while Terry Waite and Peter Settler have a fine ear for less blatant massage of the truth. None of the three is distracted by concern with the morality of lying (which is no surprise in Settler's case as he lies when he needs to); rather, they try to work out why the liar lies. For example, a kidnapper may tell Crowe that a hostage is very ill or even dying: "The health of the victim is a sort of strand of negotiation that goes on. Very often it gets a bit of play acting on both sides."

Crowe uses intuition, circumstantial evidence and expert advice to decide whether or not a kidnapper is lying. If the victim does seem ill or injured, the captor is obviously trying to reach an agreement while he still has a live hostage — a dead body is not much of a shield and tends not to draw a ransom. If Crowe decides the victim is well he puts himself in the kidnapper's shoes and tries to work out the reasons for the lie. In one case the kidnappers sent a photograph to the family to prove they had cut off the tip of the captive's middle finger. Crowe said "Our medical people told us the guy might die from infection if it wasn't treated. In the photograph they had tucked the top of the finger underneath and it was possible to see its shadow, so we were pretty confident it was a fake." The observation told Crowe the kidnappers were under pressure to reach an agreement but were unlikely to harm the victim. This conclusion tipped the sense of control towards the negotiator. The family stayed calm and the negotiator applied appropriate tactics in dealing with kidnappers who now had less credibility and confidence, and could be induced to cut their ransom demand.

Doug Anderson's business negotiations tend to be more benign, but his success depends just as much on empathy. When negotiating in China he is alert for unvoiced reasons for stalled negotiations:

> Like any negotiation, anywhere in the world, you must try to have some per-
> ception of how the other party is thinking. What is important to them?
> Once, back in the late 1980s, we had ordered two ships from the Hudong
> shipyard. Our people up there had come to a brick wall, so I went to help
> them. We had a stalemate on price. I could tell that it was a Chinese 'face'
> thing. They wanted to say to their workers in the yard, and their Party
> people, that this was the price. I said to my colleagues "Perhaps we could let
> them have their price and say 'We'll pay you over three years'. That gives us
> what we want [in overall cost] and they can still say they got their price."

Anderson's colleagues did not think his proposal would work, but next morning when he put it to the woman leading the Chinese team she accepted at once: "For them it was important to get their price of $20 million, or whatever it was. The fact that it was really $19 million, because they weren't getting it all up front, and were going to pay interest on the deferred payments, wasn't the issue. It was a face issue." His empathy led to a solution based on his preference for subtle control and the right result rather than the image of overt controller that is so dear to the Chinese.

Further to Meg McDonald's experience with the American who saw at least one negotiation as a clash, empathy is an important mark for working out a counterpart's concept of negotiation, including the level of trust and confidentiality to be expected during and after the transaction. Sir Alan Donald made this point when we discussed loyalty to the culture of professional diplomacy, which assumes confidentiality is a tenet of private negotiations. He showed me his annotated copy of Chinese Premier Deng Xiaoping's collection of essays *On the Question of Hong Kong* (1993). In 1982 and 1984 he was at confidential meetings between Deng and British Prime Minister Margaret Thatcher, and later found that Deng had breached etiquette in 1993 by including details of the meetings in the book when negotiations over the Hong Kong Handover were at their most tense. The implicit threat was that Britain's negotiators might be quoted in public if the Chinese did not like what they heard. Negotiators dealing with the Chinese must constantly project into their shoes to pick up signs of an unspoken threat to put confidential discussions on the public record if they do not get their way in the negotiation. Hong Kong Governor Chris Patten refers to "the usual debilitating Chinese tactics of delay and leak" (1998: 64). The non-Chinese negotiator must know when to hold his tongue, based on how he expects the Chinese to take what he is about to remark or argue. As the point applies to what the Chinese want to hear or do not want to hear, the foreign negotiator who understands them is under constant pressure that may, in paradox, work against the patience and calmness associated with clear-minded empathy.

Although the veterans appear to be more empathetic than most negotiators, none would claim flawless empathy in all places at all times. Questioning is at the core of empathy, and sometimes the question is wrong or vague; sometimes the answer, sometimes both. Sometimes the veteran is stuck for any question at all in an unfamiliar environment. Like all good negotiators, Robin Talbot knows the limits of his empathy and other attributes. He does not doubt his ability to delve into the minds and emotions of people in the Americas and Europe — to ask the right questions and get the right answers — but he avoids negotiating in Asia because he does not seem to think his empathy is strong enough there. In tough negotiations to take over a family-owned company in the USA, he knew the main shareholder "didn't want to sell because he was in love with the business". At the same time, Talbot inferred from the demeanour of the man's wife that she did want to sell even though she did not say so: "You just knew there was something there. We thought 'We'll work on her.' " Talbot sent a colleague to see her "on innumerable occasions, and kept convincing her to sell. That would secure her kids' future and hers." The woman worked on her husband and the deal was done.

In contrast, Talbot has always found it difficult to delve into Asian minds and emotions: "With some cultures I feel very uncomfortable. I could never cope with doing a deal in Asia." He does not mean you should avoid Asia if a deal is available: "If you can't do it [in China] yourself, recruit a Chinese person who can go with you and explain. You've got to learn to think like them. In any negotiation you've got to put yourself in the other's shoes."

Sir Alan Donald prefers socks to shoes when he talks about the negotiator's empathy as both reflexive and comparative, a theme common to many veterans. He paraphrased one of Sun Tzu's maxims:

> Know the enemy and if you do not know yourself, you will be successful fifty percent of the time. If you know yourself and do not know the enemy, you will be successful fifty percent of the time. But if you know the enemy and yourself, you can be successful one hundred percent of the time.[10]

Then he said:

> Echoing that thought, I was always mindful of Wellington's idea of thinking beyond the hill. He was very good at seeing into the mind of the French generals that came up against him in the Peninsular War, and he was really putting himself into the socks of the other side to get a clear understanding of where they were at and what they were trying to do, and what *he* was trying to do.[11]

Sir Alan's military analogies belie his benign negotiating style, and they are interesting because they echo the reflexive and comparative spirit of most veterans' empathy.

Further to the military theme on French soil, listen to the narrator in *The Negotiators*:

---

10. See Sun Tzu (1988 [400BC]: 82) for a direct translation of the original.

11. "The prolonged struggle [1808-14] for the Iberian Peninsula between the occupying French and a British army under Sir Arthur Wellesley (subsequently the Duke of Wellington), supported by Portuguese and Spanish forces." (Chambers 2005)

> And in truth, carried away by my own words, I was feeling as a Huguenot. I
> put myself in the Admiral's place in order to weigh his advantages.... I have al-
> ways proceeded in this way. It is easy for me to shift my feelings to one side
> or the other. I turn towards the other man; I become familiar with his situ-
> ation; I mould myself on his destiny and, living in his place, I begin to experi-
> ence his fortune and misfortune. Henceforth my concern is not to impose my
> point of view on him, as to persuade him to adopt the one I consider best for
> him—which always agrees with the interests of my own cause. (Walder 1960:
> 11–12)

The narrator seems to be more of a puppeteer than Sir Alan. Like the other
veterans, he said nothing to suggest a link between empathy and sharp
practice (although some people might question some of Settler's and others' tactics), but that does not mean empathy always leads to cooperative
strategies and collaborative tactics. Nor does it mean the veterans told all.

Empathy is a fairly simple idea but the practice is another matter. For
instance, undisciplined attempts at projection can cause confusion—How
do I see them? How do they see me? How do they think I see them? How
do they think I think they see me? To avoid paralysis, the veteran knows
just how many Chinese boxes to open.

**Flexibility** is the readiness to modify one's strategies, tactics and expectations to match the changing demands and knowledge that flow from the
open system of contextual forces and the complex interplay of the negotiators. It is the capacity to adjust one's behaviour to the nuances of each negotiation rather than try to work to a formula or restrictive pattern. Flexibility is crucial to international negotiation in particular, with its complex
variations in cultural, political, historical and other forces. It is about adapting to the differences between one negotiation and another, and to
changes that take place in the context of a given negotiation.

The veteran is not fazed by uncertainty and is always ready to adjust to
advantage, whether or not circumstantial change has been forecast or anti-
cipated. Griffiths has a better grasp of this concept than most writers and
uses flying as an analogy for hostage negotiation:

> A pre-conceived framework based on accumulated experience serves the
> same useful purpose as the pilot's pre-take-off checklist.... This ensures that
> nothing essential is overlooked in the pressure of the moment. Once air-
> borne, the pilot may have to respond flexibly to emergencies and deviations
> from the norm—icing, engine failure and so on. The hostage negotiator is in a
> similar situation and a too-rigid adherence to prescribed theories of negoti-
> ation can equally lead to disaster.... The only rule in a hostage situation is that
> there are no rules, only guiding principles (2003: 142, 153)

Griffiths says hostage-takers may be highly-educated people who have
studied negotiators' strategies and tactics in earlier cases, and know their
strengths and weaknesses. The empathetic negotiator senses this and is
flexible enough to try new tactics if others do not work or are unlikely to
work (143). All of these observations are valid for negotiation in general.

There are parallels with negotiation in the way the military strategist
Von Clausewitz sees context as an open system of uncertain influences on

the conduct of war. In warfare, just like a game of cards or a negotiation, flexibility goes with uncertainty:

> In short, absolute, so-called mathematical, factors never find a firm base in military calculations. From the very start there is an interplay of possibilities, probabilities, good luck and bad, that weaves its way through the length and breadth of the tapestry. In the whole range of human activities, war most closely resembles a game of cards. (1832: 86)

The military historian Brent Nosworthy sees the players themselves as part of a fitful system that demands flexibility:

> An officer's plans could, and probably would, be affected by his opponent's actions and plans. In other words, the actions of those on one side almost always had to be modified because of the actions and tactics of those they were fighting against. Combat was, is, and always will be a truly complex interplay of dynamic systems.... *Ad hoc* [tactical] variants born out of necessity thickly populated every crucible of battle. (1995: 33, 453)

It would be whimsical to take military analogies too far, for fear of characterising negotiation as necessarily adversarial; but, as recognised by Sir Alan Donald and other veterans, military tacticians and other writers have a sharp sense of the relationship between successful action, flexibility and a grasp of context as an open system.

In keeping with Jacob Crowe's warning that specific anticipation is not always possible when a tapestry is being woven before one's eyes, he says "I know from my police background that you need to remain flexible and be prepared for the unexpected. If they throw you something that is totally unexpected, you or your communicator has to respond appropriately and not give part of your game away."[12] He is talking here about flexibility within a given negotiation but elsewhere in the interview he extols flexibility across negotiations. He knows that the styles and tactics he used in London sieges would not have suited his hostage negotiations in Latin America or the Philippines.

Crowe is typical of the veterans when he refers again and again to the negotiator's need to cope with risk and uncertainty, which he associates with strategic, tactical and stylistic flexibility. Doug Anderson's tactical flexibility on payment schedule and price with the Hudong shipyard distinguished him from his more rigid and risk-averse colleagues. His flexibility matches his keen sense of changing context — of the tapestry that is woven and rewoven as he is trying to understand it. The pattern may change without warning. Anderson describes the norm for negotiation in China as slow and tortuous, "but the Chinese have shown that when they decide they want to do something they can move quickly. For such an enormous country as China, you can't generalise. You might do another deal in another part of China and it might take four times as long." He says the negotiator must adjust to specifics. Meg McDonald says "You have to allow room for pathways you haven't thought of to come out. You have to be

---

12. In Crowe's case, the paradox of preparing for the totally unexpected suggests a superior sense of anticipation, not a shortfall.

flexible enough to get to your objectives." She would applaud Hugh Davies' ploy of trading off an outside Handover Ceremony for an inside one in order to get the strong international element the British had wanted but the Chinese had resisted up to that point.

Terry Waite comes close to defining negotiation in terms of flexibility, with a flexible negotiator as agent for a flexible principal. He says he is "not keen on a formula for negotiation", then says what this means for an organisation: "The board needs to understand the complexities of an issue, so that the whole company is almost in a negotiating stance, a constantly flexible stance."

**Opportunism**: Before or during the negotiation the veteran is ready to seize opportunity created by unexpected incidents or information. Opportunism is about taking advantage of unanticipated incidents or knowledge. In the Bali case, Settler often recognises and exploits unexpected information, such as the interrogator's nostalgia for his visits to Australia as a seaman and his desire for his children to get an education that he cannot afford to give them. Settler cultivates an almost 'one Australian to another' relationship with a man in need of a bribe. Settler also gains ground when the unforeseen opportunity arises for him to lie by saying the source of Gregory's AIDS was a woman, not a man. This seems to reduce the apparent Indonesian need to punish Gregory for picking up the virus in a homosexual act.

Rather than fear the unexpected, the veteran harnesses it. Meg McDonald links opportunism with cooperation:

> Win-win is too simplistic for it but you have to allow room for pathways you haven't thought of to come out. Cooperative and opportunistic, I think, is the best way to describe it, because you really have to work with some unlikely bedfellows at times to get to where you have this crossing over of interests [which means] you might find yourself working even complicitly with your deepest, darkest enemy.

Sometimes the negotiator or an adviser discovers useful information well before the negotiation and makes a plan to use it if the conditions arise or can be created. This is a form of anticipation that does not have the spontaneity of opportunism as I define it, although the two are cousins. For example, Kirk Wolcott, an adviser to Jimmy Carter on conflict resolution, told me Carter discovered well before he was due to meet Bosnian Serb leader Radovan Karadzic that the ethnic cleanser of Muslims and other non-Serbs was a poet. Carter's staff tracked down the poetry for an obvious purpose—to equip Carter to steer the discussion: "President Carter has written a book of poetry. During a lavish dinner in Bosnia, Karadzic asked if he could read aloud some of his own work. President Carter already knew some of it and was able to comment on it, and they traded poems over dinner. That type of thing builds trust."[13] Anticipation

---

13. This dinner sounds painful. It reminds me of Herbert Giles's comment about the Chinese Emperor Ch'ien Lung, who took the throne in 1735: "His one amiable weakness was a fondness for poetry; unfortunately, for his own" (1911: 211).

is about discovering, predicting, planning and engineering; opportunism is *ex tempore*.

On the other hand, the meeting itself was founded on opportunism. Wolcott said it took place only because Carter seized an out-of-the-blue opportunity:

> We've had some strange things. Our involvement in Bosnia came about because we got a telephone call from a plastic surgeon in Beverly Hills. He said the conflict had reached a point where no one was talking to the Bosnian Serb leader and they thought President Carter could help. We said "What does a plastic surgeon in Beverly Hills have to do with this?" It turned out that he was born in Bosnia and was a childhood friend of Karadzic. They had gone to medical school together. We had a meeting with him and that led to our going to Bosnia.[14]

Other opportunities may not arise until hesitant negotiators are face to face and having trouble getting down to work. Opportunism is associated with the unexpected 'way in' or the icebreaker that induces trust and gets negotiations moving at the outset, or helps overcome a stalemate. Sam Passow, Research Director of London's Centre for Dispute Resolution, gave an example of American and Chinese trade negotiators struggling to find a way into a transaction. The American had a conspicuous scar on his face and he sensed that the Chinese negotiator wondered about it, so he said "The Japanese did this to me in World War Two". The Chinese negotiator seized the opportunity by lifting his shirt and showing a body scar caused by a Japanese bayonet. "All went smoothly from there," said Passow.

When Robin Talbot saw that the main shareholder in a targeted company was reluctant to sell but his wife was ambivalent, she became the medium in an excellent example of opportunism. Such impromptu revision of the cast and script is opportunistic, and different from the way Jimmy Carter's script often includes his wife as a character whose role is to work on the wives of his counterpart negotiators. According to Carter adviser Kirk Wolcott, "[Carter] says she just takes notes but I have heard that it's much more than that, and often she'll connect with a leader's wife, and later the wife will go back to the leader and say [something like] 'You are missing the larger point. You've got to think about your people.' " This is a standard Carter tactic and not to be confused with opportunism.

Opportunism is a constructive response to surprise; it is about being alert for unexpected ways of finding a way into a negotiation or gaining control of it. The narrator in *The Negotiators* says it best:

> I have always observed that in negotiations the unexpected element brings great profit for the man who knows how to make use of it. Every delegation arrives with a ready-made programme of ideas and arguments. There is nothing in its instructions that has not been turned over and pondered a score of times. Hence, any innovation, even if favourable, disturbs that preconceived order and produces a moment of uncertainty from which the more alert intelligence can profit before the others. (Walder 1960: 8)

---

14. For a detailed and less constrained version of this anecdote and its broader context, see Brinkley (1988).

**Potency** is the capacity to control negotiations in the face of great complexity, belligerent counterparts, risk, uncertainty and constant contextual change. The veterans are all confident about being in control (even when talking about temporary setbacks) but they are not arrogant, and they consult insiders and outsiders as needed. Their ego is robust but not bloated. They know they are good at what they do and expect deference in much the same way as other top-class professionals; but they are polite and listen well—there is none of the fingers-in-ears omniscience that marks some academics and other highly educated professionals.

Ambassador Don Kenyon's comment typifies the informants' reluctance to let self-confidence get in the way of respect for others: "You've got to show your opponent respect. You've got to recognise that this person on the other side is just as clever as you are, and they're not going to take kindly to someone assuming that they are not." (Like many of the veterans, Kenyon sometimes uses adversarial language that contradicts his reported approach to negotiation.)

Some veterans criticise their performance but occasional self-deprecation does not dent their confidence in always regaining full control. Again, Don Kenyon is typical:

> You often go back and think to yourself "Gee, I didn't play that very well," either from a defensive or offensive position. I'm sure that happens to everybody. But then you adjust and make sure you don't make the same mistake twice. Nobody gets into a situation where you commit yourself irrevocably without scope for reflection. You don't go back to your hotel room and say "I screwed up this whole negotiation." Nobody worth their salt gets into that situation. You always give yourself time for reflection. You often think "Oh no! We'll fix that tomorrow." Or you ring them.

Veterans know where they go wrong from time to time but rather than dwell on error they use the water under the bridge to help them learn to be even better controllers. They are always moving on, always tenacious and patient as they steer themselves and their counterparts towards agreement.

Controlling is one of four managerial functions listed early in most university textbooks on management. The other three are planning, organising and leading; the four tend to get equal weight. Although the books do not say so, these functions all concern the manager's capacity to coordinate his and others' activities as an element of control, with preconceived or evolving strategy and tactics in mind. In negotiation—a form of management—planning, organising and leading are functions of a player who strives to control the transaction. It is about getting all parties to do what you want, without the others feeling impotent or manipulated unless you want them to feel that way.

Some veterans warned that the controller as blatant puppeteer may lose control of the process and outcomes because less powerful people do not like to be puppets. Terry Waite seems to think American negotiators are crude control freaks: "America gets away with a lot in negotiation because it has enormous economic power and muscle. But the come-back is fantastic resentment which America doesn't understand." One of the reasons the World Trade Organization negotiations failed at Seattle in 1999 was said to be the autocratic attitude of the US Trade Representative, Charlene Barshefsky, who chaired the meeting with a touch of annoyance because the USA could not control the agenda as it had during GATT negotiations. She countered by trying to treat the negotiations as bilateral rather than multilateral, and so caused regular delays in plenary sessions by prolonging meetings with individual countries. According to Geoff Raby, the lead Australian negotiator at Seattle, delegates in general were "pissed off" by Barshefsky as master puppeteer and chief "head-butter". She worsened the normal tension in the WTO between bilateral "horse trading" and multilateral "Geneva driven" negotiations.[15]

In discussing the mark of empathy, I have already covered aspects of Meg McDonald's serene confidence in her capacity to control her own team. She also recognised her need, as a relatively weak player at Kyoto, to play chess with real people outside her team, to bring other small players on side in order to create strength in numbers and so have more control over the big players. Consistent with Lawrence Susskind's findings on strategic alliances in *Environmental Diplomacy* (1994), McDonald used skilful management (a word used often by her) to recruit less powerful players into a coalition without trying to overwhelm them:

> At the beginning of the Kyoto process we were on our own. By the end we had built a coalition of countries. It was pretty fragile in the beginning—a very unlikely group of Japan, Norway, Iceland and Australia. Then, towards the end, Russia joined. We all wanted different things, but we were arguing for equity and differentiation. That [understanding] proved to be absolutely decisive. A couple of developing countries were sympathetic, including Brazil, which is a very important player.

This managerial control and coordination, with McDonald at the helm, led to the USA deciding "they had to become part of this differentiation crowd. The USA was isolated and couldn't out-gun the Europeans, but by joining us [there was] sufficient critical mass as well as political mass to stand up against the Europeans." McDonald's low-key managerial potency is typical of the veterans, as shown by the two cases in Part Three and in all the interview transcripts.

* * * * * *

Although I have explored each of the seven marks in its own right, with some crossover, they are interactive as symbolised by the dotted lines in Figure 8.1. The strength of each mark varies among individuals—some people are more empathetic than others; some have a stronger sense of negotiation as theatre, and so on. The interdependence of some marks is stronger and more logical than it is between others. For example, empathy, diagnosis and anticipation are inseparable in the sense that a negotiator who is an adept anticipator must also be empathetic and skilled at

---

15. When Raby returned from Seattle, the Australian Foreign Minister said to him: "Well, Ambassador, you have failed."

diagnosis. Opportunism implies flexibility. But an empathetic person might not be a great opportunist. Robin Talbot's empathy allowed him to see that the wife would like to sell the company. As he is very opportunistic he went to work on her, whereas a lesser negotiator might not have seen the opportunity; or having seen it, another virtuoso might have decided not to exploit it.

The number, labels and categories of the marks must be arbitrary to some extent as they represent patterns in my interpretation of what the negotiators told me about themselves; and in a couple of cases, about one another. I considered including a mark to highlight the extraordinary communication skills of my veterans but decided it was too obvious as people do not become veteran negotiators without superior ability to listen to other people's ideas and express their own. I also considered 'intuition' but decided there were not enough specific quotes to justify it as a separate mark. As I became more familiar with my transcripts and interview notes I redefined and relabelled the marks, and changed the number from five to eleven, and then back to the seven that capture a set of powerful attributes common to my veterans but weighted according to individual differences. These attributes seem to help them control and coordinate negotiations and be good boundary players—they communicate well across national, cultural and other borders.

## BOUNDARY PLAY

The seven marks arm the veterans with finesse that eludes most negotiators. In keeping with my model of negotiation, this links the marks with superior ability to manage tensions. Circumstantial evidence makes sense of this claim but it would be a wild goose chase to use statistics or any other research tool to try to prove direct cause and effect. Given the evidence in the two detailed cases in Part Three and the discussion of the seven marks, it also makes sense to say the veterans have an extraordinary ability to cross metaphorical boundaries—some are more like brick walls than beaches—as they manage the tensions inherent in all negotiations.

Negotiation on any topic, in any place, involving people of any background, will highlight myriad differences between the parties even if interests and aims are common. The mix of differences, which tends to be more complex in international than domestic negotiations, separates the parties—there is a cardinal boundary between 'them' and 'us' that must be breached for the communication to take place. The cardinal boundary comprises more specific ones, such as national, cultural, social, organisational, emotional, educational, professional, intellectual, political, historical, personal, religious, linguistic, paralinguistic, ideological and psychological, as evidenced in the cases and the discussion of the marks. The successful international negotiator-as-tension-manager is always a subtle and adept 'boundary player' who thrives on such complexity.

Two areas of theory provide insight into the relationship between boundary play and international negotiation. They may help analysts to look for connections between the marks and adept tension management when defining and analysing scenarios. The first, from social and cultural anthropology, concerns ethnicity; the second area, from organisational theory, is about the transitional zone between an organisation and its external environment (Starbuck 1983), and the manager as 'boundary role person', an ugly but useful label invented by Adams (1983).

## Ethnicity and Boundary Play

An ethnic group and a negotiation team are not of the same order, but simple ethnicity theory does provide insight into the nature of the relationship between negotiating parties and the circumstances under which boundaries between the parties may be breached.

One of the distinguishing features of an ethnic group is a membership that identifies itself, and is identified by others, as constituting a category of people that is distinguishable from other categories of the same order (Barth 1969: 10–11). There are claims, credible or spurious, to distinctive combinations of culture, language, race, and so on. There is a parallel with negotiation: the broad identity of each party distinguishes it from other parties even though common aims are possible.

Ethnicity is a device for control of interaction between groups. Each group maintains the boundary with other groups to promote an internal sense of identity and purpose, and to ensure that interaction between groups is strategic rather than haphazard or casual. The boundary and the rules for crossing it increase the chances of success in the competition for control of economic and other resources.

In international negotiation, the players cannot simply discard the boundary between 'them' and 'us' to negotiate without constraint. The complexity of cultural and other factors that have created the boundary cannot be eliminated wholesale. On culture as one variable, Salacuse (1993) says good international negotiators have learned to cross the cultural divide, but "cultural ... bridging requires the cooperation of the parties at both ends of the divide, and no negotiator will permit a bridge to be built if he or she feels threatened or sees the bridge as a long-term danger to security" (206). Rather, negotiators try to build and cross selectively a bridge across the boundary—as with ethnic interaction, the crossing is strategic, focused, purposeful, limited and probably temporary. The cases and the discussion of the seven marks are rich in such boundary play.

An example from Jakarta illustrates the analogy between ethnic interaction and the negotiation process. No doubt there are other perspectives on this sort of meeting, but one non-Chinese manager claims you must take great care when negotiating with Chinese people who come to Jakarta from Singapore and Hong Kong to do business:

> The Chinese trick is to have a few people working on the same task as you. They take the best of what they can pick up from everyone along the way, and try to avoid paying anything to anyone. When we are trying to strike a deal, and it seems clear that they are very interested in what I can do for them, I work my way around to suggesting some payment up front into a trust account. They say "That's not how we do business. We'll take it else-where." "Go ahead," I tell them. "If you guys are as rich as you say you are, what's $5000 deposit to you?" They confer, and argue, and procrastinate. It goes backwards and forwards, and the angle changes. But they rarely go else-where. They agree to the deposit but they don't like me for it.

In this case, the Chinese and non-Chinese negotiators are separated by a real ethnic boundary that is reinforced by the parties' different approaches to doing business. The boundary is crossed, in a very limited way, as they negotiate an arrangement that each expects to be gainful. The Chinese want the other man's consulting skills; he wants their fee. The jockeying for position may be construed as a clarification of rules governing the lim-ited boundary crossing between the parties. This exchange also shows shrewd 'calculated insensitivity' by the non-Chinese manager as he man-oeuvres the Chinese into a position where they need to save face by accept-ing his terms.

Often there are actual ethnic boundaries to cross, as in the Jakarta ex-ample and in most international negotiation. Even if ethnic differences are minor or non-existent, negotiators are always in a relationship that is ana-logous to inter-ethnic relations. Membership of a negotiation team, like membership of an ethnic group, is reinforced by a boundary that reflects some form of actual or potential competition and conflict; but member-ship is meaningless if the boundary is impregnable and negotiation cannot occur.

## The 'Boundary Role Person' in Grey Space

The negotiator as boundary player is similar to the organisational "boundary role person [BRP]" (Adams 1983). Adams gives marketing, sales, purchasing and despatch as examples of specialist BRP roles. English (1995, 2001) shows how the boundary role is striking in the international manager, who tends to have multiple rather than specialist roles and always operates across national, cultural and other borders. The features Adams says distin-guish the BRP from other members of the organisation include greater psychological and often physical distance from other members of the or-ganisation than they have from one another. I would add intellectual dis-tance—the international operator must learn to understand and deal with the unfamiliar in order to continue with the assignment; cognitive disson-ance is more likely to stimulate questioning of the self and others (English 2001).

Adams's BRP represents the organisation but is more oriented to the external environment and tends to be closer to the agents of other organ-isations. These features are accurate in general for the international negoti-ator. In my study, not a single veteran representing an organisation seemed 'mainstream', at least during negotiations. I did not doubt the veterans' loyalty to the organisation, but their reporting suggested they were negotiating in some sort of limbo, more or less remote from their constituents but not divorced from them. International managers gave the same impression in my earlier study.

However he may see the various boundaries, perhaps as a physical thing at one extreme and a state of mind at the other, the faithful player who represents an organisation also seems to have a paradoxical sense of separation from it. Turner (1992) sees the negotiator as the meat in the sandwich between constituents and other parties to the transaction. The negotiator knows the constituents expect certain behaviour and results, but also knows that he or she must negotiate in ways and for purposes acceptable to the other party or parties (235). Moreover, the negotiator's sense of personal image on the international circuit is an interest that should not be taken lightly by his or her constituency. This is clear from the *agent ↔ principal* tension of Cutcher-Gershenfeld and Watkins (1999), discussed in Chapter 3.

The concept of the boundary in organisational and communication literature is important for understanding negotiation in general and international negotiation as a variation involving more complex boundary play. There is not only the boundary inherent in 'them' and 'us'. There is also a transitional zone in *negotiator ↔ constituents* that requires careful management by the negotiator. This may be difficult for diplomats in particular because pressure to play the game according to professional expectations may mean the cosmopolitan diplomatic club is as much of a constituency as the diplomat's home government.

Starbuck says an organisation, like a cloud or magnetic field, is not crisply discrete from its external environment:

> [An organisation] comprises a distinctive section of social space. But as one approaches the boundary, the boundary fades into ambiguity and becomes only a region of gradual transition.... One can sometimes say "Now I am inside" or "Now I am outside", but [one] can never confidently say "This is the boundary". (1983: 1071)

In the model of negotiation context described in Chapter 4, the 'immediate zone' is a temporary organisation distinguished from the external 'macrocosm' that influences it. Starbuck's concept supports the idea of an unclear boundary in *negotiator ↔ constituents*, to the extent that constituents are outside and within the immediate zone.

In the search for boundaries to play—Another one there! And another!—the nest of Chinese boxes again comes to mind. For instance, there may be a case for treating the individual negotiator as a third zone in the locus. I choose to open only enough boxes to give me the conceptual tools I need to demonstrate the prominence of boundary play as an aspect of tension management in my data.

## Boundary Play and Empathy

Attempting to understand the other point of view—the empathy mark—is the first step towards communicating across the boundary between 'them' and 'us'. The accomplished negotiator tends to talk about negotiation and its context in terms of tension between different perspectives on the same issues. Successful negotiators take great pains to understand other points of view and compare them with their own. The other party's point of view is encapsulated in 'them'; my point of view as negotiator is an element of 'us'. The process of trying to understand and be understood—to communicate—involves transmitting verbal and other messages, receiving feedback, digesting it, sending more messages based on that feedback, and so on (Figure 8.2). This is boundary play as communication, with empathy at its heart. Perhaps the figure represents broadly the entire negotiation process.

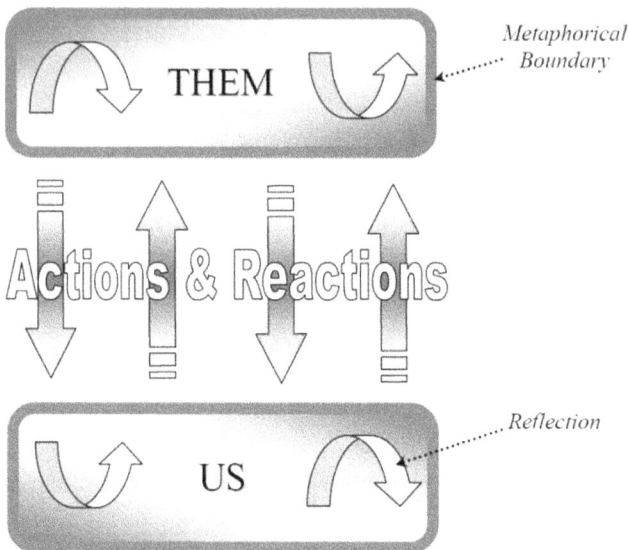

**Figure 8.2:** Boundary Crossing, Empathy and Communication

Projection into the shoes of the 'other' is usually associated with a search for common ground as a foundation for agreement, but this does not necessarily signal an ongoing collaborative approach, or a tendency to give ground. In fact, an empathetic negotiator may choose to adopt a competitive strategy and combative stance for all or part of a negotiation. The astute negotiator is not a monostylist.

Although empathy is essential to effective boundary play, projection into other shoes does not always lead to appropriate action. The negotiator makes strategic and tactical decisions, but some of them may be wrong. For instance, Ramberg says the USA and the USSR would have concluded the Seabed Arms Control Talks in 1967-1970 much earlier if they had used a collaborative style instead of a competitive one in which each side took a fixed position it *knew* was anathema to the other (Ramberg 1977: 133). Communication across the boundary was poor even though empathy was strong. To extend Salacuses's point about cultural bridging, even if communication and understanding are excellent there is no guarantee of consensus as the parties' interests, let alone their positions, may be too far apart. Crossing the beach is a complex and uncertain journey. A narrow strip of sand may turn out to be the Sahara.

↔ ↔ ↔

# Chapter 9

## « Tension Management as Contextual Intelligence »

### THE ESSENCE OF CONTEXTUAL INTELLIGENCE

In other literature, variations on the seven marks describe negotiator traits. In 'toolkit manuals' and some academic works, traits that may be learned or honed are prescribed for novices or experienced players who want to improve their practice. My study uses the marks to illuminate negotiation, and to suggest that a negotiator who applies them to advantage as a boundary player is a good tension manager who can continuously extract manageable order from chaos by identifying or sensing tensions and the forces that generate them; and, of course, can manage content and process characterised by those forces and tensions. To be a good tension manager is to have high 'Contextual Intelligence' (CI). This includes awareness that not all tensions are malleable, and that it would be unwise or futile to even try to manage every tension we experience ourselves or perceive in others. High CI also includes awareness that 'managing' tensions includes dealing with their behavioural influence, which may be benign or malignant, without necessarily trying to change or eliminate them.

Tension management and CI are synonymous. International negotiating is a specialised form of CI; it is the explicit or implicit ability to identify, understand and manage significant tensions in the constantly changing context of international negotiation. I make the temporary label change from tension management to CI for the comfort of analysts in negotiation and other fields who know psychology and might find it useful to relate tension management to the no-man's-land of intelligence modelling, well summarised by Davidson and Downing (2000), on whom I rely for much of the next few pages. If theory fogs your eyes, jump to Chapter 10 or take my earlier advice to switch to Walder's *The Negotiators*.

To explore the fit with psychological models of intelligence I first need to define the general idea of intelligence that underpins CI. When I think of someone who is more or less intelligent than other people, I am comparing their ability to extract relevant order from informational chaos, make apt choices for physical or non-physical responses, and so have significant control over their own and other people's behaviour in a given environment, and some control over other elements of that environment. By that definition, a hostage negotiator needs to be very intelligent:

> At the time of initial response to a crisis, the situation is almost always chaotic, emotions are high and the perpetrator is in control. We need to move the situation towards stability, calmness and containment. We need to tie up the loose ends, define the terms of the standoff and gradually impose our control. (Miron & Goldstein 1978: 5).

A highly intelligent person can extract complex or simple order according to need and can do so, or has the potential to do so, in diverse roles and settings. At the other extreme, a very unintelligent person is limited to extracting simple order for simple purposes in a narrow range of settings. The definition makes no direct link between intelligence and morality or socioeconomic status: a professor of postmodernism or a pope may be more or less intelligent than a serial axe-murderer, a mathematics genius, a politician, a *shakuhachi* composer, a shaman or a card-sharp.

## CONTEXTUAL INTELLIGENCE AND STANDARD MODELS

### Neural Efficiency

Davidson and Downing summarise intelligence modelling into four broad types: neural efficiency, hierarchical, contextual, and complex systems. *Neural efficiency* theorists say intelligence is a function of the speed and accuracy with which the brain operates. They claim IQ scores correlate with neurophysiological measures, such as consistency and efficiency in the transmission of information through the cerebral cortex, the amount of energy used by the brain for a given task, and the speed with which electrical impulses move throughout the body. Davidson and Downing find problems with this model that I need not mention, but I do have an extra one. Electrodes attached to negotiators to test their intelligence would be a nuisance as they try to release hostages, or flit across the globe to do business deals or stop wars, so I do not think the neural efficiency method could yield data specific to CI in international negotiation. Perhaps a neural efficiency boffin could create a convincing laboratory experiment that would differentiate my veterans from the rest of us in ways specific to CI in negotiation; but I doubt it.

## Intelligence Hierarchies and the $G$ Factor

*Hierarchical* models are also about measurable proxies for intelligence, based on generalisations from the results of a range of mental ability tests given to many people. Psychologists are not sure what intelligence is but they claim their tests measure it, just as we might measure elusive traits like lust and frigidity according to their display in bed. The general theory is that the relationship between scores on various psychometric tests gives clues to the forms and structure of intelligence, which is seen as a composite of abilities measured by those tests. The abilities, usually called 'factors' or 'primary mental abilities', include numeracy, verbal skills, induction, spatial visualisation, perceptual speed and accuracy, and memory. Intelligence is hierarchical because one or a few general factors subsume a larger number of more specific lower-order factors. The higher-order factors are needed to explain correlations between lower-order factors as evidenced by psychometric tests. Some theorists argue for two strata and others for three.

Hierarchy theory continues to evolve from Spearman's (1904, 1927) idea of $g$—a general factor of intelligence—and Thurstone's (1938) primary mental abilities (listed in the previous paragraph) that he says are independent of one another and therefore not governed by a general factor. Spearman's $g$ is an umbrella capacity to perform psychometric tests. As refined by Cattell (1963), $g$ subsumes two components at a common level: fluid intelligence ($gf$) is an innate ability to abstract, reason, see patterns and infer, that does not depend on experience or context; crystallised intelligence ($gc$) relies on $gf$ but is a set of functional skills and knowledge acquired and refined through experience and education over a lifetime.[1]

The $gf$-$gc$ model has two strata: as second-order factors, $gf$ and $gc$ are at the top; they subsume over forty first-order factors, including Thurstone's 'primary mental abilities'. At the top, Horn (1986) "organizes the second-order abilities functionally according to their level of information processing. The $gf$ and $gc$ factors represent the highest levels of cognitive function," labelled *"relation education* (or inference)" (Davidson & Downing

---

1. Although hierarchy theorists agree that broad factors subsume more specific abilities, ego may eclipse science when disputes about finer detail turn psychology conferences and peer review into guerrilla warfare. Warriors brawl over the existence and nature of $g$, the extent to which $gf$ and $gc$ are innate or acquired, fixed or changeable, and whether it is good form to split $g$ into $gf$ and $gc$. See Jensen (2002) and other papers in Sternberg and Grigorenko (2002), *The General Factor of Intelligence: How General Is It?* Jaeggi et al. (2008) claim to show for the first time that $gf$ itself can be improved (by memory training), whereas previous claims are suspect because they report a raising of $gf$ only by practising on the very tests that measure it.

2000: 38). Also within the top order, but at a lower level of information processing, is "*perceptual organization* [which] provides input to the relation education level"; it includes processing speed and the abilities to visualise information and process sound (38). The third level within the top order is "*association processing* [which] includes the ability to acquire and retrieve information from short-term memory and the fluency of information retrieval from long-term memory" (38). Horn's lowest level of function within the second-order stratum is "*sensory reception* [which] consists of … the ability to detect a large amount of visual information in one's environment and hold it in iconic memory", and the ability to detect sound "and hold it in echoic memory" (Davidson & Downing 2000: 38). Fluid intelligence, short-term memory and processing speed tend to decline with age; crystallised intelligence and long-term memory may increase or stabilise.

Carroll is the main exponent of the three-stratum hierarchy (1993). He sees intelligence as a pyramid, ascending from very specific skills and abilities at Stratum I to more general factors at II and III. Strata I and II are much the same as the two orders in the *gf-gc* model but with a third-order general factor (much the same as Spearman's *g*) at the apex.

Hierarchy theory may give some insight into negotiation as tension management, but might be useful only to the extent that standard psychometric tests associated with the theory would surely confirm the veterans' superior primary mental abilities and higher-order factors; that is, cognitive function.

The hierarchy theory is limiting because it equates intelligence with intellect as evidenced by test scores. Comparison with patterns of scores by people who are known to be poor negotiators, but do well on tests overall, might differentiate the intellect of strong negotiators from that of other people. Even so, any explanatory link with negotiator prowess is tenuous because high scores on IQ and other psychometric tests do not make a good negotiator, let alone a great one characterised by my concept of high contextual intelligence, which requires high intellect but is far from confined to it. The seven marks are at the heart of CI but are about much more than intellect. Perhaps an expert in psychometrics could devise tests to see if and how the marks relate to first-order and second-order factors, governed by *g*, that hierarchy theorists have already identified, defined, and labelled in some other way. It would be a major challenge to define the marks as sets of testable, measurable variables that could be related to existing psychometric tests of intelligence. How would we measure anticipation, empathy, opportunism or sense of drama in a real negotiation? Scoring by a trained observer might be feasible if proxies were to be devised but their chances of being credible are slim. Moreover, the results would be questionable if only because a lot of significant, spontaneous action goes on in private away from the main game and is usually not available for scrutiny by any method. The picture of a given player or group would be far from complete. Perhaps analysts desperate to link negotiation skills with hierarchy theory could comb negotiator interview transcripts and other reports, score the players for evidence of tension management skills, including the seven marks, and relate the scores to standard psychometric tests of intelligence.

## Contextual Models of Intelligence

I was unaware of the third type of intelligence model—*contextual*—when I coined the label 'contextual intelligence' as a synonym of tension management. I will return to my CI concept after touring the established contextual models of intelligence.

These models react against "an absolutist position on intelligence [that] assumes ... intelligence involves species-wide mental processes and responses ... and that the theories and assessment techniques of Western cultures apply to individuals everywhere" (Davidson & Downing 2000: 40). Rather, contextual models assume that the meaning and display of intelligence vary according to context, especially cultural context. There is plenty of cross-cultural research to show that behaviour considered intelligent in one cultural setting may be seen as idiotic in another. For example, the Kpelle of Liberia classify and match objects by function rather than linguistic category, and therefore pair a knife and potato instead of classifying the former as a tool and the latter as food. They say a fool would sort by linguistic category, "the style of sorting considered to be intelligent in many cultures" (40). Brazilian street children calculate well in their heads if problems relate to items they sell but not very well with numbers out of context. I remember being on patrol with New Guineans who thought I was a fool for wanting to know the distance between villages rather than the number of cigarettes a chain-smoker would consume en route. Assuming every smoker walks and smokes at much the same rate, their method made better sense on a hike across an open plain in the morning and up a mountain in the afternoon.

The place of culture varies among contextual models. Some theorists see it as one of many abstract, concrete, internal and external influences on intellectual performance, while for cultural relativists "intelligence is defined in terms of its specific meaning within a cultural context.... The extreme form of relativism implies that intelligence has no universal attributes" and therefore scores cannot be compared across cultural contexts (Davidson & Downing 2000: 40–41).[2] No matter where they sit on the spectrum from multiple influences to extreme cultural relativism, the contextual models are enlightening because they rely on empirical research to open our minds to the idea that intelligence relates to time and place, not just scores on a universal set of psychometric tests taken in a laboratory or other contrived situation. The models "stress the importance of connecting cognitive-psychological research to the real-world realities it is

2. The extreme relativist stance may originate in debate about racial differences in intelligence scores (politically taboo in academia since the 1970s) and the validity of the race concept itself.

supposed to explain" (41). The theory also counters addicts who equate research and knowledge with numbers and only numbers.

The contextual models have a lot of evolving to do. At present they "do not provide definitive specifications on when and how to integrate context into research on intelligence. Different types and amounts of integration are likely to produce different results and views on intelligence" (Davidson & Downing 2000: 41). The theory does not explain individual differences in performance within a given context; it does not "specify mechanisms to account for how and why some individuals acquire particular types of knowledge or select certain strategies whereas other individuals within the same context do not" (41).

My concept of tension management as CI is compatible with the contextual models to the extent that both are about applied intelligence in real-life situations, including international negotiation. I define context as tensions and the forces that generate them, whereas the psychological models, apart from the extreme cultural relativist variety, see context as a diverse, variable set of internal and external influences on mental performance and on the idea of intelligence itself. A skilled tension analyst could probably identify and define tensions generated by those influences. CI and the other models all concern the ability to sense or decipher contextual forces, extract meaningful order from them, and react appropriately.

Contextual models relate intelligence to environmental influences on the ability to perform mental tasks. As the seven marks suggest, CI includes but is much more than the ability to perform mental tasks. 'Diagnosis' is largely a mental or intellectual skill, but 'empathy' combines social, affective, intuitive and mental ability. Another difficulty is the deterministic flavour of the contextual models, which are about mental ability at a given time in one place under specific cultural and other conditions. This does not match the influence that negotiators and other people can have on forces, tensions and their effects; moreover, CI is more general and therefore portable. CI is a better fit with *complex systems models*, the fourth category of intelligence modelling, and in particular with Robert Sternberg's theory of Successful Intelligence.

## Complex Systems: Multiple and Successful Intelligences

These models combine aspects of the neural, hierarchical and contextual models and so appeal to people with an eclectic bent and an interest in open systems. Intelligence is "a complex system that includes interactions between mental processes, contextual influences, and multiple abilities. According to the complex systems models, intelligence is dynamic and can change when environmental conditions change" (Davidson & Downing 2000: 42). The authors might have added that in these theories applied intelligence is not simply determined by environment but can change it, as shown by the way my veterans manage contextual tensions and the forces that generate them. In negotiation, CI is about reading context—extracting order from chaos—and moulding it to the advantage of one or more players, which is not to say all tensions and forces can or should be managed at the negotiator's whim.

Davidson and Downing categorise the complex systems models as triarchic, multiple and bioecological. I will handle them in reverse order because my main interest is in the first, which provides the best home for CI and the associated idea of extracting order from chaos. I will not dwell on the bioecological model. It has little relevance because it concerns intellectual development from cradle to grave, as cognitive potential blooms or lies dormant according to the environment and the timing and quality of the individual's interaction with it. My concern is the veterans as they are now, not how they might have learned to perform within and after the cradle. I am not blind to the natural endowment and privileged nurture of most of my veterans but I will save the nature-nurture debate for the pub.

### Gardner's Multiple Intelligences: A Near Fit

Gardner (1983) says intelligence is a set of discrete abilities, not a single thing (such as $g$) that subsumes and determines specific abilities. His Multiple Intelligences (MI) interact and may overlap but are independent in the sense that test results for one will not predict another. There are at least eight equal intelligences, an increase from the original seven, a number chosen because Gardner "views seven as a good working number and one that is large enough to express diversity and yet small enough to be manageable" (Sternberg 1990: 267).[3] As with bioecological models, the presence and development of these intelligences depend on genes and environment.

Apparently influenced by cultural relativism in contextual theory, Gardner says the intelligences are abilities that equip "an individual to solve problems or fashion products that are of consequence in a particular cultural setting" (Walters & Gardner 1986: 165). Standard abilities have evolved as humans have adapted to a range of environments, and are played out in culture-specific ways. His original seven intelligences are linguistic, logico-mathematical, spatial, musical, bodily-kinaesthetic, intrapersonal (reflexive), and interpersonal; he adds naturalist in Gardner (1998). In a later paper he says everyone has eight or nine basic intelligences but that no two people have the same profile of strengths and weaknesses (2000). Intelligences may bolster one another: try to imagine a good xylophonist with low bodily-kinaesthetic intelligence. Linguistic skills influence interpersonal relations. This is what Gardner seems to be getting at when he says high linguistic intelligence, associated with clear thinking, explaining and convincing, may help negotiators but "it is dangerous to assume that negotiation is a purely rational process" (2000: 322).

---

3. By coincidence I ascribe seven marks to my veterans. My choice has nothing to do with Gardner or my faith in 'lucky seven'.

The gist of the first seven intelligences is clear enough. Naturalism is more cryptic; it is our ability to see and understand patterns and relationships in the natural world. Davidson and Downing say the first three "are related to abilities measured by conventional intelligence tests [whereas] the other five are valued in most cultures even though they are not measured by conventional intelligence tests" (2000: 44). They say Gardner sees some value in psychometric testing but does not rely on it because he thinks "the narrow scope of these measures severely limits $g$'s explanatory and predictive value" (44). He draws on sundry sources of data, including neurophysiological research into brain structure and function, and the observed performance of normal and abnormal people in diverse cultural settings and different domains, such as music and mathematics.

Gardner's attempt to free up the idea of intelligence and its measurement is refreshing but there are conceptual and other difficulties. For instance, the label 'intelligence' in MI theory is not always convincing. Take bodily-kinaesthetic ability. An ungainly girl is two metres tall, adores ballet, knows all about it, and would love to star in Swan Lake; but she is smart enough to know her body cannot take her there or anywhere else that demands bodily-kinaesthetic finesse. She becomes a psychiatrist. Another girl is 150 centimetres tall, nimble, loves ballet, knows all about it, and gets to pirouette with the Bolshoi company. When she is too old to dance well (Does her intelligence drop?) she also becomes a psychiatrist. If all other 'intelligences' are equal for the pair, is the second girl more intelligent because she can exploit her dancer's body and exceptional motor ability before moving to another field that does not require those attributes? Gardner's arithmetic says she is; common sense says she is not. Even if we accept the existence of multiple intelligences, does it follow that someone who cultivates more of them to a higher level than someone else is more intelligent? If we deny $g$ or something similar, that line of argument can lead to a claim that some people are more intelligent because they are more intelligent; or that intelligent people are intelligent because they are demonstrably intelligent. There is a sense of something missing.

The seven marks of my veterans could be squeezed into or added to Gardner's array of intellectual and non-intellectual intelligences. The marks include intellectual skills (for example, diagnosis and anticipation) and intelligent reaction to what those intellectual skills dig out and analyse. Empathy is intellectual but also has non-intellectual elements of intelligence, such as intuition and emotional control. Nonetheless, the fit with MI theory is uneasy because I would have to think of the marks as discrete intelligences unrelated to any form of umbrella intelligence. The idea of CI, derived from my veterans, assumes an overarching capacity to integrate and orchestrate the marks as the players extract manageable order from chaos and manoeuvre their way through negotiations as tension managers. From my dealings with them, it would be naive to doubt that they have a superior, generalised ability they could use well in other realms. Some people are better equipped than others to learn how to operate in many domains and cultural settings, at a given time and over time. Gardner does not deny a general factor but he sets it aside in favour of demonstrable abilities because it is too hard to pin down. Notwithstanding, to ignore this mammoth in the living room does not make any more sense than to say 'love' is too hard to grasp so we should see a gift of flowers as love itself, not as an expression of love.

### Sternberg's Successful Intelligence: The Nearest Fit

Gardner's theory of MI is engaging but does not embrace CI with comfort. A better partner is Sternberg's Successful Intelligence [SI] (1997, 2002), a theory I had not heard about before developing my 'manageable order from chaos' theory of intelligence, and then the more specific concept of CI. SI is compatible with Gardner's MI to the extent that both are about applied intelligence which equips us to adapt to a given environment and role; both include but go beyond intellectual skills. Unlike MI, in which various forms of intelligence are discrete and largely independent, Sternberg's model integrates interactive elements in a structure that better represents the way people seem to use their intelligence. Like Gardner, he thinks hierarchical nesting of mental abilities under $g$ is too limiting: "the construct of intelligence needs to serve a broader purpose, accounting for the bases of success in all of one's life" (2002: 455). At the same time, the SI model gives a strong but not exclusive position to analytical skills and is therefore a good match with my general concept of intelligence as stated in the third paragraph of this chapter.

Successful Intelligence is "the ability to achieve success in life in terms of one's personal standards, within one's sociocultural context. One's ability to achieve success depends on capitalizing on one's strengths and correcting or compensating for one's weaknesses through a balance of analytical, creative, and practical abilities in order to adapt to, shape, and select environments" (2002: 448). Sternberg's theory is built upon a "triarchy" of sub-theories: *internal, external* and *experiential.*

The *internal* sub-theory concerns three classes of information-processing [cognitive] abilities within the individual.[4] Sternberg hypothesises that the three processes—metacomponents, performance components, and knowledge acquisition components—underlie all aspects of intelligence and are universal approaches to problem-solving, even though definitions of problems and intelligent solutions vary across cultures. The first of the three processes, metacomponents, comprises higher order, internal "executive processes [that] plan what to do, monitor things as they are being done, and evaluate things after they are done. Examples are recognizing the existence of a problem, defining the nature of the problem, deciding on a strategy for solving the problem, monitoring the solution of the problem,

---

4. Sternberg favours categories and sub-categories based on three-way splits and structures, which are popular in academic and other analysis but do make his work briefly confusing from time to time. The tension construct also reflects the popularity of 'three': left pole, right pole, and the relationship between them.

and evaluating the solution after the problem is solved" (2002: 456). He might have added 'or after quitting because the problem is unsolvable', which good negotiators and other managers always do. Performance components, the second class of internal information-processing, concern an individual's ability to work out how to relate the metacomponents to the external environment—how to implement the instructions from the mental executive; how to do the job. The third process, knowledge acquisition components, is about the individual's ability to learn how to get knowledge and information, and decide what is relevant to solving problems; and later to apply the learning to new problems. All three componential processes are associated with the competence of successful and therefore intelligent people.[5]

The *external* sub-theory in Sternberg's triarchy is about three ways of applying the three internal mental processes to the intelligent individual's real-world environment: adaptation to the environment at hand; moulding the environment to match the individual's capacity to deal with it; and selecting an alternative environment if necessary.[6] Intelligence is not random use of the mental processes but deliberate and apt use of them to adapt to, mould and select environments. High intelligence is not just about cognitive versatility and speed, but knowing one's strengths and weaknesses in specific situations, making the most of the former and fixing or compensating for the latter. Not everyone is dealt aces in life, so "how and how well an individual adapts to, shapes and selects environments must always be viewed in terms of the opportunities the individual has" (Sternberg 2002: 456).

*Experiential*, the third sub-theory in the triarchy, deals with "the importance of coping with relative novelty and of automatization of information processing" (456). With experience, an intelligent person learns to select, distil and use new and old information to cope with new problems and so increase the chances of success. Subconscious, automatic processing evolves with experience, so that conscious, deliberate processing is not always needed. Intelligent people know they do not have to sit in a quiet corner and reinvent the wheel, and so they become increasingly confident and efficient when facing new problems or tasks. Such intelligence has universal respect, regardless of cultural and other differences of opinion about what is and is not intelligent behaviour.

The three analytical processes of the *internal* sub-theory—metacomponents, performance, and knowledge acquisition—are always used to some extent when any problem or task is faced, but the way in which they are used and their relative weight depend "on whether a given problem requires analytical thinking, creative thinking, practical thinking, or a combination of these types of thinking" (Sternberg 2002: 457). Success

---

5. The argument makes sense even though it seems circular.
6. The external sub-theory is also called "contextual" in some of Sternberg's earlier work.

depends on appropriate balance of the three types of thinking, without which the individual cannot adapt to, shape and select environments.[7] It follows that 'successfully intelligent' people have significant *control*, for particular purposes in a given environment, over their own and other people's behaviour, and some control over other elements of that environment. Such control can come only from an ability to extract appropriate order from chaos in environments that suit the strengths and play down the weaknesses of the players—in this study, the veteran negotiators. The control factor is weak in other intelligence models but it is a powerful link between CI, SI and my general idea of intelligence defined earlier: the ability to extract relevant order from informational chaos, choose apt responses, and so have significant control over their own and others' behaviour in a given environment, and some control over other elements of that environment. CI is the ability to continuously extract manageable order from chaos by identifying or sensing tensions and the forces that generate them, and to manage problems characterised by those forces and tensions. To be a good tension manager is to have a high level of CI and to succeed according to Sternberg's criteria. Perhaps CI is best seen as a variation on SI. International negotiating, a specialised form of CI, is the explicit or implicit ability to identify, understand and manage significant tensions in the fluid context of cross-border transactions.

The seven marks and their use by the veterans encompass the *analytical*, *creative* and *practical* aspects of SI. 'Diagnosis' takes in Sternberg's 'analytical' ability with comfort: "Analytical intelligence is involved when the components of intelligence (which are specified by the componential subtheory of the triarchic theory) are applied to analyse, evaluate, judge, or compare and contrast" (2002: 464). Diagnosis also includes intuition, an ability not mentioned by Sternberg. Perhaps he sees it as a form of automatisation, which would make sense if we assume conscious experience fosters successful intuition that influences decision-making and therefore should not be ignored just because it is difficult or even impossible to quantify.[8]

Sternberg does not define *creative* intelligence but he associates it with "how well an individual can cope with relative novelty" (467). The two cases in Part Three, and much of the discussion on marks and boundary play in Chapter 8, are enough to classify the veterans in general as prodigies for their creative approach to new negotiations and novelty as the transactions twist and turn. *Practical* intelligence, the third aspect of SI, "involves individuals applying their abilities to the kinds of problems that confront them in daily life, such as on the job or in the home. [It] involves applying the

---

7. For details of testing and other research used to support this conclusion, see Sternberg (2002).

8. Lost bushwalkers, divorced people and other gamblers may realise too late that gut feeling is unreliable. For a psychological study of its power in business and other realms, see *Inside Intuition* by Eugene Sadler-Smith (2007), and David Myers (2002), *Intuition: Its Powers and Perils.*

components of intelligence to experience so as to (a) adapt to, (b) shape, and (c) select environments" (469).[9] Again, the cases and the discussion of the seven marks show the veterans are deft at adapting their strategy, tactics and style to match the negotiation context, which they also shape to suit their purposes, just as their counterparts try to do—the players shape context as a sub-negotiation, in particular by applying the 'drama' mark. 'Selecting' means renouncing one environment in favour of another, sometimes after failure due to personal flaws; at other times after fruitless attempts to adapt to or shape the first environment. Robin Talbot found he could not negotiate well in Asia so he got other people to do it for him there and applied his own skills in Europe and the Americas. Geoff Goon had trouble negotiating deals in Asia and Fiji but found his niche in the Middle East. Where my veterans 'selected' by moving from one occupation to another there was no evidence of failure or incompetence in the former. After Hugh Davies' role in Hong Kong, other likely postings with the British Foreign Office seemed humdrum so he took his skills to the business world of Prudential (Asia). Jacob Crowe had a stellar career as a policeman before he became a private hostage negotiator. In a more focused sense, within the realm of negotiation, one example of selecting is refusal to negotiate in the first place if no agreement seems likely; another is withdrawal from a lost cause after negotiation stalls. Temporary avoidance as a tactic to steer a transaction is shaping rather than selecting. All these examples of managerial response to context are consistent with SI and my theory of CI.

## THE EXECUTIVE FUNCTION, SI AND CI

After reading a draft of this chapter, Dr Donald Round, a neuropsychologist at Boston's McLean Hospital, sent me an email suggesting I relate 'executive function' (EF) to the intelligence required of successful negotiators. He sees EF as a sort of cognitive manager or supervisor; as "the overarching ability to pick and choose among lower level cognitive abilities, to plan for the longer term, defer gratification, and so on." He directed me to Friedman, Miyake et al. (2006: 172), who say EF comprises a set of theorised "processes that control and regulate thought and action."

---

9. Social Intelligence, a popular theory in management and organisational psychology, concerns people's ability to cooperate because they understand what makes one another tick. Sternberg sees it as part of practical intelligence (2002: 471). I agree. As CI is consistent with Successful Intelligence, the former includes social intelligence. A related theory is Emotional Intelligence, "a type of social intelligence that involves the ability to monitor one's own and others' emotions, to discriminate among them, and to use the information to guide one's thinking and actions" (Mayer & Salovey 1993: 433). The empathy and diagnosis marks cover the ability in that definition, so CI also includes EI. Note that EI is about intellect and not to be confused with emotionalism as a bogus form of intelligence touted by self-help sages.

The formal literature of cognitive psychology tends to see EF as having three components: *inhibiting* is the deliberate suppression of habitual, impulsive and distracting responses carried over from experience to new situations; *updating* is revision of the working memory to select, assimilate, manipulate and apply new information relevant to a task at hand, and to delete wrong or irrelevant information; and *shifting*, also known as *cognitive flexibility*, is the ability "to flexibly switch perspectives, focus of attention, or response mappings" (Diamond 2006: 70) and "to quickly and flexibly adapt behavior to changing situations" (Davidson, Amso et al. 2006: 2037). Shifting includes moving among sub-tasks of a broader mental task.

Evidence of *inhibiting* would be a negotiator's informed decision to adopt a collaborative style because he thinks his normal, preferred combative style would work against him in a current negotiation. As the negotiation proceeds he discovers germane facts, some at odds with his existing knowledge and assumptions about the negotiation content and process, so he *updates* his working memory. To cope with the complexity of Kyoto, Meg McDonald had to *shift* her analysis and responses continually among myriad sub-tasks without losing her grasp of the broad negotiation—she needed to work with the trees and the forest.

Although the relationship is not absolute, the idea of EF as higher level cognitive control over lower level cognitive abilities is consistent with the SI triarchy's *internal theory*, discussed earlier. The metacomponents issue instructions to the performance components, which work out how to implement the instructions; the knowledge acquisition components equip the person to learn how to get knowledge and information relevant to the task examined by the performance components. These three internal processes guide activity encompassed by the *external* and *experiential* theories, the two more pragmatic elements of the SI triarchy. The relationships within the triarchy reflect Diamond's summary of the relationship between EF and lower-order cognitive abilities:

> *Executive function* ... is required whenever going 'on automatic' would be insufficient and especially when it would lead one astray. Classes of situations in which executive functions are required include (1) novel tasks and situations that require (2) concentration, (3) planning, (4) problem solving, (5) coordination, (6) change, (7) conscious choices among alternatives, or (8) overriding a strong internal or external pull (Diamond 2006: 70).

These "classes of situations" are a good match with those faced and managed so well by the veterans, whose high CI is distinguished by astute application of the seven marks to negotiation as tension management. Perhaps the umbrella intelligence that binds and guides the marks is best seen as a variation on EF.[10] Whether or not that proposition is reasonable, Donald Round's conclusion stands firm: "Obviously, successful negotiators need EF in spades."

In summary, SI is CI's most compatible model of intelligent behaviour in general and negotiation in particular. The theories are united by the idea of people learning to apply their intelligence, with more or less success, to extracting manageable order from informational chaos and taking control of their lives, including their role as negotiators. In that respect at least, my veterans are at the high end of the intelligence spectrum. People who tend to foul up negotiations are likely to be weak overall on the seven marks which define a strong negotiator and will therefore have lower CI and SI in that role. Such people may be weak, middling or strong managers in other contexts, perhaps depending on the complexity, degree and speed of contextual change—an area that calls for more explicit development by Sternberg in his discussion of the adapting, shaping and selecting elements of practical intelligence.

There is plenty of evidence in Chapters 1 and 2 that tension-based thinking is a feature of intelligent behaviour across diverse cultures and roles, from scientists who analyse the physical world, to artists and philosophers and chefs, and people who organise and manage the nexus of supernatural and temporal according to classes of left and right, as proposed by Hertz (1909). His work evokes an embrace by human arms, a symbol of people wresting chunks of manageable order from informational chaos as they try to control their lives through a balance of the analytical, creative and practical abilities proposed by Sternberg. People with a fine sense of balance extract or impose order to suit particular purposes without trying to fool themselves into thinking their intelligence can ever come close to ordering their entire universe.

↔ ↔ ↔

---

10. Further to the contentious general factor of intelligence, Friedman, Miyake et al. (2006) tested the relationship between EF and $g$ in young adults. They found that updating, but not inhibiting or shifting, correlated highly with traditional psychometric measures of $gf$ and $gc$. Based on their own and many other studies, they say "the current finding that not all EFs are related to psychometric intelligence suggests that traditional measures of intelligence are missing some fundamental supervisory functions" (178).

# Chapter 10

## « The Play's the Thing »

### FROM THEORY TO ACTION

My main purpose has been to describe and justify a theoretical framework for international negotiation analysts who might or might not be practitioners. The focus has always been on analysing content and process, not on selling tension management as a conscious negotiation technique. This does not mean the theory cannot help negotiators to polish their practice; indeed, it might help them to understand what they do and how they do it, and perhaps work out how to do it better by identifying, defining and trying consciously to manage the tensions that influence their own and other players' craft. As a process for helping negotiators to make sense of actual and expected experience, I recommend scenario definition and will focus my advice there. Later I offer some general suggestions from above the fray about *what* to do with tensions once a scenario has been defined; but it would be rash to offer precise advice about *how* to do it within the fray because each negotiation is unique in complex and unpredictable ways within a realm, let alone across realms. Another reason for holding back on precise advice about how to do it is fear that an over-intellectualised approach to the minutiae of action will work against the tactical spontaneity and intuition displayed by outstanding negotiators as they respond to reality that might not match forecasts. A practitioner creating scenarios for a future or current negotiation should see them as provisional, just as a SWOT analysis or medical diagnosis is always open. Excellent negotiators seem to anticipate various futures, always knowing that none is likely to be "the one". That attitude may give them an advantage because their mindset equips them to run with the unexpected. On the other hand, the blow by blow detail of 'how we *did* it' is a reasonable topic for an intellectual post mortem, provided we are at least mildly sceptical about the accuracy and completeness of any rational story we stitch together with hindsight. There is likely to be more than one credible story.

Scenario definition is meant to be a scanning device for independent analysts, but the formal process may be a good representation of the practitioner's ongoing scrutiny of a transaction as he or she employs the seven marks to identify forces and control the play. For the practitioner, tension management represents the scrutiny, decisions and associated action. A hostage negotiator, diplomat or business manager trained in tension dynamics and scenario definition is likely to understand transactions better than before and therefore improve his or her potential to influence contextual forces and reach agreement. This position makes sense even though it would be difficult to test for clear cause and effect, but training in scenario definition at least offers negotiators another way of thinking about practice, and a tool that may improve their craft. Scenario definition might be useful to mediators because part of their job is to help conflicting parties to define the conflict. The mediator becomes sculptor.

A negotiator wanting to apply the theory of tension management to practice would need to understand these concepts and processes: the generic tension; tension dynamics (properties and conditions); tension categories (content and process); the locus as the seat of forces that generate tensions; the immediate and macrocosmic zones of the locus; the negotiation context as an open system of forces and the tensions they generate; the scenario as an ordered segment of context; scenario definition; the seven marks of the veteran; boundary play; and contextual intelligence, including its affinity with Sternberg's 'successful intelligence'. The *international* negotiator also needs to understand forces and tensions associated with cross-border as well as domestic transactions. For instance, in the former there tend to be greater differences between the players because of influences such as nationalism, diplomatic power, culture, language, political ideology, perceptions of history, and the economic strength of the players' countries.

The definition of tension management in Chapter 4 is for analysts in general who are looking for implicit and explicit examples. Negotiators may manage tensions without necessarily being conscious of doing so, but anyone who wants to manage them deliberately needs a modified, operational definition that includes scenario definition and calculated action. Hence, tension management for practitioners is: (a) scenario definition; (b) any calculated action that alters the balance or intensity of tensions and therefore their influence on negotiator communication and other behaviour, and on negotiation results; and (c) any calculated attempt to avoid action that would modify tensions and their influence. Under (b), a managerial act may change more than one tension. Parts (b) and (c) are responses to part (a) scenario definition. For the player, a scenario created during a negotiation or at the outset is a summary of tensions that ought to be considered when decisions are to be made about managing content and process.

When I asked Malcolm Lyon and Meg McDonald if they thought I should try to create a tension-based analytical framework that might be useful in negotiator training as well as to scholars, he hesitated but she was enthusiastic. He said negotiation was best learned through experience with a mentor who could compile a good brief, not through training in analytical techniques; or in anything else for that matter. The traditional brief was the thing; frameworks and training programs were unnecessary. To the contrary, Meg said Kyoto taught her that negotiators needed all the help they could get to extract manageable order from context. No doubt no one ever morphed from negotiation stumbler to maestro after a quick course on how to use a scanning tool, but I also doubt that anyone created worse briefs or became a worse negotiator by learning how to scan context better. I respect a good brief but I do not think a long apprenticeship with a veteran is the only way to learn how to prepare one. Anyway, scanning techniques have long been used by negotiators to prepare for and track the play in many realms. Examples are the generic checklists for diplomats and business negotiators discussed in Chapter 5 (Winham 1979, Salacuse 1991). There I say why the checklists fall short of scenarios but might help negotiators define the latter, and then prepare associated briefs and action plans for managing tensions.

One expert on diplomatic negotiation offers a checklist for diagnosing player mindsets but is even more interesting for his argument that "well-prepared candidates for working in this kind of arena would be people carrying a methodology in their heads that is interdisciplinary and an intellectual capacity for integrating all the diverse incoming information and interplay of pressures that bear on the problem at hand" (Fisher 1988: 15). He advocates conceptual systems as tools that negotiators can use "to make cumulative experience applicable to new problem situations. Does the old hand have twenty years' experience or one year's experience twenty times?" (19). Novices and old hands who learn to define scenarios are likely to raise their contextual intelligence, make more of their experience, and so improve their craft as tension managers. This is consistent with Sternberg's research findings that analytical, creative and practical aspects of Successful Intelligence can be taught and learned (2002: 466–470).

There is no formula for learning how to be a deliberate tension manager, but a good start would be to study the finer points of the tension and learn to define scenarios, as explained in Chapter 5 and summarised in Figure 5.2. Participants in my programs have been quick to understand tension management as action associated with a grasp of tension dynamics. For instance, during discussion of *sensitivity ↔ insensitivity* in an executive program, one person suggested the poles were not absolute because no one would be entirely sensitive or insensitive to an unfamiliar culture or broader context at any given time. Moreover, suggested someone else, an individual's tendency to sensitivity or insensitivity might vary from one transaction to another. That is, the participants saw the poles as competitive and complementary extremes on a continuum. Further discussion led to unanimous agreement that training in cross-cultural adjustment would generate a form of tension management, as trainees would be encouraged to bias their behaviour towards the sensitivity pole.

It is true that Davies and Settler use their normal repertoire to manage implicit tensions without having to formally assess contextual forces, express their influence as explicit tensions, and consciously manage balance and intensity. On the other hand, the searching and questioning process of defining scenarios for pending, current and completed (or aborted) negotiations should assist an already skilful practitioner to better extract manageable order from chaos: What tensions *that I can see* are inherent in this negotiation? Which ones seem to be most significant to me and the other players? Why do the tensions exist? What forces generate them? What are their properties and conditions? How, why and when do tensions change? How should I react to these tensions?

The questioning encourages flexible thinking and gives order to the negotiation context while discouraging shallowness and definitive vision. The method does not dilute issues or the associated positions, interests and desired results. The content tensions in the Part Three cases arise from meticulous exploration of issues; the process tensions make conceptual sense if isolated from real negotiations but much more sense if they are related to real cases. It follows that practitioners who define tensions should gain deeper insight into issues and become better armed to devise strategies and tactics that match the scenario. Although common process tensions are recommended for international scenarios, the set is reinterpreted for each case. *Other (? ↔ ?)* is a warning to keep an open mind. The process elicits both specifics and general principles, including the idea that culture is not always dominant, nor a strait-jacket. Moreover, the practitioner should remember that he or she deals with real people, not statistical samples, and should ponder *person ↔ group* in the light of Avruch's (1998) rejection of homogenous, external culture that determines individual cognition and action.

Culture in the Hong Kong and Bali cases brings out the general principle that negotiators who understand the forces that create a tension can modify their own and others' behaviour accordingly, which is not to say the forces or the tensions are eliminated; rather, that their influence may be controllable. For example, it would be absurd to try to eliminate culture and most other forces but the negotiator can try to reduce problems caused by them and take advantage of any of their positive influence on the negotiation. Negotiators should not allow the psychological idea of tension as anxiety to intrude, as tension management does not assume tensions and the forces that create them are negative. Perhaps all tensions are ultimately positive and productive if they generate communication leading to agreement.

No scenario can be cast in concrete, as the negotiation context is always changing. Scenarios are not absolute in another sense that concerns differences in the way people see their world, even if they come from a common socio-cultural background. In a classic urban study of witnesses to crime and other events, Irving Goffman found that witnesses of much the same background reported the same events with bizarre inconsistency (1974).[1] In the Part Three cases the players did not define the scenarios that I present. I defined them, based on information obtained from the players and other sources. Your scenario for those cases might differ from mine, depending on such influences as your personal history, negotiation experience, nationality, grasp of the issues, and role (if any) in those negotiations. If all players in a given negotiation were trained in scenario definition they might better understand one another's positions and interests through comparing similarities and differences in scenarios. Serial attempts to develop a common scenario, working from separate team or individual scenarios, could be a part of the negotiation itself, especially to provide focus in the early stages. If Hugh Davies and his Chinese counterparts had been used to creating common scenarios the process might have been a good foundation for negotiating a quicker agreement. On the other hand, the players still might not have agreed because of social, political, cultural or other checks, including unforeseen events.

Using the process described in Chapter 5, a negotiation team might define and refine scenarios under the eye of an expert in the method. For confidential transactions in any realm, this person might be a trained internal adviser or a member of the team. With or without such a guide, a common scenario should be recorded for the team but individuals might add private tensions associated with personal concerns. There might be private conflict associated with the negotiator's need to balance concern for substantive issues with concern for personal image in the eyes of constituents and other negotiators (Wilson 1992). Sir Alan Donald says the diplomat is faced with not wanting the public to be deceived or misinformed, but the government, not the public, is the diplomat's constituency. As reported in Chapter 2, former Israeli Foreign Minister Abba Eban examines the ethical dilemmas of diplomats who must face "the confrontation between power and conscience" (1998: 39) as they attempt to reconcile

---

1. One of my favourite examples, not reported by Goffman, is the dispute among witnesses to Soviet Premier Khrushchev's alleged shoe-banging at the UN General Assembly on 13 October 1960 (or was it the 12th ?), in protest against an anti-Soviet speech by Filipino delegate Lorenzo Sumolong. Some say Khrushchev took off his shoe and banged it on the desk; others that he took it off but did not bang it; others that he did not take off his shoe, but brandished a third shoe—some say a sandal—that he might or might not have banged. (Taubman 2003).

the doctrine of state sovereignty with the principle of universal human rights. Bartos identifies a tension between "the individual (competitive) desire to maximize one's own utility and the collectivistic (cooperative) desire to reach a fair solution" (1977: 13). Negotiators are not automatons. They carry unique experience, cultural knowledge and other traits that influence the way they see and are seen, and the way they negotiate. If a diplomat is feeling venomous because her husband has bolted, this is likely to affect her negotiation about state matters, so she should define one or more private tensions to add to her record of the scenario created by the team. She might settle on *marriage ↔ divorce* and *fidelity ↔ infidelity*, which have simple labels but rich meaning for her. She might add codes denoting her judgment on the relationship as it stands, how it might end up, and how her diagnosis and prognosis might influence her diplomatic negotiation. This example is a reminder that not all tensions are common to all players, and even if they are common their intensity and the way they influence behaviour will vary between individuals and, over time, within them.

My reluctance to offer advice on how to micro-manage tensions may suggest my feet and head are made of clay, or worse. Negotiation, in particular the international sort, tends to be so intricate and varied that such advice would be fanciful, even though my academic habit tempts me to give it anyway. If such advice were not fanciful we should see it by now for 'co-opetition', one of the constants in the business negotiation literature—the tension between "cooperative moves to create value jointly and competitive moves to gain individual advantage" (Lax & Sebenius 1986: 30). Some scholars say the authors should have said precisely how to manage the tension to back up their assertion that it affects all tactical and strategic choice. Some have tried to fill the gap. Allred is typical: "Given how fundamental this dilemma is to the field, it is surprising how little sound prescriptive advice exists for dealing with it" (2000: 388).[2] His survey of students in a negotiation course inspired a prescriptive framework based on the dual concerns model.[3] He links "best practices" and "strategic practices" with various types of short-term and long-term relationships that are characterised by blends of assertiveness, cooperativeness, trust, distrust, minor interests, and major interests.

"Best practices" are "those that tend to work well in all situations" and "strategic practices" are "those that tend to work well in certain situations and poorly in others" (387). An example of a "best asserting practice" is "working to see that, where possible, one's own needs and interests are met"; a "strategic asserting practice" in "cooperative, long-term relationships with minor interests at stake" is "using one's power and authority to win a favorable outcome *less*"; in "competitive, distrustful, short-term relationships with major interests at stake" the prescribed strategic asserting

---

2. Allred uses "tension" and "dilemma" as synonyms. In the same paper he causes minor confusion by also using "tension" to mean anxiety.

3. Discussed in Chapter 3.

practice is "using one's power and authority to win a favorable outcome *more*" (391; emphasis in original). Some strategic asserting practices can turn a good relationship into a bad one, so a negotiator should not use them unless he is sure the other party is competitive and untrustworthy (396). A negotiator wanting to create as well as claim value should ponder relationships and interests before taking off a shoe (or sandal) to hammer the table.

Lax and Sebenius (1986) reads as if the authors do not prescribe ways to manage their signature tension because it is too broad, and because they assume a good negotiator who understands it will have the wit to better channel and apply his skills in specific transactions. If that is what they mean they make good sense. Although Allred's axioms on asserting and other practices also make sense they are unsurprising and do not really prescribe ways of managing the tension at ground level. This is less to criticise Allred and other prescribers than to accept the limitations of prescribing for the complex and fluid activity of negotiation. Broad ideas about *what* to do and not do with some tensions might be useful, but specific advice on *how* to go about it would be rash without knowing a great deal about the details of a transaction in context, and would be no wiser than telephoning an artist to suggest colour selection and brush technique for an unseen canvas on an unknown subject.

Therefore I have little to say about managing specific tensions. To novices, there may be some value in advice that would be self-evident to veterans. For example, if there is too much focus on positions in *positions* ↔ *interests*, try to steer the play towards interests without ignoring the reality and resilience of positions. If a collectivist approach is working against an agreement within a reasonable time, find a way to moving the balance towards the individualism pole. If your style is collaborative but the other party is too combative, perhaps move your style towards the 'combat' pole as a temporary tactic to induce the other party to modify its negotiation strategy. If there seems to be disadvantage through treating a counterpart team as a group, identify and cultivate individuals whom you can influence to your advantage. For a content tension, concede or engineer movement away from your preferred balance as a trade-off for favourable movement in another content tension. If you cannot or should not change the balance of a tension, consider trying to reduce or raise its intensity to foster agreement. In *content* ↔ *process*, if the latter pole takes over, remind the other players why you are there and try to move the balance further to the left. Where appropriate, create new tensions as part of environmental control in the spirit of Sternberg. That level of advice might be too obvious even to a novice who has read Chapter 4 and knows how to define scenarios.

More precise advice on what to do and how to do it cannot be separated from deep analysis of tensions in specific contexts which we cannot come close to understanding in full. The best I can do from above the fray is to remind practitioners that a refined understanding of balance and intensity should guide any conscious attempt to manage tensions. The range of skills needed to do the managing is covered in myriad, sometimes hackneyed how-to-do-it books. Like academic works, they never see the generic tension and so lack analytical guidance based on a construct representing so much human effort to order and manage existence. I agree with Robin Talbot, probably the most experienced of my business veterans, that the best available work in this genre is still *You Can Negotiate Anything*, Herb Cohen's 1980 classic. Cohen does not refer to the tension even though it is inherent in his work, and like many American writers he may be too confident about win-win as a universal value; but practitioners should read him anyway, and think about his ideas while learning to define scenarios. If anyone decides to read only one book it should be Cohen, or Francis Walder's profound and brilliant novel, *The Negotiators* (1960); or Faure and Rubin's *Culture and Negotiation: The Resolution of Water Disputes* (1993), from which I have cited several articles.

As well as defining scenarios and linking action to tension balance and intensity, negotiators might find it useful to gauge their own contextual intelligence, and test their empathy by gauging the CI of colleagues and counterpart players. Estimates no finer than high, medium and low would be realistic, but negotiators who like statistics might use a single Likert scale or develop a more complex set of measures for the seven marks and other elements of CI. I do not know a negotiator who would want to do so but some academic analysts might want to try. One indicator of CI might be whether or not an individual demonstrates a fine balance of *content* ↔ *process*, and so understands that too much concern with one or the other pole might impede communication. Negotiators searching for the best balance in their own practice should examine their own cognitive propensities, and those of any team members, not just those of counterparts. This is in keeping with the principle that the key to collaboration may be a search for individual differences, not just broad cultural and other similarities (Smith & Berg 1997).

Like Sternberg's Successful Intelligence, CI is applied intelligence that can improve with experience. Therefore both are learnable within limitations defined by the blend of nature and nurture in the individual. As the seven marks and boundary play are proposed as factors of CI, in theory they are more or less learnable, and practitioners might study and try to emulate them. A veteran is differentiated from a novice not so much by the presence and absence of the seven marks and boundary play as by their prominence, refinement, and skilful use. I do not see why practitioners at any level cannot hone and better apply their diagnostic ability, sense of drama, opportunism, empathy, and so on.

Many academic and other courses on negotiation, in the realms of business and diplomacy if not hostage release, are based on win-win theory and 'toolkits'. At least for the sake of variety, it might be a good idea to teach participants to understand, evaluate, compare, modify and apply scenario definition and other scanning systems, such as the Phatak-Habib framework and the checklists of Winham and Salacuse. Using lectures, seminars, case studies and simulations as media, the same courses could include any other matters raised in this book about the idea of negotiation as tension management.

## FINALE

My theory of context and negotiation, like most theories of anything, is a work in progress. There is much scope for research across disciplines into the theory itself and its usefulness to practitioners, their advisers, and academic analysts. For example, do tensions have significant traits apart from conceptual affinity, balance, balance tendency, and intensity? Do negotiators trained to define scenarios report better strategies and tactics, better understanding of issues, and better agreements? Do they claim to have finer insight into the content and process of previous negotiations? If players learn to create and review scenarios, do they become better at seeing and managing wrong assumptions that underpin the way they and other people frame negotiations? Do they become better judges of when to withdraw from a negotiation? How do individualism and collectivism relate to the tension management skills of single negotiators and teams? Do cognitive style and culture influence the negotiator's ability to learn and apply tension management theory? How do the tension and its polar labels relate to other research into handedness, symmetry and asymmetry? Seminars involving practitioners and academics, a method used by Winham (1979) to compile his checklist for diplomats, could explore these questions and design research projects to tackle them. Perhaps novelists could dig even deeper. A linguist might relate theories of language to the process of identifying tensions, putting them in words, and managing them. A barmy philosopher or biologist might wonder if there is a gene, perhaps with evolutionary advantage, that predisposes human beings to frame and manage all or part of their lives as tensions.

$$\longleftrightarrow \quad \longleftrightarrow \quad \longleftrightarrow$$

*If your book could persuade some of our new soldiers to read and mark and learn things outside drill manuals and tactical diagrams, it would do a good work. I feel a fundamental crippling incuriousness about our officers. Too much body and too little head.*

T. E. Lawrence [of Arabia], letter to historian B. Liddell Hart, 1933

# References

ABC (2000) Lines of Communication: Program 1—Contact. Radio National Open Learning, 9 December. Australian Broadcasting Corporation.

ABC (2004) Interview with Canon Andrew White. Radio National AM, 15 September. Australian Broadcasting Corporation.

Adams, J. S. (1983) The structure and dynamics of behavior in organizational boundary roles. In: M. D. Dunnette (ed.), *Handbook of Industrial and Organizational Psychology.* Wiley: New York. 1175–1199.

Allred, K. G. (2000) Distinguishing best and strategic practices: A framework for managing the dilemma between creating and claiming value. *Negotiation Journal,* 16(4), 387–397.

AMORC (2006) *The Rosicrucian Order AMORC [Ancient and Mystical Order of the Rose Cross].* Available from: http://home.wxs.nl/~amorc.nl/ enhistne.html [Accessed 7 June 2006].

Auerbach, A. H. (1998) *Ransom: the Untold Story of International Kidnapping.* Henry Holt and Company: New York.

Avruch, K. (1998) *Culture and Conflict Resolution.* United States Institute of Peace Press: Washington, DC.

Avruch, K. (2000) Culture and negotiation pedagogy. *Negotiation Journal*, 16(4), 339–346.

Babbitt, E. F. (1999) Challenges for international diplomatic agents. In: R. H. Mnookin, and L. E. Susskind (eds), *Negotiating on Behalf of Others: Advice to Lawyers, Business Executives, Sports Agents, Diplomats, Politicians and Everybody Else.* Sage: Thousand Oaks. 135–150.

Barth, F. (ed.) (1969) *Ethnic Groups and Boundaries: The Social Organization of Culture Difference.* George Allen and Unwin: London.

Bartos, O. J. (1977) Simple model of negotiation: a sociological point of view. In: I. W. Zartman (ed.), *The Negotiation Process: Theories and Applications.* Sage: Beverly Hills. 13–27.

Bateson, G. (1936) *Naven: A Survey of the Problems Suggested by a Composite Picture of the Culture of a New Guinea Tribe Drawn from Three Points of View.* Cambrige University Press: Cambridge.

Bateson, G. (1973) *Steps to an Ecology of Mind: Collected Essays in Anthropology, Psychiatry, Evolution and Epistemology.* Paladin: St Albans, UK.

Beeston, R. & Farrell, S. (2004) Kidnapping for ransom a fast-growing industry. *The Weekend Australian*, 18–19 December, Sydney, p. 13.

Bernard, H. R. (2002) *Research Methods in Anthropology: Qualitative and Quantitative Approaches.* 3rd edition. Alta Mira: Walnut Creek, CA.

bin Laden, O. (2001) I tell them that these events have divided the world into two camps, the camp of the faithful and the camp of the infidels. Video broadcast 7 October 2001. *The Weekend Australian*, 13–14 October, p. 28. Prologue to article by Paul Kelly.

Blackman, C. (1996) Negotiating commercial agreements in China: A discussion of Australian perceptions and strategies. In: J. Selmer (ed.), Conference Proceedings, *Cross-Cultural Management in China*, Hong Kong Baptist University, 26–28 August, Vol. 1, 24–30.

Blackman, C. (1997) *Negotiating China: Case Studies and Strategies.* Allen and Unwin: Sydney.

Blake, R. R. & Mouton, J. S. (1964) *The Managerial Grid.* Gulf Publishing: Houston.

Boulding, K. (1962) *Conflict and Defense: A General Theory.* Harper Torchbooks: New York.

Brett, J. M. (2001) *Negotiating Globally: How to Negotiate Deals, Resolve Disputes, and Make Decisions Across Cultural Boundaries.* Jossey-Bass: San Francisco.

Brinkley, D. (1998) *The Unfinished Presidency: Jimmy Carter's Journey Beyond the White House.* Penguin: New York.

Buckman, G. (2005) *Global Trade: Past Mistakes, Future Choices.* Fernwood Publishing: Halifax.

CAER (2006) *Just How Business is Done? A Review of Australian Business Approach to Bribery and Corruption.* Centre for Australian Ethical Research: Sydney.

Cambria, J., DeFilippo, R. J., Louden, R. J. & McGowan, H. (2002) Negotiation under extreme pressure: The 'mouth marines' and the hostage takers. *Negotiation Journal*, 18(4), 331–343.

Camp, J. (2002) *Start With No: The Negotiating Tools that the Pros Don't Want You to Know*. Crown Business: New York.

Cardno, C. & Piggot-Irvine, E. (1997) *Effective Performance Appraisal: Integrating Accountability and Development in Staff Appraisal*. Longman: Auckland.

Carr, E. H. (1961) *What is History?* Macmillan: London.

Carroll, J. B. (1993) *Human Cognitive Abilities: A Survey of Factor-Analytic Studies*. Cambridge University Press: Cambridge.

Carter, J. (1982) *Keeping Faith: Memoirs of a President*. Collins: London.

Carvill, B. (2005) Minds and hearts in the making. *Minds in the Making*, 2(1). Available from: http://www.calvin.edu/minds/vol02/issue01/bcarvill.php [Accessed 23 December 2007].

Cattell, R. B. (1963) Theory of fluid and crystallized intelligence: A critical experiment. *Journal of Educational Psychology*, Vol. 54, 1–22.

Chambers (2005) *The Chambers Dictionary of World History*. 2nd (new) edition. Chambers Harrap: Edinburgh.

Chambers Dictionary (2006) *The Chambers Dictionary*. 10th edition. Chambers Harrap: Edinburgh.

Chen Ming-Jer (2001) *Inside Chinese Business: A Guide for Managers Worldwide*. Harvard Business School Press: Boston.

Chenery, S. & Sellick, R. (2002) The new king of Siam. *The Weekend Australian Magazine*, 14–15 September, pp. 12–15.

Ching, F. (1998) China's attitude to the rest. *Far Eastern Economic Review*, 9 July, p. 32.

Chubb (2007) *Kidnap/Ransom and Extortion Insurance*. Pamphlet, Chubb Executive Protection. Available from: http://www.csi.chubb.com [Accessed 20 March 2007].

Clutterbuck, R. L. (1987) *Kidnap, Hijack and Extortion: The Response*. St Martin's Press: New York.

Cohen, H. (1980) *You Can Negotiate Anything*. Angus and Robertson: London.

Cohen, M. R. (1946) *A Preface to Logic*. Routledge: London.

Cohen, M. R. (1949a) *Studies in Philosophy and Science*. Frederick Ungar: New York.

Cohen, M. R. (1949b) *A Dreamer's Journey*. The Free Press: Glencoe, Illinois.

Cohen, M. R. (1953) *Reason and Nature: An Essay on the Meaning of Scientific Method*. 2nd edition. The Free Press: Glencoe, Illinois.

Cohen, R. (1993) International negotiation: Does culture make a difference? An advocate's view. In: G. O. Faure and J. Z. Rubin (eds), *Culture and Negotiation: The Resolution of Water Disputes*. Sage: Newbury Park. 22–27.

Conger, J. A. (1998) Qualitative research as the cornerstone methodology for understanding leadership. *Leadership Quarterly*, 9(1), 107–121.

Conrad, J. (1902) Heart of Darkness. In: *Youth: A Narrative and Two Other Stories*. Blackwood: London.

Cooper, H., Davis , B. & Johnson, I. (1999) To brink and back: In historic pact, US opens way for China to finally join WTO. *The Wall Street Journal*, 16 November, pp. 1, A19.

Copland, A. (1957) *What to Listen for in Music*. Mentor Books: New York.

Courtis, J. (1998) *Commentaries on the Secret Symbols of the Rosicrucians: Tabula Smaragdina Hermetis* [Emerald Tablet of Hermes]. Available from: http://www.crcsite.org/printTabula.htm [Accessed 7 July 2006].

Covarrubias, M. (1937) *Island of Bali*. Alfred A. Knopf: New York.

Crelinsten, R. D. & Szabo, D. (1976) *Hostage-Taking*. Lexington Books: Lexington, Mass.

Cross, J. G. (1977) Negotiation as a learning process. In: I. W. Zartman (ed.), *The Negotiation Process: Theories and Applications*. Sage: Beverly Hills. 29–54.

Crystal, D. (1997) *English as a Global Language*. Cambridge University Press: Cambridge.

CSAA (2000) *On the Beach*. Conference of the Cultural Studies Association of Australia, 4–6 December 2000, University of Queensland. Available from: http://english.uq.edu.au/conferences/csaa-conf-2000/home.html [Accessed 26 April 2001].

Cutcher-Gershenfeld, J. & Watkins, M. (1999) Toward a theory of representation in negotiation. In: R. H. Mnookin and L. E. Susskind (eds), *Negotiating on Behalf of Others: Advice to Lawyers, Business Executives, Sports Agents, Diplomats, Politicians and Everybody Else*. Sage: Thousand Oaks. 23–51.

Davidson, J. E. & Downing, C. L. (2000) Contemporary models of intelligence. In: Robert J. Sternberg (ed.), *Handbook of Intelligence*. Cambridge University Press: Cambridge. 34–49.

Davidson, M. C., Amso, D., Cruess Anderson, L. & Diamond, A. (2006) Development of cognitive control and executive functions from 4 to 13 years: Evidence from manipulations of memory, inhibition and task switching. *Neuropsychologia*, 44(11), 2037–2078.

De Jomini, Baron (1837) *The Art of War*. Translated from French by G. H. Mendell and W. P. Craighill, 1977. Greenwood Press: Westport, CT.

Deng Xiaoping (1993) *On the Question of Hong Kong*. New Horizon Press: Hong Kong.

Dening, G. (1980) *Islands and Beaches: Discourse on a Silent Land, Marquesas 1774–1880*. Melbourne University Press: Melbourne.

Dening, G. (1998) *Readings/Writings*. Melbourne University Press: Melbourne.

Deresky, H. (2006) *International Management: Managing Across Borders and Cultures.* 5th edition. Pearson Prentice Hall: New Jersey.

Diamond, A. (2006) The early development of executive functions. In: E. Bialystok and F. I. M. Craik (eds), *Lifespan Cognition: Mechanisms of Change.* Oxford University Press: New York. Chapter 6, 70–95.

Dickens, C. (1859) *A Tale of Two Cities.* Chapman and Hall: London.

Dodgson, C. & Cust, L. (1915) Notes. *The Burlington Magazine for Connoisseurs,* 27(150), 248–251.

Dowsett, G. (1987) The semi-structured interview. *Australian Journal of Adult Education,* 27(2), 29–32.

Druckman, D. (2002) Content analysis. In: V. A. Kremenyuk, *International Negotiation: Analysis, Approaches, Issues.* Jossey-Bass: San Francisco. 288–312.

Eban, A. (1998) *Diplomacy for the Next Century.* Yale University Press: New Haven.

Edelman, M. (2001) *The Politics of Misinformation.* Cambridge University Press: Cambridge.

Eliade, M. (1959) *The Sacred and the Profane: The Nature of Religion.* Harcourt, Brace and World: New York.

Encyclopedia Britanicca (2006) Heracleitus. *Encyclopaedia Britannica.* Ultimate Reference Suite DVD.

English, T. (1995) The Double-headed Arrow: Australian Managers in the Business Context of Asia. Unpublished PhD thesis, University of New England.

English, T. (2001) Tension analysis in international organizations: A tool for breaking down communication barriers. *International Journal of Organizational Analysis,* 9(1), 61–86.

English, T. (2002) Defining tension scenarios: A managerial approach to international negotiations. In: L. Bennington (ed.), *Proceedings of the 16th ANZAM Conference: Enhancing Business and Government Capability.* Beechworth, Victoria, 4–7 December. Australian and New Zealand Academy of Management: Melbourne. CD-ROM.

Ernst, B. (1985) *The Magic Mirror of M. C. Escher.* Tarquin: Stradbroke, UK.

Evans, A. & Doz, Y. (1992) Dualities: A paradigm for human resource and organizational development in complex multinationals. In: V. Pucik, N. Tichy and C. Barnett (eds), *Globalizing Management: Creating and Leading the Competitive Organization.* Wiley: New York. 85–106.

Fall, B. B. (1964) *Street Without Joy.* Revised edition. Pall Mall Press: London.

Fang, T. (1999) *Chinese Business Negotiating Style.* Sage: Thousand Oaks, California.

Faure, G. O. (2002) International negotiation: The cultural dimension. In: V. A. Kremenyuk, *International Negotiation: Analysis, Approaches, Issues.* San Francisco, Jossey-Bass. 392–415.

Faure, G. O. & Rubin, J. Z. (eds) (1993) *Culture and Negotiation: The Resolution of Water Disputes.* Sage: Newbury Park.

Feldmann, T. B. (1999) Media issues affecting hostage negotiation. Unpublished manuscript supplied by the author.

Fisher, G. (1988) *Mindsets: The Role of Culture and Perception in International Relations.* Intercultural Press: Yarmouth, Maine.

Fisher, R., Kopelman, E. & Schneider, A. (1994) *Beyond Machiavelli: Tools for Coping with Conflict.* Harvard University Press: Mass.

Fisher, R., Schneider, A., Borgwardt, E. & Ganson, B. (1997) *Coping with International Conflict: A Systematic Approach to Influence in International Negotiation.* Prentice Hall: New Jersey.

Fisher, R., Ury, W. & Patton, B. (1991) *Getting to Yes.* Business Books Limited: London.

Forbes, C. (2007) *Under the Volcano: The Story of Bali.* Black Inc: Melbourne.

Forsyth, F. (1989) *The Negotiator.* Bantam Press: London.

French, P. (1995) *Younghusband: The Last Great Imperial Adventurer.* Flamingo: London.

Friedman, T. L. (1999) *The Lexus and the Olive Tree.* Farrar Straus and Giroux: New York.

Friedman, N. P., Miyake, A., Corley, R. P., Young, S. E., DeFries, J. C. & Hewitt, J. K. (2006) Not all executive functions are related to intelligence. *Psychological Science*, 17(2), 172–179.

Gardner, H. (1983) *Frames of Mind: The Theory of Multiple Intelligences.* Basic Books: New York.

Gardner, H. (1998) Are there additional intelligences? The case for naturalist, spiritual, and existential intelligences. In: J. Kane (ed.), *Education, Information, and Transformation.* Prentice Hall: Englewood Cliffs. 111–132.

Gardner, H. (2000) Using multiple intelligences to improve negotiation theory and practice. *Negotiation Journal*, 16(4), 321–324.

Gauguin, P. (1923) *The Intimate Journals of Paul Gauguin.* Translated from French by Van Wyck Brooks. Heinemann: Melbourne.

Giles, H. A. (1911) *The Civilisation of China.* Thornton Butterworth: London.

Goffman, E. (1974) *Frame Analysis: An Essay on the Organization of Experience.* Harvard University Press: Cambridge, Mass.

Graves, R. (1996) *The Greek Myths.* Folio Society: London. Original Penguin: London, 1955.

Gregersen, H. B., Morrison, A. J. & Black, J. S. (1998) Developing leaders for the global frontier. *Sloan Management Review*, 40(1), 21–32.

Griffiths, J. C. (2003) *Hostage: The History, Facts and Reasoning Behind Hostage Taking.* André Deutsch: London.

Gudykunst, W. B. & Kim, Y. Y. (1997) *Communicating with Strangers: An Approach to Intercultural Communication.* 3rd edition. McGraw-Hill: Boston.

Gudykunst, W. B. & Ting-Toomey, S. (1988) *Culture and Interpersonal Communication.* Sage: Newbury Park.

Gulliver, P. H. (1988) Anthropological contributions to the study of negotiations. *Negotiation Journal,* 4(3), 247–255.

Gunatilleke, G. (2001) *Negotiations for the Resolution of the Ethnic Conflict.* Marga Monograph Series on Ethnic Reconciliation, No. 1. Colombo: Marga Institute.

Hall, E. T. (1976) *Beyond Culture.* Doubleday: New York.

Hammersley, M. & Atkinson, P. (2000) *Ethnography: Principles in Practice.* 2nd edition. Routledge: New York.

Hampden-Turner, C. & Trompenaars, F. (1994) *The Seven Cultures of Capitalism.* Piatkus: London.

Handy, C. (1994) *The Empty Raincoat.* Random House: London.

Harlan, M. (2006) *Texas Hold'em for Dummies.* Wiley: Hoboken, NJ.

Hawkins, L. & Hudson, M. (1990) *The Art of Effective Negotiation.* Business Library: Melbourne.

Hegel, G. W. F. (1821) *Philosophy of Right.* Clarendon Press: Oxford. Translated from German by T. M. Knox, 1952.

Hertz, R. (1909) Le pre-eminence de la main droite: Étude sur la polarité religieuse. *Revue Philosophique de la France et de l'Etranger,* 34(2), 553–580.

Hertz, R. (1973) The pre-eminence of the right hand: A study in religious polarity. In: R. Needham (ed.), *Right and Left: Essays on Dual Symbolic Classification.* University of Chicago Press: Chicago. 3–31. Translation of Hertz (1909).

Hewitt, G. (1991) *Terry Waite: Why Was He Kidnapped?* Bloomsbury: London.

Hoang, P. B. (1997) Globalization vs. customization in international marketing: An attempted integration of current literature. *Journal of International Marketing and Exporting,* 2(1), 25–34.

Hofstede, G. (1989) Cultural predictors of national negotiation styles. In: F. Mautner-Markhof (ed.), *Processes of International Negotiations.* Westview Press: Boulder.

Hofstede, G. (1994) *Cultures and Organizations: Software of the Mind.* Harper Collins: London.

Hofstede, G. (1998) Attitudes, values and organizational culture: Disentangling the concepts. *Organization Studies,* 19(3), 477–492.

Hofstede, G. (2001) *Culture's Consequences: Comparing Values, Behaviors, Institutions and Organizations Across Nations.* 2nd edition. Sage: Thousand Oaks.

Hofstede, G. & Usunier, J. C. (1999) Hofstede's dimensions of culture and their influence on international business negotiations. In: P. Ghauri and J. C. Usunier (eds), *International Business Negotiations.* Pergamon: Oxford. 119–129.

Hopmann, P. T. (2002) Negotiating data: Reflections on the qualitative and quantitative analysis of negotiation processes. *International Negotiation Journal*, 7(1), 67–85.

Horn, J. L. (1986) Intellectual ability concepts. In: R. J. Sternberg, *Advances in the Psychology of Human Intelligence*. Erlbaum: Hillsdale, NJ. Vol. 3, 35–77.

Huntington, S. (1993) The clash of civilizations? *Foreign Affairs*, 72(3), 22–49.

Iklé, F. C. (1964) *How Nations Negotiate*. Harper and Rowe: New York.

Jacoby, R. (2008) Determined not to keep it simple. *The Australian*, 5 March, Sydney, p. 29.

Jaeggi, S. M., Buschkuehl, M., Jonides, J. & Perrig, W. J. (2008) Improving fluid intelligence with training on working memory. *Proceedings of the National Academy of Sciences*, 105(19), 6829–6833. Early Edition online. Available from: http://www.pnas.org/cgi/doi/10.1073/pnas .0801268105 [Accessed 10 June 2008].

Jandt, F. E. (1985) *Win-Win Negotiating: Turning Conflict into Agreement*. Wiley: New York.

Janosik, R. J. (1987) Rethinking the culture-negotiation link. *Negotiation Journal*, 3(4), 385–395.

Jensen, A. R. (2002) Psychometric *g*: Definition and substantiation. In: R. J. Sternberg and E. L. Grigorenko (eds), *The General Factor of Intelligence: How General is It?* Lawrence Erlbaum Associates: Mahwah, NJ. 39–53.

Joint Liaison Group (1996) Agreed Minute of the Sino-British Joint Liaison Group on the Handover Ceremony for Hong Kong. [Enclosure 1 to Finance Commmitee Paper FCR(96-97)64 of 25 October.] Home Affairs Branch, Hong Kong Government: Hong Kong.

Jung, C. G. (1963) *Memories, Dreams, Reflections*. Recorded and edited by A. Jaffé. Translated from German by R. and C. Winston. Collins, and Routledge and Kegan Paul: London.

Kahane, D. (2003) In theory: Dispute resolution and the politics of cultural generalization. *Negotiation Journal*, 19(1), 5–27.

Kalé, S. (1999) How national culture, organizational culture and personality impact buyer-seller interactions. In: P. Ghauri and J. Usunier, *International Business Negotiations*. Pergamon: Oxford. 21–38.

Kanayama, M. (1996) Cross-cultural management and international negotiations: The case of Sino-Japanese joint ventures. In: J. Selmer (ed.), Conference Proceedings, *Cross-Cultural Management in China*, Hong Kong Baptist University, 26–28 August, Vol. 1, 209–214.

Keesing, R. M. (1991) Asian cultures? *Asian Studies Review*, 15(2), 43–56.

Kelly, J. (1993) *Facts Against Fictions of Executive Behavior: A Critical Analysis of What Managers Do*. Quorum Books: Westport.

Kheel, T. W. (1999) *The Keys to Conflict Resolution: Proven Methods of Resolving Disputes Voluntarily.* Four Walls Eight Windows: New York.

Kidnap and Ransom (1999) *Kidnap and Ransom: A Secret War.* Television documentary. Directed by D. André. Produced by France 2 and Capa Presse TV.

Kimball, R. (2002) *Lives of the Mind: The Use and Abuse of Intelligence from Hegel to Wodehouse.* Ivan R. Dee: Chicago.

Kissinger, H. (1960) *The Necessity for Choice: Prospects of American Foreign Policy.* Chatto and Windus: London.

Kissinger, H. (1977) *American Foreign Policy.* 3rd edition. W.W. Norton: New York.

Kozicki, S. (1993) *The Creative Negotiator.* Gower: Pyrmont, NSW.

Kuhn, T. (1977) The essential tension: Tradition and innovation in scientific research. In: *The Essential Tension.* University of Chicago Press: Chicago. 225–239.

Lang, W. (1993) International negotiation: Does culture make a difference? A professional's view. In: G. O. Faure and J. Z. Rubin (eds), *Culture and Negotiation: The Resolution of Water Disputes.* Sage: Newbury Park. 38–46.

Langness, L. L. (1987) *The Study of Culture.* Revised edition. Chandler and Sharp: Novato, Calif.

Larsen, R. E. (1959) Morris Cohen's principle of polarity. *Journal of the History of Ideas*, 20(4): 587–595.

Lawrence, T. E. (1933) Letter to B. H. Liddell Hart, 26 June. *T. E. Lawrence Studies.* Reference DG 768–9. Available from: http://telawrence.net/telawrencenet/letters [Accessed 20 July 2008].

Lax, D. A. & Sebenius, J. K. (1986) *The Manager as Negotiator.* The Free Press: London.

Lévi-Strauss, C. (1969) *The Raw and the Cooked.* Harper and Row: New York. Translation of *Le Cru et le Cuit*, 1964.

Levy, R. I. & Hollan, D. W. (1998) Person-centered interviewing and observation. In: H. R. Bernard (ed.), *Handbook of Methods in Cultural Anthropology.* Altamira Press: Walnut Creek. 333–364.

Lewicki, R. J., Saunders, D. M. & Barry, B. (2006) *Negotiation.* 5th edition. Irwin McGraw-Hill: Boston.

Lewin, K. (1951) *Field Theory in Social Science.* Harper and Row: New York.

Lewis, P. H. (1969) *The Social Context of Art in Northern New Ireland.* Field Museum of Natural History: Chicago.

Leys, S. (2005) *The Wreck of the Batavia: Anatomy of a Massacre.* Black Inc: Melbourne.

Liddell Hart, B. H. (1967) *Strategy.* Frederick A. Praeger: New York. Revised edition of 1954 original.

Lloyd George, R. (1992) *The East-West Pendulum.* Woodhead-Faulkner: London.

Lowi, M. & Rothman, J. (1993) Arabs and Israelis: The Jordan River. In: G. O. Faure and J. Z. Rubin (eds), *Culture and Negotiation: The Resolution of Water Disputes*. Sage: Newbury Park. 156–175.

Maccoby, M. (1978) *The Gamesman*. Bantam Books: New York.

March, R. M. (1988) *The Japanese Negotiator*. Kodansha International: Tokyo.

Martin, W. M. (2005) Bubbles and skulls: The phenomenology of self-consciousness in Dutch still life painting. In: M. Wrathall and H. Dreyfus (eds), *The Blackwell Companion to Phenomenology and Existentialism*. Blackwell: Oxford. 559–584.

Mayer, J. D. & Salovey, P. (1993) The intelligence of emotional intelligence. *Intelligence*, 17(4), 433–442.

McBeth, J. (2001) Indonesia: Waiting for Gus Dur. *Far Eastern Economic Review*, 12 April, p. 28.

McGregor, D. (1960) *The Human Side of Enterprise*. McGraw-Hill: New York.

McManus, C. (2002) *Right Hand, Left Hand: The Origins of Asymmetry in Brains, Bodies, Atoms and Cultures*. Harvard University Press: Cambridge, Mass.

Melville, H. (1957) *Moby Dick or The Whale*. Rinehart Press: San Francisco. Original Harper and Bros: New York, 1851.

Metcalf, P. (1982) *A Borneo Journey into Death: Berawan Eschatology from its Rituals*. University of Pennsylvania Press: Philadelphia.

Miall, H., Ramsbotham, O. & Woodhouse, T. (1999) *Contemporary Conflict Resolution*. Polity Press: Cambridge.

Miron, M. S. & Goldstein, A. P. (1978) *Hostage*. Behaviordelia: Kalamazoo.

Mnookin, R. H., Peppet, S. R. & Tulumello, A. S. (1996) The tension between empathy and assertiveness. *Negotiation Journal*, 12(3), 217–230.

Mnookin, R. H. & Susskind, L. E. (eds) (1999) *Negotiating on Behalf of Others: Advice to Lawyers, Business Executives, Sports Agents, Diplomats, Politicians and Everybody Else*. Sage: Thousand Oaks.

Moorehead, C. (1980) *Fortune's Hostages: A Study of Kidnapping in the World Today*. Hamish Hamilton: London.

Morgan, G. (1986) *Images of Organisation*. Sage: Beverly Hills.

Mulder, J. (1992) *Non-Stop Negotiating: The Art of Getting What You Want*. Penny Publishing: Sydney.

Myers, D. G. (2002) *Intuition: Its Powers and Perils*. Yale University Press: New Haven.

Naisbitt, J. (1995) *Megatrends Asia: The Eight Asian Megatrends that are Changing the World*. Nicholas Brealey: London.

Nalebuff, B. J. & Brandenburger, A. M. (1996) *Co-opetition*. Harper Collins Business: London.

Needham, R. (ed.) (1973) *Right and Left: Essays on Dual Symbolic Classification*. University of Chicago Press: Chicago.

Needham, R. (1987) *Counterpoints*. University of California Press: Berkeley.

Neuman, W. L. (2003) *Social Research Methods: Qualitative and Quantitative Approaches.* 5th edition. Pearson Education: Boston.

Nicolson, H. (1963) *Diplomacy.* 3rd edition. Oxford University Press: London.

Nisbett, R. E., Peng, K., Choi, I. & Norenzayan, A. (2001) Culture and systems of thought: Holistic versus analytic cognition. *Psychological Review*, 108(2), 291–310.

Nosworthy, B. (1995) *Battle Tactics of Napoleon and His Enemies.* Constable: London.

Oxford English Dictionary (1980) *The Shorter Oxford English Dictionary on Historical Principles.* 3rd edition. Oxford University Press: Oxford.

Patten, C. (1998) *East and West.* Macmillan: London.

Peng, K. & Nisbett, R. E. (1999) Culture, dialectics and reasoning about contradiction. *American Psychologist*, 54(9), 741–754.

Phatak, A. V. & Habib, M. H. (1996) The dynamics of international business negotiations. *Business Horizons*, 39(3), 30–38.

Pizer, S. A. (1998) *Building Bridges: The Negotiation of Paradox in Psychoanalysis.* Analytic Press: Hillsdale, NJ.

Powdermaker, H. (1933) *Life in Lesu.* Williams and Norgate: London.

Prochnau, W. (1998) Dispatches: Adventures in the ransom trade. *Vanity Fair*, May, pp. 69–81.

Provis, C. (1996) Interests vs positions: A critique of the theory. *Negotiation Journal*, 12(4), 305–323.

Pruitt, D. G. & Rubin, J. Z. (1986) *Social Conflict: Escalation, Stalemate, and Settlement.* New York: McGraw-Hill.

Pruitt, D. G. & Carnevale, P. J. (1993) *Negotiation in Social Conflict.* Open University Press: Buckingham.

Purdy, D. (2005) *The Illustrated Guide to Texas Hold'em.* Sourcebooks: Naperville, Ill.

Putnam, L. L. & Holmer, M. (1992) Framing, reframing and issue development. In: L. L. Putnam and M. E. Roloff (eds), *Communication and Negotiation.* Sage: Newbury Park. 128–155.

Putnam, L. L. & Roloff, M. E. (1992) Communication perspectives on negotiation. In: L. L. Putnam and M. E. Roloff (eds), *Communication and Negotiation.* Sage: Newbury Park. 1–17.

Pye, L. (1985) *Asian Power and Politics.* Harvard University Press: Cambridge.

Pye, L. (1992) *Chinese Negotiating Style.* Quorum: New York.

Raiffa, H. (1982) *The Art and Science of Negotiation.* Harvard University Press: Cambridge, Mass.

Ramberg, B. (1977) Tactical advantages of opening positioning strategies: Lessons from the Seabed Arms Control Talks 1967–1970. In: I. W. Zartman (ed.), *The Negotiating Process: Theories and Applications.* Sage: Beverly Hills. 133–148.

Rammal, H. (2005) International business negotiations: The case of Pakistan. *International Journal of Culture and Management*, 15(2), 129–140.

Reading, H. F. (1977) *A Dictionary of the Social Sciences*. Routledge and Kegan Paul: London.

Reber, A. S. (1985) *Dictionary of Psychology*. Penguin: London.

Richards, C. & Walsh, F. (1990) *Negotiating*. Australian Government Publishing Service: Canberra.

Riessman, C. K. (1993) *Narrative Analysis*. Qualitative Research Methods Series, No. 30. Sage: Thousand Oaks.

Rijksmuseum (2008) Johannes Torrentius, *Emblematic Still Life*. Available from:
http://www.rijksmuseum.nl/aria/aria_assets/SK-A-2813?lang=en
[Accessed 10 June 2008].

Rose, C. (1989) *Negotiate and Win: The Proven Methods of the Negotiation Workshop*. Spa Books: UK.

Rubin, J. Z. (2002) The actors in negotiation. In: V. A. Kremenyuk (ed.), *International Negotiation: Analysis, Approaches, Issues*. Jossey-Bass: San Francisco. 97–109.

Sadler-Smith, E. (2007) *Inside Intuition*. Routledge: Abingdon, UK.

Salacuse, J. W. (1991) *Making Global Deals: Negotiating in the International Marketplace*. Houghton Mifflin: Boston.

Salacuse, J. W. (1993) Implications for practitioners. In: G. O. Faure and J. Z. Rubin (eds), *Culture and Negotiation: The Resolution of Water Disputes*. Sage: Newbury Park. 199–208.

Salacuse, J. W. (1998) Ten ways that culture affects negotiating style: Some survey results. *Negotiation Journal*, 14(3), 221–240.

Schoemaker, P. J. (1995) Scenario planning: A tool for strategic thinking. *Sloan Management Review*, 36(2), 25–40.

Schön, D. A. (1983) *The Reflective Practitioner: How Professionals Think in Action*. Basic Books: New York.

Schulzinger, R. D. (1975) *The Making of the Diplomatic Mind: The Training, Outlook, and Style of United States Foreign Service Officers, 1908–1931*. Wesleyan University Press: Middletown, CT.

Sebenius, J. K. (2001) Six habits of merely effective negotiators. *Harvard Business Review*, 79(4), 87–95.

Sebenius, J. K. (2002) The hidden challenge of cross-border negotiations. *Harvard Business Review*, 80(3), 76–85.

Shue Lam Yip (1995) *Doing Business in China*. McGraw-Hill: Toronto.

Smith, K. S. & Berg, D. N. (1997) *Paradoxes of Group Life: Understanding Conflict, Paralysis, and Movement in Group Dynamics*. New Lexington Press: San Francisco.

Smith, P. B. (2002) Culture's Consequences: Something old and something new. *Human Relations*, 55(1), 119–135.

Snowden, D. (2002) Complex acts of knowing: Paradox and descriptive self-awareness. *Journal of Knowledge Management*, 6(2): 1–13.

Snyder, A. (2000) Borrowed and beautiful. *The Weekend Australian*, 11–12 November, p. 30.

Sontag, S. (1977) *On Photography*. Picador: New York.

Speake, J. (ed.) (1979) *A Dictionary of Philosophy*. Pan Books: London.

Spearman, C. (1904) 'General Intelligence,' objectively determined and measured. *American Journal of Psychology*, Vol. 15, 201–293.

Spearman, C. (1927) *The Abilities of Man: Their Nature and Measurement*. Macmillan: New York.

Standish, R. (1943) *Bonin*. Peter Davies: London.

Standish, R. (1949) *Gentleman of China*. Peter Davies: London.

Starbuck, W. H. (1983) Organizations and their environments. In: M. D. Dunnette (ed.), *Handbook of Industrial and Organizational Psychology*. Wiley: New York. 1069–1123.

Sternberg, R. J. (1990) The systems metaphor. In: *Metaphors of Mind: Conceptions of the Nature of Intelligence*. Cambridge University Press: New York. 261–283.

Sternberg, R. J. (1997) *Successful Intelligence*. Plume: New York.

Sternberg, R. J. (2002) Beyond *g*: The theory of successful intelligence. In: R. J. Sternberg and E. L. Grigorenko (eds), *The General Factor of Intelligence: How General Is It?* Lawrence Erlbaum Associates: Mahwah, NJ.

Sternberg, R. J. & Grigorenko, E. L. (eds) (2002) *The General Factor of Intelligence: How General Is It?* Lawrence Erlbaum Associates: Mahwah, NJ.

Stevenson, R. L. (1886) *The Strange Case of Dr Jekyll and Mr Hyde*. Scribner: New York.

Strathern, M. (1990) *The Gender of the Gift: Problems with Women and Problems with Society in Melanesia*. Studies in Melanesian Anthropology, Vol. 6. University of California: Berkeley.

Sun Tzu (1988) *The Art of War*. Shambhala Dragon Editions: Boston. Chinese classic *circa* 4th century B.C. Translated by Thomas Cleary.

Susskind, L. (1994) *Environmental Diplomacy: Negotiating More Effective Global Agreements*. Oxford University Press: New York.

Taubman, W. (2003) Did he bang it? Nikita Khrushchev and the shoe. *International Herald Tribune*, 26 July.

Thomas, K. & Kilmann, R. (1974) *Thomas-Kilmann Conflict Mode Instrument*. Consulting Psychologists Press: Palo Alto.

Thomas, W. I. (1966) *On Social Organization and Social Personality*. University of Chicago Press: Chicago.

Thurstone, L. L. (1938) *Primary Mental Abilities*. University of Chicago Press: Chicago.

Turner, B. A. (1988) Connoisseurship in the study of organizational cultures. In: A. Bryman (ed.), *Doing Research in Organizations*. Routledge: London. 108–122.

Turner, D. B. (1992) Negotiator-constituent relationships. In: L. L. Putnam and M. E. Roloff (eds), *Communication and Negotiation*. Sage: Newbury Park. 233–249.

Vincent, B. (2001) Crossed signals: Shanghai wants to hear more English spoken ahead of the Apec summit—so long as it isn't on the radio. *Far Eastern Economic Review*, 26 April, p. 58.

Vines, R. & Naismith, L. (2002) Exploring the foundations of knowledge management practice. In: B. Cope and R. Freeman (eds), *Developing Knowledge Workers in the Printing and Publishing Industries*. Common Ground: Melbourne. 35–58.

Volkema, R. J. (1999) *The Negotiation Toolkit: How to Get Exactly What You Want in Any Business or Personal Situation*. Amacom: New York.

Von Clausewitz, C. (1832) *On War*. Edited and translated by Sir M. Howard and P. Paret, 1976. Princeton University Press: Princeton, NJ.

Wadley, N. (1978) *Gauguin*. Phaidon: Oxford.

Waite, T. (1993) *Taken on Trust*. Hodder and Stoughton: London.

Walder, F. (1960) *The Negotiators*. Heinemann: London. First published in France as *Saint-Germain ou La Négociation*, 1958, Librairie Gallimard. Translated from French by Denise Folliot.

Walsh, E. (1996) Profile [of Charlene Barshefsky]: The Negotiator. *The New Yorker*, 18 March, 72(4), 86–97.

Walters, J. M. & Gardner, H. (1986) The theory of multiple intelligences: Some issues and answers. In: R. J. Sternberg and R. K. Wagner (eds), *Practical Intelligence: Nature and Origins of Competence in the Everyday World*. Cambridge University Press: Cambridge. 163–182.

Walton, R. E. & McKersie, R. B. (1965) *A Behavioral Theory of Labor Negotiations: An Analysis of a Social Interaction System*. McGraw-Hill: New York.

Watkins, M. & Winters, K. (1997) Intervenors with interests in power. *Negotiation Journal*, 13(2), 119–142.

Web Gallery of Art (2006) Notes on Torrentius's *Emblematic Still-Life*. Available from: http://www.wga.hu/html/t/torrenti/allegory.html [Accessed 5 July 2006].

Weiss, S. E. (1993) Analysis of complex negotiations in international business: The RBC perspective. *Organizational Science*, 4(2), 269–300.

Weiss, S. E. (1994) Negotiating with 'Romans'—Part I. *Sloan Management Review*, 35(2), 51–61.

Weiss, S. E. (1996) International negotiations: Bricks, mortar and prospects. In: B. J. Punnett and O. Shenkar (eds), *Handbook for International Management Research*. Blackwell: Cambridge, Mass. 209–265.

Wilson, P. J. (1973) *Crab Antics: The Social Anthropology of English–Speaking Negro Societies of the Caribbean*. Yale University Press: London.

Wilson, S. R. (1992) Face and facework in negotiation. In: L. L. Putnam and M. E. Roloff (eds), *Communication and Negotiation*. Sage: Newbury Park. 176–205.

Winham, G. R. (1979) Practitioners' views of international negotiation. *World Politics*, 32(1), 111–135.

Womack, D. F. & Walsh, K. (1997) A three–dimensional model of relationship development in hostage negotiations. In: R. G. Rogan, M. R. Hammer and C. R. Van Zandt (eds), *Dynamic Processes of Hostage Negotiation: Theory, Research and Practice*. Praeger: Westport, CT. 57–75.

Wright, L. L. (1996) Qualitative international management research. In: B. J. Punnett and O. Shenkar (eds), *Handbook for International Management Research*. Blackwell: Cambridge, Mass. 63–81.

Yates, J. (1989) *Control Through Communication: The Rise of System in American Management*. Johns Hopkins University Press: Baltimore.

Zartman, I. W. (1993) International negotiation: Does culture make a difference? A skeptic's view. In: G. O. Faure and J. Z. Rubin (eds), *Culture and Negotiation: The Resolution of Water Disputes*. Sage: Newbury Park. 17–21.

# Index

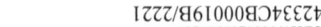